PITT LATIN AMERICAN SERIES

Pitt Latin American Series

Cole Blasier, Editor

The Hovering Giant

COLE
BLASIER

The Hovering
Giant

U.S. Responses
to Revolutionary
Change in
Latin America

University of Pittsburgh Press

Library of Congress Cataloging in Publication Data

Blasier, Cole.
  The hovering giant: U.S. responses to revolutionary change in Latin America.

  (Pitt Latin American series)
  Includes bibliographical references and index.
  1. United States—Foreign relations—Latin America. 2. Latin America—Foreign
relations—United States. 3. Revolutions—Latin America. I. Title.
F1418.B646   327.73′08   75–9130
ISBN 0–8229–3304–7
ISBN 0–8229–5264–5 (pbk.)

Dedicated to Martha Hiett Blasier

Contents

Illustrations

Castro with U.S. Ambassador to Cuba Philip W. Bonsal
Castro with Vice-President Richard M. Nixon
Castro with Soviet Premier Nikita Khrushchev

Chapter 8, following page 266
John N. Irwin, U.S. emissary, with Peruvian President Juan Velasco Alvarado
James Greene, chief U.S. negotiator, at the signing of the general settlement
   between the United States and Peru
Salvador Allende, president of Chile, at a press conference

Figures

Tables

Preface

Anyone who devotes oneself to a theme as broad and elusive as U.S. responses to revolutionary change should be able to explain why. Except for the avoidance of nuclear war, few problems that confront mankind seem more significant to me than how rich and powerful nations respond to the efforts of poorer and weaker nations to build a better life. Those efforts which take the form of revolutionary change pose a hard test for Great Powers, who often perceive them as threats to their own vital and not-so-vital interests. The drama unfolds in Africa, Asia, Eastern Europe, and Latin America.

In the last region the U.S. government bears heavier responsibility than in most other areas of the world because of its relatively greater power there and its longer and more intense involvement. That responsibility includes taking into account how its acts affect neighbors—not just identifying and protecting U.S. interests. In conflicts between these parties, settlements arrived at through negotiations have proved more viable than those imposed by force.

Successful compromises usually require the parties to know a good deal more about one another and about themselves than have most U.S. leaders and Latin American revolutionaries. When I first looked into this subject in the late 1960s I was unable to find any comprehensive account of U.S. responses to any individual Latin American revolution, much less any authoritative comparative studies. Nobody seemed to be well informed about how the United States responded, or why. Since that time a few well-documented studies have improved our knowledge of specific aspects of U.S. responses in individual countries.

Most generalizations about U.S. responses to revolution have been in the polemical literature, which is spotty, bitterly controversial, contradictory, and vast. Some of these writings make sense, but it is difficult to sort out the probable from the improbable. The most satisfactory interpretations have been offhand or incidental speculations of a handful of scholars and diplomats.

In the face of this ignorance and confusion, I concluded that the most useful function I could perform would be to bring together in one volume a comparative description and explanation of U.S. responses to individual Latin American social revolutions. I reasoned that a better understanding of the past would help U.S. leaders and Latin American revolutionaries conduct themselves more effectively in their mutual relations. That assumption is not based on a perception of the policy-making process as rational, orderly, or consistently manageable. I do not believe it is. Knowledge of the past will not necessarily solve these or any other of mankind's problems, but it can help. Men of power often are ignorant of, conceal, or defy facts; my commitment to this study is based on my continuing faith that they cannot be or do so forever.

My original purpose was not simply to make parallel case studies, but also to use those case studies to identify and explain recurring patterns of U.S. official behavior. That is one of the reasons why the study is organized, not by individual countries, but according to stages in the revolutionary process and characteristics of U.S. responses.

My approach to this subject was not facilitated or burdened by explicit doctrinaire predispositions. Conservative, liberal, and radical writers all have made arguments of one sort or another which I consider persuasive, but I do not identify totally with any single school—no doubt partly because these terms are vague labels which serve as useful shorthand.

Initially, I found little theoretical work in international relations helpful. A number of recent works, however, are relevant and insightful and are cited in the notes to chapter 7. My conclusions tend to confirm some of their hypotheses and call others into question. The relationship of my approach to "transnational" and "bureaucratic" perspectives is discussed in chapter 1. Conclusions about the utility of these perspectives can be drawn from chapter 7 and elsewhere. I have also been attentive to the work of Marxists and dependency theorists, and issues concerning them are discussed frequently, particularly in the conclusions.

My findings have clustered around two major themes. The first deals with revolutionary seizures of U.S. direct investments in the countries concerned and the U.S. responses thereto. My graduate-student assistants and I have spent many weeks assembling what one would have thought was elementary information already available: namely, what property was seized, its approximate value as reflected in claims or evaluations, and what, if any, compensation had been paid. Books by Eric Baklanoff and George Ingram, cited in chapter 4, notes 30 and 59, from Praeger Publishers, which were published just as this study was going to press, will provide future researchers with information that I lacked. The other major theme deals with the impact of U.S. global strategies toward Germany or the Soviet Union on U.S. responses in Latin America.

My research has brought to light for the first time new information about the four countries whose relations with the United States constitute the core of this volume: Mexico, Bolivia, Guatemala, and Cuba. With respect to Mexico, my most important contribution is to clarify the record of German-Mexican relations as they relate to U.S. responses during World War I and on the eve of World War II. Similarly, the German archives have cleared up charges of Nazi involvement with the MNR in Bolivia, and I have been able to assemble other evidence explaining U.S. involve-

ment in the Villarroel and MNR governments. The section on U.S. relations with
Arévalo in Guatemala may be the first study of its kind, and there is much new
evidence showing the hows and why of U.S. involvement in Guatemalan affairs
under Arbenz. Although my account of U.S.-Cuban relations contained new information and interpretations at the time it was written, it is now primarily useful for its
analysis of these events in the light of my specific theme. On the whole, this book's
most important contributions to the historical record probably are its disclosures
about Bolivia and Guatemala because the relations of these countries with the United
States have received far less scholarly attention than those of Mexico and Cuba.

My work began before the Peruvian military overthrew Belaunde in late 1968 and
was largely finished before the fall of Allende in Chile in September 1973. It was not
until that latter event and the U.S. Peruvian settlement of February 1974 that the U.S.
responses to these two social revolutions could be characterized as having taken
clearly recognizable shape. Much information about both countries remains to be
made public before definitive evaluations may be made of U.S. responses to either
revolution. The continuing revelations in 1974 and 1975 about U.S. policy toward
the Allende government in Chile suggest that so far we may have seen only the tip of
the iceberg.

Knowledge about U.S. relations with these two countries during these crucial
years is likely to become available only gradually, and definitive studies will probably not be possible until the diplomatic archives are opened to the public, if then. At
the present rate that means a lag of more than a quarter of a century. Reaching
conclusions now about the Peruvian and Chilean cases involves substantial risks of
error, but they are the same risks that are involved, to a much lesser degree, in
analyzing events at greater historical distance. For example, for this study I have been
able to consult the U.S. diplomatic archives only for the Mexican revolution and the
very early years of the Bolivian and Guatemalan revolutions. If research is to have
much current utility, we cannot afford to wait until the U.S. government decides to
make its records available to the public. Moreover, readers will probably have an
intense interest in the extent to which work on earlier revolutions helps us to interpret
recent events in Peru and Chile.

As a result, I decided to focus my central attention on the four earlier revolutions
about which we know a good deal, that is, up to the Bay of Pigs, and draw conclusions
about patterns of U.S. official responses in these four cases. Those conclusions are
based on extensive research in primary and secondary sources over a span of a half
dozen years. In an epilogue, chapter 8, I have tested these conclusions against the
necessarily more superficial study, based primarily on secondary sources, of U.S.
responses to the recent revolutions in Peru and Chile. This analysis emphasizes the
distinction in research method and reliability between the first seven chapters and the
last one.

The book is organized according to stages in the revolutionary process and the
nature of U.S. responses. The table of contents includes the subheadings in each of
the chapters so that readers who are interested in tracing chronologically the U.S.
responses to a particular country can do so with ease.

Although a policy-oriented study, this book devotes little attention to specific policy recommendations. There are a number of reasons for this. First, I thought it was more important to establish what U.S. policies had been before suggesting what they should be. That has proved a large task in itself. Second, I did not want controversy about specific recommendations to interfere with or to undermine whatever authority my conclusions may have. With a record before them, readers themselves will be better able to form conclusions about what U.S. policy should be. A distillation of my own views about the lessons of history are contained at the end of chapter 8.

Readers who want specific recommendations for the mid-1970s should consult *The Americas in a Changing World*, the report of the Commission on United States Latin American Relations which is being published by Quadrangle Books in 1975. Prepared by a panel of businessmen, educators, and journalists, the report's thirty-three recommendations represent an enlightened approach for reconciling the conflicting interests of the United States, on the one hand, and Latin American nations, on the other.

As my work has progressed, I have published by-products of my research as articles and contributions to studies of specific countries. The articles deal with controversial episodes whose analysis has required more argument and evidence than I felt appropriate for this book. They are "The United States, Germany, and the Bolivian Revolutionaries (1941–1946)," *Hispanic American Historical Review*, 52, no. 1 (February 1972), and "The United States and Madero," *Journal of Latin American Studies*, 4, pt. 2 (November 1972). The contributions to books were published in multiauthor works edited by my colleagues at the University of Pittsburgh as part of an informal effort involving comparative studies of social revolution. These chapters are "The United States and the Revolution," in James M. Malloy and Richard S. Thorn, eds., *Beyond the Revolution: Bolivia Since 1952* (University of Pittsburgh Press, 1971) and "The Elimination of United States Influence," in Carmelo Mesa-Lago, ed., *Revolutionary Change in Cuba* (University of Pittsburgh Press, 1971). I draw heavily on all four of these studies here. Each contains material which did not seem appropriate for use in this book, and I have added fresh material here on each country so that this volume provides the most authoritative and comprehensive treatment for these countries with respect to its central theme.

I have found German archival sources to be very rewarding in dealing with the revolutionary movements' ties with Germany. Soviet sources have been of limited usefulness because Soviet scholars appear to lack access to their own diplomatic archives and to Communist party documents and use roughly the same sources as scholars in the West. The translations from these and other languages used here are my own, except as otherwise indicated.

There is one glaring omission among my source materials, the total absence of any reference to Latin American diplomatic archives. I made routine efforts to gain access to archives in Bolivia and Guatemala mainly as a matter of principle, since the political situation in both countries at the times of my visits largely ruled out such a possibility. As a simple illustration, most of the published works dealing with the Arévalo and Arbenz period were removed from the national library in Guatemala.

The Mexican government has announced its intent to make some archives available; my informal inquiries through well-connected intermediaries indicated, however, that I was unlikely to be able to use them before my press deadline.

Readers may find my treatment of U.S. policies of the past sharply critical of U.S. officials and Latin American revolutionaries. That is as it should be since my main purpose is to encourage constructive criticism and discussions toward the larger purposes of mutual understanding and reconciliation. If a tone of self-righteousness has crept into my work, I regret it. With the benefit of hindsight it is far easier to criticize the past conduct of others than to act constructively in the present.

Many specialists have read and commented on individual sections of this manuscript: E. David Cronon and Friedrich Katz (Mexico); William D. Broderick, the late Carter W. Goodrich, James M. Malloy, and Richard S. Thorn (Bolivia); Kalman Silvert (Guatemala); Rolando Bonachea, Philip W. Bonsal, Ernesto Betancourt, and Carmelo Mesa-Lago (Cuba); and Abraham Lowenthal and José Moreno (Dominican Republic). I have also received many helpful suggestions of a general character from others who read all of the manuscript or its conclusions: Philip W. Bonsal, Heinrich Brünner, Richard W. Cottam, Peter Carsten, Reid R. Reading, and Robert S. Walters. The publisher's editors, Louise Craft and Sally Mennen, also made useful criticisms.

Thanks are also due to many Latin American and North American leaders who gave generously of their time in interviews, many of which are acknowledged in the notes. I much appreciate the assistance given to me by librarians at the Library of Congress and at the Hillman Library at the University of Pittsburgh. Eduardo Lozano, the Latin American bibliographer of the latter library, has been immensely helpful to me from the beginning to the end of my task. I also want to express my thanks to my former graduate-student assistants, Herbert Braun, Gerald Lemega, and especially to Judith Ludvik who has worked with me for the last three years.

Most of the research and writing for the study was completed while I was simultaneously teaching in the Department of Political Science and serving as Director of the Center for Latin American Studies at the University of Pittsburgh. I appreciate the unfailing cooperation of the Chairman of the Department, William J. Keefe, and the moral and material support of the Director of the University Center for International Studies, Carl Beck. My greatest debt, however, is to Ms. Shirley Kregar, the Administrative Specialist in the Center, without whose executive skills and editorial assistance this book would not have been feasible.

Cole Blasier

University of Pittsburgh
February 28, 1975

The Hovering Giant

1 Introduction: Revolutionary Change

Revolutions have been among the most dramatic political events in the twentieth century, possibly exceeded in their global repercussions only by the two world wars. Much of the attention of U.S. leaders and the U.S. public has been devoted to coping with revolutionary upheavals in Russia and China and in developing countries, such as Mexico, Cuba, and Vietnam. Revolutions in Latin America have been of special concern in the United States partly because U.S. vested interests there tend to be greater than in other developing areas and because the United States has long regarded Latin America as vital to its strategic interests.

The old regimes in Latin America have been vulnerable to revolutionary ferment because many have been characterized by poverty and dictatorship. Seeking to make government more responsive to popular needs, revolutionary leaders have overthrown old regimes and initiated revolutionary change in Mexico, Bolivia, Guatemala, and Cuba, and in the 1970s in Peru and Chile.

These societies have often been perceived as separate national entities when in fact they are an integral part of the international system. For this reason revolutionary change in these countries has had far-reaching international repercussions, particularly in the United States, which has interlocking relationships with virtually all its Latin American neighbors. Such revolutionary upheavals have affected U.S. economic interests, military arrangements, and political relations. Conflict with the old regimes has often been transformed into conflict with the United States.

The consequences of revolutionary change have been among the most demanding and frequently recurring problems the United States has been forced to face in Latin America since the early part of this century. In turn, U.S. responses to these revolutionary upheavals have had a deep and lasting impact on the societies concerned.

Revolutionary change burst to the surface in Mexico on the eve of World War I, in Bolivia and Guatemala during World War II, and in Cuba in the late 1950s. Revolutionary ferment appeared to be brewing in the Dominican Republic in the early 1960s, and revolutionary change itself began in Peru and Chile as the 1970s began. The U.S. government and the public at large have focused more attention on social revolutions in Latin America than on those anywhere else in the Third World, except in Indochina.

In the following chapters I describe, compare, and explain U.S. responses to revolutionary change in Latin America. The main cases discussed are Mexico (1910–1940), Bolivia (1943–1964), Guatemala (1944–1954), and Cuba (1956–1961). These four cases are discussed in chapters 2–6 and the findings summarized in chapter 7. U.S. responses to the process of revolutionary change since the Cuban Revolution (1961) are discussed in the Epilogue, chapter 8. The last chapter examines the process in recent years in terms of the major findings of chapter 7 with particular reference to the Dominican Republic, Peru, and Chile. Readers should note that chapters 2–7 are based mainly on primary sources, while the Epilogue, chapter 8, is based mainly on secondary sources.

The term "revolutionary change" means an exceptionally rapid, comprehensive, and profound form of social change,[1] usually accompanied by violence and resulting in an abrupt and explosive break with the past. This social process redefines man's relationship to land, machines, and other men, thereby reordering the composition of social groups and their relationships to one another.

Land is seized and redistributed, mineral and industrial properties are taken over by the state, and revolutionary political movements seize control of government. Previously authoritative groups are suddenly excluded from access to power.[2] The social structure and values of the old regime are swept aside; new structures are established and revolutionary values proclaimed. The best-known examples of revolutionary change are the French, Bolshevik, and Chinese Communist revolutions. The Latin American nations most transformed by revolutionary change are Mexico, Bolivia, and Cuba. Peru and Chile must now also be considered for inclusion in this latter group.

The revolutionary process in these countries can be divided into three stages (see table 1). In the first stage, *rebel movements* organized and overthrew the old regime, usually dominated by military dictators (chapter 2). In the second stage, the rebels gained control of the governmental apparatus and, instead of revolutionizing society, established *reformist governments*; some of these governments were overthrown by force (chapter 3). After an interval, the revolutionaries returned to power and established *revolutionary governments*. At this point, the third stage and revolutionary change itself began: the revolutionaries gained control of and revolutionized the political and governmental systems, seized land and other properties, and introduced changes in foreign relations (chapters 4–6). Sometimes the expressions "revolutionaries" or "revolutionary movements" are used to emphasize the continuity of the process without special reference to any particular stage.

The three-stage revolutionary process can also be applied to revolutions outside Latin America. In China, for example, there were the rebel movements against the Manchus, the reformist governments of Sun Yat-sen and Chiang Kai-shek, and revolutionary change under the Chinese Communists. Similarly, the overthrow of the czar marked the end of the first stage in Russia, the brief provisional government had

TABLE 1
STAGES IN THE REVOLUTIONARY PROCESS

	Old Regime	Stage 1: Rebel Movement	Stage 2: Reformist Government	Stage 3: Revolutionary Government
Mexico	Díaz (1876–1911)	Madero	Madero (1911–1913)	Carranza through Cárdenas (1915–1940)
Guatemala	Ubico (1931–1944)	Arana Arbenz Toriello	Arévalo (1945–1951)	Arbenz (1951–1954)
Bolivia[1]	Peñaranda (1940–1943)	Villarroel	Villarroel/Paz (1943–1946)	Paz or Siles (1952–1964)
Cuba[2]	Batista (1952–1959)	Castro	Castro (Jan.–May 1959)	Castro (May 1959–)

The following are variations in the revolutionary process:

1. Hernán Siles led the MNR forces in an urban insurrection against a military junta in April 1952.

2. In September 1933 Ramón Grau San Martín overthrew Manuel Céspedes, a successor to the dictator Gerard Machado (1925–1933). Governments headed by Grau (1944–1948) and Carlos Prío Socorrás (1948–1952) may also be considered reformist governments. Castro, however, repudiated those governments and launched a rebel movement of his own. I have dated the onset of revolutionary change in Cuba from the proclamation of the agrarian reform in May 1959.

a reformist character, and the Bolsheviks introduced revolutionary change. In Peru and Chile the administrations of Belaunde and Frei can be viewed as reformist governments superseded by revolutionary change under Velasco and Allende.

Revolutionary change in Latin America has had serious repercussions in the United States because the United States has dominated the Caribbean economically and politically since the end of the nineteenth century, and its ties with all the Latin American countries have been especially great since World War II. With the defeat of Nazi Germany and the retreat of Great Britain after 1945, U.S. influence spread deeper into South America. In fact, it penetrated most sectors of Latin American societies, reaching its apogee during the early years of the Alliance for Progress.

United States investment, which rapidly expanded beyond the extractive industries and public services into manufacturing, became the most dynamic force in the economies of many countries. United States direct private investment in Latin America has been and is greater than in any of the other developing regions of the world.[3] In fact, U.S. investment in Mexico in 1913 and in Cuba in 1959 was far greater than U.S. investments in Russia or China on the eve of revolution,[4] or for that matter, greater than in almost any contemporary developing country outside the hemisphere today.

United States trade with Latin America has long been greater than with other developing regions of the world.[5] Most of the exports of the countries of the north and a large share of those in the south are bought by the United States. In return it supplies the bulk of imports to many countries. Through private branch banking, U.S. economic assistance agencies, and international agencies under U.S. influence or control, the United States has been the major external source of Latin American finance capital. Much economic aid has been administered with the assistance and supervision of U.S. officials who served as advisers in industry, agriculture, finance, public administration, education, and health.

The United States also has provided much military equipment, munitions, and military training for Latin American armed forces through outright grants, sales of surplus equipment, and long-term credits on favorable terms. United States military assistance missions have been located in most countries in addition to the military attachés from the three services in U.S. embassies. The United States has maintained army, navy, or air force bases in Cuba, Puerto Rico, Trinidad, and the Canal Zone, in addition to satellite tracking stations in South America. There also appears to have been in the area a vast network of clandestine intelligence operations, most of which are not a matter of public knowledge to this day. Some of these are known to have included covert support for the anti-Communist labor federations that ultimately expelled Communist leaders from many if not all trade unions in the area.

Even the Latin American churches did not escape influence from the United States. The U.S. Catholic hierarchy and Protestant missions exerted great influence, partly through their control of funds for evangelical and charitable activities. Although independent of official U.S. controls, the large U.S. foundations have provided much risk capital for scientific and humanistic research. Many countries have relied heavily on U.S. media for news and television programming.

In these complex relationships, the United States has been the most powerful nation in the hemisphere on which individual Latin American countries have been dependent.[6] In great measure dependency has been the inevitable result of disparities in economic and political power. With its technology, productive capacity, markets, financial resources, and military power, the United States has easily maintained its bargaining advantage. United States leaders have been able to influence the domestic and foreign policies of individual Latin American countries whereas the latter have had virtually no chance of influencing domestic U.S. developments or U.S. policies toward nations other than themselves. Sometimes only dimly perceived, often deeply felt, dependence on the United States became a major concern of revolutionary movements in Latin America. In fact, revolutionary activities have been directed not only at incumbent governments and the system that sustained them but also at the United States and the international arrangements integral to the national reality.

My analysis of the conflict between revolutionary movements and the United States unfolds in terms of Latin American actions and corresponding U.S. reactions. The focus will first be on the actions of revolutionary leaders and the reactions of the presidents of the United States and their senior associates (secretaries of state, senior officers in the Department of State and other agencies dealing with Latin American affairs, and U.S. ambassadors to the countries concerned). Finally, the impact of U.S. reactions on the countries concerned will be discussed briefly.

The Issues Posed

The single most important question is why a nation as large and powerful as the United States sponsored paramilitary forces to suppress or attempt to suppress revolutionary movements in countries as small and weak as Guatemala and Cuba? Why with its overwhelming economic, political, and military power was the United States unable to achieve a negotiated settlement of outstanding disputes with these countries?

The United States has not suppressed all revolutionary movements in Latin America. It became the principal supporter and ally of revolutionary governments in Mexico and Bolivia. Why was reconciliation achieved with these two countries and suppression not attempted as in Guatemala and Cuba?

Two well-known explanations of U.S. interventionist policies need testing. One explanation frequently offered has been the alleged threat of international communism or Soviet imperialism. What was the nature of U.S. official perceptions with regard to Communist or Soviet influence in the countries concerned, and were these perceptions correct? What did the United States really mean by the Communist threat? Do the Mexican and Bolivian revolutionaries' experiences with Germany and the resultant implications for U.S. policy throw any light on U.S. responses to the orientations of revolutionary governments vis-à-vis the Soviet Union?

The second explanation has been that U.S. intervention has been motivated by private business interests who have used the U.S. government as a weapon to help them exploit Latin American countries economically. Do the alleged rapacious appetites (for profit) of U.S. "imperialists" explain the U.S. intervention in Guatemala in 1954 and in Cuba in 1961? In answering these questions it will be important to describe and explain not only U.S. conduct but also that of the revolutionaries. What was the relative influence of the parties on the outcome? Closely related to this is an examination of who was primarily responsible for framing the U.S. responses. Was the nature of the response affected by the level of government at which it was decided?

Another question relates to whether there were recurring patterns of U.S. behavior in each of the three stages of revolutionary change. How did U.S. officials respond to Madero and Castro in the first stage, that is, before they seized power, and how did the conduct of these two men affect U.S. policies? Put another way, were there consistent patterns of behavior toward rebel movements? If not, why not? What were the patterns of U.S. behavior in the reformist stage? United States officials were implicated in efforts to overthrow reformist presidents in all four countries. Why such hostility? What was the responsibility in this respect of U.S. ambassadors and military representatives?

What was the impact of revolutionary change on U.S. private interests? How much did U.S. investors lose through expropriation and to what extent were they compensated?

In a more general vein, what instruments did the United States use to achieve its ends? How did U.S. blandishments and sanctions work? What was the impact of U.S. policies on the Latin American countries concerned and on U.S. interests there and elsewhere? What were some of the long-term consequences of U.S. policies? What are the implications of some of the findings with respect to recent U.S. policies toward revolutionary governments in Peru and Chile?

Answers to these and other questions are advanced beginning in chapter 2. My major findings are summarized in chapter 7, and these are reexamined in the light of recent events in chapter 8.

Analytical Perspectives

The following chapters describing and explaining U.S. responses to the revolutionary process in Latin America are designed to increase mutually beneficial relations in the future. Although the main purpose is not a study of the decision-making process in the White House and the Department of State per se, the evidence presented and the kinds of interactions singled out for study correspond to analytical categories much discussed in recent political-science literature on the decision-making process.

The "bureaucratic politics" perspective in the Halperin-Kanter reader on foreign policy, for example, describes "foreign policy decisions and actions as a non-frivolous game—the result of regulated interaction of several individuals and domestic organizations (usually intra-governmental), planning strategies, bargaining with one another, each struggling to achieve a particular objective." This perspective emphasizes the "centrality of those individuals who are members of the national security bureaucracy."[7] Readers will find such *intra*governmental bargaining important in my explanation of U.S. responses to Madero in 1913, to the Mexican oil expropriations in 1938, to the Arbenz government in 1954, and to Castro in 1960.

Closely related to this perspective, and sometimes included in it, is consideration of the impact of domestic politics on foreign policy. Domestic political factors, for example, are especially important in my explanations of the U.S. official decision to use force in the Guatemalan and Cuban episodes. I present relatively little material on "bureaucratic politics" inside individual Latin American governments, but this work deals extensively with the domestic politics of individual countries as it relates to revolutionary change and U.S. official policies.

Material in the following chapters which is illustrative of the "bureaucratic politics" perspective will not be labeled as such, but discussions of this category of interactions appear in the concluding sections of chapters 2, 3, 5, and 6. Comment on the utility of this perspective in analyzing U.S. responses is made in chapter 7.

Another perspective, among whose leading advocates are Robert Keohane and Joseph Nye, favors the analysis of world politics according to a "transnational relations" paradigm. This perspective asserts that study of "classic" interactions, involving governments and international governmental organizations, is not enough. The paradigm also includes the study of the interactions among nongovernmental groups in society as well as the interactions of those groups with governmental entities and their subunits. Thus, transnational relations are defined as interactions in which at least one of the parties is a nongovernmental actor.[8]

Transnational as well as intergovernmental relations are treated in the following chapters. The main theme of two of the five core chapters involves transnational relations. Chapter 2, for example, deals with the relations between the U.S. government and rebel movements. Chapter 4 deals primarily with Latin American government seizures of the property of U.S.-owned multinational corporations. Discussion of the activities of labor, paramilitary organizations, and political parties constantly recurs.

Continuity and Change

The revolutionary process in Latin America has spanned well over half a century from Madero's rebellion of 1910–1911 to the Allende government in Chile (1970–1973). In analyzing that process I will compare rebel, reformist, and revolutionary governments widely separated in time and space. An effort will be made to take into account the different geographic and temporal settings.

What is most striking, however, are the similarities in that process wherever and whenever it has taken place, both with respect to Latin American actions and U.S. reactions. The revolutionary movements have invariably sought greater public control over the economy, over political life, and over foreign relations with broader representation of the interests of industrial and rural labor. The United States has consistently emphasized the protection of U.S. private investment and shown concern over the relations of the governments with the Great Power rivals of the United States. United States foreign policy instruments have been similar: the granting or withholding of recognition, commodity purchases, credits, arms sales, grants, and, in extreme cases, the sponsorship of armed intervention. The same or similar problems have continued to recur throughout the years.

The great divide in the international scene was the year 1947, the beginning of the Cold War. Even the fear of communism that developed thereafter was by no means the first international ideological conflict that had touched the Americas. Roosevelt and Hull feared Nazi influence in Mexico before and during World War II and in Bolivia during the war. There had been a touch of U.S. hysteria about nazism in Latin America at that time just as there was about communism later.

What most distinguished the Cold War from earlier periods was the intensity of U.S. fears that communism is contagious.[9] This went beyond the fear of Soviet nuclear and military might per se.

The Soviet-American tensions during the Cold War were based partly on genuine conflicts of interests and values. The two strongest players in almost any arena are apt to be at odds. Each regards the other as threatening. Beginning in 1945 the United States was virtually the only government that could seriously threaten the Soviet Union and vice versa. Both actually did take steps that the other correctly considered threatening. The U.S. interest in a free and independent Eastern Europe was a threat to Soviet defensive strategy vis-à-vis Germany. Soviet sponsorship of the expansion of international communism affected U.S. interests around the world. Soviet and American interests and beliefs clashed on many issues.

Fostered initially by the Truman administration to mobilize U.S. resources for the reconstruction of Western Europe, anticommunism gained a viselike grip on the public at large. The hysterical proportions which it reached were first and foremost due to ignorance. Stalin shut off the Soviet Union from the West; what Americans did not know and did not understand they feared. Soviet capabilities were exaggerated to inhuman proportions.

Soviet policies and ideologies also posed a direct challenge or offended most vested interests in the United States: property owners, union leaders, the free press, the churches, Jews, and Eastern European immigrants. Anticommunism became a rallying point for diverse interests; it united liberals, conservatives, and reactionaries. The consensus was so broad, the majority so great, that the pressures for conformity approached a kind of social tyranny.

The effect on U.S. policy toward Latin America was to distort the judgment of U.S. leaders, officials, and the public. Fears of communism prevented them from evaluating the political developments in Latin American countries objectively. So much emphasis was placed on following Communist activities that diplomats and journalists underestimated and overlooked other groups. United States observers lost their perspective. Vigorous critiques of communism and recommendations for strong anti-Communist measures were interpreted as evidence of group loyalty. Advocacy of moderation and restraint with respect to the Communist issue was suspect. Groups with vested interests in the status quo used anticommunism for self-serving purposes. Proponents of social change were placed on the defensive.

The extent of U.S. fear of communism was demonstrated in the extreme hostility of the U.S. responses to the Guatemalan and Cuban revolutions and the Dominican revolt. U.S. policy makers were afraid that the communism allegedly infecting these countries would spread elsewhere in Latin America. In some quarters there appear to have been fears, perhaps unconscious, that communism in Latin America might even be catching in the United States. Another development was a shift in the purposes of U.S. military assistance from defense from external enemies to defense of the internal order from subversion. Military assistance was complemented by U.S.-sponsored programs in police assistance as well.

Another important Cold War development was the introduction of clandestine operations as a major instrument of U.S. policy in Latin America. The most dramatic cases were the U.S.-sponsored armed movements of exiles from Guatemala and Cuba. The United States appears to have provided clandestine support for anti-Communist organizations such as labor unions.

The peak of U.S. anticommunism in Latin America was reached in the Dominican intervention of 1965. Critical reactions to the intervention in the United States and Latin America led to a soberer view of international realities. The crushing of Che Guevara in Bolivia in 1967 was the symbol of the end of a phase of Communist activity in the hemisphere. Meanwhile, détente with the Soviet Union and the chastening effects of the Vietnam War led ultimately to a lower U.S. profile in Latin America, the phrase that characterized President Nixon's policies in the region.

As the 1970s opened, revolutionary ferment continued, especially in Peru and Chile, but Washington appeared convinced, as it had not been in the case of Castro, that these countries' foreign policies, whatever their other features, did not seek Soviet interference in the hemisphere. Active domestic opposition with U.S. covert support, when also joined with that of the Chilean armed forces, proved too much for Allende, and he was overthrown by a military coup in September 1973, a development which appears to have evoked a sigh of relief in the Nixon administration. In February 1974 the United States and Peru reached a settlement of a broad range of issues, the most vexing of which had been Peru's expropriations of U.S.-owned properties.

Revolutionary ferment abated in Latin America as 1975 approached. The only existing revolutionary government in the area with which the United States had not yet come to terms was the Cuban, and even Castro had largely ceased to support actively guerrilla movements elsewhere in the Americas. What was probably only a temporary lull in the process of revolutionary change gave U.S. leaders a rare opportunity to reassess the past in a relatively calm period of inter-American relations. What, then, are the lessons to be learned from the United States' long experience in Latin America which will help meet the challenges of revolutionary change in the future?

I

Prelude to Revolutionary Change

Rebel Movements: Flexibility

All the rebels treated in this study were winners, at least for a time (see table 2). Each movement gained full control of the machinery of government in its respective country and was recognized by the United States, with whom normal diplomatic and trade relations were carried on, in some cases for many years.

Later chapters will describe how the United States responded to the rebels in power; this chapter deals with the rebels before they gained control of their respective governments.

Rebels

The men who seized the initiative and separately led the rebel movements against dictatorial governments in the four countries selected here have backgrounds surprisingly alike. All came from well-established, small-town families of affluent, or at least moderate, means. Most were of middle class or in the case of Francisco I. Madero of Mexico of upper-class background. All were writers, at least of a sort.

TABLE 2
REBEL MOVEMENTS

	Dictator	Rebel Leader	Decisive Event	Date	Tactic
Mexico	Díaz (1876–1911)	Madero	Battle of Ciudad Juárez	1910–1911	Armed revolt
Bolivia	Military junta	Siles	Attack on armed train, La Paz	1952	Urban insurrections
Guatemala	Ubico (1931–1944)	Arana Arbenz Toriello	General strike, Guatemala City	1944	Demonstrations, strikes
Cuba	Batista (1933–1944, 1952–1958)	Castro	Battle of Santa Clara	1957–1959	Urban resistance, guerrilla warfare

Prepared by Herbert Braun and Judith Ludvik.

Juan José Arévalo wrote poetic essays and books on education and philosophy. Madero was the author of the famous *Presidential Succession in 1910*. Víctor Paz Estenssoro of Bolivia and Fidel Castro of Cuba, although more interested in social action than in writing, were eloquent speakers whose public statements were widely published and circulated.

Most of these rebel leaders had characters of a sentimental or passionate nature; they could easily qualify as romantics and, in varying senses, idealists. The only exception was Paz Estenssoro who was a coolly intelligent economist and lawyer. And only Paz had held high administrative responsibility—heading the Ministries of Economy and Finance—before becoming president.

All the rebels, except the Bolivian, sought to overthrow dictators long established in power. Most of the dictators had come to power in violation of legal or constitutional norms, and all retained control extralegally or by self-serving constitutional manipulations. They ruled, often brutally, through political oppression.

The rebels shared a deeply entrenched, passionate, and relentless hostility toward the dictatorial regimes, sparing themselves no personal sacrifice to combat them. None established fortunes of their own, although Madero managed his family's properties for many years. Madero and Castro suffered imprisonment. All lived in exile, most for long periods; Arévalo and Paz, for example, lived for many years in Argentina.

The rebels' passionate opposition to dictatorship distinguished them more than their political or social views. They stood mainly for political democracy, with free elections and civil rights, and for social gains that had long been taken for granted in the United States. Castro was explicit about these matters, particularly in regard to a return to the Constitution of 1940. All of the rebel leaders, except Castro, were eventually elected president of their respective countries in free elections. Those who came to espouse radical views, namely Castro and, to a lesser extent, Arévalo, did so some time after they had seized power, not before.

Most were educated in a milieu typical of that of other Latin American intellectuals of their time—oriented toward Europe rather than the United States. The greatest foreign cultural influences on Madero were French, and his residence in Paris as a student influenced him the rest of his life. Arévalo and Paz spent many years in Argentina where foreign cultural influences were predominantly European. Both had traveled far more in Europe than in the United States. Castro was the only one of the four leaders whose development was not profoundly shaped by European influences.

Madero was the only one of the four revolutionary leaders who had more than a superficial knowledge of the United States. He attended St. Mary's College in Baltimore, Maryland, in his early teens, studied agriculture at the University of California, Berkeley, and lived in exile in the United States. Madero manifested respect for political practices in the United States in discussing democracy in his book on the presidential succession.

Arévalo and Paz Estenssoro knew a good deal about U.S. relations with Latin

America, and they looked critically at U.S. behavior, just as many Latin American intellectuals have before and since. Discussion of U.S. policy, if any, in their early works was temperate and reasonably detached. Paz Estenssoro was outspokenly critical of U.S. "imperialism," but he was also explicit about Bolivia's unavoidable economic dependence on the West and especially on the United States. Arévalo was not particularly interested in U.S. policy.

In spite of his fund-raising trips in the United States, Castro probably knew less about the United States than the other leaders. This was partly because he simply had not had time, arriving at the leadership of his country at a far younger age. Castro's early speeches have surprisingly little to say about the United States and U.S. interests despite their immense role in Cuban history. In his "History Will Absolve Me" speech, Castro does express concern that "over half the best lands under cultivation are in the hands of foreigners" and "the lands of the United Fruit Company and the West Indian Company run from coast to coast in [Oriente] province."[1] In this statement, Castro also called for the nationalization of the power and telephone companies, though not identifying them as U.S.-owned. Overt attacks on U.S. imperialism were notably absent from Castro's statements.

Some believe that Castro held back attacks on the United States for tactical reasons. He himself explained later, "Radical revolutionaries . . . do not announce programs that might unite all our enemies on a single front."[2] But Castro's near silence on such important issues should not be explained away that easily. There are all sorts of ways he could have safely discussed U.S.–Cuban relations if he had had the knowledge to do so. Castro also confirmed his ignorance of this subject when he admitted "idealistic" and "utopian" views on foreign policy.[3]

Castro and the other rebel leaders, however, were associated with men who had more radical and doctrinaire views about the United States. For example, Che Guevara in the early years was a readier critic of the United States than was Castro. Juan Lechín was more critical than Paz Estenssoro. Arévalo eventually took a bitterly critical position toward U.S. policy in polemical works,[4] but his resentment was formed after, not before, he assumed presidential office.

The United States as a Revolutionary Base for Mexico and Cuba

Madero and Castro both used the United States as a base for revolutionary activities, Madero primarily to organize armed units and Castro as a means of publicizing his cause. Official U.S. agencies had extensive dealings with both Madero and Castro during their rebellions.

Refugees have long sought to organize rebel movements in the United States against incumbent Mexican governments. Francisco I. Madero put U.S. soil to more effective use for this purpose than any other Mexican activist, but he was by no means the first. One of his rivals within the broader Mexican revolutionary movement, Ricardo Flores Magón, was convicted for violating the neutrality laws in 1908 and detained in prison in the United States.

Madero's decision to flee to the United States and launch a revolutionary movement there did not come until after his campaign for the presidency in the 1910 elections gained momentum and Díaz had imprisoned him. With the electoral route to power closed, Madero opted for revolution—organized and supplied partly from the United States. After escaping from prison, he fled to San Antonio, Texas, from which he issued his first major revolutionary manifesto, the Plan of San Luis Potosí. In attempting to organize and lead his revolution from the United States, Madero risked arrest and imprisonment by the U.S. authorities for violations of the neutrality laws.

As a result, the manner in which the U.S. government implemented the neutrality laws and its policies toward the Díaz government had an important bearing on the prospects of Madero's rebel movement. U.S. relations with Díaz were subject to numerous crosscurrents. On the one hand, U.S. private interests were not always treated by Díaz as they might have wished, particularly insofar as competition with British and other European interests was concerned. Also, the United States and Mexico had backed opposing factions in Nicaragua, a further source of tension.

Nevertheless, relations between the two governments were relatively good. Díaz had brought an era of stability and prosperity to Mexico which contrasted sharply with the economic and political chaos that characterized postindependence Mexico and many other nineteenth-century governments in Latin America. President Taft made an unprecedented visit across the Mexican border in 1909 and sent a prestigious delegation to the Mexican centennial celebration in September 1910. Taft and Ambassador Wilson admired Díaz's achievements and welcomed the protection he afforded U.S. investors in Mexico.

The luminous celebration of the centennial and the sentiments of U.S. officials did not blind them to Díaz's personal weaknesses or to the weaknesses of his regime. Ambassador Wilson called attention to Díaz's "senile vanity" and "tendency toward maudlin sentimentality,"[5] and pointed out that his autocratic authority rested on army and police controls. He called attention to the excessive concentration of land, the impoverishment of the poor, and the incompetence and corruption around Díaz, particularly in the judiciary. Ambassador Wilson also predicted the turbulence unleashed by the revolution and the inevitable passing of Díaz.[6] Taft was concerned about the succession as well and expressed hope that the deluge expected with Díaz's passing could be deferred until after his own term had expired. This hope proved futile.[7]

President Taft and his ambassador were not hostile toward Díaz as a person or necessarily to his administration as such, but they were fully aware of its increasing precariousness and the explosive forces churning beneath the surface of Mexican society. In this sense both were observers standing at one side, helpless to stem the avalanche. Their major interest was not to buttress Díaz's crumbling edifice, but to protect American interests in the rapidly approaching collapse. A massive effort to save Díaz apparently was never seriously considered.

The foregoing helps explain why Madero was able to launch his revolution from

U.S. soil. Almost alone and with few resources in a foreign land, he could not have hoped to survive had the U.S. authorities proceeded resolutely against him. At the least, he needed to count on their not applying U.S. neutrality laws harshly against him. Fortunate in this respect, Madero carried out his revolutionary plans against Díaz without being seized by the U.S. authorities. He maintained a large correspondence by mail to Mexico, issued proclamations, statements, and circulars, purchased arms and other military supplies, and recruited men for the revolutionary forces—but all the while he was wary of arrest and frequently changed his address. The Díaz government filed its protests against Madero's activity in both Mexico City and Washington from the beginning, in November of 1910, well into the early months of 1911. Mexican diplomats in both capitals kept the United States well informed of Madero's movements and repeatedly called for his detention and prosecution under U.S. laws.

One result of these seemingly endless demarches was a mass of diplomatic correspondence on the subject, as well as numerous exchanges of messages between Washington and the U.S. authorities along the border. But Madero remained at large actively fomenting the revolution.

The Department of State, with the advice of the Department of Justice, was inclined to interpret U.S. laws in a narrow fashion, that is, in a way favorable to the revolutionaries. Secretary Knox explicitly excluded Madero's propaganda against the Díaz regime as a violation of the U.S. neutrality laws because of the U.S. Constitution's guarantees of freedom of speech and of the press.[8] Secretary Knox explained to the Mexican ambassador that the neutrality laws did not prohibit the export of arms or the transport of men for revolutionary purposes abroad, only the launching of a military expedition across the U.S. border.[9]

Such an interpretation of the neutrality laws made it difficult to prefer charges against Madero. The U.S. attorney of western Texas wired Washington on December 2, 1910, in answer to a request for the arrest of Madero, that he had insufficient evidence to show a violation of the neutrality laws.[10] In addition, public opinion in the Southwest was frequently hostile to Díaz and sympathetic to Madero, as Mexican consuls reported to their foreign minister.[11] As a result, officials in Washington hesitated to press cases with doubtful evidence in an unsympathetic venue.

The most authoritative analyses maintain that the U.S. government usually interpreted the neutrality laws in a manner sympathetic to the followers of Madero.[12] Díaz's successor as provisional president, Francisco Léon de la Barra, contended that "the American government, although it ostensibly gave its support to General Díaz, was impotent to prevent neutrality violations since, while having placed a cordon of troops along the entire border, shipments of arms and munitions passed through every day and multitudes of sympathizers of the rebellion entered Mexico anyway. Public opinion, in addition, was already notoriously opposed to the [Díaz] government."[13]

Among the persistent contentions in the historical interpretation of the Mexican Revolution is that U.S. private groups with vested interests in the revolution were among the major groups that financed Madero's efforts. Presumably, one of the major motives for these alleged contributions was Standard Oil's efforts to out-maneuver its British competition in Mexico. The charges had sufficient color to cause Secretary Knox, with the president's approval, to send a warning to the president of Standard Oil about violations of the neutrality statutes.[14] The latter categorically denied the charges, and there appears to be no conclusive evidence to this day that the company actually made contributions to Madero's cause, although there may have been tentative discussion between intermediaries. In fact, it appears that Gustavo Madero diverted some $500,000 received in a contract with French railroad interests and that the Madero family (including Francisco) put up nearly an equivalent amount. The total came to about $1 million which has been judged to be about what Madero spent. One or two U.S. citizens from San Antonio may also have made small contributions.[15]

Madero's concern about being arrested by the U.S. authorities proved justified, and an order for his arrest was finally sent to federal officers in the western district of Texas.[16] To avoid arrest, Madero crossed the frontier into Mexico near Ciudad Juárez on February 14, 1911, with a force of 130 men. It is of interest that about 50 of the men were U.S. volunteers.[17]

Not long after his flight across the border as a fugitive from U.S. justice, Madero, as the self-declared provisional president of Mexico, wrote a note to the U.S. secretary of state explaining the causes and purposes of the insurrection. In elegant and dignified style he expressly recognized Mexico's treaties and other obligations entered into before November 30, 1910, and guaranteed his government's responsibility for damages and injuries to persons and companies of governments which recognized him, effective on the date of recognition. This adroit message of reassurance, delivered at the end of March 1911 by his confidential agent in Washing-ton, was a clear expression of his favorable disposition toward the U.S. government and his willingness to commit himself to a friendly policy in concrete ways.[18]

Castro also found the United States important as a base of operations against a dictatorial regime. Although Castro organized and trained his paramilitary forces in Mexico, he came to the United States to raise money in Bridgeport, Union City, New York, Miami, Tampa, and Key West.[19] Much of the money he needed to finance his expedition came from Cubans there. One of the largest gifts was later made by former President Carlos Prío Socorrás who turned some $40 or $50 thousand over to Castro at the border city of McAllen, Texas, in September 1956.[20] Part of the Prío funds were used to purchase the pleasure yacht *Granma* from U.S. citizens resident in Mexico. U.S. citizens not of Cuban descent appear to have contributed little to Castro's operations, except for the "taxes" collected toward the end of his campaign from U.S.-owned companies located in Cuban territories "liberated" by Castro.

Castro may have collected some $100,000 in the United States, but few arms actually got through to him in Cuba before Batista's collapse.[21] Once in the Sierra, Castro relied primarily on arms captured or stolen from the regular army or turned over to his movement by civilian sympathizers. The U.S. government attempted to enforce its neutrality laws, arresting Cubans and seizing arms and supplies involved in the resistance activities against Batista, many of which were associated with groups other than Castro's. Some 190 Cubans were charged with violating the neutrality laws and 170 convicted. United States authorities seized arms, munitions, and other materials valued in excess of $500,000.[22]

The United States was also important to Castro as a base for his psychological and political campaign against Batista. The Cuban public media, newspapers, magazines, and radio were for the most part closed to him, especially during those periods when censorship was in force. Yet one of his major objectives was to reach the Cuban people in order to mobilize them against the dictator. United States communications media gave him the exposure he needed. Herbert Matthews of the *New York Times* published a lead story on Castro in February 1957 following a secret visit to the guerrillas in the Sierra, and the *New York Times* continued to give him good coverage. *Life* and *Look* featured him in picture stories, and he received television coverage as well. When censorship permitted, some of this material appeared in the Cuban press, and the frequent travelers between the island and the mainland brought back the story in print and by word of mouth. Cubans also had easy access to U.S. radio broadcasts. It was, in fact, the U.S. media which helped spread Castro's message and gave him stature, especially in the early part of his campaigns before the 26th of July Movement went on the air with Radio Rebelde.

In the meantime, the U.S. government was involved in actions which directly impinged on the political struggle in Cuba. Batista was accustomed to maintaining his authority with the acquiescence, and sometimes the support, of the U.S. government. One of the cornerstones of his political strategy was friendly relations with the United States. Like other Caribbean dictators, he consistently cultivated the U.S. government by catering to U.S. business interests and collaborating with the Department of State in diplomatic matters. The latter could almost invariably count on Batista's government voting in support of the U.S. position in the Organization of American States and at the United Nations.

The Cuban government had signed a military assistance agreement with the United States early in 1952 just before the coup, and the agreement was routinely implemented when Batista came into office. Under the agreement, Cuba received about $12 million in military assistance from 1953 through 1958 (see table 3). In addition, Cuba bought military equipment with her own funds in the United States. Although the level of military grants was not high, it is interesting to note that the level nearly doubled during the guerrilla campaigns of 1957 and 1958. The U.S. government maintained a military mission in Havana which included in 1958 about eleven officers and men from the army, nine from the navy, and eleven from the air force.[23]

Castro deeply resented the fact that the United States helped train and equip the regular Cuban military forces which were used against his guerrillas, and he appealed time and again to the United States to terminate military assistance and withdraw the military mission. Concerned about the use of U.S. supplies and equipment in an

TABLE 3

U.S. MILITARY ASSISTANCE TO CUBA

Grants and Excess Stocks	
Year	U.S. Dollars (in millions)
1953	0.4
1954	1.1
1955	1.5
1956	1.7
1957	3.2
1958	3.6

SOURCE: Worksheets provided by the Office of Statistics and Reports, Bureau for Program and Policy Coordination, Agency for International Development.

internal Cuban struggle, the Department of State in September 1957 called the attention of the Cuban authorities to the restrictive provisions of the Mutual Defense Assistance Agreement.[24] The agreement provided that U.S. military assistance was to be used for the defense of the Western Hemisphere, and the "prior agreement" of the United States was required for its use for other purposes.

Meanwhile the U.S. government was prosecuting members of the Cuban resistance movement for violations of the U.S. neutrality laws. The indictment on February 13, 1958, of former President Carlos Prío Socorrás focused public attention on the plight of the Cuban resistance and the mounting opposition to Batista within Cuba. At about this time a Castro representative in Washington, Ernesto Betancourt, called the attention of various members of the Congress to U.S. military assistance to Batista. The subject came up in the testimony of the then assistant secretary of state for American republic affairs, Roy R. Rubottom, before the Foreign Relations Committee on March 5, 1959. Senator Mike Mansfield pointed out the inconsistencies in U.S. policy: "A government which came into power by usurpation [referring to Batista's 1952 coup against Prío], and which maintains a military dictatorship, can buy arms or have arms given it by the United States, but a constitutionally elected President [Prío] is put in jail for trying to assist in the overthrow of that government."[25]

As a result of a variety of pressures and its own concerns on the subject, the Department of State suspended the shipment of 1,950 rifles to Cuba on March 14. At a news conference on April 8, Secretary Dulles explained: "We allow arms to go to other countries primarily to meet international defense requirements—in this case, the needs of hemispheric defense. . . . we don't like to have them go where the purpose is to conduct a civil war."[26] Except for the correction in May 1958 of an earlier delivery error, no more arms were given or sold to the Batista government thereafter.

Batista pressed his need for arms in his conversations in Havana with U.S. Ambassador Smith to the very end, and military equipment was, of course, needed to suppress Castro. In a sense, however, Batista's chief problem was troop morale and rising popular indignation at home. The U.S. arms embargo established on March 14 was thus more significant politically than militarily. The public announcement of its existence was a clear indication of U.S. determination to disassociate itself from Batista's suppression of the guerrilla movement and was a severe blow to Batista's political prestige and authority.

Despite Castro's continuing and insistent requests, the United States refused to withdraw its military mission from Cuba, which remained until after Batista's fall from power. In reply to José Miró Cardona's letter of protest on the subject to President Eisenhower, the Department of State replied: "The United States government believes that its missions in Cuba are serving the purpose for which they were established. Governments and administrations change from time to time in both Cuba and the United States but hemispheric defense needs present a constant problem, the solution of which calls for a cooperative program carried out on a steady, long range basis."[27]

In contrast to Madero's revolt in which a major source of friction was the actions of Mexicans affecting U.S. territory, the main U.S. problem during the Cuban insurrection of 1958 was the treatment of American citizens in Cuba. There were recurring incidents when U.S. civilians or the military were kidnapped or otherwise fell into the hands of rebel forces. Perhaps the most serious case was Raúl Castro's kidnapping of some twenty-four servicemen on liberty from the Guantánamo naval base and, a little later, of civilians from nearby industrial plants. His purpose was to protest what he believed was the Cuban armed forces' use of U.S. facilities in their campaign against his rebel forces. U.S. consular officers negotiated the release which was gradually effected over a period of weeks. United States troops also moved outside the limits of the Guantánamo base to protect its water supply but were hastily withdrawn when rebel interference appeared unlikely.

These incidents are interesting not so much for their actual significance as for their potential implications. Castro very much feared that Batista might somehow involve the U.S. forces in the struggle or that the United States would use some pretext, such as the protection of U.S. lives and property, to intervene on Batista's side against the guerrilla forces. Under the provocation of the Raúl Castro kidnappings, Fidel Castro's fears were not entirely groundless. Ambassador Smith unsuccessfully urged that U.S. Marines be landed to effect a release and expressed his belief that Batista would have granted permission.[28] Both the rebel forces and authorities in Washington, however, were anxious to avoid U.S. military involvement. After a period of tension and negotiation, each of these minor but potentially explosive incidents was resolved.

The possibility that the U.S. government maintained covert contact with Castro's rebel movement in the Sierra should not be ruled out. Ambassador Smith recommended to the Central Intelligence Agency (CIA) that an agent be placed in the Castro forces, although he "assume[d] that this was never done, or they [the CIA] would have been better informed."[29] Many observers believe that one of the journalists who spent time with Castro was working for the CIA, and this same man was subsequently identified by Che Guevara as an agent.[30] Unlike many of the other newsmen who were assigned to Castro, this particular journalist's by-line has appeared little, or not at all, before or since.

Confrontations

The U.S. government was involved in the climactic confrontations between the rebel movements and the incumbent dictatorships in all four countries. The United States played a prominent role in the events surrounding the fall of Porfirio Díaz and Fulgencio Batista. The U.S. response in these two countries will be examined first. This will be followed by a discussion of how U.S. officials reacted to the fall of the old regimes in Guatemala and Bolivia where their involvement was relatively less important. The timing and manner of U.S. recognition was vital to all four successor governments.

Mexico: Díaz's Resignation

Although revolutionary outbreaks had occurred in various parts of Mexico toward the end of 1910, Francisco Madero's participation in the field against Díaz began on February 14, 1911, when he crossed into Mexico. It ended with the Treaty of Ciudad Juárez and the resignation of Díaz on May 25. The United States scrupulously guarded its neutrality during these months.

Neutrality was achieved in the face of temptations and complications, some of the United States' own making. For example, when Madero slipped across the border and out of reach of U.S. authorities, the governor of Texas asked President Taft whether he should cross the Rio Grande to capture Madero. President Taft advised the governor to hold the matter in abeyance, particularly on the grounds that the Mexican government was sure to refuse permission.

President Taft's order of March 8, 1911, sending 20,000 troops to man the northern side of the border with Mexico raised further complications. The president justified the measure in order to "prevent insurrectionary expeditions from American soil" and to "have a healthy moral effect to prevent attacks upon Americans and their property in any subsequent general internecine strife." He called assertions that he intended intervention "gratuitous," while making clear his readiness, with authority from the Congress, to protect American lives and property in Mexico.[31]

The troops remained on U.S. soil and the feared intervention never took place. The major test of the president's resolve came when shots fired during the struggle strayed across the border into Douglas, Arizona. At that point the governor raised the possibility of military action across the border to the town of Agua Prieta. The president stayed the governor's hand, and the crisis passed.

Some Mexicans on both sides of the struggle were alarmed by the U.S. mobilization. José Yves Limantour who had returned to President Díaz's side in the crisis was "greatly relieved" to learn that the "United States had not the slightest intention of intervening, unless the present Mexican Government should fall and not be succeeded by a responsible one."[32] President Díaz appears to have been less alarmed initially by the mobilization, having expressed to Ambassador Wilson his belief that the military movements "strengthen the hands of the Mexican government."[33]

As the revolutionary crisis deepened, the Díaz administration began to view the U.S. military action in a somewhat different light. Vice-President Ramón Corral was quoted as having charged that "the revolution in Mexico is being fomented by the Americans with a view of forcing intervention."[34] Ambassador Wilson lodged a protest and Corral denied having made the statement.[35]

Similarly, Ambassador Wilson was sensitive to certain allusions of the foreign minister, possibly reflecting adversely on the motives behind the troop movements. These underlying tensions were resolved in further conversations, if only superficially. Meanwhile, the U.S. troops remained at home, and revolutionary violence mounted, culminating in the rebels' successful confrontation with federal troops at Ciudad Juárez and Madero's seizure of that city where he established his provisional government.

At that point the Mexican government complained in Washington that the rebel-held city served as an entrepôt for supplies from directly across the border. President Taft refused to interfere. He agreed that the possession of Ciudad Juárez gave the insurrectionists a great advantage but that this grew out of the "weakness or misfortune of the Mexican government, for which we are not responsible, and it does not change . . . the right of persons in our jurisdiction to carry out legitimate business."[36] Also, it is of interest that the American consul in Ciudad Juárez reported on May 11, 1911, that he was dealing with the de facto government of Madero there. He reported that the provisional governor under Madero "seems anxious to favor Americans and work in harmony with them in the establishment of law and order."[37]

Meanwhile, President Díaz's government in Mexico was in disarray, his health was failing, and his troops had lost control in many parts of the country. Faced with what seemed irresistible pressures, he formally announced on May 8 his intention to resign. In the closing paragraph he referred to "the imminent dangers which threaten our social system and the autonomy of the nation," a statement that may be interpreted as a reference to the U.S. mobilization.[38] The earlier statements attributed to his subordinates Corral and de la Barra also suggest that Díaz may have meant to explain his resignation partly as an effort to avoid foreign intervention. Since he was not more explicit on this point, it is difficult to determine what his real feelings were. In any case opposition within the country combined with his inability to resist effectively was clearly the major cause of his downfall. Moreover, the U.S. troops conducted themselves with restraint along the border and did not move into Mexico at that time.

The conflict between the forces headed by Madero and the Díaz government was resolved by a negotiated settlement which named Francisco Léon de la Barra, formerly the Mexican ambassador in Washington, to preside over a government of transition until presidential elections could be held. De la Barra was well known in Washington and served Díaz as minister of foreign relations at the end. When de la Barra formally assumed the provisional presidency May 25, 1911, President Taft and Secretary Knox sent their congratulations.[39] The continuity of diplomatic relations was not, therefore, broken between Díaz's fall and Madero's election and subsequent assumption of the presidency on November 6, 1911.

Cuba: Batista's Flight

In late 1958, as Batista's position deteriorated and the pressures of the resistance grew, the United States became increasingly concerned about the bloodshed and disorders that were wracking the island as well as about Cuba's future after what appeared to be Batista's impending collapse. Ambassador Smith clung hard and long to the hope that Batista would fulfill his pledge to conduct genuinely free elections which would permit a transition toward a democratic and popularly elected government. Even Ambassador Smith, who had pressed Batista so hard to arrange for the popular election of a successor, claimed that the results of the November 3, 1958, elections, rigged to confirm Batista's candidate, "would not be acceptable to the people."[40] At the same time Smith had also rejected Castro as an acceptable leader when he indiscreetly remarked to the press that the United States would never "be able to do business with Castro."[41]

Sometime late in 1958 the Department of State decided to press for a solution in Cuba without either Batista or Castro, that is, to try to find some third force between what U.S. officials felt were two extremes. To this end former Ambassador William D. Pawley was sent to Cuba on an unofficial and secret mission to talk Batista into resigning in favor of a military junta. Pawley said that the men they "had selected . . . were Colonel Barquín, Colonel Borbonnet, General Díaz Tamayo, Bosch of the 'Bicardi' firm and one other . . . all enemies of Batista."[42] In the December 9 meeting Batista refused to step down in favor of these men. Pawley attributed Batista's refusal to the fact that he, Pawley, was not permitted to link the proposal directly to the U.S. government. When this mission failed, the Department of State sent Ambassador Smith to ask Batista to resign indicating that "there were Cuban elements which could salvage the rapidly deteriorating situation."[43] Ambassador Smith, however, was not authorized to tell Batista who they were.

Castro, meanwhile, was concerned about foreign interference and the imposition of a military junta and had long voiced this concern in his proclamations from the Sierra.[44] He feared that the resistance forces might be denied the fruits of their impending victory. A Castro representative in Washington, Ernesto Betancourt, protested publicly the efforts by Ambassador Smith and U.S. military officers to change the U.S. hands-off policy.[45] As the political crisis in Cuba approached a climax, the U.S. Department of State appears to have hoped that the government succeeding Batista would be broadly representative, that is, not under Castro's exclusive domination.[46]

When Castro's troops and other resistance forces routed the Cuban Army and discipline in the latter collapsed, the United States refused to change its position or try to save Batista. His designation of a military officer to succeed him when he fled the country in the early morning hours of January 1, 1959, infuriated Castro. The latter was quoted as describing this as an effort to "prevent the triumph of the Revolution."[47] In his first broadcast after Batista's flight, Castro violently protested the coup as snatching "victory away from the people" and called for a general strike to force the unconditional surrender of Batista's forces.[48]

Castro's prestige as the symbol of the revolution, the disposition of his guerrilla forces, and his astute political tactics easily overcame the efforts of those who sought to promote an alternative to Castro in the form of a military junta or independent participation by his rivals within the Cuban resistance. Castro was the hero of the revolution, and he rapidly established his authority within the country.

By that date U.S. officials accepted these developments as beyond their control. The best course, they seemed to believe, was to try to reason with Castro as best they could, hoping for but not necessarily expecting the best. The U.S. government recognized the new government headed by Manuel Urrutia, Castro's designee, on January 7 before Castro had completed his triumphal march to Havana from Oriente province. Ambassador Smith was promptly removed from his post and Philip W. Bonsal, then U.S. ambassador to Bolivia—which was experiencing its own social revolution—was named as his successor. Despite the frictions and mutual suspicions of the past, the United States showed by these initial actions its acceptance of the new government and its desire to work with it.

Guatemala: The Fall of Ubico

Unlike the Mexican and Cuban cases, the U.S. government had relatively little connection with the Guatemalan revolutionary movement and the overthrow of Ubico in 1944. Since 1931 the relations of the U.S. government and particularly U.S. private interests with Ubico had, for the most part, been very good indeed. Ubico had cooperated with U.S. efforts to counteract Nazi and German influences in Guatemala, while not being disposed to grant each and every U.S. request out of hand. Charges that Ubico was pro-German or pro-Italian were not borne out by his conduct toward the United States in this respect.

Ubico was, however, out of step with U.S. policy in a more profound sense. While he was a great admirer of Francisco Franco of Spain and the traditions and style of the Falange, currents of opinion in the United States rode on a high tide of democratic idealism, deliberately drummed up in the prosecution of the war against the Axis and authoritatively expressed in the Atlantic Charter. It was in fact these very ideals with which the Guatemalan revolutionary movement attempted to associate itself in its efforts to overthrow Ubico, claiming its own affinity for the democratic ideals of the West and the repudiation of Axis totalitarianism.

Some officials in Washington were vaguely troubled by the persistence of dictatorial regimes in Latin America and looked ahead to a new and more democratic postwar era. Nelson Rockefeller, then assistant secretary of state for American republic affairs, visited Ubico in March 1944. According to Ernesto Rivas, then Ubico's private secretary, Rockefeller requested Ubico to comment on a written statement of U.S. policies for the postwar. Ubico was conservative in a fiscal sense and did not favor Guatemala's accepting large development loans, the means by which the United States planned to influence Latin America. By giving a negative response to Rockefeller about the plan, Ubico was, Rivas maintained, figuratively submitting his resignation.[49] Even if the details of this encounter are not completely correct, the episode as described reflects tensions developing between the two governments; I have not been able to find in the diplomatic correspondence any authoritative expressions of regret at Ubico's subsequent fall or any U.S. effort to sustain him in power.

In fact, the reporting of the revolutionary developments of 1944 from the embassy in Guatemala City is largely objective and appears to reflect a lack of deep involvement with either side. Ambassador Boaz Long reported the rising tide of opposition to Ubico on June 21 and predicted that "a climax may be approached by June 30 or soon thereafter." At that time, he reported his refusal of a request from an Ubico cabinet member to arrange for American doctors and nurses to help the government in the face of an impending strike of Guatemalan medical professionals.[50] On June 25 Long criticized the "intransigent attitude of the Government and today's ruthless policy measures."[51] In Washington, Laurence Duggan wrote the secretary of state that Ubico "has completely dominated the country but in fairness it must be said that Guatemala has no real tradition of liberty and that in return for the suppression of freedom, he has given the country a peaceful, progressive and in general honest administration."[52] The U.S. government's attitude toward Ubico could be summed up as not bitterly hostile but simply not supportive in the crisis.

The military junta which succeeded Ubico on July 1 promptly assured the embassy of its "pro-democratic and pro-American sentiments," and the university leaders and professionals who had led the anti-Ubico movement kept in close touch as well.[53] When General Ponce, a member of the transitional military junta, informed the embassy of his assumption of the presidency on a provisional basis, within a few hours Washington authorized the embassy to continue relations with the Ponce government. In a summary dispatch, Long expressed his qualified optimism about future U.S. relations with Guatemala and reported:

> The period of transition from the ironclad rule of General Ubico to the relatively liberal administration under General Ponce, has taken place with remarkably little disorder. The machinery of government is continuing to function smoothly and the outward life of the country has apparently settled back to normal. The newspapers are enjoying their first taste of freedom in years . . . the next five months will see intensified political activities and considerable state of political ferment.[54]

The U.S. embassy and officials in Washington appeared to be pleased with the developing political transition in Guatemala.

Francisco I. Madero wounded at Casas Grandes, Mexico, May 1911. (Library of Congress)

Armed units in Guatemala, October 1944. (Wide World Photos)

Fidel Castro (second from left) during a fund-raising trip to New York City, November 1955. (Wide World Photos)

Ambassador Long, however, did sound a note of alarm at the end of September noting signs that the Ponce administration might seek to perpetuate itself in office. Speaking for the Department of State, Norman Armour did not believe that the United States should threaten to withdraw recognition if Ponce refused to proceed with elections, but did authorize Long to express, as representing opinion in the Department of State, that "we feel . . . greater affinity, a deeper sympathy, and a warmer friendship for governments which effectively represent the practical application of democratic processes."[55]

Just as the embassy seemed able to adjust happily to the departure of Ubico, so too did it accept the overthrow of Ponce by the Guatemalan revolutionary movement. When Ponce, facing armed opposition, requested the embassy to supply bombs for his air force, the embassy replied firmly in the negative.[56] When two of the leaders of the revolution, Senator Jorge Toriello and Captain Jacobo Arbenz, asked permission to use the American embassy to communicate with the Ponce government, the chargé d'affaires, William C. Affeld, Jr., complied. And in a further exchange with Ponce, the revolutionary group refused to meet any place other than the American embassy. The settlement between the two contending forces was completed in the embassy at midday in the presence of members of the diplomatic corps, and when other diplomats agreed to sign, the chargé did so also, specifying his signature as that of a "witness."[57]

The chargé d'affaires summarized his impressions of the political situation on October 24:

> The movement which overthrew Ponce was well planned and efficiently executed as has been the effort to restore public order and confidence. The behavior of the Junta and its volunteer police has been correct in regard to citizens' private property . . . the Revolutionary Government . . . is made up of sound and responsible persons with emphasis on the younger elements. . . . The present basis of government enjoys wide sympathy and popular support.[58]

By October 31, the Department of State expressed its view that the new government had met many of the requirements of recognition, and formal recognition was extended after consultation with other American governments on November 7.

Bolivia: The Fall of Peñaranda

The U.S. government has probably had no more complex or intense relationships with a revolutionary movement than with the Bolivian Movimiento Nacionalista Revolucionario (MNR). The MNR overthrew two governments dominated by Bolivian tin interests that had negotiated agreements for tin purchases with the United States. The first, the Peñaranda government inaugurated in 1940, was overthrown by a group of military officers led by Gualberto Villarroel in alliance with the MNR in 1943. The Villarroel government lasted until 1946 when political parties associated with the tin interests came into power again and remained in control until

April 1952. In that year the MNR overthrew the government in an urban insurrection, thereby initiating Bolivia's social revolution. The complex relations between the MNR and the United States in 1943 to 1946 and 1952 to 1964 will be described in chapters 3 and 5 respectively.

What is pertinent here is that the United States had almost nothing to do with the military coup of December 1943 or the urban insurrection of April 1952. The United States maintained close relations with the Peñaranda government in the early 1940s but was not in a position, nor did it try, to defend that government against the 1943 coup. The United States did not welcome Villarroel and the MNR to power and recognized his government only after considerable delay, as chapter 3 will explain.

Similarly, the United States had worked closely with the traditional governments during the years from 1946 to 1952, but on the eve of the 1952 revolution reached a deadlock with the Bolivian government over the price of tin. Stuart Symington of the Reconstruction Finance Corporation (RFC), which managed the U.S. strategic stockpile in tin, sought to keep prices down and was not disposed to offer what the Bolivians asked.[59] The U.S. government's brusque dealings with the Bolivians did not strengthen the incumbent government's prestige, and the deadlock placed the Bolivian administration under severe strain. The tin sales crisis, however, was only a minor and superficial symptom of the deeper political and economic crisis which led to the Bolivian Revolution of 1952. This time the United States waited nearly two months to recognize the new government.

The United States did not significantly help or hinder the traditional Bolivian governments or the rebel opposition in December 1943 nor in April 1952.

Origins of Flexibility

The United States maintained normal and close relations with the dictatorial governments in these countries during most of their tenure of office. It sought to maintain order along the Mexican border and, generally, to promote trade, protect U.S. investments, and counter the influence of hostile European powers. Achieving these objectives required maintaining contact and influence with the men who controlled the countries, whatever their political coloration.

At the same time, the Department of State sought to avoid undue entanglements once a government's weakness and unpopularity became manifest. The expediency that governed relationships with dictatorial regimes was demonstrated when the latter faced collapse before rebel opposition. United States representatives reported the weakness and divisions within the dictatorships and predicted their imminent fall. Aware of widespread popular opposition and not wishing to back losers, the United States did not come to their rescue. Taft's mobilization of troops along the Mexican border as a precautionary measure did not help Díaz on the eve of his fall, but embarrassed him instead. The U.S. embargo on arms to Cuba in 1958 was a severe political blow to Batista, and eventually U.S. envoys pressured him to resign. U.S. relations deteriorated with Ubico in Guatemala in 1944 and with the Bolivian government in 1952 on the eve of their political demise. The United States refused to help sustain either in power. Thus, the United States was at best neutral toward Ubico and the Bolivian dictatorship and took adverse actions with respect to Díaz and Batista. Most of the measures which the United States took against the dictatorial regimes, especially in Cuba, benefited the rebel forces.

The programs and policies of the various rebel movements all appeared to be designed to attract U.S. support or at least neutralize U.S. opposition. (This was true even in the case of the MNR.)[60] All the rebel movements sought to reassure the Department of State and the American public about their objectives.

For example, Madero, upon leading his forces into Mexico, sent a formal note to the Secretary of State in which he agreed to assume responsibility for U.S. claims when formally recognized. The Guatemalan rebels successfully insisted that their takeover of the government in October 1944 be solemnized in ceremonies at the American embassy. Bolivian leaders visited the American minister in La Paz on the eve of their coup to explain their position and to hint at their plans. During his guerrilla campaign, Castro maintained contact with U.S. officials through intermediaries in the United States and Cuba and skillfully cultivated U.S. news media.

All of the rebel movements were nationalistic in that they sought national independence from foreign influence. In all cases, however, the "anti-imperialist"—often meaning "anti-American"—aspects of their programs were muted during the struggle for power. All sought to avoid unnecessary friction with the United States.

An open society in the United States facilitated the rebel activities of Madero in 1911 and of Castro in 1956 to 1959. Both used the United States as a base for organizing and equipping rebel forces and mounting political and psychological warfare against the dictatorships. Madero and Castro were popular with the American public as Davids bent on slaying Goliaths. Little attention was paid to the Guatemalan rebels' unseating of Ubico, episodes overshadowed by the climactic events of World War II. The U.S. authorities did not usually attempt to suppress rebel activities against foreign governments and were slow to enforce rebels' violations of U.S. neutrality laws.

The fact that there is widespread support for constitutional methods and orderly reform in American society did not in itself hamper U.S. relations with foreign political leaders supporting armed revolt. The rationale behind flexibility in relations with the revolutionaries was not to promote these leaders' interests but rather to protect those of the United States. American representatives sent in full reports and maintained complex, not unfriendly, informal relations with the rebel leaders in most of the countries. Even in Cuba where the U.S. ambassador eventually spoke out against Castro, consular officials, journalists, and others with official contacts kept in touch with Castro's guerrilla forces. There was surprisingly little hostility. Many of the movements, such as Madero's, were treated sympathetically initially, and others, such as the Guatemalan and Cuban movements, were seen as expressions of popular uprisings against dictatorial government. When the rebel forces seized control of their respective governments, the U.S. government continued relations or, with one exception,[61] recognized them all promptly. Friction with the United States developed mainly after the rebels had strengthened their control over their respective governments.[62]

Policy disagreements within the U.S. government appear not to have been great concerning Bolivia and Guatemala where the rebels' coups were played out in a few days. When Díaz was losing his grip on Mexico in 1910–1911, President Taft exerted a restraining influence on U.S. law enforcement agencies and the military whose primary concern was the maintenance of order and security along the Mexican border.

Perhaps the most important division within the U.S. government in these cases occurred over policy toward Cuba. Officials in the Department of State encouraged an evenhanded policy in the civil conflict in Cuba in 1957–1959, while the U.S. ambassador, a political appointee and businessman, was critical of Castro and favored more responsiveness to Batista—an orientation which he claimed did not find the necessary official support in Washington. As a result of congressional pressure and the approval of President Eisenhower and Secretary Dulles, the Department of State arranged the suspension of military assistance to Batista but was either unable, or did not seek, to force the withdrawal of the U.S. military mission to the Batista government. Until more archival material becomes available, the termination of military assistance but the continued assignment of the military assistance mission to Havana may be interpreted as representing a compromise between civilian and military officials. Quite apart from foreign policy considerations per se, the military appears to have favored retaining at least some staff, funds, and influence in Cuba. Castro's reaction to Ambassador Smith's public criticism and the maintenance of the U.S. military mission was violent, and both constituted major causes of his mistrust of the United States during the early months of his takeover in Cuba.

With respect to Mexico, Guatemala, and even Cuba, U.S. official policies toward the rebel movements were sympathetic or at least not generally antagonistic, an orientation that contrasted sharply with the extremely hostile U.S. policies toward Latin American guerrilla movements in the 1960s. Guerrillas in the 1960s identified the United States as a major enemy from the beginning, and U.S. agencies helped suppress them by supplying arms, training, etc., to governments in power. The experience of the 1960s has sometimes obscured the far less hostile relations of earlier years. The reasons for the recent deterioration of U.S. relations with rebel movements will be discussed in chapter 8.

3 Reformist Governments: Hostility

In taking over governments, all the rebel leaders followed a reformist model at first, leaving the existing social structure largely intact. They were not antagonistic initially to the interests of the middle class. Representatives of the old elite retained the economic bases of their political power and thus influence in government and politics as well. To offset that influence and to secure backing for reform, the new governments drew industrial and rural labor into the political arena, in some cases for the first time.

The leaders of the reformist governments who will be discussed in this chapter are Francisco I. Madero in Mexico (1911–1913), Gualberto Villarroel and Víctor Paz Estenssoro in Bolivia (1943–1946), and Juan José Arévalo in Guatemala (1945–1951).

The revolutionary process in Cuba followed a pattern similar in some ways to that of Mexico, Bolivia, and Guatemala. A rebel movement led by Ramón Grau San Martín and Fulgencio Batista established a reformist government in Cuba at the end of 1933 not long after the overthrow of the dictatorial regime of Gerardo Machado. After Grau was forced out in early 1934, Fulgencio Batista dominated Cuban politics and government for a decade. Grau was elected president in 1944 and was succeeded by Carlos Prío Socorrás from 1948 to 1952. The two Grau administrations and the Prío administration were Cuba's closest experiences to the reformist governments of the other three countries, although the Cubans did not go as far down the road of social reform.

Unlike the reformist movements in the other three countries, Grau's party, the Auténticos, went into a decline after 1952 and did not return to power. This is one reason why this chapter will not analyze the U.S. response to the Grau and Prío governments. Another is that U.S. policies toward Cuba from 1944 to 1952 followed long-established patterns and were not important in explaining the Auténticos' successes and failures.

Rejecting Grau's leadership and political following, Fidel Castro seized the banner of social change and established his own rebel movement. Castro came to power on a reformist platform but followed reformist policies for only a few months.

His reformist stage was so short and closely related to the onset of revolutionary change that U.S. responses to Castro during early 1959 will not be discussed here but in chapter 6 dealing with revolutionary change.

The major emphasis of the reformist platforms in Mexico, Bolivia, and Guatemala was political: the elimination of a self-perpetuating dictatorial regime and the restoration, or institution, of governments more representative of popular interests (see table 4). Madero, Villarroel, and Arévalo had their take-over of power confirmed by elections under constitutional provisions. Madero and Arévalo achieved what was then a high watermark in the exercise of civil liberties in Mexico and Guatemala. In Bolivia the participation of authoritarian military officers and some instances of brutal repression, such as the political executions in late 1944, marred the Villarroel government's record on civil liberties.

The reformist governments also introduced innovations in economic and social policy designed to meet more effectively the material and social needs of the populace at large. Labor unions were allowed to organize and become more active than ever before, and legislation in favor of improved working conditions was introduced. Legislation was passed to improve the lot of the rural poor, and in several countries the Indian populations gained new, if still only symbolic, stature. Social security legislation was passed. New expenditures were made to finance social welfare measures.

None of these reformist governments tampered in any profound way with the existing social structure. The existing capitalist framework was left intact, and large domestic and foreign interests were not subject to expropriation. All of the governments were favorably disposed, at least initially, toward the United States, which in turn was friendly, at least initially, toward all the new governments, except the Bolivian.

The Madero and Villarroel governments were overthrown by a counterrevolutionary coup d'etat; only Juan José Arévalo served out his full term and was succeeded by a constitutionally elected president. The ultimate fate of these governments contrasted sharply with their auspicious initial prospects with respect both to domestic reform and, except for Bolivia, to good relations with the United States. In their declining fortunes, U.S. officials played important roles.

Madero in Mexico (1911–1913)

The Taft administration and its representative in Mexico City, Ambassador Henry Lane Wilson, were ready to work with the new Mexican leadership that took over after President Porfirio Díaz's resignation in May 1911. They had viewed Díaz sympathetically as a person but also as a kind of political anachronism. As a result, they had been neither surprised nor disheartened by his overthrow. The revolution's leader, Francisco I. Madero, was a popular figure in the United States, especially in the Southwest. If the Taft administration did not fully share the public enthusiasm for this David who had slain Goliath, this was due to its innate conservatism and the natural and healthy skepticism which characterizes bureaucracies.

Madero's social program was moderate in comparison with those already prevailing in Europe and the United States; it was noteworthy mainly because it contrasted with Díaz's authoritarianism. Mexico posed its greatest challenges to U.S. adaptability *after* Madero left office, when revolutionary social forces burst to the surface.

TABLE 4

REFORMIST GOVERNMENTS: SOCIAL CHANGE

	Mexico Madero, 1911–1913	Bolivia Villarroel/Paz, 1943–1946	Guatemala Arévalo, 1945–1951
Agricultural reform	Survey and recovery of illegally alienated national lands; agricultural experiment stations established	—	Agricultural development program; attempt to promote cooperatives
Industry/ commerce	Official study of oil exploration; plan for electrification of central plateau	Increased taxes on tin; foreign exchange controls (tin)	Increased governmental control over petroleum resources; national bank established
Labor measures	Established Department of Labor; studies on reduction of hours, strikes, minimum wages; National Labor Office settled 70 strikes	Labor's role strengthened by growth of miner and peasant unions; workman's compensation and other labor laws	Expansion of membership of industrial/agricultural unions; new labor code, courts, and social security law
Indigenous affairs	Official investigation of Indian education	Feudal service abolished; first national Indian congress	First Indian congress
Political parties	Multiparty	Multiparty	Multiparty
Elections	Presidential, October 1911	Parliamentary, July 1946	Presidential, December 1944
New constitution	—	—	1945
Education	New rural public schools; large budgetary increases; National Congress on Primary Education	New rural schools; education code; literacy campaign	Expansion of rural education; literacy campaign

Table prepared by Herbert Braun and Judith Ludvik.

NOTE: This table permits only rough comparisons of these reformist governments. For more authoritative and complete information, readers should consult studies on individual countries, such as: Stanley Ross, *Francisco I. Madero, Apostle of Mexican Democracy* (New York, 1955), chapter 15; Herbert S. Klein, *Parties and Political Change in Bolivia, 1880–1952* (Cambridge, 1969), chapters 11 and 12; and Richard Adams, *Crucifixion by Power: Essays on Guatemalan National Social Structure, 1944–1966* (Austin, 1970), chapter 3.

Madero was elected to the presidency in October 1911 and took office in November. During the transitional government, the revolutionary forces he had headed were weakened, first by internal quarrels and second by a rapidly regrouping opposition. When Madero assumed the presidency, his deep commitment to democratic institutions allowed the opposing camps full freedom, thereby complicating his efforts to maintain order and implement his program of moderate social reform. The Madero administration lasted only fifteen months.

Madero's cabinet was a mixture of conservative and revolutionary forces including three holdovers from the transitional government. The army and the police continued largely under the control of officers inherited from the Díaz dictatorship. Madero did not disturb the former followers of Díaz in their key positions in government and the economy. The other side of the coin was that his personal supporters did not become well established, and Madero failed to capitalize on his revolutionary following to build a broad and firm base of political support.

Madero was and remained immensely vulnerable politically, depending on critical or hostile military officers for the maintenance of order and, ultimately, for his own personal safety. During his term, Madero faced two major uprisings (Emiliano Zapata's and young Pascual Orozco's), the Reyes conspiracy, and a barracks revolt in Veracruz under Félix Díaz, all before the coup de grace in Mexico City in February 1913.

Ambassador Henry Lane Wilson, the brother of Senator John L. Wilson, came to Mexico in 1910 at the end of the Díaz regime on his third diplomatic assignment. Following services to William McKinley in the presidential campaign of 1896, he was sent as minister to Chile and later to Belgium. The only ambassador among many ministers, Wilson served as dean of the diplomatic corps in Mexico. He was thus in a strategic position to influence the conduct of other foreign representatives there.

Relations between the United States and Mexico deteriorated rapidly after Madero became president, eventually resulting in intimate U.S. involvement in the events surrounding his overthrow. First, a brief description and explanation of that deterioration is essential, especially since Madero's own political and social programs represented a move toward U.S. programs and both sides appeared favorably disposed to one another from the start. Second, the U.S. involvement in Madero's overthrow will be summarized and evaluated.

The Growing Rift

The estrangement between the governments in Mexico City and Washington after Madero came to power was in part due to the continued disorders, revolts, and instability which persisted after Díaz's fall. Having passed through one of the most tranquil periods in their own history, many Americans did not look sympathetically on the revolutionary tumult which shook Mexico. U.S. officials were often unable to hide the contempt with which they viewed disorders there, having forgotten the Civil War and other violent episodes of U.S. history. Nor was the United States accustomed to such unsettling developments, whether along the U.S. border or in the interior of Mexico, partly because of the seeming serenity that had characterized most of the Díaz era.

A major objective of U.S. policy was the maintenance of public order in neighboring Mexico—with little appreciation in the United States of the price Mexico had paid to achieve order under Díaz or understanding of the causes of revolutionary ferment. Moreover, the character and social goals of Mexican revolutionaries were alien to many U.S. leaders of that day. At that time the revolutionary upheaval that led to Díaz's overthrow and Madero's assumption of the presidency held few or no obvious advantages to the material interests of the United States; and the accompanying disorders resulted, if only incidentally, in the death of U.S. citizens, damage to their property, and other losses and inconveniences.

Madero was not hostile to foreign capital and was prepared to accept it, but his administration did not aggressively promote foreign concessions in the manner of Díaz. Moreover, Madero had a more developed national sensitivity, particularly about discrimination against Mexicans in favor of foreigners. Perhaps the best-known case of friction arose from Madero's enforcement of the requirement that employees of the national railways pass a written examination in Spanish. Many employees who were U.S. citizens did not qualify and left the country.

Madero's political idealism and sense of social justice, particularly insofar as these adversely affected vested interests, were not well received by many of the affluent in Mexico City nor by their close social and business associates in the U.S. colony. Several leaders of the latter were close friends of Ambassador Wilson, feeding his growing hostility to Madero. As a result, the buffetings to which all vested interests were subject, not the least the United States, caused many observers to view Madero's administration critically.

Ambassador Wilson himself wrote of Madero in a vituperative vein, reflecting nostalgia for the more orderly Díaz era, political differences with the incumbents, and personal animosity toward the president. If anything, his reports exaggerated the disorders from which the country suffered and the indecisiveness and burdens of the Madero administration. Moreover, his messages carried an emotional charge, an irascible disdain for trends in Mexico and a self-righteous, unyielding, and imperious manner partly explicable by his own disappointments and frustrations and the tensions arising from personal maladjustment in the Mexican scene. As early as July 11, 1911, Wilson was reporting:

A permanent disrespect for constituted authority . . . a defiance of the
law . . . lack of respect for property rights, violence, and
rapine. . . . general apprehension created throughout the Republic is
profound. . . . the economic situation grows steadily worse . . . . the labor-
ing classes have quit work and are making demands. . . . a formidable
opposition . . . is springing up against Mr. Madero [who] lacks in that decision of character, uniformity of policy, and close insight which is so
essential.[1]

One of the ambassador's major responsibilities was the protection of American life and property; and the propriety of his informing himself of the conditions of the American community and the representation of their interests, under certain circumstances, was not questioned by the Mexican government nor by Madero personally. Yet the trials to which Americans were put by the revolutionary situation were not, on the whole, greater than those of the Mexicans themselves or other foreigners.

Wilson's insistence on Americans' "rights" became a kind of obsession, a means of simultaneously carrying out what he conceived as his high responsibilities, as well as serving as a means of venting his frustrations in aggressive behavior toward the Mexicans, many of whom he appeared to hold in contempt. Wilson seemed to take an almost satanic relish in castigating Madero and his associates for failing to maintain order and in using what he interpreted as their discomfiture for imposing his will. For the most part, Madero and his ministers resisted Wilson's importunities both firmly and fairly, parrying his thrusts with tact, dignity, and finesse that infuriated the ambassador. The more Wilson fumed, the less his results, until his conduct toward the government as well as toward Washington exceeded the limits of normal diplomatic behavior.[2]

Wilson did not fully appreciate that Mexicans held the protection of American interests in their own country as a matter secondary to their own affairs. This is not to say that responsible Mexican leaders, especially those from the old school, did not respect international practices as interpreted by the Great Powers or that they were not embarrassed by the internal tumult. It simply meant that for Madero maintaining control over the Mexican government and political scene and carrying out his own domestic program was far more important than what he considered the incidental injuries suffered by foreigners. Yet Ambassador Wilson put his own country's and foreign interests first and insisted that the Mexicans do so too. He even thought that protection of American lives and property was a sufficient pretext to make demands about the military dispositions of the government,[3] and, as will be shown below, to affect the issue of the presidency itself. Wilson's belief in the incapacity of Madero to protect what he considered the legitimate U.S. interests was coupled with ever greater insistence that Madero comply. It seemed not to occur to Wilson that Americans did not have to come to Mexico, and that those who did assumed risks from which no government, Mexican or U.S., could protect them.

Wilson went to extremes, but his general orientation was not all that unusual in those days. Then and since, the leaders and envoys of Great Powers have sought to manipulate the affairs of small countries, sometimes by bringing the full weight of economic or military weapons to bear. The Taft administration often considered ways of bringing Mexico into line and was not above brandishing weapons to do so. But as those ultimately responsible, Taft and Knox were far less ready than Wilson to take the risks and pay the price that direct action would have involved.

In early 1912 the rebellion of Pascual Orozco in the north and particularly the battle for Ciudad Juárez endangered Americans and their property just across the border. President Taft and Ambassador Wilson both made public statements presumably designed to have a calming effect but which had just the opposite. In the ensuing panic, Washington appears to have been seriously considering intervention as one of several options.[4] Wilson helped organize military units staffed by, and for protection of, the foreign colony.

Wilson also attempted to generate support from the British and German ministers for the Great Powers to send marines to Mexico City. British Minister Stronge reported "that he [Wilson] only waited a request from any two of his colleagues representing Great Powers in order to take the initiative."[5] The German minister reported that any such action would draw Mexico into war with the United States and that the British minister believed England would "do everything in her power to avoid such intervention."[6] He also thought it was in Germany's interest to postpone any such action. When President Taft learned of Wilson's approach through the British, the Department of State tersely ordered Wilson "on no account to make any such suggestion [for landing troops] except after consultation and with instruction."[7] Ambassador Wilson's categorical denial of the British report is not very convincing, particularly since his version conflicted with statements of the British and German ambassadors.

A summation of the many issues which arose between the United States and Mexico during Madero's first year in power is contained in the U.S. note of protest of September 15, 1912,[8] and the Mexican reply of November 22.[9] What appeared to exercize the Americans most were crimes committed against U.S. citizens whose authors escaped punishment. The U.S. note presents a long list of such cases, only three of which occurred under Madero's government. The U.S. note also protested the treatment of certain American business interests in Mexico, in several instances vaguely, and the Mexican reply demonstrated that there was a valid Mexican side to each issue.

What is perhaps most conspicuous about the U.S. note is its threatening and insulting tone. At the beginning the note referred, for example, to the "federal administration at present in control of Mexico City" from which it was an easy step to infer a slur that the administration did not control much else. The note also contrasted "the supineness" of the federal government with U.S. tolerance and patience and charged that the Madero government was "either apathetic or incompetent, or both." The unnecessary reference to Mexican jails as "insanitary [sic] and filthy," one of Wilson's personal touches, was a gratuitous insult. The note also insisted that the government either establish law and order or "confess . . . that it is powerless to do so," in which case the United States would consider what measures it should adopt. Threatening to abandon a policy of "pronounced friendliness" if the Mexicans didn't act promptly, the note clearly committed the United States to further action in the event of Mexican noncompliance. The Mexican reply treats all the cases in copious detail, while objecting to a tone and form at variance with diplomatic courtesy.

Some sense of the relative importance the Department of State attributed to the various issues raised in this note was more clearly evident when the issues were reconsidered later in connection with the possible recognition of the government which succeeded Madero. The department emphasized, above all, claims for damages to American life and property arising out of political disturbances. Various border questions appeared to be of secondary importance, while only one business case, that of the Tlahualilo Company, was made an issue (apart, of course, from those interests damaged by revolutionary violence).[10]

Ambassador Wilson returned home on leave toward the end of the year and met with President Taft and Secretary Knox in Washington.[11] Foreign Minister Lascurain was also in Washington in December and made a favorable impression on Taft and the secretary, and the administration expressed willingness to try again to work with Madero.[12] Washington decided to take up various issues between the two nations individually, overriding Ambassador Wilson's insistence that negotiations be conducted only on a single collective settlement of all U.S. claims.

While Lascurain was in Washington, Madero wired him urgent instructions to meet with President-elect Wilson with the specific request that Henry Lane Wilson not be allowed to remain in Mexico City under the new Democratic administration. The cable also stated that the Madero administration had informed Washington earlier that Wilson was persona non grata but decided later to postpone insistence on his removal.[13]

Meanwhile, other events had led to a sharp reversal in the fortunes of Henry Lane Wilson. Most important was the defeat of the Republican party in the presidential elections of 1912. Woodrow Wilson's victory meant a likely end to Wilson's diplomatic career as a political appointee. Nor did he have any reason to expect that Madero would urge the president-elect to continue his appointment. Even if Ambassador Wilson did not yet know of Madero's cable to Lascurain mentioned above, he surely must have been aware of Madero's personal hostility. In addition, Wilson's brother, the former senator and political power, had died that fall. Thus on his return to Mexico City early in 1913, Ambassador Wilson could expect to be out of a job within a matter of months.

One apparent result was that in January 1913 the ambassador's reporting took on a renewed sense of urgency and doom. In his long roundup dispatch in early February, only two weeks before Madero's fall, the ambassador vented his animosity toward the Mexican president:

> The sound condition of the public finances . . . [under] General Díaz has given place to disorder and dissipation. . . . the government [resorts] to all sorts of quack economic remedies. . . . [Madero's] family connections have been . . . a scandal. . . . [The government] is impotent in the face of domestic ills and disorders and truculent, insolent, and insincere in its international relations . . . responsible for the sacrifice of thousands of human lives, the destruction of vast material interests, aggravation of the condition of the poorer classes, for unspeakable barbarities and for desolation and ruin over a third . . . of the Republic. . . . [Madero] has himself become a despot, practicing all forms of tyranny. . . . The presidential election . . . was

farcical. . . . The agents of the Government . . . spread false impressions as
to actual conditions . . . discredit and impugn the motives of
the . . . diplomatic representatives of our Government.[14]

The embassy's sympathy for the opposition to Madero became increasingly
evident. That fall, after Wilson had left on home leave, the chargé d'affaires
expressed his own sentiments with remarkable candor in reporting the collapse of
Félix Díaz's revolt in Veracruz: "The collapse of this revolt greatly complicates the
general situation. Temporary success of the Government will only result in prolong-
ing the trouble. We should have warships in every Mexican port. . . . the Madero
administration is absolutely impotent to bring about even a semblance of peace and
order."[15] On January 18, 1913, the ambassador recommended "vigorous and drastic
action with the purpose of securing redress for our wrongs, an abatement of the
situation, and perhaps, incidentally, the downfall of a Government which is hateful to
a vast majority of the people of this country, and which has given us innumerable
evidences of its bad faith, inefficiency, hostility, and insincerity."[16]

In fact, Secretary Knox was sufficiently concerned to warn President Taft about
the ambassador's "increasing pessimism . . . upon the political situation in Mexico
which appears . . . unjustified, if not indeed, misleading. . . . the Ambassador
[shows] a disposition to drive the Department to action . . . which he for reasons of
his own seems set upon . . . to force the Government's hand in its dealing with the
Mexican situation as a whole."[17]

When the Cuban minister asked Wilson at this time whether he thought the
Madero government might soon fall, the ambassador replied, "Its fall will not be
easy, nor is it impossible"—which gives a curious insight into the trend of his
thinking.[18]

Madero's Overthrow

Francisco Madero was overthrown as president of Mexico by a barracks revolt
beginning on February 9 and ending in his arrest on February 18, 1913. General Félix
Díaz who led the revolt was able to hold out for so long because he was plotting with
General Victoriano Huerta to overthrow Madero almost from the beginning. Huerta
became Madero's general in charge of the defense of the city shortly after the revolt
broke out. Ambassador Wilson was in touch with both Generals Díaz and Huerta
during most of the ten-day period.

The shooting and shelling between the opposing forces endangered the lives and
property of foreigners as well as Mexicans. Since many were Americans, Ambassador Wilson put extreme pressure on the Madero government to provide protection
for them and their property. He also urged protests about their treatment as a means of
keeping in touch with the principals, that is Madero, Díaz, and Huerta, thereby
having an opportunity to affect the outcome of the contest. Several times the
Department of State suggested that the Americans withdraw from the danger zone,
and the Mexican foreign minister pointedly offered them quarters on the outskirts of

the city. Wilson explained with some heat that the removal of the embassy would be a "calamity" and that "Americans cannot be advised to go to a safer place because there is none. Outside the firing range there are bandits and inside there are bullets."[19]

While making representations about U.S. lives and property, Wilson threatened Madero with U.S. military intervention. His threats were credible because the Department of State, at Wilson's request, had arranged on February 10 for the Department of Navy to send several warships to Mexican waters.[20]

In his report to Washington, Wilson told Madero and Félix Díaz that "vessels had been ordered to the various seaports, as well as transports with the marines which could be landed if necessary and brought to maintain order and afford protection to the lives and property of foreigners."[21] The German and Spanish ministers in Mexico City at that time have since confirmed the threats Wilson made to Madero.[22] Ambassador Wilson tried unsuccessfully to secure authority to direct these warships and troops himself.

What made his threats of U.S. troop landings in Mexico City so significant was that he linked them to recommendations that Madero resign. Wilson used two channels for this purpose. First, he urged Foreign Minister Lascurain to work for Madero's resignation to avoid U.S. military intervention. Lascurain must have reported his conversation to President Madero and in addition, following Wilson's recommendation, presented the threat of U.S. military intervention to the Mexican senate, controlled by the opposition to Madero. This explanation is not inconsistent with Wilson's own reporting and is specifically confirmed by an independent entry in the German minister's diary. The German minister said Wilson told the foreign minister "he would have 3,000 to 4,000 American troops at his disposal and 'then he will establish order here' . . . tell the President to get out; in a legal way; . . . call in the senate."[23] Lascurain did in fact take the matter up with the senate and, although a quorum was not present, a group of twenty senators unsuccessfully tried to see the president and passed on their recommendations for his resignation to Madero's brother instead.

Wilson's other channel to force Madero to resign was through representatives of the European powers, the British, German, and Spanish ministers. He persuaded them to have the Spanish minister approach Madero directly on their behalf and seek his resignation. The Spanish minister called on Madero on February 15 and made his statement. Madero replied to him vigorously, "Foreigners have no right to interfere in Mexican politics," and abruptly left the room.[24] The foregoing version of the foreign diplomats' demarche to Madero through the Spaniard is confirmed independently by the statements of all three ministers.[25]

Alarmed by these threats, Madero wired a protest to President Taft asking him to avoid a "conflagration with consequences inconceivably more vast than that which it is desired to remedy."[26] He also sent a message to Taft through the Mexican embassy in Washington that "the ambassador, in view of local circumstances, will try perhaps to disembark marines and this will produce an unnecessary international conflict of terrible consequences."[27] Surprised by this furor, and after consulting the now-infuriated Ambassador Wilson, Taft replied that Madero must have been misinformed and that the United States was not planning a military intervention. Madero was much relieved by Taft's reply and cast aside further thoughts of resignation.[28] Ambassador Wilson's maneuvers, at least insofar as Madero's resignation was concerned, failed.

In his efforts to eliminate Madero, Ambassador Wilson had greater success in his dealings with Generals Díaz and Huerta. The two generals were in touch with one another through intermediaries almost from the beginning of the revolt and actually met face to face on February 11, two days after the revolt broke out.[29] Ambassador Wilson was in communication with Félix Díaz through confidential messengers from the first day of the revolt as well as with General Díaz in person on several occasions thereafter.[30] In his reports to Washington, Wilson presented Díaz in a most favorable light and consistently reported that public opinion favored him over Madero.

General Huerta sent Ambassador Wilson a confidential messenger on February 14, if not on the previous day, who informed the ambassador that it would be "possible to have him [Huerta] and Díaz come to an understanding, if the Ambassador thinks that would be a good idea."[31] Wilson met with the emissary privately and, remaining in touch with Huerta through messengers, reported to Washington on February 17, the day before Madero's arrest, that "General Huerta . . . will remove Madero from power at any moment . . . the purpose of delay being to avoid violence or bloodshed. I asked no questions and made no suggestions beyond requesting that no lives be taken except by due process of law."[32] A confidential agent of President Woodrow Wilson who came to Mexico several months later reported from reliable sources that Huerta's emissary had been quoted on several occasions and overheard by different people saying that he had promised Ambassador Wilson that Madero would not be killed when he was arrested.[33]

That very night Ambassador Wilson played host to a reception at the embassy after which Generals Huerta and Díaz agreed that Huerta would become provisional president, Díaz's nominations would form the cabinet, and Huerta would support Díaz for the permanent presidency. Their pact was signed in the American embassy in the presence of the ambassador.[34]

Ambassador Wilson appears to have committed himself to secure U.S. recognition of the Huerta government in exchange for the Mexican government's favorable consideration of the important issues outstanding in U.S.–Mexican relations, particularly as outlined in the U.S. note of September 15, 1912.[35] This appears as a reasonable inference from Wilson's messages to Washington thereafter and his insistent clamoring for U.S. recognition. In fact, he mobilized the diplomatic corps to meet with Huerta in formalities that gave the appearance of recognition, even though such an act required express validation by the individual foreign offices. Carried away by what he must have then considered a great diplomatic coup, Wilson instructed the consulates to help rally Mexicans around the Huerta government, indicating that "the new government . . . will be recognized by all foreign governments today."[36] And, in fact, the Department of State did appear to be on the verge of recognizing the provisional government, having indicated once again those matters from the note of September 15 which it held to be particularly important.

The murders of President Madero and Vice-President Pino Suárez intervened. Thereafter the Taft government cooled noticeably toward Huerta and left the question of recognition to the new administration. (President Wilson never recognized Huerta and ultimately used military force in Mexico, partly in an effort to unseat the general.)

Ambassador Wilson's animosity toward President Madero was well known to General Huerta before Madero's murder and when Huerta asked Wilson whether Madero should be sent into exile or thrown into a lunatic asylum, the ambassador replied, "Do that which [is] best for the peace of the country."[37] Later, partly to protect himself, Ambassador Wilson and the German minister did get Huerta's pledge that Madero would be spared, a pledge which Huerta either did not wish or was unable to fulfill. Wilson was implicated in Madero's death by the fact that his previous actions largely disqualified him from any influential role to protect Madero, plus the fact that he might have done more to save the deposed president. Primary responsibility for the crime, however, rests with the military squad which killed him and those superiors who gave the order.

During the ten-day revolt, Ambassador Wilson, as he himself admitted, proceeded frequently without instructions. Alarmed by his telegrams, the Department of State consistently tried to restrain him and refused almost all his requests for undefined military or diplomatic powers. Three times the department asked that he lead Americans out of the zone of danger.[38] The department refused his request for drastic instructions on the grounds that they "might precipitate intervention . . . and might subject American interests to increased dangers."[39] The department also refused Wilson's request for powers to direct troops.[40] Also, Washington showed its concern in advance about Madero's life and urged Wilson to use his influence to save him.[41] And, as indicated above, President Taft's denial of intentions to intervene nipped in the bud Ambassador Wilson's efforts to force Madero's resignation.

Conclusions

All the evidence suggests that Henry Lane Wilson sought to overthrow Madero almost from the start of the Díaz barracks revolts on February 9. He was in touch with Díaz that very day and with General Huerta, the other leading member of the conspiracy, no later than February 14. Wilson's campaign—through the foreign minister and a group of senators as well as through leading members of the diplomatic corps—to force Madero's resignation on threat of U.S. military intervention failed. It failed primarily because Wilson lacked authority to direct the ships and troops sent to Mexican waters and had no instructions to threaten intervention. In addition, President Taft reassured Madero that intervention was not planned. Most remarkable is the fact that Ambassador Wilson was able to bend influential members of the diplomatic corps and the Mexican foreign minister to his will, as well as provide a pretext for Mexican senators to seek Madero's resignation.

Wilson's actions were, of course, a flagrant intervention in Mexican affairs, not only exceeding but actually in conflict with his instructions from Washington. The men who overthrew President Madero were General Huerta and his associates, who arrested him and bore responsibility either for murdering him or not protecting him from assassination. Wilson's maneuvers and animosity toward Madero, coupled with his assurances that Great Power recognition would be forthcoming, surely strengthened the general's resolve to revolt.

Once Félix Díaz's revolt in Mexico City was under way, the Department of State in Washington did almost everything it could to restrain and control Ambassador Wilson. Secretary Knox demanded explanations of him time after time, refused his request for further authority, cautioned him to reduce the risks to American interests, made clear that military threats were not in order, and denied both to Wilson and to Madero the U.S. intention to intervene. The fears about Wilson's course of action expressed in many of the department's telegrams were prophetic. Once the revolt was under way, the department hardly had time (less than a week) to take decisive action. And, in view of current information in its possession and Ambassador Wilson's misleading reports, it would have been almost too much to have expected the department to remove him on the spot.

The Department of State appears to have made two major errors in its conduct with regard to Ambassador Wilson. First, its promptness in sending warships to Mexican waters at the ambassador's request made his threats of intervention credible. Actually in those days the dispatch of troops toward the Mexican border or warships to Mexican or other waters was almost routine. The episode of Madero's overthrow shows to what serious misunderstandings this practice could lead.

More important, Washington erred not so much in failing to remove Ambassador Wilson in the final days as having appointed him in the first place—or not having removed him far earlier. The department had had ample time during his career of some fourteen years to become acquainted with the man's instability and unreliability. His reporting during the first year of the Madero government, his recommendations to Washington from the embassy, and the meetings with him in December 1912, should have convinced Taft and Knox that his prompt removal was essential. How dangerous Knox considered him was revealed in the confidential letter to the president at the end of January 1913. The administration waited too long and both countries paid the price.

Francisco Madero was one of the best friends of the United States in Latin America and, in some ways, a better friend than Porfirio Díaz, though less likely to collaborate with large foreign economic interests. Moreover, Madero's political ideals and economic programs represented a far more moderate and gradual readjustment of Mexican society than that of his revolutionary successors. Later, the United States was forced to come to terms with more radical governments requiring greater adjustments from the United States than had Madero. Moreover, Henry Lane Wilson's erratic meddling in Mexican domestic matters and his association with the fall of Madero left indelible stains on the relations between the two countries.

Villarroel in Bolivia (1943–1946)

The Bolivian government corresponding most closely to the other "reform-ist" governments was that of Gualberto Villarroel (1943–1946). The Villarroel government continued the trends in social and economic policies introduced by the "military socialists" of the 1930s[42] and temporarily broke the dominance of the tin-owning elite. Villarroel led the greatest sustained effort up to that time of reforming Bolivian society.

The Villarroel government had more military participation than the civilian regimes of Madero and Arévalo, and Villarroel himself was an army man. Although elections were held, the Villarroel government respected civil liberties and political pluralism less than the other two reformist governments, as the political executions of 1944 indicated.

The impetus for Villarroel's reforms came from the Movimiento Nacionalista Revolucionario (MNR), a group of young civilian reformers who intermittently held important posts in Villarroel's government. The leaders of the MNR had complex relations with the U.S. government before Villarroel came to power, discussion of which is essential to understanding the U.S. response to his government.

Before Villarroel

Early U.S. relations with the Bolivian revolutionaries (MNR) were shaped by the repercussions of the MNR's opposition to the settlement of a dispute with the Standard Oil Company and its leadership in Bolivian labor unions.

After the outbreak of war in Europe, the United States wanted to strengthen its relations with Latin American countries for reasons of national security, especially to organize them in defense of the Western Hemisphere. To encourage political and military cooperation, as well as to insure the provision of strategic materials, the United States was prepared to offer Latin American countries economic assistance.

Completing these arrangements with Bolivia, however, was greatly compli-cated by the fact that the Bolivian government had seized the properties of the Standard Oil Company in 1937 and never paid compensation. The United States was unwilling to provide economic assistance to a government which had seized U.S. private investments without compensation. The United States was also concerned about access to oil in the Western Hemisphere, and the Bolivian seizure set a disturbing precedent for negotiations in Venezuela and elsewhere. The case was blocking an agreement with the United States for continental defense.

Tempted with the prospects of economic assistance and less committed to the move against Standard Oil than predecessor governments, the Peñaranda administra-tion which took office in 1940 sought a compromise with the United States. Political opposition to a settlement in the Bolivian congress was led by the MNR which made strong nationalistic appeals against giving in to Standard Oil. The U.S. and Bolivian governments sought a pretext for overcoming Bolivian opposition to the Standard Oil settlement, thereby clearing the way for Bolivian participation in hemispheric de-fense and economic assistance.

The British government, which was then desperately seeking U.S. and Latin American support against Germany, provided that pretext by fabricating a German plot for a Nazi putsch in Bolivia. British intelligence officers devised a letter from the Bolivian military attaché in Berlin to the German minister in La Paz containing plans for a coup.[43] The British arranged for the U.S. minister in La Paz to give a photocopy of the fabricated document to the Peñaranda government. United States officials refused to confirm the authenticity of the letter, but it is not certain that they knew it was a fraud.

On the basis of this document and other considerations, the Peñaranda government declared the German minister persona non grata and expelled him from the country. Also, the government declared a state of siege and imprisoned some of its leading critics, including leaders of the MNR, thereby temporarily silencing its most vocal opposition. The MNR was not singled out for mention in the fabricated letter, but the government's action associated the MNR thereafter with "Nazi-fascism."

On August 1, ten days after the alleged "putsch" and the government's efforts to suppress it had been made public, the Bolivian minister in Washington received a note from the Department of State proposing a long-term plan of collaboration to foster continued mutually beneficial economic relations between the United States and Bolivia. The Japanese attack on Pearl Harbor in December and the sympathy this aroused in Bolivia for the United States, further facilitated compromise. On January 27, 1942, the two governments reached an agreement providing for the settlement of the Standard Oil claim and on the next day, January 28, signed a $25 million economic development program for Bolivia.[44] Simultaneously the Bolivian government announced the severance of diplomatic relations with the Axis.

There is no evidence that the United States attempted to suppress the MNR leaders in 1941 or label them Nazis, but because of the party's earlier and continuing opposition to the Standard Oil settlement and the government's action, the United States thereafter associated them with "Nazi-fascism." The effect of the "Nazi putsch" episode, in which the United States was involved, made the MNR a victim of the Peñaranda administration's maneuvers in domestic and international politics as well as of U.S. anti-German policy in Latin America.

Another aspect of U.S. policy affecting the MNR was the former's position on the side of the traditional parties and in opposition to the MNR in labor disputes in 1942 and 1943. Ernesto Galarza, an official of the Pan American Union, charged the American ambassador, Pierre Boal, with having used his influence with President Peñaranda to discourage passage of a labor code. Boal apparently sought to avoid price increases for tin which innovations in the code would require and for which the United States would have to pay. The Department of State backed up Boal by urging that "no steps . . . be taken that might result in the creation of situations which would inhibit the full performance of contracts made in good faith."[45] In defending its opposition to the code, the Peñaranda government charged that the labor disturbances had been fomented by Nazis. The charge of nazism was a clear reflection on the MNR in view of the latter's influence in the miners' union.

The Catavi "massacre" of December 1942 and the furor created in the United States over Boal's position on the labor code, however, led to remedial action by the Department of State. The U.S. government sent a commission headed by Judge Calvert McGruder to study labor conditions in Bolivia, and a report was issued recommending reforms in the mines. So that labor's interests would be better represented, a labor attaché was sent to the embassy in La Paz, the first of the labor attachés that have since been sent to missions around the world.

Nonrecognition of Villarroel

On December 20, 1943, a group of young military officers overthrew the Peñaranda government and made a political unknown, Major Gualberto Villarroel, president. He appointed three members of the MNR to his cabinet. Víctor Paz Estenssoro, the leader of the MNR group and the new minister of finance, was perhaps the most powerful civilian in the new government. Paz had called on the American ambassador before the coup to make clear his willingness to collaborate with the United States in the war effort, and high officials of the new Villarroel government sought to reassure Washington about its position on the war within hours of its assumption of control.

The Department of State was reserved and suspicious from the start and Secretary Cordell Hull commented in connection with the Villarroel coup that "the hemisphere is at present under sinister and subversive attack by the Axis, assisted by some elements within the hemisphere itself."[46] On January 10, Secretary Hull circulated to the other American republics, except Argentina, a confidential memorandum describing the pro-Axis orientation and activities of the MNR.[47] Among the many charges against the MNR were anti-Semitism, hostility to the Allies, and collaboration with the Axis. The memorandum charged specific contacts with Axis agents, the receipt of financial support from the Axis, and implied that the Axis was controlling MNR activities. The purpose of the memorandum was to persuade other American republics to withhold recognition from the new regime. The U.S. action was especially damaging to the Villarroel government because it meant the suspension of U.S. assistance—including lend-lease—and the political isolation of Bolivia.

In the weeks that followed, U.S. officials made it clear that Villarroel would need to remove the three MNR members from his cabinet as the price of U.S. recognition and U.S. support for recognition by the other American republics. Laurence Duggan told the Villarroel representative in Washington that "the revolutionary junta as it now stood contained elements which were wholly inacceptable and whose Axis taint was such that their continued presence precluded recognition by this Government" and that so long as these elements remained there would be no recognition.[48] When the pressure continued, the three MNR ministers, including Víctor Paz Estenssoro, left the cabinet, and following a visit from U.S. diplomat Avra Warren and consultation with other governments, the United States and the

Latin American republics recognized the Villarroel government at the end of June 1944.[49]

To what extent were the U.S. charges against the MNR valid? The charge of anti-Semitism was made to link the MNR with the Nazis, and, in fact, the MNR program and its policies did have anti-Semitic elements. A number of Bolivians—including some MNR members—were agitated by competition from an influx of Jewish refugees displaced by the Nazis in Europe. But the MNR leaders, like most Bolivians, were of mestizo or Indian blood and their anti-Semitism had nothing to do at all with Nazi views of racial superiority. Paz said that the MNR opposed the "Jewish avalanche . . . because it constitute[d] unproductive immigration. . . . The Jews have created serious problems relating to subsistence and housing in almost all Bolivian communities."[50]

The MNR also had an antiimperialist coloration which related especially to the United States and Great Britain. Resentment of U.S. and British wealth and power made them more susceptible to Nazi criticism of the Western Allies. The MNR maintained that the Bolivian government should insist on higher prices in the sale of its raw materials to the United States and other countries. Also the MNR favored greater government intervention in the economy than had ordinarily been welcome in the United States. Nor had the MNR been a supporter of Bolivian adherence to the United Nations declaration. Nevertheless, the MNR leadership recognized the realities of the Bolivian situation and had reaffirmed time and again its willingness to cooperate with the United States in the war, both before the Villarroel coup and many times thereafter. Moreover by early 1944 Germany's chances of winning the war appeared increasingly dim.

Members of the MNR had had social contact with Germans as they had with nationals of other countries, their newspaper had received subsidies to run Nazi releases on the war just as other Bolivian papers had received subsidies from one side or the other, and some members may have sympathized with the German cause.

Various U.S. charges in the case have implied but have not actually specified that the MNR was controlled by Nazi Germany. In fact, there is no evidence that it was and evidence available suggests the contrary. A confidential dispatch from the American embassy in April 1944, only recently available for public examination, offers an authoritative judgment: "No definite proof was ever available, even at the time of the 'Nazi-Putsch' to establish direct connection between the MNR and the Nazi party. At the present time it seems doubtful that the party was anything but a completely national one. . . . Good material for Nazi influence, if there is any such party."[51]

The MNR represented the strongest civilian pillar of the Villarroel government and the force within the cabinet for reform and moderation. Its political influence was demonstrated at the 1944 elections and Villarroel's calling the MNR back to the cabinet at the end of the year. Yet the U.S. nonrecognition policy threw the Villarroel government off balance from the start and it never really established its equilibrium.

The Overthrow of Villarroel

Like the Toro and Busch military socialist governments in the 1930s, the Villarroel administration was adamantly opposed by the tin mining interests which had dominated Bolivian politics in the twentieth century. Denied formal MNR participation in the government by the U.S. nonrecognition policy initially, Villarroel never succeeded in developing a coherent social and economic program of his own and the accompanying mass following which it might have produced. U.S. opposition to the MNR had the effect of strengthening the government's military elements. Moreover, the political opposition continued to label the MNR "Nazi-fascist" at a period, the middle 1940s, when such an association was particularly damaging.

The United States contributed to the discomfiture of the Villarroel government and its MNR participants by the publication in February 1946 of the Blue Book leveled at the Perón regime in Argentina.[52] Although the purpose of publishing the charges was not, apparently, to discredit Villarroel, the Blue Book contained a section which repeated publicly many of the charges which had been made earlier on a confidential basis against Víctor Paz Estenssoro and the MNR. The Bolivian section was included to show how Germany and Argentina had posed a Nazi-fascist threat to the continent. The effect of the State Department's action was to stir up again the animosities of the wartime period and to complicate further relations between the two governments. One author interpreted the publication of the Blue Book as giving the green light to proceed with a conspiracy against Villarroel.[53]

The United States complicated the political life of the Villarroel government in other ways as well. Negotiations of a new tin contract taking effect when the existing contract expired in June 1946 were perhaps the single most important pending issue. As usual the two parties disagreed on what constituted a fair price. The more interesting aspect of the discussion was that the United States was negotiating not only on how much to pay Bolivia for tin but also how the Bolivians would distribute the proceeds. The latter touched on long-time tensions between the owners of the tin mines and the MNR-sponsored government.

The specific points at issue included taxes, foreign exchange proceeds, and Bolivian government expenditures. The mine owners, such as Mauricio Hochschild who was also meeting separately with State Department officials, favored taxes on profits rather than on production units. The Villarroel government wanted to tax output per se since collections could be more easily verified this way. The U.S. discussion of tax questions may have been interpreted by the Bolivian government as pressure to ease up in their efforts to collect back taxes from the mine owners. Another major issue was the government's insistence on control of the percentage of foreign exchange from tin sales the mine owners would be permitted to keep. This was a major plank of the MNR platform, and Bolivian ambassador to the U.S. Víctor Andrade insisted that 40 percent was quite enough despite the owners' desire for more.[54] Finally, the mine owners hoped that their own tax burdens could be lowered if the federal budget could be trimmed.

In all the above issues the U.S. negotiators took positions which coincided with those of the mine owners and against the Bolivian government. Mr. James Wright of the Department of State pressed, as a "purely personal opinion," for the taxation of tin on the basis of company profits rather than production units.[55] Assistant Secretary of State Spruille Braden and his associate decided to discuss with the Bolivians the "whole problem, including taxes, exchange, and budget,"[56] that is, Bolivian *internal* affairs. Another interesting aspect of the tin negotiations was that, while the Villar-roel government was refusing to make troops available to the mine management for use against miners, the American embassy was making representations to the government about the safety of U.S. citizens in the mines.[57]

A defense of the Villarroel government and an indictment of U.S. policy during this period is contained in an elaborately documented report by Ernesto Galarza published in May 1949.[58] It is interesting that many of the charges he made then about U.S. policy were confirmed in State Department documents for Bolivia for 1946 made public in 1970, as cited above.

United States negotiators could not have been expected to be totally unconcerned about domestic Bolivian problems, particularly since the United States was prepared to approve prices for tin above the world market price. (Officials have justified the premium by reference to U.S. needs, Bolivia's high costs, and political-strategic considerations). At the same time, the record makes clear that the official U.S. government position had the effect of associating the United States with the position of the mine owners against the Villarroel government. As late as July 17, 1946, Ambassador Víctor Andrade pleaded with Mr. Braden either to reach an agreement for the purchase of Bolivian tin or to free Bolivia of restrictions on selling to other buyers. Andrade reportedly threatened to take the matter up with the United Nations as a discriminatory practice to free trade if Braden would not reach a decision.[59]

Braden yielded, but too late, for the movement that culminated in Villarroel's murder four days later was already under way. Almost as if to escape responsibility for what had transpired, the State Department wired Ambassador Flack on July 24 that "Department and RFC [Reconstruction Finance Corporation] replying to inquiries re tin negotiations . . . that agreement in principle reached few days ago between RFC and Bolivian producers covering deliveries . . . through balance calendar year."[60] The "final agreement" was concluded August 14.

Another arena of controversy in the concluding months of Villarroel's administration was in La Paz, where the U.S. chargé d'affaires was in frequent dispute with the Villarroel government. One of the issues was the conduct of the Bolivians who managed the Panagra and Grace interests. The Bolivian government charged them with involvement in the antigovernment disturbances in June and the U.S. embassy recommended that they be replaced by U.S. citizens. Assistant Secretary Braden and other U.S. officials were much concerned about the developing climate of violence in the country, including a violation of the U.S. embassy premises. On its side, the Bolivian government called the U.S. chargé "unfriendly" for allegedly having called together the diplomatic corps to consider collective representations about the June events.[61]

By mid-July, Joseph Flack, who shared the chargé's critical views of the Villarroel government, assumed his duties as the U.S. ambassador. On July 18, when the revolt was already under way, Ambassador Flack accompanied the dean of the diplomatic corps and the papal chargé on a visit to Foreign Minister Pinto:

> We saw Pinto at once, and the Dean, acting as chief spokesman, said that our visit was not in any sense an intervention in Bolivian internal affairs, nor did we come as diplomats or ambassadors, but as friends of Bolivia with humanitarian motives to urge clemency in dealing with the students a number of whom had been killed during the day and a larger number gravely wounded. The Dean added that he felt that the students were animated by enthusiasm in defending their institution and did not merit being treated as an alien army or as a subversive political element.[62]

In fact, the university was a focus of anti-MNR activity. The revolt of the students against Villarroel was the spearhead of the successful rebellion that led to his overthrow and murder on July 21.

When the shooting was over and Villarroel's elimination complete, Ambassador Flack did not conceal his jubilation in his telegram reporting the event to Washington:

> For Braden. A popular revolution in every sense of the word has just occurred in Bolivia. . . . this may prove first democratic government in Bolivian history. Immediate prospects are greatly improved relations with the United States. . . .
>
> Because of lengths Argentines went to uphold cruel and Fascist Villarroel dictatorship, reprisals in form [of] failure [to] ship needed food may be anticipated. This revolution an irreparable blow [to] formation of anti–United States bloc so dear Perón's heart. I therefore urge that we be prepared [to] ship any food necessary on any terms to prevent this democratic movement falling victim to Fascist reaction because of people's hunger. Also that tin negotiations be brought to prompt satisfactory conclusion as soon as recognition is accorded.[63]

The United States recognized the new government on August 12. Within two months, Ambassador Flack published his account of the revolution in the quasi-official *Foreign Service Journal*,[64] a most irregular practice for an ambassador still accredited to the successor government.

To my knowledge, virtually no one has charged the United States with primary responsibility for the fall of the Villarroel government. Domestic developments were probably far more significant, but the United States contributed pressures which led to the government's collapse, not the least of which was the absence of U.S. agreement to buy Bolivian tin.

Conclusions

The MNR paid a heavy price for its opposition to the Standard Oil settlement, opposition which ultimately led to the U.S. nonrecognition policy. The MNR insisted from the beginning that tin, not oil, was the main question, yet intransigently opposed the oil settlement. This action incited the opposition of the powerful Standard Oil Company and the U.S. government and helped array them both on the side of the MNR's political enemies. Further, the U.S. government permitted itself to be used as a channel for British intelligence in 1941 to promote wartime collaboration with Bolivia to which the MNR had interposed itself as an obstacle, partly because of the deadlock on the oil settlement. As a result, MNR opposition in the Standard Oil settlement and unwillingness to come out behind the Western Allies early in the war, helped shape U.S. policies, including at first nonrecognition of, and later opposition to, the Villarroel government—both of which were damaging to the MNR's first major effort in national leadership.

United States policies toward the MNR and the Villarroel government were motivated by a short-term "win-the-war" approach. The U.S. anti-MNR position, however, appears not to have appreciably advanced U.S. interests even with respect to the war. The MNR leader, Paz Estenssoro, had believed that Bolivia had no choice but to collaborate with the United States and, by 1944, the MNR knew that Germany had lost the war. As a result, the nonrecognition campaign against Villarroel was not only unnecessary to secure U.S. wartime objectives, but caused long-term misconceptions and distortions in American policy.

Charging the MNR with Nazi-fascism and making that label stick was a major part of the strategy of the tin mining and other traditional interests in Bolivia. In a sense, the United States fell for exaggerated or false charges, arraying itself on the side of the traditional interests against their major opposition, the MNR. After Germany's defeat, the United States continued to press the same charges and took positions against the Villarroel government that paralleled that of the political opposition and together led to its fall.

Like other revolutionary movements, the MNR had a number of faults which did not commend it to the United States. The MNR started out as an elite organization with close ties to the military and rather closer German connections, however tenuous, than the United States might have wished. The attraction nazism may have held for some MNR leaders may have been due less to its totalitarianism than to its opposition to the western tin interests believed to be oppressing Bolivia. What was perhaps most significant about the MNR was that it embodied, as much as any other Bolivian political party, aspirations of the less affluent sectors of Bolivian society, particularly the tin miners and later the peasants. Under Villarroel, the MNR was instrumental in the sponsorship of the first Indian congress in Bolivian history. Also, it concerned itself in very concrete ways with Bolivian social and economic development, and its nationalistic policies, though raising complications for the United States, foreshadowed the goals of the Alliance for Progress.

No doubt it would have been expecting a good deal for the United States to swing behind the MNR in the 1940s as it did later in the 1950s. United States leaders were understandably reluctant to take such chances during the war. But the United States might have consulted its own interests more carefully. The charges of Nazi-fascism were exaggerated, if not totally incorrect. Much of the U.S. campaign against the MNR was self-defeating, particularly since the latter gave every indication both in late 1943 and in early 1944 of its readiness to cooperate with the United States in prosecution of the war against the Axis. The Nazi-fascist issue blinded the United States to a clear-eyed appraisal of the MNR and served as a pretext for certain Bolivian groups to get the United States to act in accord with their vested interests. As a result, the United States contributed to the collapse of the reformist Villarroel government in 1946. In the six-year interregnum that followed, the political and economic weaknesses, if not bankruptcy, of traditional interests were demonstrated time and again. The government was easily overthrown by a relatively small group of revolutionaries in the urban insurrections of 1952. Thereafter, the Bolivian government embarked on more radical programs. What was most interesting about the later relationships was that the United States was better able to come to terms with the MNR with its revolutionary policies in the 1950s than with its reformist policies in the 1940s.

Arévalo in Guatemala (1945–1951)

The young Guatemalans who helped overthrow Ubico in June 1944 and seized power for themselves in October 1944 were doctors, lawyers, teachers, students, and other members of the middle class who sought a sharp break with the nation's dictatorial past. Guatemala's new leaders embarked on what Marxists call a bourgeois-democratic revolution which seeks to make the capitalist system more responsive to popular needs within a democratic framework. Many returned from exile in neighboring countries and Europe and lacked previous governmental experience. They seized on the Atlantic Charter as a symbol of their ideals and sought to put them into practice in Guatemala.

The new Guatemalan government began its life under auspicious circumstances. The seizure of government did not involve civil war and loss of life, as in Mexico, nor international controversy, as had the seizure of power in Bolivia in 1943. The new leaders sought constructive domestic reform, their attitudes toward the United States were still favorable, and they were optimistic about the future. Their presidential candidate, Juan José Arévalo, was an idealistic teacher and writer whose views at that time were independent but not antagonistic toward the United States.

After Arévalo's election and assumption of the presidency in March 1945, he devoted his major energies to strengthening the political foundation of the country. Political parties of all persuasions were allowed to form, freedom of speech and press were largely respected, labor unions were encouraged to recruit members and bargain collectively, and Guatemala experienced the excitement and confusion of political and intellectual liberation following a long authoritarian regime. Arévalo established a national bank, a social security system, an institute for economic development, and turned attention to the large Indian population.

United Fruit Company

The Arévalo government was also concerned about the immense influence of large U.S. corporations in the country's economic and political life. The United Fruit Company, controlled by U.S. stockholders, was the largest private enterprise in the country with many thousand employees.[65] Bananas, the company's main product, were an important source of foreign exchange, although far overshadowed by Guatemala's major export, coffee. The company owned hundreds of thousands of acres suitable for bananas, only a fraction of which was cultivated.

United Fruit's agricultural interests were, however, less significant politically than its control over the Guatemalan transportation network. The company owned a controlling interest in the International Railways of Central America (IRCA), whose northern arm was the sole overland connection between Guatemala City and the Atlantic coast. The company also owned the only port at the rail terminus on the coast, and the company's ships handled many of the nation's exports. IRCA shipped United Fruit products at preferential rates, and products from the Pacific coastlands were shipped overland across the entire width of the country to the Atlantic port. Pacific ports handled little traffic. Since there was no highway to the northern coast, IRCA had a near monopoly on the transport of the country's foreign trade, imports and exports alike. Thus, nationalist resentment of United Fruit was based not simply on the company's large landholdings but also on its control of the nation's central transportation network. Foreign companies also controlled the nation's international communications, one of which, Tropical Radio, was a subsidiary of the United Fruit Company.

Nationalist and "antiimperialist" sentiment was also aroused by the fact that the major source of electric power in the country was controlled by foreign interests. Electric Bond and Share, the owner preceding American and Foreign Power, owned the power company, Empresa Eléctrica de Guatemala which supplied about four-fifths of the country's electric service.[66]

Critics of foreign companies in Guatemala have maintained that those companies gained access to the nation's resources through unscrupulous methods and exploited them unfairly at the expense of the local population. Critics have charged that the companies' overwhelming wealth permitted them to suborn local political leaders.

Charges such as this are common in anti-American propaganda in the area and have sometimes been carefully documented, as in the study of three large foreign corporations in Guatemala by Alfonso Bauer Paiz. Bauer Paiz has charged that most Guatemalan dictators have secured U.S. recognition and support, which were essential for them to come into power or stay in power, by concluding contracts with U.S. companies at Guatemala's expense.[67] He charged that these contracts proved "the prostitution of democracy" to U.S. business interests.

Bauer Paiz has examined in detail port and railroad arrangements, production, profits, investments, in fact, almost the entire scope of the United Fruit Company's operations. His conclusion was:

All the achievements of the Company were made at the expense of the impoverishment of the country and by acquisitive [mercantile] practices. To protect its authority it had recourse to every method: political intervention, economic compulsion, contractual imposition, bribery, tendentious propaganda, as suited its purposes of domination. The United Fruit Company is the principal enemy of the progress of Guatemala, of its democracy and of every noble effort directed at its economic liberation.[68]

Two years later another serious study prepared by Stacy May and Galo Plaza reached diametrically opposed conclusions with respect to United Fruit operations in six Central American countries. While not taking on "the probably impossible task of appraising the rights and wrongs of . . . the days of banana pioneering," May and Plaza concluded: "We are willing to believe that the early 'banana hands' did not always fully exemplify the virtues and rectitude associated with ideas of chivalry. But the same could be said of the political and commercial environments in which they had to work. On balance, it is doubtful that they seriously depreciated the prevailing ethical currency."[69]

The two authors also carefully studied the company's operations in Central America in the light of its contribution to the host countries' economies:

> The contribution of the United Fruit Company to the economies of the six countries [including Guatemala] is enormously advantageous when regarded from the viewpoint of their national interest. . . . it has been leaving within the production area more than $7.00 for every dollar in profits withdrawn . . . its operations in the six countries have yielded a return to their economies several times larger per acre of land and for each agricultural worker employed than any agricultural activity developed through local initiative and capital financing. . . . Upon all *strictly economic measurements* that can be applied, the suggested test for justifying the worth of a foreign private investment to host countries—by clear demonstration that it brings them greater gains than they could have hoped to achieve without it—is answered in terms too conclusive to admit debate.[70]

The study also alleges that the company's earnings were not equivalent to the earnings of the average company of its size engaged primarily in domestic business in the United States. From 1899 to 1955 the profits after taxes reportedly averaged under 13 percent of net assets which compared with the only roughly comparable figure of 14.9 percent prepared by the First National City Bank for 1,843 leading U.S. manufacturing corporations.

What may have actually happened in the past is less important politically than what local political leaders and their followers *believed* happened. On that count, the Guatemalan leaders became increasingly critical and ultimately hostile toward United Fruit's record. May and Plaza, for example, readily admit that its image was far blacker than its performance.[71] Moreover, readers should bear in mind that the May/Plaza study was devoted to economic considerations. Some Guatemalans might have preferred to forego any conceivable economic advantages that association with the United Fruit Company offered in order to avoid what they considered decisive *political* disadvantages.

Labor Disputes

The deterioration and tensions in relations between the U.S. and Guatemalan governments during Arévalo's presidency may not be fully understood without reference to the international labor movement and particularly the relations between Guatemalan and U.S. labor leaders. The Guatemalan labor movement had immense significance after 1945 because it became, in a sense, the most important organized political group behind the revolutionary governments of Arévalo and Arbenz. Arévalo counted on organized labor to support his social and economic reforms and as a major obstacle to those domestic and foreign groups which hoped to regain the privileges and influence they had enjoyed in earlier eras. Organized labor made the decisive contribution in the successful armed defense of the Arévalo government in the 1949 street fighting following the assassination of Colonel Arana, the leader of the revolutionary party's right wing.

Guatemala's most influential labor leaders were supporters of the pro-Communist and pro-Soviet Confederación de Trabajadores de América Latina (CTAL) led by the Mexican, Vicente Lombardo Toledano. The Confederación de Trabajadores de Guatemala (CTG), led by Víctor Manuel Gutiérrez, was a member of the CTAL from its founding in 1944, and the other large labor confederation, the Federación Sindical de Guatemala (FSG), decided to join the CTAL in 1950, subject to the unification of the Guatemalan labor movement as a whole.[72]

Pro-Communist labor leaders were successful in Guatemala not because the Communists were strong there when Ubico fell. On the contrary, Ubico had eliminated or sent Guatemalan Communists into exile in the 1930s, and unlike in many other Latin American countries, communism had weak roots in Guatemala.[73] The absence of Guatemalan experience with a strong Communist party has sometimes been advanced as a reason why it gained influence rapidly in the late 1940s.

Widespread support for the CTAL and its pro-Communist leadership represented a strong rebuff to the initiatives of U.S. labor leaders, such as Serafino Romualdi who sought, with official U.S. government approval and probably financial support, to establish an anti-Communist federation of labor unions in Latin America opposed to the CTAL. Romualdi visited Guatemala in May 1947 on such a mission and not only failed to win the FSG over to his side but antagonized them as well. Romualdi's contact in Guatemala, Arcadio Ruiz Franco, lost his position with the FSG and was banned from his own union as punishment for his dealings with Romualdi. The leader of the FSG, Manuel Pinto Usaga, publicly denied any intention of the FSG to affiliate with the anti-Communist Confederación Interamericana de Trabajadores (CIT) formed in Lima, Peru, in January 1948.[74] The politically significant result of these maneuvers was that, unlike labor in many Latin American countries, the Guatemalans rebuffed the U.S.-supported anti-Communist movement and retained ties with the pro-Soviet organizations.

Another major source of friction between the Arévalo administration and the United States was the new labor code introduced in 1947. Markedly favoring labor at the expense of management, the code sought to right the balance in a society where management had long dominated. As a former minister of labor under Arévalo commented, "A capitalist democracy ought to compensate with the means at its disposal (some of which are legislative) for the economic inequality between those who possess the means of production and those who sell manual labor."[75]

One of the most controversial provisions of the law dealt with severance pay. A presumption in favor of a discharged worker was made with regard to entitlement to such pay, and the burden to prove the contrary rested with management. One result was that management found discharging certain workers costly because severance pay was so high.[76] Most of the inspectors who looked after the implementation of the law and many of the judges who enforced it were sympathetic to labor rather than management. According to Richard Adams, "For the first time in history employers found themselves suddenly on the short end of the power relationship."[77]

The labor code affected many financial interests in Guatemala, but the companies controlled by U.S. capital were especially vulnerable. United Fruit was the largest employer in the country, with more than 10,000 employees. Provisions of the law made more stringent requirements on companies with more than 500 employees. Since there were few such companies, United Fruit complained bitterly that the thrust of enforcement was directed against itself on a discriminatory basis, a charge which the Department of State backed up.[78] As a result of the new labor code and what was believed to be government bias in favor of the unions, the United Fruit Company considered its control over its own operations threatened. This came as a bitter pill to the company because the pay and working conditions of its employees were far better than those of most Guatemalans.

The United Fruit Company's managers had always worked closely with the vested financial interests and government leaders before and during the Ubico administration, and adversity had the effect of strengthening their personal and business ties with the domestic vested interests which opposed the Arévalo government. Disputes between labor and management hampered or suspended the company's operations during the last three years of Arévalo's presidency. Strikes, slowdowns, or shutdowns occurred each year, usually accompanied by recriminations between the company and the government.

The Arévalo administration also disappointed other U.S. financial interests not yet established, which sought a foothold in Guatemala. One was a major U.S. boat company seeking, with the support of the U.S. ambassador, to open up the lumber resources of the Petén. The company's representative began dealing with the influential military leader, Colonel Francisco Javier Arana, and negotiations were suspended following his assassination.[79] Similarly, U.S. oil companies wished to begin explorations in Guatemala and pressed the Arévalo government for concessions. The Guatemalan leaders' experience with one large U.S. corporation, United Fruit, made them leery of intimate collaboration with others, in spite of tempting economic benefits that oil concessions might bring. Arévalo linked approval for oil concessions to U.S. support for Guatemalan claims to Belize against the British—a commitment the United States was unlikely to make—and the deal fell through.[80]

Ambassador Patterson

The Arévalo government's posture vis-à-vis U.S. business interests, present and prospective, disturbed U.S. officials. Difficulties with regard to U.S. business began under Edward J. Kyle, the first U.S. ambassador to serve after World War II. Kyle was succeeded in 1948 by Richard C. Patterson, Jr., a business impresario and former chairman of the board of Radio Keith Orpheum. Promotion was his specialty and U.S. business interests in Guatemala were his major concern. Before arriving in Guatemala, Patterson made some of the earliest speeches alerting the country to the dangers of international communism with dramatic illustrations from his ambassadorial experience in Yugoslavia.

Members of the government developed an intense dislike for Ambassador Patterson. Luis Cardoza y Aragón, a writer and ambassador under Arévalo, takes the United States to task for sending Guatemala such a "violent and vulgar functionary" guilty of "intermeddling and ill-breeding."[81] The former foreign minister under Arévalo, Raúl Osegueda, tells how Ambassador Patterson tried to tempt President Arévalo with money and girls.[82]

Attention is devoted to Ambassador Patterson because his fate in Guatemala was a symbol of the deterioration in relations with the United States. Patterson's central complaint against the government appears to have been its treatment of U.S. business. He considered the defense of those interests one of his major responsibilities, whether this related to United Fruit or to other Americans who were disappointed in their hopes of making use of Guatemala's timber or oil resources.

The underlying tensions in the relationship broke through to the surface in a seemingly minor incident at the Central American Olympic Games which took place in Guatemala City in February 1949. The Puerto Rican athletes present were honored by the Puerto Rican shield and a popular Puerto Rican song instead of the American flag and the Star Spangled Banner. During the parade, the loudspeaker proclaimed that the new Guatemala was leading the fight "to liberate colonies from imperialist powers," it not being clear whether the statement referred to the Guatemalan claim on British Honduras, the Puerto Rican independence movement, or both.[83] Expressing his surprise and indignation, Ambassador Patterson made a formal protest. The Guatemalans thereafter ran up the Stars and Stripes and played the U.S. national anthem.

About one month later the hostile relations between Patterson and the government reached a climax. The Guatemalan embassy in Washington orally requested Ambassador Patterson's recall on the grounds that "he was interfering in the domestic politics in grave danger to his person."[84] Ambassador Patterson left immediately for Washington. The department categorically rejected the charges, but he did not return to Guatemala.

In a presidential report in 1951, Arévalo elaborated on this episode:

> For several years agitators from sectors opposed to the popular revolutionary movement had been seeking the official intervention of foreign powers in order to solve Guatemalan political problems. Subordinate functionaries of foreign missions assigned to Guatemala conspired more than once along with . . . Guatemalans to overthrow the constitutional system. . . . [In 1950] because of this kind of plot they even compromised the chief of an honorable diplomatic mission. My government . . . accumulated trustworthy information as evidence of the complicity of the eminent diplomat. Under these circumstances the immediate recall of this man . . . was requested.[85]

In a statement published in 1955, Arévalo explicitly linked Patterson to conspiracy: "In his last phase Patterson went so far as to preside over secret sessions of conspirators."[86]

International Difficulties

Meanwhile, Guatemala had been striking out on an independent course in foreign policy which, if not in conflict with major U.S. objectives, was frequently a source of annoyance and concern. The United States had long since accustomed itself in foreign policy matters to resistance from Mexico, Argentina, and Chile, but was not used to the small countries of the Caribbean basin striking out persistently on their own.

The Guatemalan revolutionary government took such a line from the outset, believing at first that such initiative did not conflict with U.S. policy. For example, the Guatemalan government broke diplomatic relations with many of the Caribbean dictators, such as Somoza, Trujillo, and Peréz Jiménez. That position proved a complication for the United States which found the dictators' support on international questions useful. The Arévalo government also reiterated nationalistic demands for British withdrawal from British Honduras and asked the United States for support. The latter was on record as being opposed to colonialism in principle, but in practice was not disposed to challenge Great Britain in the Americas just at the moment she sought her collaboration under the Marshall Plan in Europe. Thus, in the spring of 1948, at the Inter-American Conference in Bogotá, the United States expressed its opposition to any "extension" of European colonies in the Americas, as well as its unwillingness to become embroiled in disputes between its friends over existing possessions there.[87]

At the Rio Conference in 1947, the Guatemalan delegation vigorously pressed to make the treaty applicable not only to threats to the peace but also to the "democratic" structure of member states, which went further than the majority wished to go. In a defeated but prophetic proposal, the Guatemalans also called for abstention from "lending aid, direct or indirect, to any aggressions . . . against . . . signatory states . . . which aim to change the constitutional regime . . . by means of force."[88]

In the negotiations on economic matters in Bogotá in 1948, Guatemala explicitly opposed articles regarding the treatment of foreign investment approved by many other delegations. The Guatemalans said that the provision about "prompt, adequate, and effective" compensation for expropriated properties should be subject to each country's constitution, and that articles involving protection for foreign investors should be interpreted in such a way as to make clear that aliens, as well as nationals, are subject to the law of the country concerned.[89] Already by the late 1940s the Guatemalan government had formally taken an independent position on issues of concern to the United States.

Ambassador Patterson's recall from Guatemala City marked, in effect, a break in friendly relations between the two governments. No ambassador was named to succeed him during the balance of President Arévalo's term, which the latter called both a kind of "punishment" and a peaceful interlude.[90] Arévalo was sufficiently distrusted that the United States refused to sell him arms beginning in 1948. The Guatemalans correctly considered this refusal a significant indicator of U.S. hostility. Arévalo said Guatemala had to embark for five years on a "humble search" for arms for its "little" army.[91] In the early 1950s when other Latin American countries were concluding Mutual Defense Assistance agreements with the United States, Guatemala was noticeably among the absent.

The Korean War broke out shortly after Ambassador Patterson's recall and the most intense period of the Cold War began. Anticommunism became the order of the day, and President Arévalo was quick to affirm his solidarity with the United States in the Korean conflict on a trip to New York. At the same time, he reiterated Guatemala's opposition to foreign intervention in Latin America and the negative aspects of foreign investment there.[92]

Meanwhile, the United Fruit Company's difficulties and Ambassador Patterson's recall had attracted the attention of many influential congressmen. The United Fruit Company was remarkably successful in conveying its side of the story in the Congress. In 1949 and 1950 such leading representatives as Christian Herter, Mike Mansfield, and John McCormack and Senators Lister Hill, Henry Cabot Lodge, Claude Pepper, and Alexander Wiley spoke from the floor opposing discrimination against the United Fruit Company. The senators and representatives from Massachusetts were reflecting in part the interests of their constituents; the United Fruit Company was headquartered in Boston. According to Mr. McCormack, 90 percent of New England's foreign investment was in Latin America.[93] Senator Hill expressed his own appreciation of the United Fruit's use of the port of Mobile in his state of Alabama.[94]

The alleged discrimination against the United Fruit Company under the new labor code came up first in connection with President Truman's Point Four Program.

Several senators said that Point Four was based on the principle of a two-way street and suggested that countries like Guatemala which discriminate against American business should not receive such assistance. Senator Lodge reported that he was informed that the actions against the company in Guatemala "can be traced directly to Communist influences."[95] The congressional spokesmen against Guatemala came from both political parties and from conservatives and liberals.

Senator Alexander Wiley of Wisconsin, a Republican, made one of the most flamboyant speeches against the "Reds" in Guatemala. He was incensed at the affronts to the American flag at the Olympic Games, Ambassador Patterson's recall, and the attacks on American business and the American government in Guatemala. While claiming to despise jingoism and to oppose exploitation, he maintained that "we are battling for the minds of men throughout the world and the people of the world will have nothing but contempt for the American giant unless we take stern action." Senator Wiley had nothing but praise for Ambassador Patterson, an "effective, able, diplomat—the kind the Reds cannot stomach, the kind they would like to replace by U.S. milquetoasts."[96]

The *New York Times* and the *New York Herald Tribune*, although more restrained than Senator Wiley, both ran editorials supporting the State Department's rejection of the charges against Ambassador Patterson and strongly critical of the Arévalo government. Both also ran feature stories on Guatemala critical of the government and sounding the alarm about the Communist "threat."[97]

The United Fruit Company clearly had a strong case to make, given the prevailing standards of treatment expected by foreign companies in small countries and its own earlier treatment there. As a Canadian observer commented, "While the provision [for special benefits for workers of companies with more than 500 employees was] not expressly limited to foreign enterprises, it would be difficult to deny that the number of enterprises falling within the provision [was] obviously restricted and that the special treatment (which, in fact, create[d] two unequal classes among the workers) [was] a source of friction with the foreign companies."[98]

What is surprising, however, is that there was virtually no expression of the Guatemalan side of the story in the Congress or in the New York editorials. For example, Guatemalan national resentment about how the United Fruit Company allegedly had gained its hold was not mentioned, nor was the fact that the company had almost exclusive control of Guatemala's major railroads, port, and of many of the ships which carried its foreign trade. The newspapers also did not suggest, as did a World Bank mission to Guatemala a year later, that "foreign companies should refrain from any direct or indirect political activity against the government."[99] No serious effort appears to have been made to examine the Guatemalans' complaints against Ambassador Patterson or to assert the long-established right of any government to request the recall of a foreign diplomatic representative. Perhaps the most notable omission was any reference to the many social and economic reforms which had been introduced in Guatemala since Ubico's fall and the sharp contrast in the democratic practices of the Arévalo administration as compared with the dictatorial methods of many of his predecessors.

During the administration of Juan José Arévalo, Guatemala developed further in the direction of liberal democracy than many other Latin American countries. Guatemala, too, was the largest Central American neighbor of the United States both in terms of population and area. Yet there is virtually no indication that President Truman or Secretary of State Acheson had any serious idea of what was happening in Guatemala or cared. Both, for example, scarcely mention Guatemala in their memoirs. In the early months of 1951—the last of the Arévalo administration—the political rift between the two countries was almost complete. The U.S. embargo on sales of arms to Guatemala continued, Ambassador Patterson was not replaced, and Guatemala's prospects for U.S. economic assistance were even dimmer than for most Latin American countries.

President Arévalo's deep and bitter disillusionment with the United States was one of the major, thinly veiled themes of his presidential address as he left the presidency in 1951:

> I took over the presidency possessed with romantic fire, believing as always in the intrinsic nobility of man. . . . I believed that Guatemala could govern herself . . . without submission to foreigners. . . . Roosevelt's speeches told us . . . that the horror of the killing would return our liberties to nations and to men. . . . In order to achieve the dignity [of each one of our inhabitants] we had to collide with the specific social and economic structure of the country: . . . a culture, a polity, and an economy in the hands of three hundred families, inherited . . . or acquired from foreign establishments. . . . Indigenous . . . mercenaries tried every strategem and every influence of foreign circles to prevent the discussion and approval of the [Labor] Code. . . . they financed conspiracies in the shadows. . . . The Banana magnates, compatriots of Roosevelt's, rebelled against the audacity of a Central American president who placed the honorable families of the exporters on the same legal basis as their compatriots. From this alliance . . . emerged a pact of war against Arévalismo. . . . That was when the ingenuous and romantic school master discovered from the presidency of his country the extent to which brilliant international sermonizing about democracy and human liberties is perishable. . . . I came to confirm that, according to certain international norms, . . . little countries don't have a right to sovereignty. . . . The arms of the Third Reich were broken and conquered . . . but in the ideological dialogue . . . Roosevelt lost the war. The real winner was Hitler.[100]

Conclusions

The Arévalo government, favorably disposed initially toward the United States, was modeled in many ways after the Roosevelt New Deal. In this sense it represented one of the most progressive political developments in Latin America in the immediate post–World War II period. Arévalo, who was freely elected, sought to strengthen the bargaining position of organized labor and favored improving the living and working conditions of rural and urban labor—all within a democratic capitalist framework.

The Truman administration, preoccupied with problems in Europe and Asia, devoted relatively little attention to Guatemala. A government which one would have expected President Truman to have much in common with was largely ignored by senior officials. Local and foreign interests, such as the United Fruit Company, feeling threatened by Arévalo's reforms, succeeded in discrediting him in the United States. In the person of Richard Patterson, the United States sent an ambassador who conceived of himself as a protector of U.S. private interests. As a militant anti-Communist, Patterson successfully advocated U.S. opposition to the prolabor and social reformist Arévalo government. Although Patterson's interference in Guatemalan domestic politics may never have been authorized by the Department of State, the United States gradually adopted a policy of hostility toward Arévalo, the most important component of which was the refusal to sell arms to his government. United States policies contributed to the narrowing of Arévalo's political base and to the gradual polarization of domestic politics. These latter developments made Arévalo increasingly dependent on the Left and ultimately resulted in the radicalization of Guatemalan politics under Arbenz.

Origins of U.S. Hostility

The Madero, Villarroel, and Arévalo governments came into office with social and economic programs that contrasted sharply with those of predecessor governments and embodied many objectives already achieved in the United States and Western Europe. All the governments were confirmed in elections which were relatively free in the light of the nations' political traditions. None seriously challenged the capitalist framework. All were well disposed initially toward the United States.

The United States opposed the Villarroel government from the beginning. United States relations with Madero and Arévalo were good initially but deteriorated rapidly. At the end, all three reformist presidents were viewed with hostility by important sectors of the U.S. establishment, public and private. United States officials were intimately involved in the fall of Madero and Villarroel. In Guatemala, the American ambassador was sent home on charges of fomenting a coup d'etat. Why was the United States unable to come to terms with governments which came closer to approximating expressed American ideals than most Latin American governments in the past?

The process of transition from dictatorship to politically more competitive systems, a process in which these governments were engaged, was at best painful and disorderly; in the more open societies previously pent-up political and economic forces were liberated. The result was confusion, conflict, and violence. The new

Henry Lane Wilson, U.S. ambassador to Mexico, 1910–1913. (Library of Congress)

Francisco I. Madero, president of Mexico, 1911–1913 (seated, third from left), with other leaders of Mexican revolutionary movement. (U.S. Signal Corps, photo in The National Archives)

United States Ambassador Joseph Flack (left) presents his credentials to Gualberto Villarroel, president of Bolivia, 1943–1946, in the presence of the Bolivian minister of foreign relations. (Wide World Photos)

Spruille Braden, assistant secretary of state for American republic affairs, 1945–1947. (Department of State)

Juan José Arévalo, president of Guatemala, 1945–1951. (Organization of American States) Richard C. Patterson, Jr., U.S. ambassador to Guatemala, 1948–1951. (Department of State)

reformist governments came into direct conflict with vested interests, both domestic and foreign. New economic and social policies adversely affected established business and financial arrangements, and complaints by local businessmen were often sympathetically heard by their American trading or investing partners. Many Americans who had necessarily dealt with the old leadership before were forced to come to terms with new organizations and new men. The brunt of discontent arising from adjustments in the break with the past were borne by the new governments.

These governments set out on a path of reform not only in domestic affairs but foreign relations as well. National pride and nationalistic ambitions made them less willing than their predecessors to compromise what they felt were vital national interests for the sake of attracting foreign capital or U.S. diplomatic support. Madero attributed less importance to foreign concessions than Díaz and enforced laws requiring employees of the foreign-owned railways to know some Spanish. Villarroel's efforts to control foreign exchange generated through tin sales and to strengthen labor's hand against management became an issue in tin negotiations with the United States. Arévalo took the side of organized labor against the United Fruit Company and refused concessions to U.S. oil companies.

On the basis of unsubstantiated charges, the opposition to the Bolivian and Guatemalan reformist governments succeeded in pinning them with totalitarian labels. The Bolivian revolutionaries (MNR) were charged with Nazi-fascism, charges which were based partly on evidence fabricated by British intelligence. The charges about Nazi control were never proved and the policies of the MNR in power did not follow the Nazi pattern either. Arévalo's critics charged him with communism, but convincing evidence of Soviet connections was never made public. The fact that Communists played a role in the Arbenz government cannot properly be used against Arévalo.

In fact, the Madero, Villarroel, and Arévalo governments did not represent political extremes of the Right or Left, but were, broadly speaking, centrist. Many of their domestic programs were deliberately or coincidentally modeled on U.S. practices. None was anti-American initially, especially in comparison with certain other local political parties. Nevertheless, U.S. embassy officials became aggressively hostile toward them.

The role of U.S. ambassadors was crucial in explaining the tensions that developed with the three governments. Ambassadors Henry Lane Wilson and Richard C. Patterson were political appointees with prior ambassadorial experience. With ties to influential figures in the Republican or Democratic parties, they dealt with the Department of State with more independence than most professional diplomats. Each had a flamboyant style of his own and pressed his views forcefully upon Washington.

Wilson and Patterson had complicated and tense relationships with the presidents of the governments to which they were assigned, exhibiting personal hostility toward them on numerous occasions. In addition, they had close personal and professional ties to vested private American interests critical of the incumbent government and were proud and demonstrative about their efforts to protect these interests.

Wilson, and possibly Patterson, looked on the president as a kind of rival. They resented his not consulting them more and expected him to be responsive to their recommendations about government policies. Acutely conscious of their role as representatives of the dominant Great Power in the area, both used pressure tactics in their relations with the government. Their views and tactics inevitably led them into deep involvement in domestic affairs. Wilson asked that U.S. troops be sent to Mexico and that he exercise command over them. Threatening armed intervention, he tried to force Madero's resignation through third parties. When these efforts failed, he plotted Madero's overthrow with the latter's chief of staff. Patterson maintained contact with Guatemalan military officers and was accused of plotting Arévalo's overthrow. Even Joseph Flack, a career man, tried to stay the hand of the Bolivian government against its armed opposition and rejoiced when that government fell.

The extent and character of conflict within the U.S. government over U.S. responses to the three governments is difficult to determine conclusively.

In the Mexican case of 1911–1913, the president and secretary shared many of Ambassador Wilson's reservations about Madero but were strongly opposed to Wilson's interference in domestic politics and his threats of U.S. armed intervention. Wilson's tactics were a reflection of his personal ambitions and his personal associations with private U.S. interests who felt threatened by Madero. The Taft administration responded to Wilson's request by sending naval forces into offshore areas, but refused to place them under the ambassador's command. The U.S. military does not appear to have played an active role in policy decisions. The Department of State was unable to control an eccentric and irrational envoy in the rapidly developing political crisis.[101]

Hostility to Villarroel was widely shared within the U.S. establishment. United States private interests and former President Peñaranda, who had paid a visit to President Roosevelt, probably convinced both the president and Secretary Hull that the MNR was tainted with nazism. Factual information and wiser counsels on this complex subject appear never to have reached their ears, a not surprising result of the tumultuous climax of World War II. And the Nazi label stuck well into 1946 when Perón's government, with which the MNR maintained relations, became a major international issue. The U.S. military had assisted in the implementation of what was viewed as a U.S.-sponsored anti-Nazi program in Bolivia, namely in the evacuation of German and Japanese nationals from that country. (United States military officers do not appear, however, to have established close relations with leading military figures in Villarroel's cabinet.) The Bolivian situation also provided an opportunity for the Federal Bureau of Investigation (FBI), in charge of U.S. intelligence operations in the Americas, to flex its muscles against Nazi Germany.

The appointment of Spruille Braden in 1945 to take charge of U.S.–Latin American affairs placed a man with a long record of hostility to the MNR and close associations with Bolivian tin interests in a decisive position to influence U.S. policy.

The strong pressures he exerted on the Villarroel government in the tin negotiations of mid-1946 helped set the stage for the coup.

It is not surprising, therefore, that the new U.S. ambassador, Joseph Flack, who arrived in Bolivia on the eve of the coup with a hostile orientation toward the MNR, was pleased by its overthrow. There were U.S. officials in La Paz and Washington during and after the war who attempted to correct the record with respect to the MNR's relations with Nazi Germany and its social policies. Such efforts, however, had little chance of success in the face of the hostility toward Villarroel shared by the White House, Assistant Secretary Braden, influential Bolivian tin interests, and Ambassador Flack.

There was probably much agreement in Washington with the embassy's coolness toward Arévalo. An interesting but little remarked aspect of U.S.–Guatemalan relations was the failure of the U.S. labor leaders to build a strong anti-Communist labor movement in Guatemala as they had succeeded in doing in so many other Latin American countries. It seems probable that this failure may have solidified the opposition to Arévalo within the U.S. intelligence community, and heightened official U.S. perceptions of Guatemala as a danger area. No doubt fears of this sort also were partly responsible for the U.S. military's coolness toward Arévalo. The most important symbol of tensions in military matters was the absence of a Mutual Defense Agreement and the arms embargo the United States tried to enforce against the Arévalo government.

A major question that remains unanswered is whether there was any significant opinion in the Department of State and other civilian agencies favoring closer ties with and greater understanding for Arévalo's programs. As Cold War tensions deepened in the late 1940s, it would have been difficult to sponsor such views and oppose the anti-Arévalo orientation of the Truman administration, supported as it was by the influential Ambassador Patterson, the United Fruit Company, other private U.S. interests, and many U.S. congressmen and senators. The virtual absence of any reference to Guatemala in the memoirs of President Truman and Secretary Acheson suggests not only that proponents, if any, of alternative policies toward Arévalo had little impact, but also that Guatemala had a low priority in Washington in those days.

Another interesting question is the extent to which private interests, as distinct from public officials and entities, influenced outcomes. As indicated throughout the chapter, private interests were involved in a different fashion in all three cases. In Mexico many such interests opposed Madero's reforms and helped foment opposition to his government. Men who represented some of these interests were close personal friends of Ambassador Wilson. In addition to having disagreements with Madero, Ambassador Wilson tended by conviction to share many of his friends' views about the necessity of protecting U.S. private interests.

Like Wilson, Ambassador Patterson came to Guatemala considering protection of U.S. private interests one of his major missions. It is likely that he would have been critical of many of Arévalo's policies irrespective of whether U.S. managers sought to influence him. What seems likely in Guatemala more than elsewhere, although difficult to prove, is that U.S. companies used their political and economic influence to bolster opposition to the Arévalo government inside Guatemala.

In Bolivia the most powerful companies, the tin interests, were not U.S.-owned. As in Guatemala and Mexico, these interests not only worked actively against the government but also had better access to and more sympathetic hearings from U.S. embassy officials and Washington than the new government. This was partly a result of long-established contacts from former times when they and their political collaborators had dominated the local governments and their access was a natural reflection of the then existing political and social order.

In the three countries, U.S. and Latin American private interests probably did not control U.S. officials in a strict sense, but both tended to think alike. Private interests may have achieved their greatest impact by encouraging influential U.S. officials to hold negative perceptions of the reformist governments. Bolivian private interests appear to have been especially successful with respect to U.S. cabinet officers and embassy officials. In the Guatemalan case, U.S. private interests influenced Capitol Hill as well.

The Madero and Villarroel governments were forcefully overthrown. Madero was succeeded by a military dictator, Victoriano Huerta, who became an anathema to the Woodrow Wilson administration and was eventually forced to resign under the guns of a U.S. occupying force. The Villarroel government was overthrown by an unlikely coalition of traditional political parties and the Bolivian Stalinists, ironically, on the very eve of the Cold War. Only Arévalo managed to serve out his constitutional term of office. Jacobo Arbenz who followed him adopted a whole series of policies which the United States viewed with more alarm than those of Arévalo.

The ultimate consequences of U.S. opposition to these three reformist presidents were governments which took an even more independent line and created more serious problems for the United States than the reformist presidents had themselves.

Revolutionary Change

Seizures of U.S. Properties: Compensation Required

The end of the reformist governments concluded the second stage of the revolutionary process. Their fate disillusioned and radicalized all the revolutionary movements. Immediately, or as soon thereafter as they could regain power, the surviving revolutionary leaders embarked on far-reaching programs involving revolutionary change (see table 5).

The revolutionary movements sought to break the control of old elites over important sectors of the economy, control which had served as the basis for that old elites' political dominance. In all cases, changes in ownership patterns were an important element in the revolutionaries' strategy of gaining or strengthening control over the nation.

Revolutionary Change

Land reform was the most far-reaching change in each country partly because agriculture was the major occupation except in Cuba. Division of large landholdings into small plots was the dominant form of redistribution in Mexico, Bolivia, and Guatemala. Cooperatives, called ejidos, were also established on a large scale in Mexico. State farms ultimately became the main mode of land tenure in Cuba, although nearly a third of the land was left in individual, small holdings subject to state controls.

Revolutionary changes were also made in the industrial sector. Extractive industries, such as oil in Mexico, tin in Bolivia, and nickel in Cuba, were nationalized. Public utilities were also expropriated in several countries. Until Allende took over in Chile, however, Cuba was the only Latin American country which had nationalized manufacturing concerns on a large scale.

Revolutionary changes also occurred in national politics. The organization of industrial workers was intensified, and national labor federations became a major source of support for the new governments. The organization of peasants and other agricultural workers began or was accelerated and rural influences in politics grew. Indigenous culture was recognized and promoted in countries with large Indian populations.

TABLE 5
REVOLUTIONARY GOVERNMENTS: SOCIAL CHANGE

	Mexico (1915–1940)	Bolivia (1952–1964)	Guatemala (1952–1954)	Cuba (1959–1972)
Land	Haciendas disbanded; lands redistributed, 25.6 million hectares to 1.6 million owners (1940):[1] 25% ejidos, 75% private (1960)[2]	Haciendas disbanded; lands redistributed to 145,000 owners (1964)[6]	Restrictions on hacienda size; distribution of 1 million hectares to 100,000 owners (June, 1954)[8]	Large holdings, commercial farms, sugar lands, and mills nationalized; 70% state farm, 30% small private plots (1970)[11]
Extractive industries	Nationalized major foreign oil companies (1938)	Encouraged oil exploration and production by public corporation and foreign companies; nationalized 3 largest tin companies (1952)	Refused to grant foreign oil concessions	Nationalized oil refineries and nickel mines (1960)
Electric power	Federal Electricity Commission to regulate and gradually take over private plants (1939)[3]	—	Temporary intervention of U.S.-owned plant; construction of public plants[9]	Nationalized (1960)
Railways	Expropriation of privately owned shares in national railways, public management (1940)[4]	—	Main rail line (IRCA) seized (returned late 1954)[10]	Nationalized (1960)
Labor unions	Mass mobilization, linked to party and government bureaucracy	Mobilization, especially in mines, later challenged revolutionary government	Incipient mass mobilization of industrial and rural workers	Mass mobilization, subordination to Castro
Suffrage	Tripled between 1917 and 1940[5]	Expanded ten times (1952-1964)[7]	—	No national elections

Political parties	One party dominance, symbolic opposition parties	Uneasy one-party dominance challenged by splinter and other opposition parties	Revolutionary coalition, opposition parties permitted	Totalitarian mass party
Military	Subordinated to civilian control by 1940	Extensive reform, resurgence and palace coup	Initial support; later, palace coup	Old army disbanded, revolutionary army subordinated to Castro

Table prepared by Herbert Braun and Judith Ludvik.

1. Departamento Agrario, *Memoria*, 1945–1946, Part II (Statistics) (Mexico, 1947), as cited in James Wilkie, *The Mexican Revolution* (Berkeley and Los Angeles, 1967), pp. 188, 194.

2. Of entire national territory, in Frank Brandenburg, *The Making of Modern Mexico* (Englewood Cliffs, N.J., 1964), p. 253. In 1940, about 49% of the *cultivated* lands were in ejidos, a percentage that had dropped to 47% by 1960; Clark Reynolds, *The Mexican Economy* (New Haven, 1970), p. 139.

3. Brandenburg, *Modern Mexico*, p. 279. The American and Belgian monopoly ended and thereafter only Mexican companies could obtain new concessions.

4. Ibid., p. 294.

5. Pablo Gonzalez Casanova, *Democracy in Mexico* (Oxford, 1970), pp. 198–99.

6. Víctor Paz Estenssoro, *Mensaje del presidente de la república, Dr. Víctor Paz Estenssoro* (La Paz, 1964).

7. Dirección Nacional de Información, Bolivia, *10 Años de Revolución* (La Paz, 1962), p. 243.

8. From either expropriated or state-owned land, in Guillermo Toriello, *La batalla de Guatemala* (Santiago, Chile, 1955), pp. 30–42.

9. Part of five-year electrification plan, ibid., p. 145.

10. IRCA was intervened temporarily due to labor strife, ibid., p. 144. Counterrevolutionary regime returned control to foreign owners.

11. Carmelo Mesa-Lago, "Economic Policies and Growth," in *Revolutionary Change in Cuba*, ed. Mesa-Lago (Pittsburgh, 1971), pp. 282–83. No private plots were "created" by revolutionary reform. Private holdings remaining have an average size of 13.8 hectares, and they are integrated into their national association (ANAP) under the supervision of INRA (Instituto Nacional de Reforma Agraria). Although these participate in cooperative arrangements, they are cultivated individually, not collectively.

One large mass political party came to dominate government and politics in each of the four countries, but the extent of their political power varied. Powerful opposition parties continued in Guatemala under Arbenz, had slightly less influence in Bolivia in 1952–1964, and have long served mainly as symbolic representation in Mexico. In Cuba, opposition parties were eliminated and a newly organized Communist party was given the monopoly of political power.

The political composition of the armed forces was radically affected in Mexico, Bolivia, and Cuba. The Guatemalan armed forces, however, remained influential under both Arévalo and Arbenz with continuing rivalry between the leaders of factions from the Left and Right, the latter ultimately overthrowing Arbenz. In Mexico the revolutionary leaders took over control of the armed forces, which were gradually professionalized and dominated by the political leadership. The Bolivian armed forces were also radically reorganized after the 1952 insurrection. But after being bolstered in the late 1950s to offset opposition within the revolutionary movement, they overthrew Paz Estenssoro in 1964. Taking into account the Guatemalan military's overthrow of Arbenz, Castro destroyed the pre-1959 Cuban armed forces and organized a new army completely subordinate to him personally.

All the revolutionary governments took a more independent line in their relations with foreign governments. They characterized themselves as antiimperialist, which tended to mean anti-American in Mexico, Guatemala, and Cuba. The revolutionaries' opposition was not so much against U.S. domestic or other foreign policies as against U.S. actions, public and private, which they considered damaging to their own domestic interests. All opposed what they considered excessive foreign influence in their domestic affairs.

The Seizures

Seizures of properties of U.S. companies and citizens often caused the greatest initial repercussions in U.S. official relations with revolutionary governments in Latin America. For this reason, and because of the continuing importance of property issues, this chapter is devoted exclusively to the seizures and the U.S. response to them. This permits fuller treatment of some of the important legal and economic issues involved. Later chapters deal with U.S. response, not only to seizures but to other aspects of revolutionary change in their broader political dimensions.

The seizure of property, including that of foreigners, often signals the beginning of revolutionary change. In fact, most seizures of foreign-owned property in Latin America until 1961 have occurred in the countries experiencing revolutionary change, Mexico, Bolivia, Guatemala, and Cuba.[1] Similar seizures of land and mineral properties were made in Peru beginning in 1969 and in Chile in 1971. Cases of negotiated purchase of industrial properties, such as government buying of industry in Mexico and Frei's "Chileanization" of copper, do not qualify as seizures since the arrangements were made with the consent of the former owners.

Almost all the seizures touched U.S. private rather than public property. Except for the U.S. nickel properties in Cuba, the U.S. government had almost no direct investments in the economies of the countries concerned. This chapter does not deal with damages to U.S. private interests from revolutionary violence—most of which were sustained in Mexico during the civil disturbances between 1910 and 1920 and in Cuba in the late 1950s. The Mexicans eventually provided compensation for some of these damages; the Cubans have not compensated U.S. citizens.

The revolutionary governments directed their expropriations primarily against local interests which they claimed stood in the way of social progress. But foreign-owned properties, including those of U.S. citizens, were also seized. This attack on property relationships was not an attack simply on the old elite itself but also on the old system—an important sector of which was the land, mines, and other properties owned by foreign companies and often managed by foreigners. In addition, there were many local nationals, such as exporters, importers, and bankers, who were economically dependent on foreign interests.

The following description of U.S. properties seized is organized by economic sector and based largely on table 6. (Sources are indicated in the notes to the table rather than in the notes to the text.) The next section, "U.S. Responses," is organized by country rather than by economic sector.

Land
U.S. citizens owned virtually no agricultural properties in Bolivia so that the far-reaching agrarian reform begun there in 1953 affected U.S. interests scarcely at all. Of the extensive rural properties seized in Mexico, Guatemala, and Cuba, much of the land was owned by local citizens, who bore the brunt of the agrarian reform. Nevertheless, substantial U.S. interests were also involved—amounting to more than 5 million acres in Mexico, about 400,000 acres of United Fruit property in Guatemala, and in excess of 3 million acres in Cuba. The valuation of these properties depends on which source one consults. U.S.-owned agrarian properties in Mexico were appraised by U.S. government specialists in excess of $23 million. The fair value of the United Fruit Company properties seized in Guatemala probably lies somewhere between the company claim of $15 million and the Guatemalan government evaluation of about $1.2 million. The value of U.S.-owned lands seized in Cuba may exceed several hundred million dollars. In all cases the government made provisions for but did not necessarily actually issue long-term interest-paying bonds as a form of deferred compensation.

Oil and Tin
Whereas seizures of land were directed mainly against local owners, the seizures of oil fields in Bolivia and Mexico were directed mainly against foreign owners. In both countries the oil industry was dominated by foreign interests.

One of the thorniest conflicts of principle in the various Latin American oil controversies, and especially the Mexican, involved rights to the subsoil. The seizures in Bolivia in 1937 and in Mexico in 1938, however, were not precipitated by

TABLE 6
SEIZURES OF U.S.-OWNED PROPERTIES (U.S. Dollars)

	U.S. Properties	Claim	Appraisal (US = Official U.S. HG = Host Government)	Settlement
Mexico				
Land (1)	1917–1927	—	Less than $11 million (US)[1]	Claims (1917–1941) were largely compensated in the $40 million global settlement (1941)[7]
Land (2)	1927–1941: vast and moderate holdings[2]	350 claims for $75 million[3]	260 claims on 4,780,000 acres, $24,902,138 (US)[4]	Included in $40 million global settlement (1941)[5]
Railroads	1937: minority stock in National railways[6]	—	—	
Oil	1938: 5 companies[8]	$262 million[9]	$25 million (US)[10]	$23,995,991 (1942)[11]
Bolivia				
Oil	1937: lands and idle installations[12]	$3 million[13]	$1 million (HG)[14]	$1.5 million (1942)[15]
Tin	1952: 20–25% of Patiño mines[16]	—	20–25% of $7.5 million (HG)[17]	20–25% of $9,683,826 (1960)[18]
Oil/gas	1969: oil fields, installations, gas pipeline project[19]	$118 million[20]	—	$78,662,171 (1970)[21]
Guatemala				
Land (1)	1953: 233,973 acres of United Fruit[22]	$15,854,849[23]	$627,572.82 in bonds (HG)[24]	Returned (1954)[25]
Land (2)	1954: 172,532 acres of United Fruit[26]	—	$557,542.88 in bonds (HG)[27]	Returned (1954)[28]
Railroads	1953: largest national railroad (IRCA)[29]	—	—	Returned (1954)[30]
Cuba	1959-1960: cattle lands, sugar lands and mills, 2 oil refineries, 3 banks, manufacturing and public utilities, and hotels[31]	8,806 claims totalling $3,346 million[32]	$800 million (HG, 1960)[33] $956 million (US, 1959)[34] $1,760 million (US, 1971)[35]	None by 1974

Table prepared with assistance of Herbert Braun and Judith Ludvik.

NOTE. I had hoped to rely on authoritative secondary sources to determine the value and compensation, where paid, of U.S.-owned properties seized in the cases of revolutionary change discussed here. No single source of which I am aware provides this information; even data on seizures in individual categories are hard to find. In spite of the fact that this table is the product of many weeks of work on my part and that of my research assistants, it represents only the best estimates we can make and is subject to correction. Extensive research by lawyers or accountants might be necessary to unravel this complex subject. In the meantime the sources we have found in an extensive library and archival search are shown here to assist in future research.

1. I have been unable to separate the agrarian claims (1917–1927) from the other categories lumped together as general claims (1868–1927), such as business losses, taxes, and contract claims. The agrarian claims (1917–1927) were part of the $11,968,496.54 (excluding interest) of appraisals of Oscar W. Underwood, Jr. See his letter to Secretary of State Cordell Hull of October 29, 1937: DS 411.12/2447 and attached table.

2. Expropriations between August 31, 1927, and July 31, 1939, U.S., Department of State, *Foreign Relations of the United States: Diplomatic Papers, The American Republics* (Washington, D.C., 1940), vol. 5, pp. 967–68. For the estimate of claims for 1939–1941 see note 5.

3. Ibid., p. 967. Claims subsequent to August 30, 1927, and up to July 31, 1939.

4. The figure of $22,902,138 includes damages but excludes interest. American Mexican Claims Commission, *Report to the Secretary of State* (Washington, D.C., 1948), pp. 47–48. An estimated $2 million to cover seizures from 1939 to 1941 was added to the claim (see note 5).

5. Agreement of November 19, 1941. U.S., *Department of State Bulletin*, November 22, 1941, p. 400. See also the memorandum of Herbert S. Bursley to Mr. Welles of October 7, 1940, together with its attachments: DS 412.11 (41) Agreement/17. The agrarian claims (1917–1927) appraised by Mr. Underwood came to something less than $11 million, and agrarian claims (1927–1939) appraised by Mr. Lawson came to $22,902,138, both excluding interest. In addition, the U.S. claims against Mexico included an estimated $2 million in agrarian claims after the Lawson appraisals, about $5 million in other claims, and about $14 million in interest. The Department of State favored a $45 million settlement but ultimately accepted $40 million. The result was that the United States received in compensation roughly the equivalent of the U.S. commissioners' appraisals, but *without* interest.

6. On June 23, 1937, the foreign stock of the national railroads was expropriated. *New York Times*, June 23, 1937, p. 15.

7. American-Mexican Claims Commission, *Report*, pp. 47–48.

8. Seizures, March 18, 1938. U.S., Congress, House, Committee on Foreign Affairs, *Expropriations of American-Owned Property of Foreign Governments in the Twentieth Century*, July 19, 1963, p. 12. Prepared by the Legislative Reference Service, Library of Congress for the Committee on Foreign Affairs.

9. Includes oil underground. Standard Oil Company of New Jersey, *Present Status of the Mexican Oil "Expropriations"* (New York, 1940), p. 41. Bryce Wood, *The Making of the Good Neighbor Policy* (New York, 1961), notes that the companies valued their landholdings close to $200 million and their investments in equipment and drilling at about $60 million, p. 203. See also Harlow S. Person, *Mexican Oil* (New York, 1942), p. 72, who states that the companies generally stated the value of their properties to be at something over $200 million.

Notes to Table 6 (continued)

10. Duggan memorandum to Hull and Welles, June 12, 1941: DS 812.6363/7317–5/11, as cited in Wood, *Good Neighbor Policy*, p. 252. An estimate had been made by the Department of the Interior (in Memorandum, June 10, 1941: DS 812.6363/7308–1/2 as cited by Wood, ibid.). Their appraisal came to $13,538,052. E. David Cronon, *Josephus Daniels in Mexico* (Madison, 1960), p. 261. As a reason for not accepting the Interior officials' figures, Duggan stated that they were based upon data provided by the Mexican government with no consultation with the oil companies. An earlier Department of Commerce appraisal based upon statistics furnished by the companies set the value at $69 million. Paul D. Dickens, *American Direct Investment in Foreign Countries 1936*, U.S., Department of Commerce, Bureau of Foreign and Domestic Commerce, Economic Series, no. 1 (Washington, D.C., 1938), p. 36.

11. Both governments agreed upon this sum, one-third to be paid on July 1, 1942, and the balance in five equal annual installments payable on July 1 of each subsequent year with interest of 3%/year dating from March 18, 1938. U.S., *Department of State Bulletin*, April 18, 1942, pp. 351–52. The breakdown was as follows: Standard Oil of New Jersey, $18,391,641; Standard Oil of California, $3,589,158; Consolidated Oil Co., $630,151; Sabalo, $897,671; Seaboard, $487,370.

12. Seizure March 13, 1937. *FR*, 1937, 5: 277–85.

13. In a telegram to Welles, January 21, 1942, as quoted in Wood, *Good Neighbor Policy*, p. 197.

14. Without interest, as suggested by Bolivian foreign minister, *FR*, 1942, 5:587.

15. Agreement signed January 27, 1942, payment made, plus interest at rate of 3%/year from March 13, 1937. *FR*, 1942, 5:587.

16. The United States controlled 20–25 percent of Patiño, one of the three large tin companies. Source is President Paz, *U.S. News and World Report*, June 5, 1953, pp. 69–70.

17. George Jackson Eder, *Inflation and Development in Latin America* (Ann Arbor, 1968), p. 51.

18. Settlement reached July 31, 1960, Dirección Nacional de Informaciones, *Bolivia, diez, años de revolución, 1962*, p. 36. By December 1962, Patiño had received $9,683,826 (Eder, *Inflation and Development*, p. 549).

19. Seizure of Gulf Oil properties, October 17, 1969, *New York Times*, October 18, 1969, p. 1.

20. *New York Times*, September 9, 1970, p. 65.

21. The Bolivian government announced it would pay $78,662,171 for expropriated property over a twenty-year period. On September 11, 1970, this was the agreement reached. *New York Times*, September 12, 1970, p. 35:4.

22. Land seizures, March 5, 1953, U.S., Congress, House, *Expropriations of American-Owned Property*, p. 19. Lands located on the Pacific coast near Tiquisate, U.S., *Department of State Bulletin*, May 3, 1954, pp. 678–79.

23. Ibid., p. 678.

24. Guillermo Toriello, *La batalla de Guatemala* (Santiago, Chile, 1955), p. 40.

25. Returned December 1954; United Fruit gave 100,000 acres of Pacific coast land to Guatemalan government and withdrew $15,845,849 claim. *Hispanic American Report*, December 1954, p. 13. 10,000 acres of the 100,000 were good banana lands according to Stacy May and Galo Plaza, *The United Fruit Company in Latin America* (New York, 1958), p. 164.

26. Expropriation February 24, 1954, lands located near Bananera on Atlantic coast, U.S., *Department of State Bulletin*, May 3, 1954, p. 679.

27. Toriello, *La batalla*, p. 40.

28. Returned December 1954. *Hispanic American Report*, December 1954, p. 13.

29. In October 1953 the government named a Board of Temporary "Intervention" over International Railroad of Central America (IRCA) which had been controlled by United Fruit. The intervention occurred after workers went on strike to protest the company's refusal to grant higher wages. *Hispanic American Report*, October 1953, p. 13.

30. Castillo Armas' government terminated intervention in October 1954. *Hispanic American Report*, p. 132.

31. Under the first Agrarian Reform Law of May 17, 1959, expropriations of American properties such as cattle and sugar lands and sugar mills began. Further expropriations were authorized in Law 851 of July 6, 1960, and Law 890 of October 14, 1960. For a complete listing of hundreds of U.S. companies included see U.S., Congress, House, Hearings, Subcommittee on Inter-American Affairs, Committee of Foreign Affairs, *Claims of U.S. Nationals Against Cuba*, July 28–29 and August 4, 1964, pp. 40–44. On March 3, 1959, the Cuban government assumed management of the Cuban Telephone Company (*Revolución*, March 4, 1959). On August 21, 1959, the government intervened to cut the rates of Cuban Electric Light (*New York Times*, August 21, 1959, p. 12). Both of these utilities were nationalized on August 5, 1960. Philip Bonsal, *Cuba, Castro, and the United States* (Pittsburgh, 1971), p. 160. The oil refineries of Texaco and Esso were intervened on June 29 and July 2, 1960, respectively (*Revolución*, June 30 and July 2, 1960), and also later nationalized on August 5, 1960. The banks, First National City Bank of New York, First National Bank of Boston, and Chase Manhattan, were expropriated September 17, 1960 (*Revolución*, September 18, 1960); four hotels were nationalized on June 10 (*Revolución*, June 11, 1960). The Moa Bay Mining Company (Freeport Sulphur Company) was expropriated March 10, 1960 (*Revolución*, March 11, 1960), and on October 25, all remaining U.S. companies were expropriated (*Revolución*, October 26, 1960).

32. As of December 31, 1971; Foreign Claims Settlement Commission of the United States, *Annual Report to the Congress for the Period January 1–December 31, 1971* (Washington, D.C., 1972), p. 24.

33. *Revolución*, June 25, 1960, p. 2.

34. U.S., Department of Commerce, *U.S. Balance of Payments, Statistical Supplement*, rev. ed. (Washington, D.C., 1963). p. 207. The breakdown was as follows: petroleum, $147 million; manufacturing, $111 million; public utilities, $313 million; trade, $44 million; other industries, (mainly agricultural), $341 million.

35. As of December 31, 1971, the commission had made 5,887 awards totaling $1,760,124,172.08. By this same date, 1,192 claims had been denied. I am unable to account for the discrepancy in the total awards of the commission as of 1971 ($1,760 million) and the U.S. Department of Commerce appraisal of 1959 ($956 million). The value of small properties may not have been fully reflected in the 1959 estimate, Foreign Claims Settlement Commission, *Annual Report to the Congress*, pp. 24–25.

this issue or the application of eminent domain. In Bolivia the Standard Oil properties were seized under charges of fraud and in Mexico because the foreign oil companies had refused to implement a court order in a labor dispute. Both seizures brought nationalistic political pressures and sentiments to a high pitch.

The oil fields that were seized in Bolivia in 1937 were producing little oil and were of limited value. Standard Oil claimed to have invested about $17 million there. The U.S.-owned oil fields in Mexico were of far greater value and productivity. United States companies estimated their investments in Mexico at $62 million and the value of land (including oil in the ground) at $200 million.

The relationship between revolutionary governments and oil companies was also politically significant in Guatemala and Cuba, but for other reasons. The Guatemalan government of Arévalo angered U.S. companies and the U.S. ambassador by refusing to grant oil concessions to foreign companies, a decision sustained by Arbenz. The U.S. oil companies' investments in Cuba were in refining and distribution facilities and were valued together at about $147 million. After having been advanced large credits by the foreign oil companies engaged in local refining, the Castro government insisted that the Texaco and Esso companies refine crude oil from Soviet rather than their own sources. The refusals of these companies, plus that of the Anglo-Dutch Shell Company, were followed by Castro's seizure of their refineries.

The nationalization of the three large tin mining groups in Bolivia in 1952 had relatively little effect on U.S. interests. U.S. citizens owned perhaps only 20 to 25 percent of the Patiño group.

Public Utilities

Foreign ownership of public utilities has long been a politically sensitive issue in many Latin American countries. The governments of Mexico and Bolivia were both participating extensively in the ownership and control of railroads before their respective revolutions. President Cárdenas nationalized the shares of stock of the national railways remaining in private hands, and the Bolivian revolutionary government attempted to expand its control of foreign-owned lines.

Foreign control over public services was especially controversial in Guatemala. The Arbenz government took over for extended periods the management of the major rail network, the International Railways of Central America (IRCA), and the electric power company, both of which were controlled by U.S. interests before and after Arbenz.

United States owners also controlled many of Cuba's public utilities, including telephones and power. Castro intervened in the management of the telephone company early in 1959 and later lowered the rates for electric power. These were among the first U.S. industries to be nationalized in the major wave of nationalizations in mid-1960.

Except for Cuba (and more recently Chile), there have been relatively few expropriations of manufacturing industries in revolutionary situations in Latin America. Castro took over all U.S. companies which together were worth about $1 billion. Public utilities there were worth about $313 million and manufacturing firms about $111 million.

U.S. Responses

The Department of State has consistently maintained that payment of compensation is required under international law in cases involving the seizure of the property of U.S. citizens located in countries experiencing social revolution. Various terms have been used to describe the type of compensation required. What was originally phrased as "just" compensation has been more recently interpreted to mean "prompt, adequate, and effective" compensation. In actual practice the United States has been prepared to accept settlement not meeting this standard ex gratia (out of grace) while insisting on the obligation of full compliance under international law.

The Department of State developed arguments to support this position partly with respect to seizures arising out of the Mexican and Russian revolutions. In the former, Secretary of State Cordell Hull wrote to the Mexican ambassador on July 21, 1938:

> We cannot admit that a foreign government may take the property of American nationals in disregard of the rule of compensation under international law. Nor can we admit that any government unilaterally and through its municipal legislation can, as in this instant case, nullify this universally accepted principle of international law, based as it is on reason, equity, and justice.[2]

The Department of State had tended to make elaborate assertions of the rule of law as defined above, buttressed by references to more or less contemporary cases, but with citations of few precedents prior to the Mexican Revolution.[3] The logic of the U.S. argument was that membership in a community involved rights and obligations, including minimum standards of international conduct which are essential to the conduct of relations between states. Ordinarily these authorities share a concept of private property as a natural right. Such a concept is reflected in the law of many states and is further confirmed by treaty.

Certain Latin American countries, and particularly Mexico, have taken a contrary position, namely that as long as the seizures are undertaken for public purposes and are not discriminatory against foreigners, the United States may not rightfully insist upon a so-called international standard which places aliens in a more favorable position than nationals. Moreover, the argument runs, domestic laws may require compensation but that fact in itself does not establish an international obligation. Why, the Mexicans have reasoned, should a government be forced to treat aliens better than its own citizens? Here is the argument:

> The demand for unequal treatment is implicitly included in your
> Government's note for . . . it does require the payment to its nationals, inde-

pendently of what Mexico may decide to do with regard to her citizens, . . . our Government finds itself unable immediately to pay the indemnity to all affected by the agrarian reform. . . . by insisting on payment to American landholders, [the U.S. government] demands, in reality, a special privileged treatment which no one is receiving in Mexico.[4]

The Castro government has also rejected the U.S. official interpretation of the international legal norms governing expropriation on the grounds that "it is absolutely inadmissible, in view of the coexistence of two economic systems, to enunciate the principle of the sanctity of private property as a norm of international law." A Cuban authority has cited cases and legal precedents to show that "there exists in international law no principle universally accepted . . . which makes adequate compensation obligatory for expropriations of a general and impersonal character." In practice, however, the Castro government has paid compensation to certain governments, if not the United States, as the 1967 agreements with Switzerland and France show.[5]

In the Mexican and Bolivian cases where settlements with U.S. interests have been reached, the intergovernmental conflict about the properties themselves has been resolved but the legal issues associated therewith have not. Conflicts over expropriated property have probably been more important as political than legal questions. The relative power positions of the parties, relations with third states, trade and aid, military assistance, and strategic questions have often determined outcomes, rather than legal norms per se.

Mexico

Seizures are one of the main threads running through the U.S. response to the Mexican Revolution from 1910 to 1940 and are probably relatively more important in understanding U.S. relations with Mexico than with other revolutionary governments. The immediate legal and business aspects of that response will be discussed here. Other and broader aspects, including such questions as damage for revolutionary violence, diplomatic recognition, fiscal issues, arms embargoes, and Great Power rivalry will be treated in their politico-economic context in the next chapter.

The major disputes between the United States and Mexico during the first twenty-four years of the revolution, that is until 1934, were not primarily over actual seizures of U.S. properties in Mexico, although there were some, but over Mexican laws regarding expropriation. The fact that the two governments squabbled initially more over what Mexico might do, rather than what she actually had done, did not deprive the controversies of far-reaching political significance.

The thorniest issues were raised by the famous Article 27 of the Mexican Constitution of 1917, to whose possible "grave consequences" the Department of State ordered a formal protest even prior to the constitution's official promulgation.[6] Provisions in the article providing for the extensive redistribution of lands and for governmental control over oil reserves were especially significant:

Land: The ownership of lands and waters . . . is vested originally in the Nation, which has had, and has, the right to transmit title thereto to private persons, thereby constituting private property. Private property shall not be expropriated except for reasons of public utility and by means of indemnification. The Nation shall have at all times the right to impose on private property such limitations as the public interest may demand. . . . measures shall be taken to divide large landed estates.

Oil: In the Nation is vested direct ownership of all minerals . . . such as . . . petroleum and all hydrocarbons—solid, liquid, or gaseous.

The Department of State was particularly concerned about the Constitution of 1917 because it provided the most extensive constitutional limitations on aliens' rights to private properties up to that time and antedated by many months the Bolshevik Revolution. Limitations on property were also accompanied by other express restrictions on aliens in Mexico. The constitution also clearly confirmed Carranza's 1915 decree on land reform, echoing the Zapatista campaign for redistribution of landed property. If such distribution were actually effected, the U.S. authorities knew perfectly well that the Mexican treasury would not have the resources for many years, if ever, to make indemnification required by the constitution. The provision on subsoil rights also clearly asserted state control and ownership of Mexican petroleum which the foreign companies believed to be their own. The United States was sufficiently concerned about the matter so as not to grant the Carranza government de jure recognition until after the president had denied orally any "intention . . . to take over properties now in exploitation and distinctly stated that there would be no confiscation of those properties."[7]

In the following years, however, the government required certain companies to secure drilling permits, some agricultural properties were seized, and there were other types of interference with U.S. property owners as a result of which the United States was disinclined to recognize successor governments in the absence of firmer commitments to protect U.S. private interests. In 1923, for example, foreigners owned about one-fifth of the land in Mexico, of which U.S. citizens owned about one-half, or 16.6 million hectares.[8] Recognition was not granted to the Obregón government until 1923, after a compromise settlement of these and other issues had been reached in the Bucareli agreements.

The most important elements of these agreements were three. First, the Mexican government reaffirmed its intention to compensate former owners for expropriated agricultural and other properties, and the United States accepted the deferrals of such compensation in bonds with the understanding that acceptance did not constitute a precedent for payment of other expropriations. Second, the Mexican government made an informal commitment in the negotiations (the commitment was not sanctified by a treaty) that the companies which had undertaken positive acts on oil lands prior to the promulgation of the constitution would not be the object of retroactive application of the constitutional provision on subsoil rights. Third, the two governments signed "claims conventions" providing the mechanism for settling their nationals' claims against the other government, including expropriation claims.[9] As a result of these compromises and assurances, the United States formally recognized the Obregón administration.

The property rights of U.S. citizens remained largely unchallenged for the balance of Obregón's term, but when Plutarco Elías Calles succeeded to the presidency, a new petroleum code was introduced in the congress limiting the possession of oil properties acquired before 1917 to fifty years—a limitation which was subsequently revoked due partly to the diplomacy of U.S. Ambassador Dwight Morrow. Meanwhile, too, the processing of agrarian claims against Mexico went very slowly indeed and no indemnification was made to U.S. claimants.

Agrarian claims became a more controversial issue after Lázaro Cárdenas, who became president in 1934, accelerated the tempo of land reform. During his six years in office, Cárdenas distributed over twenty million hectares of land or more than twice as much as all his revolutionary predecessors put together.[10] Most of the properties seized belonged to Mexicans, but the land reform was sufficiently vast so as to affect many U.S. and other foreign citizens. Ambassador Josephus Daniels and other U.S. officials persistently protested the seizures of the property of U.S. citizens and called for compensation, almost invariably without success or apparent effect on Cárdenas' land reform policies.[11] Land reform was fundamental to Cárdenas' entire program and was hardly likely to be affected by what Mexicans considered an incidental U.S. interest. Moreover, the Mexican government did not have the funds to compensate promptly and U.S. officials knew it. The fact that President Cárdenas consistently expressed his desire and intention to provide compensation also tended to disarm U.S. criticism. In any case, the United States grudgingly put up under protest with the agrarian seizures during Cárdenas' early years.

The oil crisis of 1937 and 1938 brought the festering issue of Mexican seizures of U.S. property to a head. The problem in this instance was not a Mexican challenge to the companies' subsoil rights, nor, initially at least, the question of expropriation. The government did have plans to participate more fully in oil profits through a system of oil royalties, but a labor dispute precipitated the crisis.

The petroleum workers' unions, organized in part by political leaders of the Left, sought sharp increases in wages and improvements in working conditions in new labor contracts. When the companies refused to meet these demands, the unions struck and the subsequent oil stoppage had widespread economic and political repercussions in Mexico. An award of a labor board which went far to meet the unions' demands was eventually upheld by the Mexican supreme court. When the companies refused to implement the court's decision and defied the government, Cárdenas nationalized the defiant foreign-owned oil companies.

Secretary of State Hull was incensed by what he considered an impetuous Mexican action and sent a strong note to Mexico protesting Mexican "confiscation" of U.S. property and demanding:

My government directs me to inquire, in the event that the Mexican government persists in this expropriation, without my Government undertaking to speak for the American interests involved, but solely for its preliminary information, what specific action with respect to payment for the properties in question is contemplated by the Mexican Government, what assurances will be given that payment will be made, and when such payments may be expected. In as much as the American citizens involved have already been deprived of their properties, and in view of the rule of law already stated, my Government considers itself entitled to ask for a prompt reply to this inquiry.[12]

In view of the fact that Cárdenas had already told Daniels that the Mexican government intended to pay compensation, the Mexican authorities were stung by Hull's implied rebukes. Ambassador Daniels tried his best to soften Hull's note, and when this failed, he sabotaged Hull's efforts by agreeing with the Mexicans that the note should be considered as not having been formally presented.[13] Although this was apparently an act of insubordination, it appears likely that Daniels thereby prevented a diplomatic break between the United States and Mexico.[14]

In addition to the strong note, the Department of State also persuaded Secretary of Treasury Morgenthau to announce a boycott of the purchase of silver from Mexico, which he did on March 27, followed by a slight decrease in the price as well. Morgenthau, who was opposed to using the suspension of silver purchases as a reprisal, did so mainly in response to State Department and congressional influence. In fact, Morgenthau continued to buy silver on the open market, some of which may have originated in Mexico, and purchases from Mexico continued though at a declining rate.[15]

The oil companies, surprised and infuriated by Cárdenas' action, demanded compensation in the amount of nearly half a billion dollars, which included claims for oil still in the ground, and imposed sanctions against Mexico through their control of tankers and influence in the international oil markets. The Department of State concluded, apparently rightly, that Mexico lacked means to provide anything approaching adequate compensation at that time and that the oil companies were in no mood for a compromise settlement. As a result, the United States deferred action on the oil expropriation, in effect accepting a fait accompli under protest, and shifted its pressure to the agrarian claims.

Desirous of protecting his relations with the U.S. government, Cárdenas was disposed to work for an agrarian settlement in part to offset the bitterness engendered over oil. In November 1938 the Mexican government agreed to begin payments of $1 million a year toward the satisfaction of agrarian claims, such claims to be subsequently determined by a joint commission of the two countries.[16]

In the following three years, forces in the United States and Mexico favoring reconciliation eventually came to dominate. The United States wanted and needed a friendly Mexico on its southern border and preferred a financial settlement to continuing tension or intervention. The Mexican leaders who shared many of the prevailing U.S. views in politics and foreign relations needed U.S. markets and credits. As a result, the two powers were able to effect a global settlement of their outstanding differences in the fall of 1941 before Pearl Harbor.

The first part of Mexican concessions involved the payment by Mexico of $40 million for the settlement of outstanding U.S. claims since 1868, including pre-revolutionary claims (1868–1910), agrarian claims, and claims for other expropriated property except oil. The second part involved Mexican payment of $9 million toward compensation for the expropriated U.S. oil properties, a joint commission to determine their total value later.[17] Initially, the oil companies did not accept the government agreement. The commissioners went ahead anyway and appraised the property for $24 million plus interest and the companies ultimately accepted payment; Standard Oil of New Jersey accepted its share in the amount of $18 million in 1943.[18]

On its side, the United States agreed to spend up to $40 million to stabilize the Mexican peso, to purchase $25 million of silver a year, and to extend Mexico an Export-Import Bank loan of $30 million for the Pan American Highway.[19] Clearly, U.S. purchases and credits went a long way to offset Mexican claims payments.

Thus, some thirty years after its outbreak, the United States finally came to terms with the Mexican Revolution and particularly its impact on U.S. private interests there.

Bolivia

The Toro government's seizure of Standard Oil's installations and concession in Bolivia on March 13, 1937, was a radical measure which foreshadowed the 1952 revolution. The Toro government was a precursor of the revolutionary governments of the Movimiento Nacionalista Revolucionario (MNR) after 1952, and many of the young men who later led the MNR began their political careers under President Toro. In later years the MNR backed the 1937 seizure,[20] and the case played an important part in the subsequent history of the revolutionary movement.

The Bolivian seizure differed from the seizure in Mexico in that Standard Oil had a "concession" rather than a title to land, the grounds for seizure were fraud as compared to defiance of the Mexican supreme court, and Cárdenas promised compensation from the start. The oil companies' properties in Mexico were profitable, whereas Standard's concession in Bolivia was producing little or no oil.

The U.S. initial response to the Bolivian seizure was mild, limited mainly to an expression of regret and a hope that friendly discussions would resolve the issue. The Department of State did not question the legality of the seizure decree and the subsequent decisions of the courts nor did it pass on the company's claims or insist on any specific means of settlement. The department did, however, take the position that the company was entitled to some form of compensation.[21] To this end, and while using restraint in dealing with Bolivian officials, the United States attempted to deny Bolivia assistance from Paraguay and Argentina in the exploitation and export of oil and by refusing to extend loans or technical assistance until the Bolivian government reached a settlement with Standard Oil. Approaches to Paraguay and Argentina had little effect, but the withholding of economic assistance caused the Bolivians to be more responsive.[22]

Domestic and international events made it possible for the Bolivian government to come to terms with Standard Oil and thus be able to participate in the benefits of economic assistance from the United States. The government's expulsion of the German minister following revelations of an alleged Nazi-putsch attempt and later the Japanese attack on Pearl Harbor set the stage for a settlement with Standard Oil and the United States.[23]

In January 1941 the Bolivian government and Standard Oil agreed to a $1.5 million settlement, plus interest, and the United States authorized a $25 million loan for economic development. In the dispute, the United States had sought not to take sides, but to use indirect pressures to bring the two parties to a settlement. The U.S. loan, plus other anticipated benefits from collaboration with the United States in the war, helped persuade the Bolivians to settle with Standard Oil. The company accepted payment in 1943.

The experience the leaders of the MNR had had over this dispute with Standard Oil, as well as the experience with the U.S. nonrecognition of the Villarroel government in 1944, prepared them to cope with U.S. views on private investment. On becoming provisional president in 1952 Hernán Siles Suazo promised to respect private property.[24] Later, President Paz Estenssoro publicly affirmed his intentions to provide compensation for expropriated property.[25] The United States recognized the new government only after having received reassurance that compensation would be paid.

When the tin mines were nationalized in October 1952, the decree committed the government to pay nearly $20 million to the three large nationalized mining groups and established a procedure for effecting payment. These provisions lessened the expected negative impact abroad of the nationalization, especially on Bolivia's capacity to sell tin ores to foreign buyers. President Paz Estenssoro from La Paz and Ambassador Andrade in Washington stressed time and again that the nationalization of the tin mines was not directed against private property in general but only against the three giants of mining who had usurped the nation's right to rule itself. Government spokesmen were quick to point out that medium-sized mining companies remained and that the property of other foreign companies, such as W. R. Grace, was not disturbed. Ambassador Andrade elaborated further:

> There is genuine regret that nationalization became necessary. It is our feeling that private enterprise, under ordinary circumstance, can more quickly and effectively develop resources than can government. Bolivia's poverty is a further handicap to government exploitation of mineral resources. Nor does my government relish the bad reaction which nationalization has caused in some quarters of the United States.

We badly need and want the help of outside capital. The billions of dollars in the United States that seek profitable outlets, and the unparalleled technical skills which are a formidable part of your strength, will be welcome in Bolivia. . . . I repeat, my government will try to create an atmosphere which attracts private capital.[26]

United States officials welcomed these reassurances but sought further demonstrations of Bolivia's intentions. Moreover, prices for tin ores were falling and the United States hesitated to make large purchases with the stockpile already high. During the winter of 1952–1953 it appeared that the MNR government was not likely to survive the collapse in the tin market without foreign assistance.

These and other factors placed the MNR government under heavy pressure to reach an agreement with the owners of the big three mines. The most urgent case from the U.S. point of view was the Patiño mines, the only group believed to have U.S. stockholders. President Paz estimated that U.S. citizens owned from 20 to 25 percent of the Patiño company.[27] The government and the Patiño mines reached a provisional agreement for a full settlement in early June 1953, payments to be made out of tin sales. Similar agreements were reached shortly thereafter with the other two large groups, Hochschild and Aramayo.

About a month later, on July 6, 1953, the Department of State offered the Bolivians a one-year contract to buy tin ores at the world market price and committed itself to doubling technical assistance and studying Bolivia's further economic needs. The department's archives for the period are not yet open for examination, but the statements of Assistant Secretary Cabot give some indication of what happened. In discussing U.S. assistance to Bolivia, he stressed the importance of the preliminary agreements with the mine owners and publicly admitted: "We have had to make strong representations . . . regarding [the Bolivian government's] attitude towards American interests." While declining to discuss the "bitter charges" in the nationalization controversy, Cabot explained: "If we brought any pressure, it was on the Bolivian government, which we strongly urged to compensate American stockholders for their expropriated property."[28]

The record shows that obtaining firm commitments to compensate for expropriated property was a condition precedent to U.S. recognition of the MNR government. Arrangement for the fulfillment of that commitment with respect to the nationalized mines was a condition for continued large U.S. tin purchases and economic assistance.[29] In the fall of 1953 the U.S. emergency assistance program to Bolivia was formalized, providing for $5 million of agricultural surpluses and $4 million of essential commodities, plus a doubling of technical assistance.[30]

Guatemala

Labor disputes caused frictions in relations with the management of U.S.-owned properties in Guatemala under Arévalo (1945–1951), but seizures didn't begin until after his successor, Arbenz, took office. The Department of State appears to have made virtually no public comment on the Arbenz government's temporary seizure of the Guatemalan Electric Company and the International Railways of Central America in 1953, but the published record does contain the text, or substantial summaries thereof, of the notes exchanged between the two governments about the expropriation of lands belonging to the United Fruit Company.

Less than one month after the first expropriation of United Fruit lands, the Department of State lodged a protest dated March 25, 1953, to which the Guatemalan government replied on June 26. The department answered the latter note on August 28. The opposing lines of argument are familiar to those who followed the Mexican expropriations. The Guatemalans argued that the land reform law, having a general character applicable to Guatemalans and foreigners alike, was within the sovereign rights of the republic. They denied that it was discriminatory, asserted that payment was being made in bonds and that the basis of evaluation, namely that fixed by the company for tax purposes, was just. An important part of the government's argument was that the expropriated lands of the company were those that had been left fallow, and their state of "permanent unproductiveness" was "causing great injury [perjuicio] to the people."[31]

The most significant aspect of the Department of State's note of August 28 is that it entered directly into the controversy as a spokesman for the company, representing the company's position to the government of Guatemala on virtually all major aspects of the dispute. The U.S. government, for example, discussed at length why the company needed so much fallow land, namely to have sufficient land available until its contract expired in 1981 to replace banana lands stricken with the Panama disease. The Guatemalan government maintained that the company did not really need all that land, while the U.S. government asserted that the expropriations would make continued operations "impossible."

The August note also pointed out that the expropriated 234,000 acres of United Fruit Lands at Tiquisate constituted almost two-thirds of the 377,000 acres seized in all Guatemala thus far, raising a serious question of discrimination. Moreover the United States insisted that the application of the law should conform to the minimum standards required by international law. After citing several cases establishing precedents, the note said that Guatemala was obligated under international law to make just payment, that is, prompt, adequate, and effective compensation. Payment in bonds, the note continued, was "scarcely to be regarded as either prompt or effective payment." The U.S. government went on to make a detailed case showing how the company had tried unsuccessfully to have its properties reassessed for tax purposes. Also, since tax evaluations were commonly accepted as below real or fair value, the department maintained that fraud could not rightly be imputed when an owner sought full value for expropriated property.

The Department of State urged the Guatemalan government to settle the company claim either directly with the company, with the U.S. government, or through an international tribunal. When none of these suggestions were adopted, the department made a formal claim of $15,845,849 against the Guatemalan government.[32]

There was no indication that the U.S. government had made an independent appraisal of the expropriated property. The face amount of the bonds which the Guatemalan government offered the company was $627,572.82, based on tax evaluations.[33]

In response to the formal claim presented by the United States, the Guatemalan government called the amount submitted "absurd," charged the company with failure to comply with Guatemalan laws thereby losing its right to operate in the republic, and called the U.S. claim a frank intervention.[34] The Arbenz government was overthrown in June 1954 before the United States was able to submit a claim for the second large expropriation of United Fruit lands, namely 172,532 acres near Banan-era on February 24, 1954. Shortly before its fall the Arbenz government announced that the United Fruit Company's properties constituted less than 29 percent of all lands expropriated, the balance having belonged to Guatemalans or persons of other nationalities, thereby countering the United Fruit charge of discrimination.[35] The question of the extent to which the expropriations of the United Fruit Company were linked to the anti-Arbenz movement will be discussed in chapter 6. By 1954 U.S. fears of communism in Guatemala far overshadowed protests about land seizures.

After Arbenz fell, the new Castillo Armas administration rescinded the land reform law, new small holders were required to leave their properties, and the United Fruit properties were returned. Meanwhile, the United Fruit Company donated 100,000 acres of land on the Pacific coast, 10,000 acres of which consisted of "good banana land," for the government's resettlement program.[36]

Cuba

United States responses to the seizures of U.S. property in Cuba were politically most significant during Castro's first year in office, that is, before the sharp deterioration set in with the events beginning early in 1960. In the first few months particularly, the U.S. responses to Castro's policies affecting U.S. property were potentially significant indicators of the prospects for later collaboration between the two governments.

The Cuban intervention ("temporary" seizure) of the management of the American-owned Cuban Telephone Company in March 1959 was an early test of U.S. policy. Philip Bonsal did not believe that he, as American ambassador, should take any official notice of the intervention, and he received no instruction from Washington to do so.[37] Nevertheless, he felt it would be helpful to offer to put the minister of communications in touch with telephone regulatory officials in the United States, and an official Cuban group actually did visit the United States for this purpose.

The Cuban Agrarian Reform Law of May 17, 1959, was potentially capable of substantial effects on U.S. property interests in Cuba. Nevertheless, Ambassador Bonsal reports that he wanted to tell Castro directly of U.S. sympathy for "carefully considered and executed land reform" and that he recognized that some Cubans thought U.S. interests had unduly relied on U.S. official support in the past. In conversations with the Cuban officials, Bonsal explained that U.S. property interests would need to exhaust their local administrative and judicial remedies before expecting assistance from their own government. He sought an early meeting with Castro on the subject.[38]

Unable to secure an interview with Castro, Bonsal arranged to send the Cuban government a formal note dated June 11, 1959, on the Agrarian Reform Law.[39] The note outlined U.S. support for soundly conceived and executed programs of land reform and expressed the hope that such reform in Cuba would not impair productivity. Attention was also called to the extensive U.S. investments in Cuba and the obligation to make "prompt, adequate, and effective compensation." After referring to a provision in the Cuban constitution requiring prior payment in cash, the note urged fair treatment for U.S. investors and an exchange of views. The next day Castro called in Ambassador Bonsal, and the two discussed the Agrarian Reform Law, Castro describing the ambassador's attitude as "cordial and respectful."[40] The ambassador said that American property owners adopted a posture of compliance and that embassy officials entered into discussions concerning compensation in long-term bonds, marketable and payable in dollars. Seizures began in June, three U.S.-owned cattle ranches being among the first properties affected.

During the balance of 1959 the land reform went forward in earnest accompanied by the seizures of the property of U.S. citizens. Ambassador Bonsal was less concerned about the impact of the application of the Agrarian Reform Law on U.S. interests than damages inflicted on those interests in the absence of legal authority. There was concern about the numerous acts of arbitrary despoilment (reportedly at least fifty by early 1960) that victimized Americans in Cuba at the hands of the National Institute of Agrarian Reform (INRA):

> The productive capacity of the properties affected had been damaged well beyond the specific losses of land, cattle, and equipment misappropriated by the eager incompetents under Castro's personal supervision. . . . the actions complained of did not represent the application of the Land Reform Law or any other Cuban law; they were purely arbitrary excesses of personal power.[41]

A protest note on seizures under the land reform had been submitted on October 12, 1959, and the general position was briefly summarized in the ambassador's official statement to President Dorticós on October 27.[42] The thrust of these statements was that the United States sympathized with Cuba's programs of social and economic reform while expressing the hope that negotiations would resolve differences arising between the two countries over any effect these programs had on the rights of U.S. citizens under Cuban and international law.

These differences continued to mount, however, and after a visit to the United States early in the new year, Ambassador Bonsal returned to Cuba with a restatement of the U.S. position, this time more explicitly critical of Cuban government actions. The note protested that:

The numerous actions taken by officials of the Cuban government which are considered by the United States Government to be in denial of the basic rights of ownership of United States citizens in Cuba . . . involve principally the seizure and occupation of land and buildings of United States citizens without court orders and frequently without any written authorization whatever, the confiscation and removal of equipment, the seizure of cattle, the cutting and removal of timber, the plowing under of pastures, all without the consent of the American owners. In many cases no inventories were taken, nor were any receipts proffered, nor any indication afforded that payment was intended to be made. These acts have been carried out in the name of the National Agrarian Reform Institute.[43]

This note may have struck home, and the many other pressures focused on Castro were sufficient to provoke an outburst against counterrevolutionaries and their foreign allies on January 21. His charges were so serious that the Secretary of State recalled Ambassador Bonsal to the United States for a general review of U.S. policies toward Cuba.

The significant thing about that review, as embodied in public statements by President Eisenhower and Ambassador Bonsal at the end of January, was the continuation of the policy of restraint, particularly with regard to the seizures of U.S. properties.[44] The United States simply restated its intention of using diplomatic channels to bring violations of the rights of U.S. citizens to the attention of the Cuban government, and its hope for settlement through negotiation or, failing that, international procedures (implying arbitration). Without retreating from its original stand, the U.S. position on seizures and other aspects of Cuban relations was designed to calm troubled waters.

Meanwhile, other U.S. private interests were suffering adversity as well. Like the telephone company, the U.S.-owned electric power company was ordered to sharply reduce its rates. In October the government seized the records of all the foreign companies which had been prospecting for oil in Cuba.[45]

As the year 1960 unfolded Castro's early interference with U.S.-controlled public utilities and the seizures of agricultural properties were far overshadowed by even more dramatic and politically far-reaching U.S. initiatives described in greater detail in chapter 6. They included President Eisenhower's decision to arm a counterrevolutionary force and to cut the Cuban sugar quota, and the U.S. recommendations to the oil companies to refuse to refine Soviet crude oil. Their refusal gave Castro grounds to seize the three refineries, which he did beginning on June 29. Meanwhile, Eisenhower's plans to suspend the Cuban sugar quota came to fruition with the announcement of the suspension on July 6.

Castro had issued a decree authorizing the seizure of all U.S. properties on July 5 but waited a month after the sugar quota suspension to implement the decree. The law explicitly discriminated against U.S. owners, and compensation was provided for but only out of a fund to be composed of receipts from sales of sugar to the United

States in unlikely volume and at well above prevailing prices. This, like other seizures, was formally protested by the United States. Now, however, property seizures were only part of the mounting conflict that led to a break in diplomatic relations early in 1961, to the Bay of Pigs several months later, and the Missile Crisis of October 1962. Castro himself has estimated that U.S. properties seized in Cuba were worth some $800 million, while authoritative U.S. estimates ranged from $1 billion and up.[46]

Cuban-American relations thereafter deteriorated so rapidly, and in a sense so relentlessly, that the U.S. reaction to the seizures of U.S. property was largely for the record. In a note dated July 16, Ambassador Bonsal protested the nationalization law of July 6, 1960, as a violation of international law and in essence "discriminatory, arbitrary, and confiscatory."[47] He called it discriminatory because it was limited to the seizures of property owned by U.S. citizens, arbitrary because it was admittedly in retaliation for the sugar quota suspension, and confiscatory because of the nature of its provisions for compensation. Notes delivered on August 8 and September 29, 1960, respectively, protested the seizure of twenty-six companies and three U.S.-owned banks under the provision of the nationalization law. The U.S. government suspended the operations of its Nicaro nickel facility on September 29 because of "confiscatory" taxes and intermittent embargoes on exports.[48]

The Foreign Claims Settlement Commission has provided a procedure for making U.S. claims a matter of judicial record, and 5,887 awards in the amount of $1.76 billion had been made by the end of 1971.[49] Since funds are not available to provide compensation for the claims, the procedure provides claimants an opportunity to establish their claims in the event that compensation can eventually be arranged. Also, the procedure provided company executives with a means of reassuring stockholders that they were doing everything possible to protect their interests.

As the years go by, and more than a decade has passed now, the companies have less and less reason to hope for the return of their properties or for substantial compensation. Many of the properties have deteriorated or been rebuilt, and the Cuban economy has experienced over ten years of socialism, making a return to the old economic system difficult, if not impossible. Moreover, the companies have already benefited from tax write-offs on these losses, and any recovery would require substantial cash outlays as rebates for tax savings.

The Price of Compensation

What is the balance sheet with regard to the seizures of U.S. properties by these revolutionary governments (see table 6)? The cases of expropriation fall into three categories. In Guatemala, the expropriating government was overthrown, the expropriation measures rescinded, and the former owners authorized to resume possession of their properties. In Mexico and Bolivia, expropriation measures were carried out, have since remained in effect, and negotiated settlements were reached. In Cuba, the expropriation measures have remained in effect and compensation arrangements worked out with former French and Swiss owners, but not with former U.S. owners.

In Mexico and Bolivia, U.S. interests received far less compensation than they had claimed and after delays of many years, but the compensation received was substantial. In Mexico the payment of $40 million appears to have come close to the awards of independent government appraisers—without interest. Similarly, the $24 million paid U.S. oil companies was reached with the participation of the U.S. commissioner. In Bolivia the $1.5 million award was less than the oil companies had invested, but the explorations had been largely a failure. In the 1950s the Bolivian tin companies and the U.S. stockholders, whose participation in the compensation may have come to $2 or $3 million, did not press hard for further compensation in light of the exhaustion of tin yields and the broken-down condition of mining facilities. Big profits in tin had long since been reaped.

The Mexican and Bolivian settlements can be understood only in light of the extensive economic inducements offered by the U.S. government which made the settlements possible. In exchange for the $40 million settlement on land and miscellaneous claims and for $24 million plus interest on former U.S. oil properties for Mexico, the United States agreed to purchase about $25 million worth of Mexican silver a year, spend up to $40 million to stabilize the Mexican peso, and lend Mexico $30 million to help build the Pan American Highway. The Bolivian government paid Standard Oil $1.5 million plus interest and received a $25 million loan for economic development. The immediate financial advantages to the Mexican and Bolivian governments appear to have far offset the amounts that they committed for compensation, though the settlements should not be considered simply in dollar-and-cents terms since both parties were also involved in matters having commercial, strategic, and other implications.

United States losses in Cuba were far greater than in the other countries and probably exceed $1 billion. A substantial portion of that loss was eventually borne by the U.S. government in lowered corporate income tax receipts, due to the ability of many large multinational companies to write off their Cuban losses—an advantage not enjoyed by various small holders. The Cuban losses are roughly comparable to the economic and military grants and loans to Latin America in each of several years under the Alliance for Progress.

United States losses in Cuba were still uncompensated in mid-1974, while substantial compensation[50] or restoration had been paid for the seizures of U.S. property in Mexico, Bolivia, and Guatemala. (Arrangements to pay compensation, described briefly in chapter 8, have been made with respect to more recent expropriations in Peru and Chile.)

United States national interests appear to have been best served when a conciliatory approach was taken, as in Mexico and Bolivia. One reason the United States extended so much credit in connection with the compensation agreements was that the Mexican and Bolivian governments did not have uncommitted surplus resources available to compensate. Moreover, without such inducements, the political obstacles to raising huge funds within the country would have been immense. The charge that the U.S. taxpayer was forced to finance the payment of compensation to private U.S. holders would not be entirely fair because payment of compensation was not the sole purpose of U.S. assistance. United States assistance was also extended for the purpose of securing Mexican and Bolivian economic and military cooperation on the eve of and during World War II.

Retrospect and Prospects

The United States has long insisted that international law requires that compensation be paid for the expropriation of the property of foreign owners. This policy continues to stand as an obstacle to those political movements which hold that social progress can be achieved only through structural changes in the economy, such as far-reaching changes in the tenure of land and mines. Leaders of these movements hold that land reform is essential for economic and social development. In fact, control of private property by certain status quo groups is sometimes seen as a major bar to social progress. Expropriation is viewed as the only effective way to deprive these groups of dominant political power, even though cash to compensate is not available. People seeking radical social change may attribute little significance to demands for compensation based on legal rights or considerations of equity on the grounds that the owners of land and other properties often acquired them by theft, fraud, or bribery.

United States policies on compensation for private property conflict not only with the goals of Latin American proponents of social change but with other basic U.S. policies as well. Such programs as the Alliance for Progress have sought to promote land reform, while the countries which need it most can seldom afford to make prompt, adequate, and effective compensation in any strict interpretation of these terms. Such requirements are apt to make land reform impossible. Yet failure to insist on compensation for owners who have been expropriated is widely considered as grossly unfair since the U.S. government has encouraged private investment as a spur to development.

In coping with this dilemma, the United States has long continued to insist firmly on the principle of compensation while accepting its watering-down in practice. This may be partly due to a desire to promote social change. More important, compensation which does not meet the U.S. standard may be better than no compensation at all. As far back as 1923, for example, the United States agreed to accept long-term bonds for expropriated agrarian claims in Mexico. Later, the United States accepted installment payments for a global settlement of these and other claims. In Bolivia, the United States accepted an agreement providing for compensation to mine owners out of tin sales receipts. In Cuba, while formally insisting on prompt, adequate, and effective compensation, the U.S. ambassador was discussing deferred payment in bonds redeemable in dollars. The United States has left no doubt that it would prefer cash, but seldom, if ever, since 1933 has it stated openly that *only* cash payments were acceptable.

In adopting the Good Neighbor Policy and its core principle, nonintervention, the United States renounced the use of armed force to secure payment for expropriated properties in Latin America and has continued ever since to proclaim adherence to that policy in principle. United States-sponsored paramilitary operations against the Arbenz government in Guatemala and the Castro government in Cuba, where extensive U.S. properties had been expropriated without the payment of effective compensation, raised questions about the good faith of the United States. Some critics of U.S. policies have charged that these operations were thinly veiled efforts to protect U.S. investors, and the return of properties to the United Fruit Company after Arbenz fell gave color to this argument. My own view is that these operations were not primarily designed for such a purpose, and I offer an explanation of U.S. responses in Guatemala and Cuba in chapters 6 and 7.

In the 1930s the U.S. government also developed new procedures for dealing with expropriation disputes. In Bolivia in the 1930s, the United States refrained from being drawn into the substance of the dispute, insisting simply that compensation should be paid and urging the two parties to reach a settlement. In Mexico the United States directly entered into negotiations on a settlement of the oil dispute only when the oil companies refused to accept what the Roosevelt administration thought was a reasonable offer. In neither case did the U.S. government seek to represent the oil companies directly with the two governments concerned. As Bryce Wood has pointed out, "Following 1939 the Department of State could no longer be regarded as an international law office automatically responding to requests for the presentation to international tribunals of cases affecting U.S. companies."[51] In this connection, the United States accepted a negotiated settlement with both Bolivia and Mexico. United States practices in this respect changed when John Foster Dulles, who had long served as the attorney for U.S. corporations operating abroad, became secretary of state. In the expropriation controversy in Guatemala, the Department of State appeared to act again as counsel to the United Fruit Company, presenting peremptory demands for compensation in amounts specified by the company itself.

United States authorities have developed over the years a variety of ways to encourage expropriating governments to make compensation. Withholding recognition was successful in securing assurances about the treatment of U.S. investment from the Mexicans in 1923 and the Bolivians in 1952. The revolutionary governments were less interested in the formalities of recognition than in the private loans, government credits, or government purchases for which recognition was a prerequisite. The U.S. government purchase of Mexican silver and Bolivian tin was an important element in negotiations with those two countries. Credits for economic development enticed the Mexicans and Bolivians but were less effective with the Cubans. Castro clearly feared U.S. power with regard to the sugar-quota purchases, but the president's almost total initial suspension appears to have left Castro with little or no inducement to compromise. Sanctions may have hurt Castro but appear to have achieved little for the United States.

It is not surprising that the prospects for escalation or conciliation of disputes over expropriations have been determined largely by the willingness of the two parties to negotiate compromise settlements. When both sides demonstrated such willingness, as in the Mexican and Bolivian cases, reconciliation was achieved.

The outcome was escalation in Guatemala and Cuba. With respect to Guatemala, Secretary Dulles was not disposed to be flexible and preferred laying down the international law, no doubt partly because he looked toward escalation and overthrow. The Arbenz government, for its part, was not very successful in communicating whatever willingness it may have had to reach agreement with the United States. It probably should be recognized that when the United Fruit properties were seized, relations between the two governments were already so embittered that it would have been difficult to arrange a compromise even if both parties had ultimately been prepared to compromise.

Similarly, the United States originally appeared willing to make concessions to Castro with respect to the mode of compensation for expropriated properties, and Castro might have been prepared to provide some form of compensation if that had been the principal issue between the two parties. Castro, however, had concluded that a compensation agreement could only be part of an overall settlement, with which he doubted he could agree. Moreover, when President Eisenhower authorized the formation of an anti-Castro paramilitary force in March 1960, the necessary climate for negotiating a compromise no longer existed. Thus, the conditions for conciliation, the absence of which are likely to lead to escalation, are not only mutual willingness to work out a compromise but political relations which make negotiations feasible.

In these cases the major questions have often appeared to be legal: (1) must compensation be paid; (2) if it is to be paid, is it as a legal obligation or as a matter of grace, and (3) how should payment be made? The U.S. government does not, of course, contest the right of expropriation, and most governments, including even Castro's, are prepared to pay compensation in some cases. The main problem, once a Latin American government has decided to expropriate, usually is its inability to compensate.

Like other governments, the Latin American revolutionary governments come to terms—that is, exercise their limited capacity to pay—when they deem it in their interests to do so. In order to provide the necessary incentives and reach bilateral settlements, the United States ordinarily has been forced to look beyond private interests to broader public interests—economic, political, and strategic. What this has usually meant is that U.S. officials have found it necessary to offer inducements, often in the form of loans or commodity purchases, to secure reasonable compensation for expropriated U.S. properties as part of a total package beneficial to both sides.

While insisting on compensation, the U.S. government has a parallel policy of encouraging direct private investment in Latin America as in other countries of the Third World. It thereby has been charged with assuming a moral obligation to help protect such investments. The rationale for official encouragement has been that private investment can and does play an important role in economic development and that the development of the Third World is in the national interest of the United States. To that end, the U.S. government has sponsored a number of programs to share the risks of direct foreign investment with U.S. investors.[52] One of these programs is the Investment Guarantee Program which insures risks with respect to convertibility and war as well as to expropriation. Since 1959 the United States has signed agreements providing for investment guarantees with most Latin American governments. By June 30, 1971, $5.6 billion of guarantees had been issued in Latin America, nearly $2.6 billion of which covered expropriation risks.[53] About one-sixth of the nearly $16 billion of U.S. investment in the region was then covered by expropriation insurance.

The early public discussion of the Investment Guarantee Program emphasized its potential for stimulating development, and there appears to have been relatively little attention given to the impact the program could have on relations with governments which expropriate U.S. property. Before the U.S. government joined in risk-sharing arrangements, the central conflict in expropriation cases was between the expropriating government and the U.S. company concerned. The U.S. government retained its option of playing a peripheral role. Under the Investment Guarantee Program, the U.S. government formally became a party to expropriation controversies and itself a potential claimant under the provisions of intergovernmental agreements.

The Cuban expropriations under Castro were not covered and predated most such agreements in Latin America. Massive claims came into prospect, however, when the Allende government expropriated U.S. properties in Chile. Many of these properties were covered under the Investment Guarantee Program and coverage in Chile came to $313 million. The Chilean case shows what a heavy burden such claims can put on the program's reserves for expropriation losses, which were $85 million in 1971.[54] If Allende had not fallen, congressional appropriations might have been required to keep the program viable. The Chilean expropriations also show how the guarantee program intimately links U.S. public and private interests, raising fiscal and political complications for the U.S. government, as well as for the Chilean government and the U.S. companies concerned.

In recent years doubts have been expressed about the rationale underlying U.S. official promotion of direct foreign investment as a means of stimulating economic development. The new skepticism is not occasioned so much by the long-standing radical critique of direct foreign investment as a tool of economic exploitation and political domination as by new insights on how such investment may serve to dampen rather than stimulate local dynamism and autonomous growth.

The competition of large multinational corporations, for example, is sometimes seen as displacing or stunting the growth of local investors. The fact that so many entrepreneurs are foreigners or represent foreign companies is also sometimes believed to inhibit the development of national economic policies. In such cases, Albert Hirschman has maintained, the national interest of the United States, broadly conceived as served by the development of Latin America, may enter into "conflict with a continuing expansion and even with the maintenance of the present position of private investors from the United States."[55] He cites, for example, the incompatibility in the short run of land reform and income redistribution through taxation—important goals cited in the Alliance for Progress—with the maintenance of a favorable investment climate for private capital. As a result, he has proposed a "policy of selective liquidation and withdrawal of foreign private investment . . . in the best mutual interests of Latin America and the United States."[56] To that end he made specific proposals for mechanisms providing for compensation and the orderly transfer of properties from foreign to national ownership.

Meanwhile, President Nixon continued to insist on an international standard with respect to compensation for expropriated property. In early 1972 he asserted that the United States has a right to expect that expropriations will be "nondiscriminatory," for a "public purpose," and that "prompt, adequate and effective compensation" will be paid.[57] Moreover, the prevailing view in the American establishment is that seizure of property without compensation is a form of theft. United States officials have been reluctant to retreat an inch from this principle for fear of providing a pretext for threats to a vast array of U.S. property abroad. In 1973, for example, U.S. citizens had about $107 billion in direct investment in foreign countries, $18.5 billion in Latin America alone (see table 7).[58]

The record of the seizures of U.S.-owned properties in Latin America and the continuing public discussion suggest that there are a number of unresolved issues with respect to U.S. policies: (1) whether the U.S. government as a matter of foreign economic policy should encourage private investors to risk capital in developing areas when it is known that revolutionary seizures in some are possible if not likely and that the means to pay compensation are not available locally; (2) whether the United States should promote as a matter of public policy the adoption of "free enterprise" in developing countries while it simultaneously shares the burden of foreign investment risks there; (3) whether private foreign investment does in fact promote economic development and, if not, the type of situations when it does not do so; (4) how, from the perspective of the interests of the nation as a whole, U.S. policies on compensation and development promotion can be harmonized with the professed U.S. policies in favor of social change and friendly relations with societies where such changes are taking place.[59]

With respect to the future, revolutionary governments in Latin America will tend to give higher priority to the exercise of the right of expropriation than to the intricate questions of when and how compensation is to be paid. They are unlikely to be able to make compensation that investors will consider adequate. Such tendencies are likely to be facts of life in an increasing number of Latin American countries in spite of the outcries of the foreign investors affected.

In the United States the facts of life are quite different. The prospects of any change of the U.S. position on the "principle" of compensation for expropriated property are remote. The principle is an ideological and ethical tenet held by most

TABLE 7

SELECTED U.S. DIRECT INVESTMENT ABROAD
(PRELIMINARY 1973)

	Book Value at Year End (U.S. Dollars, in Billions)		
Developed countries			74.1
Canada		28.1	
Europe		37.2	
Developing countries			27.9
Latin American republics and			
other western hemisphere		18.5	
Mexico	2.2		
Panama	1.7		
Argentina	1.4		
Brazil	3.2		
Chile	0.6		
Colombia	0.7		
Peru	0.8		
Venezuela	2.6		
Africa		2.8	
Middle East		2.7	
Asia and Pacific		3.9	
International, unallocated			5.3
All areas			107.3

SOURCE: U. S., Department of Commerce, *Survey of Current Business,* August 1974, p. 18.

NOTE: Developed countries in Asia are included under "developed countries" and that selected subtotals only are presented for most categories.

Americans in public life, as well as being integral to the U.S. legal and social system. Political considerations make retreat from the principle even less likely. United States interests which are expropriated in foreign countries can be counted on to be vocal and influential in Washington and are likely to find many allies among U.S. investors in the United States and abroad who believe that uncompensated seizures pose a potential threat to their own interests as well.

As a result, the best prospects for compromise lie less in the realm of debates over principle and more in efforts toward mutually beneficial adjustments of material interests. As the Mexican and Bolivian cases show, the United States for its part has fared better when it has been prepared to adopt flexible positions regarding the mode of compensation. The United States has not usually found that self-righteous insistence on the fulfillment of disputed legal norms has been sufficient to secure settlements in the absence of other inducements. And on the part of the revolutionary leaders, they are likely to find isolation from capitalist markets costly and dangerous in the long run. As long as capitalist governments and economies remain powerful, revolutionary governments will have to learn to live with them and make concessions with respect to property issues.

Mexico and Bolivia: Reconciliation

The United States has had closer relations with revolutionary Mexico and Bolivia than with most other Latin American governments, except possibly the former Caribbean protectorates and Brazil. In spite of earlier friction, the Mexican and Bolivian revolutions were both climaxed by unprecedentedly friendly relations with the United States. In Mexico the global settlement of 1941 was one of the most comprehensive bilateral settlements in inter-American history and set the stage for collaboration during World War II. In Bolivia, the MNR governments of the 1950s were viewed by President Kennedy as foreshadowing development patterns sought in the 1960s by the Alliance for Progress.

The United States has had great difficulty coming to terms with most other revolutionary governments in Latin America. Relations with revolutionary governments in Guatemala in the early 1950s and with Castro after 1959 deteriorated into mutual hostility and bitterness.

The major question may be posed: why was the United States able to come to terms with the Mexican and Bolivian revolutionaries and not with those in Guatemala and Cuba? Was the reason related to differences in revolutionary programs? Was the international situation decisive? To what extent does the behavior of U.S. leaders and Latin American revolutionaries explain the differing outcomes? In this and the following two chapters an attempt will be made to answer these questions.

Let us see first how the U.S. government came to reconcile its interests with the Mexican and Bolivian revolutionaries.

Mexico (1914–1941)

Fundamental to understanding the U.S. response to the Mexican Revolution is the fact that U.S. presidents were basically sympathetic to the purposes of the revolution during its most active phases, namely in 1915–1917 and 1934–1938. Presidents Woodrow Wilson and Franklin Roosevelt both were outspoken in their approval of the general direction of Mexican development and well disposed toward their Mexican counterparts, Presidents Carranza and Cárdenas.

When Wilson became president in March 1913, he was extremely disturbed by the events leading to the overthrow and death of President Madero the preceding month. His apprehension and suspicions were sufficient to cause him to ignore the importunate demands of Ambassador Wilson for the recognition of General Huerta as Madero's successor. The president sent his friend, William Bayard Hale, to Mexico to determine the true situation and to advise him accordingly. Hale's report describing the treacherous behavior of Huerta, Ambassador Wilson's involvement in Madero's overthrow, and Madero's murder made a lasting impression on the president. Perhaps partly as a result of a shared sense of guilt about Madero's death, Wilson decided to force Huerta out of power. His commitment against Huerta's counterrevolutionary government facilitated his personal and political predisposition in favor of the Mexican revolutionaries.

As early as April 1914, Woodrow Wilson publicly demonstrated his understanding and approval of the course of the revolution in an interview with a journalist:

> I challenge you . . . to cite me an instance in all the history of the world where liberty was handed down from above. Liberty always is attained by the forces working from below, underneath. . . . That, leavened by the sense of wrong and oppression and injustice, by the ferment of human rights to be attained, brings freedom.
>
> It is curious . . . that every demand for the establishment of order in Mexico takes into consideration, not order for the benefit of the people of Mexico . . . but order for the benefit of the old-time regime, for the aristocrats, for the vested interests, for the men who are responsible for this very condition of disorder. No one asks for order because order will help the masses of the people to get a portion of their rights and their land; but all demand it so that the great powers of property, the overlords, the hidalgos, the men who have exploited that rich country for their own selfish purposes, shall be able to continue their process undisturbed by the protests of the people from whom their wealth and power have been obtained. . . .
>
> They want order—the old order, but I say to you that the old order is dead.[1]

Despite all the tensions with the various revolutionary movements, despite threats and counterthreats, despite the prospect of war between the two countries, Woodrow Wilson never abandoned his fundamental sympathy with the Mexican revolutionary cause.

Nor was Wilson's benevolent attitude toward the revolution exceptional in the United States. As José Vasconcelos, a leading Mexican revolutionary, has written:

> It was easy for us to understand the two currents of opinion: one in favor of, the other against, our country. The great mass of public opinion in the United States was in favor of the Mexican revolution because it felt that Mexico was

entitled to freedom and progress just as much as any nation. Only the small group whom we may call imperialists were of the outspoken opinion that Mexico did not deserve democracy and that a brutal dictator, an iron hand, was necessary to keep down a country of half-breeds and renegades.[2]

Rival Mexican Factions (1913–1917)

Wilson's sympathy for the revolution has been obscured by the way he treated the revolutionaries and his sporadic meddling in Mexican affairs. The latter, symbolized by his patronizing manner, blatant demands, and armed intervention, has often caused his important contribution to the victories of the leading Mexican revolutionaries to go unrecognized. During his presidency, Woodrow Wilson frequently used his diplomatic and other influences to suppress the rivals of the "first chief" of the revolutionaries, Venustiano Carranza, and to support Carranza himself.

Like Carranza, Wilson was an early and loud voice against Huerta. Within a few months President Wilson's policy had crystallized into two main elements: (1) forcing Huerta out of the Mexican presidency, and (2) achieving free elections as the basis for a popularly elected and democratic successor government. This policy was pursued initially through the president's personal representative in Mexico, the former governor of Minnesota, John Lind, and announced in a message to the Congress on August 27, 1913. In a later and even more authoritative statement of U.S. purposes in Mexico, Wilson sent a circular note to various foreign powers on November 13, 1913, stating, "If General Huerta does not retire by force of circumstances, it will become the duty of the United States to use less peaceful means to put him out."[3]

When Wilson's efforts to eliminate Huerta through persuasion failed, an incident involving what was interpreted as an insult to U.S. naval forces visiting Tampico provided a pretext for more forceful measures. Wilson ordered American troops ashore in April 1914 to occupy the port of Veracruz as a means of taking armed action against Huerta.[4] Hard pressed by domestic forces and the U.S. occupation, Huerta resigned as president in July 1914 and sailed from Mexico.

Meanwhile, Wilson had been keeping in close touch with the constitutionalist forces under the leadership of Venustiano Carranza. Carranza received U.S. representatives at his headquarters and maintained representation of his own in Washington. Also, he showed his sensitivity to the needs and interests of foreigners by formally guaranteeing, in a decree dated February 2, 1914, to entertain claims for damages suffered during the revolutions against Díaz and now Huerta.[5] Partly as a result of these assurances, Wilson moved toward a policy of support for the constitutionalists on February 3, 1914, by revoking the arms embargo, thereby allowing the latter to acquire arms legally in the United States.

Carranza was, however, intransigent toward certain aspects of Wilson's policy from the beginning. With regard to the U.S. occupation of Veracruz, Carranza wrote Wilson that the Veracruz "invasion" was "highly offensive to the independence and dignity of Mexico . . . [and] I invite you . . . to order your forces to evacuate."[6] He consistently opposed armed intervention of all sorts in Mexico and Wilson's efforts to interfere in Mexico's internal affairs. To Wilson's call for free elections and representative government, Carranza sharply rejoined that he would not admit outside interference and that he would support free elections only after Huerta had been defeated and eliminated politically.[7]

Carranza's adamant posture was one of the factors causing Wilson to set aside his plans for further armed action against Huerta but was not sufficient to persuade Wilson to withdraw immediately from Veracruz. As a result, Carranza became the beneficiary of Wilson's armed action against Huerta without himself bearing the stigma of approval of U.S. intervention. Carranza remained an authentic spokesman of Mexican nationalism and an independent voice vis-à-vis the United States. Carranza reaffirmed his position by accepting the mediation of Argentina, Brazil, and Chile in the dispute between Mexico and the United States while refusing to accept their recommendations regarding an armistice and other matters related to Mexico's internal affairs.[8]

After Huerta's resignation in July 1914, various Mexican factions led by Carranza, Villa, and Zapata struggled to dominate Mexico. During that year President Wilson considered the options of supporting one or another of the leaders or insisting that they all stand aside to give the nation a free and unfettered choice. Under pressure from Mexico and desirous of terminating U.S. involvement, President Wilson ordered American troops out of Veracruz on November 23, 1914. In doing so, the U.S. commander did not arrange to turn the city over to a particular Mexican faction, but Carranza's troops, which controlled the environs of Veracruz, took over the city after the Americans left.

By mid-1915 Carranza was gaining the upper hand in much of Mexico with the support of various generals, most notably Alvaro Obregón. These events were responsible in part for a change in U.S. policy. Wilson no longer gave first priority to free elections, but rather sought first the establishment of order by a dominant revolutionary faction, leaving the electoral question until later. Wilson and Secretary of State Robert Lansing concluded that peace could be restored most effectively by recognizing Carranza who was rapidly becoming the master of Mexico anyway.

Lansing persuaded the Latin American representatives at the Pan American Conference convened to deal with problems arising from civil conflict in Mexico to support the U.S. position and recognize Carranza de facto. The powers concerned did so beginning on October 19, 1915. That same day the Wilson administration forbade the export of munitions to Mexico while making an exception for the Carranza government.

The recognition of Carranza and the arms embargo was a severe blow to the battered but still undefeated spirit of Francisco "Pancho" Villa. He retaliated by holding some thirty Americans hostage in Chihuahua for a short time in November, killing seventeen Americans in cold blood at nearby Santa Ysabel in January, and striking across the border in force at Columbus, New Mexico, where he killed fifteen American soldiers and civilians in early March. Under presidential orders and with congressional approval, General John J. Pershing with 4,000 men under his command crossed into Mexico on March 15, 1916, in pursuit of Pancho Villa. The U.S. forces remained on Mexican soil for nearly a year, during which time the Punitive Expedition became a major issue in the presidential elections of 1916 and almost led to war with Mexico.

In the negotiations regarding the withdrawal of U.S. troops, President Wilson insisted that the United States and Mexico agree on a program which would facilitate Mexico's fulfillment of her obligations to protect the lives and property of foreigners and alleviate the conditions which had caused disorders along the border.[9] Refusing to comply, Carranza skillfully waived aside these proposals.

As negotiations dragged on, Carranza determined that he could not afford to permit Pershing to remain in Mexico indefinitely until Villa was apprehended. In order to force the U.S. troops out, Carranza decided on a military showdown that would risk war with the United States and told Pershing that American forces would no longer be permitted to move south, east, or west—only north. Military incidents ensued, but both sides used restraint and escalation was avoided. Meanwhile, in the face of Carranza's intransigent opposition to foreign interference, Wilson gave up his demand for an agreement to protect foreign interests in Mexico, and Pershing was ordered to withdraw. The evacuation was completed on February 5, 1917. Tensions between Wilson and Carranza over the Pershing expedition sometimes obscured the fact that Pershing's troops were directed against Carranza's major remaining rival.

Wilson's preference for and support of Carranza was also reflected in the U.S. government's meager relations with Emiliano Zapata, the leader and symbol of the agrarian revolution. Special agents of the United States met with Zapata from time to time, primarily to encourage him to reach peaceful agreement with rival revolutionary factions. In April through August 1914, for example, the United States attempted to mediate between Zapata and Carranza, hoping for a settlement under Carranza's leadership.[10] By May 1915 President Wilson expressed satisfaction with a report from his representative in Mexico, Duval West, who characterized Zapata as wielding "enormous power" over the peons of Morelos, but predicted that his influence would eventually be narrowed to his own region.[11]

During Carranza's most difficult struggle and in spite of his intransigence toward U.S. meddling, the Wilson administration actively opposed Carranza's most dangerous opponents, Huerta and Villa, gave no comfort to another rival, Emiliano Zapata, and permitted Carranza access to arms in the United States.

Wilson, Germany, and Mexico (1914–1917)

Woodrow Wilson's response to the Mexican Revolution, described above almost solely in terms of U.S.–Mexican relations, does not include one of the most important elements that helps to explain his actions, namely imperial Germany and World War I. In fact, Woodrow Wilson's calculations about U.S. interests with regard to the war and relations with the Central Powers appear to have been the decisive elements in many of his decisions regarding Mexico.

Wilson's activist policy against Huerta and his approval of the Veracruz landing occurred before war broke out in Europe in August 1914. Once it became clear to Wilson that deeper military involvements in Mexico would carry a bloody price and be a military liability in the face of conflict in Europe, he sought to terminate the Veracruz occupation. Note that the Veracruz landing took place several months before Britain and France were at war and was terminated in November 1914 after the major conflict was joined.

Similarly, fear of Germany played an important part in U.S. de facto recognition of Carranza on October 19, 1915. The activities of German agents in Mexico, attempting to cause strife between the neighboring countries, had been called to Wilson's and Lansing's attention. On October 10, 1915, for example, Lansing's diary entry suggested that the European war was having a decisive influence on Mexican policy:

> Obregón and the other military leaders of Carranza's factions are strongly anti-American and very friendly with the Germans.
>
> There is no doubt, however, in my own mind as to the policy which [we] should pursue for a time at least and that is *not to intervene to restore order in Mexico*. We must try to keep on good terms with Carranza and give him financial aid. We must send an ambassador to Mexico as soon as improved conditions give a shadow of an excuse. We must keep a close watch on German agents in Mexico and along the border and prevent them if possible from causing further revolution and unrest. . . .
>
> Looking at the general situation I have come to the following conclusions:
>
> Germany desires to keep up the turmoil in Mexico until the United States is forced to intervene; *therefore, we must not intervene*.
>
> Germany does not wish to have any one faction dominant in Mexico; *therefore, we must recognize one faction as dominant in Mexico*.
>
> When we recognize a faction as the government, Germany will undoubtedly seek to cause a quarrel between that government and ours; *therefore we must avoid a quarrel regardless of criticism and complaint in Congress and the press*.
>
> It comes down to this: Our possible relations with Germany must be our first consideration; and all our intercourse with Mexico must be regulated accordingly.[12]

The Wilson administration feared that military conflict with Mexico would tie U.S. hands with regard to Europe or possibly place the United States in the impossible position of fighting on two fronts simultaneously. Secretary Lansing had already identified Germany as the principal enemy and was much concerned about German intrigue in Mexico. The intensity and single-mindedness with which Secretary Lansing sought Carranza's recognition at the Pan American Conference in the fall of

1915 is explicable largely in terms of his intense desire to protect vital U.S. interests, namely security for the U.S. southern flank while facing a Europe torn by war.[13]

One of the repercussions of Wilson's recognition of Carranza and the embargo on arms to all other Mexican factions was Pancho Villa's physical attacks on Americans in Mexico and in the Southwest United States in the winter of 1915–1916. These attacks were an extreme form of provocation which Wilson dared not ignore. Note that General Pershing entered Mexico to pursue Villa before the United States became involved in the war against the Central Powers and, incidentally, in response to domestic political pressures in the presidential campaign of 1916.

Wilson revealed some of the main lines of his thinking regarding Germany in his effort to deflect the urgings of his close adviser, Joseph P. Tumulty, to take a stronger line against both Villa and Carranza. In a conversation with Tumulty in June 1916, Wilson described his determination to avoid the horrors of war and his unwillingness to pick on "poor Mexico, with its pitiful men, women and children fighting to gain a foothold in their own land."

> Tumulty, some day the people of America will know why I hesitated to intervene in Mexico. I cannot tell them now for we are at peace with the great power whose poisonous propaganda is responsible for the present terrible condition of affairs in Mexico. German propagandists are there now, fomenting strife and trouble between our countries. Germany is anxious to have us at war with Mexico, so that our minds and our energies will be taken off the great war across the sea. She wishes an uninterrupted opportunity to carry on her submarine warfare and believes that war with Mexico will keep our hands off her and thus give her liberty of action to do as she pleases on the high seas. It begins to look as if war with Germany is inevitable. If it should come—I pray God it may not—I do not wish America's energies and forces divided, for we will need every ounce of reserve we have to lick Germany. Tumulty, we must try patience a little longer and await the development of the whole plot in Mexico.[14]

As the United States moved closer to war in the winter of 1916–1917, Woodrow Wilson was forced to reconsider his determination to exact commitments from Carranza about the treatment of foreign interests in Mexico and the maintenance of public order along the border as the price for withdrawal of U.S. troops. By January 1917 Wilson appeared to have given up hope of such an agreement, deciding to withdraw Pershing's forces without it. Lansing later said that the controlling reason for the president's decision to withdraw was his determination not to run any risks of military involvement so long as there was any serious possibility of war with Germany.[15] It may be more than mere coincidence that Woodrow Wilson announced the break in diplomatic relations with Germany on February 3, 1917, and that Pershing's last troops left Mexico two days later.

Meanwhile, the new Mexican constitution drawn up at Querétaro aroused the fears of important U.S. mining and oil interests. Article 27 invested the state with rights to subsoil resources, and there were other provisions adversely affecting U.S.-owned properties. An influential committee representing U.S. interests retained the attorney Chandler P. Anderson to put pressure on the administration. Anderson sought to make U.S. recognition of Carranza contingent on Mexican treaty commitments to protect foreign owners from the retroactive application of Article 27 and from other discriminatory provisions in the constitution. Wilson was unwilling to require treaty guarantees about U.S. property from the Mexican government, believing that the Mexicans had to work these problems out for themselves.[16] Moreover, he was opposed to imperiling relations with Mexico at the approach of war with Germany. The U.S. committee was informed that Wilson believed that cordiality toward Carranza, including recognition, was the only way to prevent him from surrendering to German influences.[17] After the new constitution had been put into effect and Carranza elected president, Wilson formally received his representative in Washington in April and recognized Carranza de jure in August 1917. In this way, Wilson subordinated U.S. private interests in Mexico to broader national interests by maintaining friendly relations with Mexico in the face of a European conflict.

Mexico and Germany (1914–1918)

The relations of Carranza's revolutionary government with the United States can be understood fully only if its relations with Germany are also taken into account. Germany's orientation to the Mexican Revolution was almost the antithesis of Woodrow Wilson's. Whereas President Wilson regretted the involvement of Ambassador Henry Lane Wilson in Madero's overthrow, the German government supported the participation of the German minister, Paul von Hintze, in the conspiracy against Madero. And, in fact, it was Hintze who favored Huerta as Madero's successor, not General Félix Díaz, the American ambassador's candidate. Germany recognized Huerta in the middle of 1913 and became one of his major foreign collaborators.[18] Germany, too, had been an early critic of Wilson's strictures about Huerta's arbitrary political tactics, considering Huerta the alternative to anarchy in Mexico.[19] When Huerta decided to resign as president and go into exile, he selected a German warship, the *Dresden*, to carry him away.

Meanwhile, World War I had broken out in Europe and Germany sought by all means possible to reduce or eliminate arms deliveries from the United States to Germany's enemies.[20] To this end, a member of the German intelligence service, Franz Rintelen von Kleist, was sent to the United States in March 1915 to undertake sabotage and other clandestine activities. In analyzing the situation, Rintelen had concluded that "the only country the [United States] had to fear was Mexico. If Mexico attacked her she would need all the munitions she could manufacture, and would be unable to export any to Europe."[21]

Now that Huerta was in exile and sought to overthrow Carranza, Rintelen calculated that Huerta's designs could be put to Germany's service. Huerta arrived in New York shortly after Rintelen, and Rintelen persuaded him that they work together. According to Rintelen, their agreement of April 1915 was that "German U-boats were to land weapons along the Mexican coast; abundant funds were to be provided for the purchase of armaments; and Germany should agree to furnish Mexico with moral support. In that eventuality, Mexico would take up arms against the United States."[22]

With German help, Huerta proceeded to organize in the United States a large and well-armed force to reenter Mexico and overthrow Carranza. Most authors agree that Germany assisted Huerta with arms, money, or both though, like other clandestine operations, evidence is hard to find.[23]

Unsuccessfully seeking to deceive and evade the U.S. authorities, Huerta traveled to Newman, New Mexico, to meet Pascual Orozco, Jr., to prepare to cross the border on June 28, 1915. Large numbers of officers and men favoring Huerta were present on both sides of the border, as were caches of arms and munitions. Huerta's plans for an armed revolt against Carranza seemed clear but proving his intent in court would not have been easy. Nonetheless, two federal marshals and a concealed detachment of cavalrymen arrested Orozco and Huerta the moment they met in Newman. Huerta and Orozco were charged with conspiracy to violate the neutrality laws. During the legal maneuvers that followed, Orozco escaped his captors. Faced with President Wilson's determination not to permit him to return to Mexico, Huerta did not secure freedom until it was too late. He died of cirrhosis of the liver some six months later in January 1916, not having yet been brought to trial. Thus, prompt action by the U.S. authorities against Huerta nipped in the bud one of the two remaining threats to the new Carranza government.

Another source of disturbance along the border was an alleged plan of Mexican-Americans and Mexicans to launch a revolt in the Southwest and restore to Mexico the territories lost to the United States in 1948. Launched under the name of the Plan de San Diego, the movement appears to have been an effort to divert attention from the proposed Huerta-Orozco invasion. Germans may have backed that diversion, too. The manifesto's call for Mexico's reincorporation of its lost territories appears to have been part of a chain of events leading to the inclusion of this provision in the famous Zimmermann telegram of January 1917 to Mexico.[24]

As Huerta's life and his connections with the Germans were drawing to a tragic close, official German interest was shifting to others, this time to the disgruntled revolutionary general, Francisco Villa. Here again the German rationale was that U.S. intervention or conflict with Mexico would hamper arms deliveries to the Western Allies and hence have greater utility for Germany than sabotage.

Felix A. Sommerfeld, a Villa representative in the United States, proposed to the German propaganda agent in the United States, Bernhard Dernberg, that it would be easy to cause a U.S. intervention in Mexico. Dernberg asked for instructions and was informed by the foreign office that it favored such action as being in Germany's "best interests."[25] Friedrich Katz, who has made an exhaustive search, did not find proof in the German archives that Germany supplied arms or money to Villa before the Columbus raid. Nonetheless, he considers it probable that the German government participated in some way in support of Villa's attack on Columbus, New Mexico, on March 9, 1916. An American historian believes Sommerfeld may have instigated the Columbus raid through Dr. Lyman B. Rauschbaum, a pro-German immigrant and Villa's personal physician and adviser.[26]

The German imperial government welcomed the Punitive Expedition against Villa in Mexico, and Ambassador Bernstorff reported from Washington that, as long as the United States was tied down there, Germany was "rather secure from the aggressive action of the American government."[27] Wilson and Lansing, for their part, interpreted German interests in the same way, namely that Germany sought conflict between the United States and Mexico. As president and secretary of state, they decided to do all in their power to prevent or eliminate such involvements.[28]

Until 1916 German diplomatic and intelligence services had devoted their energies to the support of Carranza's opponents, first Huerta and then Villa, for the purpose of fanning a conflict between Mexico and the United States. Huerta's failure to return to Mexico and Villa's political and military defeats no longer made either leader a suitable pawn for German intrigue. The German minister in Mexico did not think highly of Carranza who, in spite of his declaration of neutrality, was favorably disposed toward the Allies during the early years of World War I. Aware of German support of Huerta, his enemy of the old regime, and Villa, his revolutionary rival, Carranza viewed Germany coolly until 1916. Pershing's march into Mexico radically changed Carranza's relations with both the United States and Germany.

Pershing's expedition against Pancho Villa was interpreted by Carranza as a violation of Mexican sovereignty and caused him to reappraise relations with Germany, the latter now the most effective counterweight to U.S. domination. In October 1916, for example, Mexico inquired whether Germany would inform the United States that it would not look favorably on a U.S. attack on Mexico—a naive request since Germany hoped the United States would become thus involved. In exchange for German pressure on the United States, Mexico offered to provide help to German submarines. Germany pursued this possibility through its agents there, but Katz has found no evidence that submarine bases ever became operable.[29] The Mexicans climaxed their approaches with a comprehensive memorandum of November 1916 calling for economic and military collaboration. The latter suggested German provision of arms, munitions, submarines, and military instructors to the Mexican forces. Germany received the proposals cautiously fearing that public knowledge of the German-Mexican rapprochement might lead to an increase of German-American tensions without increasing prospects of war between Mexico and the United States.[30]

Early in 1917, after Germany had decided to resume unrestricted submarine warfare and run the risk of U.S. entry into the war, the German Foreign Office took a fresh look at Mexican overtures of the previous fall. The Mexican feelers for economic and military collaboration and hints of possible submarine bases emboldened the foreign minister, Arthur Zimmermann, to propose an alliance to Mexico. The notorious Zimmermann telegram of January 15, 1917, ordered the German minister in Mexico, if the United States did not remain neutral, to propose to Mexico an alliance upon the following terms: Joint conduct of war. Joint conclusion of peace. Ample financial support and an agreement on our part that Mexico shall gain back by conquest the territory lost by her at a prior period in Texas, New Mexico, and Arizona . . . and the suggestion that Japan be requested to take part at once and that he [Carranza] simultaneously mediate between ourselves and Japan.[31]

The march of events made Zimmermann impatient, and on February 5 he sent the following orders to the German legation in Mexico:

Provided that there is no risk of the secret being betrayed to the United States, will Your Excellency take up the alliance question even now with the President. At the same time, the definite conclusion of the alliance depends upon the outbreak of the war between Germany and the United States. The President might even now throw out feelers to Japan.

If the President were to reject our proposal through fear of later American vengeance, you are empowered to offer a defensive alliance after peace is concluded, provided Mexico succeeds in including Japan in the Alliance.[32]

Zimmermann did not believe the Mexicans would be able to reconquer Texas, New Mexico, and Arizona, and his major purpose, explicitly admitted later, was to cause the United States to send troops to Mexico and not to Europe. Similarly, having little hope that Japan would join in a tripartite alliance, Mexico's good offices were being sought mainly to renew contact with Japan, difficult to reestablish directly.[33] Hardly made in good faith, Zimmermann's proposal was a deceptive maneuver designed to fan conflict between Mexico and the United States.

Meanwhile as U.S. tensions with Germany approached a climax, and in the face of Carranza's unwillingness to compromise about U.S. involvement in Mexican "internal affairs," President Wilson decided to withdraw Pershing's forces unconditionally. So as not to encourage Mexico to fall under German influence, the Wilson administration ordered Pershing out of Mexico and the last troops left the country on February 5, 1917. Pershing's departure relieved the pressure on Carranza and strengthened his hand in dealings with the Germans. German Minister von Eckhardt presented Zimmermann's proposal to Foreign Minister Aguilar on February 20, 1917.

Aguilar took note of the proposal, and Eckhardt reported on his conversation as follows:

A visit to the President at Querétaro was inopportune so I took the opportunity of a short visit here of the Minister of Foreign Affairs on the 20th of February of sounding him. He willingly took the matter into consideration, and thereupon had a conversation, which lasted an hour and a half, with Japanese Minister, the tenor of which is unknown to me. He subsequently went away to see the President where he was staying at the time.[34]

Shortly before his death, Aguilar reportedly told a colleague that he, Aguilar, had welcomed the proposal but that Carranza had spoken against it, urging, however, that no definite refusal be made.[35] According to another account, Carranza's military advisers doubted that Germany had the capacity to provide much useful military assistance and considered the Mexican reconquest of Texas, Arizona, and New Mexico not feasible. Other accounts are to the effect that Obregón also strongly opposed acceptance of the German offer and believed that the salvation of Mexico lay with the United States.[36] Postponing a definitive reply, Carranza appears to have inquired what sort of help by way of arms, munitions, and financial assistance the Germans could provide.[37]

Meanwhile, British intelligence, possessing the German code, had intercepted, decoded, and transmitted the text of Zimmermann's message to President Wilson. The latter had instructed Ambassador Fletcher on February 26, 1917, to inform the Mexican government of the contents of the Zimmermann telegram. He was also to tell the Mexicans that the contents would be made public shortly, offering them an opportunity to comment. Unable to reach President Carranza, Fletcher read the substance of the note to Foreign Minister Aguilar. The latter, in spite of his conversation with Eckhardt six days earlier, denied having "any knowledge of any representations of the character referred to" and said that "if such representations were made they must have been made directly to Carranza."[38] Fletcher spent several days with Carranza early in March and on his return to Mexico City reported Carranza's reaction to his inquiries about the Zimmermann telegram:

> He was very cautious. He said that Mexico had not received up to the present time from Germany any proposition whatever of an alliance; that for his part his sincere desire was that war should not come to this side of the Atlantic. . . . In answer to my direct question as to his attitude in case Germany should propose an alliance, he said that Mexico desires to avoid becoming involved in the war and again referred to his note [peace note of February 11, 1917], but he avoided saying directly that such a proposition would be rejected. Personally, I do not think Mexico would under circumstances accept alliance referred to. . . . I gathered that their sentiments inclined somewhat toward Germany.[39]

Carranza clearly avoided committing himself not to accept a German proposal, saying as little about it as possible.

Dissatisfied with Carranza's noncommittal response, Fletcher sent for Carranza's consideration a draft memorandum which concluded with the statement that Mexico would reject any German proposal for an alliance. Carranza struck out that part of the draft and referred again to his peace proposal, including an embargo on arms to belligerents.[40] General Alvaro Obregón, minister of war, was more outspoken in a conversation after the Zimmermann telegram was published. According to Fletcher, Obregón called the proposed alliance with Germany "absurd," that after six years of civil war Mexico should devote herself to pacification and reorganization and would be "stupid" to become entangled with a European power.[41]

As the prospect of a U.S. invasion dimmed, Carranza decided to turn the Zimmermann proposal down and so informed Eckhardt on April 14. The Zimmermann proposal, it will be recalled, was to take effect if the United States no longer remained neutral. The United States declared war on Germany early in April, and Eckhardt reported to Zimmermann that Carranza

> declared that he intends in all circumstances to remain neutral. If Mexico were nevertheless drawn in the war, we must see. The Alliance, he said, had been stultified by its premature "publication" but would become necessary at a later period. As regards munitions—Mauser 7mm—and money, he will answer after obtaining full powers from Congress, and he has the sole power of decision in his hands.
>
> Congress is dominated by the pro-German military party.[42]

During the balance of the war, Carranza's overriding aim was to stay out of the conflict and avoid further U.S. armed intervention in Mexico. Now that U.S. troops were out of Mexico, Carranza considered the need to woo Germany less urgent. So as not to jeopardize Mexico's neutral status, Carranza was careful not to be drawn into an alliance with Germany, his refusal of the Zimmermann proposal shortly after the U.S. entry into the war being his most important action in this respect. In fact, Carranza's central concern in relations with Germany was the avoidance of any development which might serve as a pretext for U.S. intervention.

Carranza, for example, did not reopen his proposals to Germany made in the fall of 1916 when the threat of war between Mexico and the United States was at its height. There is no record that he renewed his offer to Germany regarding submarines or responded to Germany's welcoming reply on that subject. (The German minister reported later that preparation had gone forward to support German submarines and that the submarines never came to Mexico. Professor Katz believes preparations probably went forward without Carranza's knowledge or against his wishes.)[43]

Earlier Carranza had brusquely waived aside a German proposal that Mexico's neutrality required an embargo on oil supplies to the Western Allies.[44] And Mexico continued to supply oil to them during the war. Carranza was adamant that the Germans should not sabotage the Tampico oil fields. In the first place, the Mexican government relied heavily on oil production for tax revenues, and the impact of sabotage on the economy would have been damaging, too. More important, Carranza feared, no doubt correctly, that German sabotage would cause the Western Allies to send troops into Mexico. An indication that Carranza's fears were justified was the temporary assignment of some six thousand U.S. Marines to Galveston, Texas, in response to reports of impending German sabotage against these fields.[45]

The continued possibility of U.S. armed action against Mexico caused Carranza to leave the door wide open to German advances. Carranza needed potential allies in the event of an attack from the United States. England and France would hardly do; they were too dependent on U.S. help in Europe. Mexico might have preferred Japan, but the latter was unwilling to jeopardize its important interests in the Far East by an entanglement with Mexico and resulting friction with the United States. Thus, Mexico viewed Germany as the principal counterweight to possible U.S. armed action during the war and U.S. domination in the postwar period.

Mexico looked to Germany for arms and munitions. And Germany complied, though by procurement in South America not from Germany.[46] Mexico also wanted a long-term loan, preferably from the United States because its financial capacity held greater promise, but money from Germany was welcome too. During the balance of the war, negotiations went forward simultaneously with both countries, playing one off against the other. Both sets of negotiations came to naught. Mexico refused to accept breaking relations with Germany as a condition of a loan from the United States.[47] And the Germans, for their part, decided against such a loan, partly because of technical difficulties resulting from the war, partly because Mexico could not offer enough in return.[48]

While Carranza skillfully avoided U.S. armed intervention, his government's relations were probably closer to Germany than to the United States and the other Western Allies. The two powers exchanged intelligence information and collaborated on radio installations; anti-Allied and pro-German propaganda was permitted by the Carranza government.[49] Germany was popular among many groups in the army and the government where the memory of U.S. interventions was still fresh. In addition, Germany was less associated in the public mind with "imperialism." As the capital of a neutral country neighboring the United States, Mexico City became a world center of espionage and intrigue comparable in some ways to Lisbon and Buenos Aires during World War II.

Germany had been cautious about involvements with Mexico before the United States joined the war—not wanting to encourage the latter to come in. Once the United States was a belligerent, however, the German government assumed the initiative in relations with Carranza. The dominant theme of German policy was, at a minimum, to keep Mexico neutral in favor of Germany and, still better, to draw Mexico into the war on the side of the Central Powers. The desirability of remaining on good terms with the Carranza government, however, limited Germany's freedom of action regarding clandestine operations in Mexico and military actions against the United States launched from Mexico.

Germany used Mexico as a major base for espionage, counterespionage, sabotage, and psychological warfare for the United States, Central America, and the Far East. There is, however, little evidence that these operations were successful, partly because they could be monitored by the Western Allies who had broken the German code. Perhaps the two most important questions with regard to U.S.–Mexican relations was the possible German sabotage of the Tampico oil fields and the use of Mexican bases to support German submarines.

In the face of Mexican opposition, the Germans ultimately decided not to sabotage the oil fields. One reason was that such action if traced to its source—a not unlikely prospect—would have ruined relations with the Mexicans for the balance of the war and prospects for German influence in Mexico thereafter. Moreover, such action would have eliminated the possibility of Mexico joining Germany against the Allies. In spite of the German military's wish to knock out Mexican oil sources, the German Foreign Office held German saboteurs in Mexico in check. The Foreign Office instructed Minister Eckhardt, who opposed sabotage, not to authorize such actions which would "endanger relations with Mexico."[50]

German agents also had apparently completed preparations to provide logistic support for German submarines from one or more bases on the Gulf of Mexico. Germany declined however, in a decision made by the emperor personally, to undertake military actions in the Gulf of Mexico for fear of endangering sources of supply in Latin America and friendly relations there.[51]

Incidentally, German policy toward Mexico had wider regional implications. The two powers worked together during the war in the establishment of an anti-American bloc of Latin American countries who stayed neutral during the conflict and were not unfriendly to Germany. Mexico was a leader of this group which also included Colombia, Argentina, and Chile.

Carranza performed a skillful balancing act throughout World War I, a crucial period during which he consolidated his own power and the revolution in Mexico. By adroit maneuvering he was able to play the two powers off, one against the other, so that neither came to dominate Mexico, and Mexicans remained the masters in their own house.

Wilson's involvements in European problems both before and after the U.S. entry into the war caused him to stay his hand in Mexico; fear that involvement in Mexico would deny him freedom of action in Europe caused him to compromise time and again with the Mexicans. Were it not for the war, the speculation seems justified that Wilson would have meddled far more in the revolution than was actually the case, and his interventions—even with the war—were by no means minor. His European interests and commitments did not permit him to protect U.S. interests along the border or in Mexico as much as he would have liked nor to provide his own moral leadership, however well intentioned and misguided, of that revolution.

Carranza's intransigence, on the one hand, with regard to Wilson's interference, and his willingness to deal with Germany, on the other, proved enormously successful. He kept U.S. forces out of Mexico after Pershing's withdrawal. He was able to capitalize on his ties with Germany while not provoking intervention from the Allies. Carranza's concessions to the Germans regarding intelligence operations and propaganda gave credibility to German hopes about drawing Mexico into the European war. One of the richest fruits of his policy was that the Germans decided not to sabotage the Mexican oil fields for fear of damaging their relations with Mexico.

German policy failed to make Mexico an ally, but did keep her neutral. This was no great achievement since Carranza was determined to stay neutral anyway. German intelligence and propaganda activities accomplished little for the Central Powers and brought Germany no significant military advantages.

In the end, the United States was an incidental beneficiary of Carranza's policies. As a neutral, Mexico supplied the Allied war effort, especially with oil. Uncertainty did require the United States to retain troops near the border; otherwise, German activities in Mexico appear to have caused little harm to the U.S. war effort.

Claims and Oil, Credits and Arms (1920–1924)

The Allied victory over the Central Powers removed the threat of German influence in Mexico which had made an accommodation with the dominant revolutionary groups seem so urgent to Wilson during World War I. Now the United States was free of concern for her own security in dealing with Mexico, particularly as that security had involved hostile European powers. And Mexico, for her part, was no longer able to play Germany off against her northern neighbor. Both powers were faced with the challenge of coming to terms within a more circumscribed bilateral relationship. Declining risks and opportunities in foreign affairs were accompanied by greater attention to domestic problems in both countries: the return to normalcy and private industrial development in the United States, pacification and reconstruction after the civil war in Mexico.

Reorientation of national goals and policies in a postwar setting marked the emergence of new leadership in both countries. Carranza's unwillingness to let his grasp of the country end with the end of his presidential term provoked armed opposition. He was assassinated in 1920 while fleeing the country. Alvaro Obregón succeeded to the presidency at the end of the year. Meanwhile, Woodrow Wilson had fallen ill during his campaign for the League of Nations and was succeeded after the 1920 presidential elections by Warren Harding. Wilson left office without having recognized either the interim or the Obregón governments. Harding's secretary of state, Charles Evans Hughes, took full charge of foreign policy in general and policy toward Mexico in particular.

The pending question of U.S. recognition of the Obregón government hung on a series of problems in the relations between the two countries. Some questions, such as the claims between citizens of the two countries between 1868 (the date of the last general settlement) and 1910, had nothing to do with the revolution at all. Other problems, such as claims for property and other damages after 1910, were occasioned by the revolutionary upheaval and the civil war. Finally, revolutionary change itself was taking place in the new social order under the aegis of the Constitution of 1917. That order, by reasserting the nation's control over Mexican natural resources in the soil and subsoil, posed a threat to U.S.-owned agricultural, mining, and petroleum properties in Mexico.

The new administration was more friendly to private business interests than the old. Secretary Hughes believed that the fundamental question with regard to Mexico was "the safeguarding of property rights against confiscation."[52] He made security for legitimately acquired property rights and interests, including the nonretroactive application of Article 27 of the 1917 constitution, a condition for U.S. recognition. Oral or even written assurances of a general sort on those points would not satisfy the secretary. One reason was that former President Carranza, shortly after assuring the United States that he would neither take over nor confiscate U.S. oil properties,[53] levied taxes which the oil companies believed excessive and required them to apply to the government for drilling permits. Hughes did not want the U.S. government to rely again on such oral assurances, which in any case were unlikely to be considered binding on successive Mexican governments. As a condition of recognition, he insisted that the assurances he sought be embodied in a formal treaty of amity and commerce.[54] Hughes ordered the U.S. chargé d'affaires in Mexico City not to attend Obregón's inauguration and formally withheld U.S. recognition.

Recognition meant far more to Obregón than a diplomatic formality. His government feared failure in solving budgetary problems and promoting economic development without a long-term foreign loan. Already under Carranza, leading New York and other bankers had refused to extend credit to Mexico nor did the U.S. government favor it.[55] Obregón was unlikely to secure needed arms from abroad for defense against domestic enemies without recognition. In short, the nation's economic welfare and internal security depended on recognition. Obregón knew from long experience that it was dangerous for any country as small and divided as Mexico not to normalize its relations with a country as large, near, and powerful as the United States. United States help to Obregón's domestic enemies, for example, could prove fatal. Since 1910 Mexico had been beset with intermittent civil war, the authority of each successive government being tested one or more times by armed revolt. To protect their very lives, Mexican leaders needed friendly relations with the United States.

Obregón's only hope of securing long-term loans depended on his coming to terms with Mexico's creditors; foreign sources of capital could hardly be expected to make capital available to him in light of Mexico's financial record. The Mexican government had ceased payments of interest on the national debt in 1912. Obregón did not believe payments on that debt could be resumed without large foreign credits. In a sense, he was caught in a vicious circle.

Obregón sought to break out of that circle by a decree announced June 7, 1921, levying an export tax of 25 percent on all petroleum and petroleum products. Petroleum was the nation's most valuable natural resource, production of which was at historic highs.[56] He explicitly linked expected revenues from the tax to the resumption of payments on the foreign debt. Thus Obregón hoped to restore faith in Mexico's credit and lay the basis for long-term loans.

With resources for resuming payments on the foreign debt assured, Obregón sent his finance minister, Adolfo de la Huerta, to meet with an international banking committee headed by Thomas W. Lamont of the J. P. Morgan Company. After weeks of negotiations, the parties drew up the so-called Lamont–de la Huerta agreement of June 16, 1922. The agreement provided that Mexico recognize a debt of approximately one billion pesos ($500 million) in bonds and securities issued before 1910, and in addition, accept a railway debt of over 500 million pesos. Also, Mexico acknowledged interest payments in arrears of 400 million pesos, and a schedule of repayments was established. As security for these payments, Mexico agreed to turn over to the International Committee of Bankers the export taxes on petroleum and proceeds from a tax to be levied on revenues from the Mexican railway system.[57]

De la Huerta hoped that as a result of this agreement, foreign bankers would extend long-term loans to Mexico. Achievement of this objective, however, was frustrated by the Department of State. President Harding insisted as a matter of public policy that his government be consulted in advance on any loans to Mexico. The Department of State informed the U.S. chargé d'affaires in Mexico in September 1921 that it would not approve any loan by American bankers to a government which had not been recognized by the United States.[58] Thus, the foreign bankers refused to discuss a loan to Mexico until after U.S. recognition had been secured. At first Obregón hesitated to approve the agreement in the absence of any commitments about loans. After some weeks delay, Obregón decided to go ahead anyway and the agreement was ratified by the Mexican congress and promulgated in September 1922.[59]

Meanwhile, pressure was building up both in Mexico and the United States in favor of a normalization of relations. The absence of recognition was crippling the Obregón government economically and politically. The U.S. interests holding property in Mexico were hurt by the repercussions of nonrecognition and urged their government to come to terms with Mexico. Representatives of the two powers met in Mexico City and drew up the Bucareli agreements in August 1923. As described in chapter 4, these agreements involved compromises over the protection of U.S. property interests and claims settlements that Secretary Hughes considered a necessary precondition of diplomatic recognition. Mexico assured the United States that specified oil properties would not be subject to the retroactive application of constitutional provisions on subsoil rights, that compensation would be provided for expropriated properties (in bonds, not in cash as the United States had initially sought), and that claims between the two governments would be settled by claims commissions. With these assurances in hand, the United States recognized Obregón on September 3, 1923.

Hope for long-term loans was not, of course, the only reason that Obregón had pressed ahead toward the accommodation with the United States reached in the Bucareli agreements. Obregón needed a reliable source of arms and munitions, the United States being both the best and the nearest. He could not, however, count on the United States for this purpose without a general political settlement symbolized by recognition.

The experience of his predecessors, most recently Carranza, was instructive with respect to arms procurement in the United States. In the latter part of 1919, U.S. relations with the Carranza government deteriorated badly. Carranza's 1918 decree restricting the operation of foreign industrial enterprises in Mexico, especially oil, provoked the hostility of influential groups in the United States who, under the leadership of such politically powerful figures as Senator Albert Fall, favored strong measures—even intervention—against Mexico. The kidnapping and arrest of the American consular agent, W. O. Jenkins, at Puebla became a cause célèbre which led to further escalation of the tension. American public opinion also looked back resentfully at Mexico's ties with Germany during the European war.

Under authority granted by Congress, the president was empowered to prohibit the export of arms and munition to Mexico, as well as to other countries. However, the secretary of state was authorized by the president to make exceptions to any such embargo. The U.S. executive thereby had a most flexible weapon to deal with established governments or revolutionary movements in Mexico.[60] Since July 7, 1919, the secretary of state had refused official Mexican requests time and again to license the export of war material to Mexico. This embargo remained in effect throughout the balance of Carranza's presidency and no doubt contributed to his political vulnerability and overthrow. After Alvaro Obregón's election to the presidency in September 1920, the embargo was relaxed slightly to permit the export of moderate quantities of small arms and ammunition. Another reason for the relaxation may have been complaints from American manufacturers that they were losing the Mexican market to European firms.

The embargo on heavy arms, such as automatic rifles, machine guns, and artillery, remained in effect for more than a year into Obregón's term and was lifted on January 31, 1922. The revocation was the result of congressional action repealing legislation from 1912 which had served as a basis for the embargo on Mexico. The repeal was a reflection of congressional views regarding arms exports in general rather than the Mexican situation in particular. Under the new 1922 legislation, the Department of State had authority to reimpose the embargo, but if it did not take affirmative action, the earlier prohibition automatically lapsed.

The politically significant development was that the Department of State inquired if the Mexican government wished to have the embargo continued. The question arises why Washington continued to maintain ecomomic pressures on Obregón while indicating willingness to relax the arms embargo. One reason was that American manufacturers of munitions, including the DuPont interests, had wanted to make sales to Mexico.[61] It appears as though President Harding decided to consult the Mexicans on the matter because negotiations leading toward recognition were proceeding favorably. When the Mexicans replied that the embargo need not be continued, the Harding administration let it lapse.[62]

In any case, the significance of Carranza's earlier experience was not lost on Obregón. Nor did the Department of State's solicitous inquiry blind him to the fact that what the department was capable of suspending, it was capable of reimposing.

Not long after the Bucareli agreements were signed, Obregón had an opportunity to test whether the accommodation with the United States would pay off as he had hoped. In December 1923 the former interim president and Obregón's one-time finance minister, Adolfo de la Huerta, launched an armed revolt against the Obregón government. The latter government requested military assistance from the United States and thereafter bought rifles, pistols, machine guns, ammunition, replacement parts for weapons, bombs, and airplanes from the War Department.[63] In the meantime, on January 7, 1924, Secretary Hughes imposed an arms embargo on Mexico, with exports to Obregón a purposely admissible exception. Thus, the Coolidge administration was deliberately discriminating against the de la Huerta forces in favor of the recognized Obregón government. As Secretary Hughes explained to the Council on Foreign Relations on January 23, 1924:

> Under General Obregón's administration there was a restoration of stability; commerce and industry began to regain confidence; there was a hopeful endeavor to put the finances of the country on a better footing; provision was made for the payment of the foreign debt. . . . this Government was glad to recognize the [Obregón] Government. . . . Two claims conventions were at once concluded . . . Diplomatic relations were resumed. . . .
> . . . suddenly there was an attempt to overthrow the established Government of Mexico by violence. . . .
> . . . the established Mexican Government asked the Government of the United States to sell to it a limited quantity of arms and munitions. . . . This government had the arms and munitions close at hand; it did not need them and could sell them if it wished. If the request had been denied, we should have turned a cold shoulder to the government with which we had recently established friendly relations and . . . have given powerful encouragement to those who were attempting to seize the reins of government by force.[64]

In addition to the arms sales, the United States helped Obregón by permitting him to transport troops and equipment across adjacent U.S. territory, by sending warships to patrol the Gulf coast of Mexico, and by protesting the rebels' closure of certain Mexican ports.[65] Hughes' policies received widespread support in political circles as well as in the public at large. In the end, Obregón's policy of seeking reconciliation with the United States paid off handsomely in putting down de la Huerta's rebellion. The movement collapsed and de la Huerta escaped into exile.

Obregón's hopes for long-term loans, however, were not fulfilled after recognition in 1923. In fact, continuing fiscal difficulties, the adverse effect of the de la Huerta rebellion on the economy, and declining petroleum output led to the suspension of the Lamont–de la Huerta agreement of 1922, and thus once again to the suspension of payments on the foreign debt. In those years the much-hoped-for foreign loans did not materialize.[66]

The cordiality that marked U.S.–Mexican relations at the end of Hughes' term as secretary of state was rapidly lost soon after Obregón's successor, Plutarco Elías Calles, became president. The security of the titles of foreign-owned oil properties was challenged once again and Calles' anticlerical policies evoked hostility in the United States, particularly among Roman Catholics. The astute diplomacy of U.S.

Ambassador Dwight W. Morrow led to a resolution of most of these differences, and relations between these two countries returned to normal channels.[67]

In the early 1930s both countries focused their attention inward to cope with the devastating impact of the worldwide depression.[68]

The Oil Expropriations

The climactic moment in the response of the United States to revolutionary change in Mexico did not come until the presidency of Lázaro Cárdenas more than a quarter century after the revolution had broken out. By that time the two countries had accumulated experience in resolving thorny issues between them.

In 1934, for example, before Cárdenas became president, the two countries settled one of the most vexatious and emotion-laden issues in their mutual relations. The special claims commission to settle claims arising out of damages suffered during the revolutionary violence in Mexico from 1910 to 1920 made virtually no progress for years after its establishment in 1923 and the expensive litigation dragged on and on. Meanwhile Mexico had reached settlements with the European powers providing for payments averaging 2.65 percent of the total amounts claimed. Adopting that standard, Mexico and the United States agreed in 1934 that Mexico would pay the United States in annual installments a total of about $5.5 million in full settlement of the claims.[69] Josephus Daniels, ambassador of the new Roosevelt administration who strongly favored compromise, signed the special protocol in April 1934—more than seven months before Cárdenas took office.

The ideological and personal affinities of Presidents Cárdenas and Roosevelt also provided a felicitous background for relations between the two new governments. Both leaders stood at the head of strong national movements for social reform which rejected authoritarianism of either the Left or the Right. Ambassador Daniels reported the following conversation with Cárdenas after the latter had only been in office a few months: "On Friday I spent an hour with President Cárdenas who sent messages to President Roosevelt. He admires our President very much and says he wishes he could give the New Deal of America to Mexico. He dispelled any idea that he is sympathetic to communism. He is chiefly concerned to give education to all children and land to the landless."[70] For his part, President Roosevelt time and again expressed his favorable personal disposition toward Cárdenas through friendly messages and policy decisions reflecting sympathy for the revolutionaries' objectives. The product of his views was a quiet and consistent determination to prevent U.S. intervention in Mexican affairs.

Cárdenas and Roosevelt also shared distaste for the Axis powers coupled with a friendly disposition toward France and Great Britain. Commonly held views on foreign as well as domestic policy often helped swing the balance in the disputes between their two governments.

Among the smoldering issues that continued to cloud relationships was a mountain of claims which had accumulated since 1868. These were in addition to the claims for revolutionary damages between 1910 and 1920 settled in 1934. Claims for land seizures under the Constitution of 1917 remained unsettled. Stepped-up expropriations under Cárdenas' land reform policy caused this category to mount rapidly. The ailing Mexican National Railways, in which there were large U.S. investments, were expropriated in June 1937. Negative reactions to this move were limited because holders of railroad securities already considered them of little value.

President Cárdenas' dramatic seizure of the foreign-owned oil properties in March 1938 came thus not as the first but after a long series of fresh blows against private U.S. interests in Mexico. Curiously, the oil expropriation did not arise simply as the result of an energetic application of the provisions of the Constitution of 1917 with respect to subsoil rights. Instead, the seizures arose out of the refusal of the foreign oil companies to carry out an arbitral award in a labor dispute. The expropriation sought to overcome the companies' defiance of the Mexican supreme court and prevent damages to the economy caused by a strikebound industry.

Cárdenas' action surprised and shocked not only the foreign oil companies but their governments as well. Ambassador Daniels told the Mexican foreign minister that the expropriation would prove "disastrous" to Mexico and "extremely embarrassing" to the United States.[71] He pleaded for a "less drastic" approach. In Washington, Undersecretary Sumner Welles tried to persuade the Mexicans to rescind the decree. And within a week Secretary Hull transmitted through Daniels a stiff note of protest which Daniels interpreted as an ultimatum. Daniels was much upset by the vehemence of Hull's reply and unsuccessfully tried to have it watered down. Next he pleaded for delay and then, without authority, agreed with the Mexicans that the note would be withdrawn especially in view of Cárdenas' assurances that compensation would be paid. In the meantime, Daniels avoided reporting the withdrawal to Hull and urged a moderate course on the president. Daniels' actions served to keep communications open between the two countries while stiff British protests led eventually to a break in Anglo-Mexican diplomatic relations.[72]

Hull's protest was backed by economic pressure. Under a recommendation from the Department of State, seconded by Senator Key Pittman of the Foreign Relations Committee, Secretary of the Treasury Henry Morgenthau, Jr., agreed to suspend temporarily U.S. purchases of Mexican silver, a major source of Mexico's foreign exchange. The U.S. government gave every indication of being prepared to fight hard to make the Mexicans back down.

The decisive underlying factor in the dispute was its possible repercussions with regard to Nazi Germany, which along with its Axis partners was Mexico's only large alternative market for oil. Other markets were controlled by the expropriated companies or firms who would make common cause on the expropriation issue. Concerned by Mexico's possible reorientation toward Germany, Secretary Hull warned Ambassador Daniels within hours of the expropriation announcement, "In following developments please consider the possibility of German, Italian, or Japanese activities, such as negotiations for the purchase of oil."[73] When this subject came up two days later in an interview with Daniels, the Mexican foreign minister replied that "Mexico . . . wished to sell to democratic nations, the United States and Great

Britain preferred. It has no relations or sympathy with Fascist countries and would not willingly sell to them. . . . [The foreign minister] denied [that Mexico had plans to sell to Japan], but [admitted] . . . that Petro-Mex had sold to a Mr. Thomas, an Englishman, who in turn sold to Japan."[74] Meanwhile, Undersecretary Welles expressed concern to the Mexican ambassador in Washington that "the Mexican government would . . . be forced to dump oil which it might produce into the hands of Japan, Germany, or Italy, which were the very governments the Mexican Government had consistently opposed on grounds of national policy."[75]

Crucially important in lessening Washington's economic pressure on Mexico was the opposition of Secretary Morgenthau, one of the most ardent foes of Nazi Germany in the cabinet. Earlier, in December 1937, Morgenthau had opposed economic pressure on Mexico even before the oil expropriations. In resisting Hull's toughness toward Mexico, Morgenthau told Roosevelt, "We're just going to wake up and find inside a year that Italy, Germany, and Japan have taken over Mexico. . . . It's the richest—the greatest store of natural resources close to the ocean of any country in the world. . . . They've got everything that those three countries need."[76] He continued his pleas for sympathetic treatment of the Mexicans arguing, "We may be able to help them pull through and have a friendly neighbor to the south of us. And I think it's terribly important to keep the continents of North and South America from going fascist."[77] When the expropriations actually occurred, Morgenthau refused to act without a formal request from the Department of State that the United States stop buying silver. He feared a repetition of Great Power rivalry in Mexico on the model of the "Spanish situation."[78] So in spite of Mexico's unwillingness to back down and the State Department's continued pressure, Morgenthau resumed spot purchases of silver from Mexico within a few months. A scholar who has had access to Morgenthau's diary comments that "the Axis threat to Mexico between 1939 and 1941 cannot be over-emphasized; many of the people in their confusion rejoiced at the prospects of joining Germany in a war against the hated gringos to the north. American help and sympathy was a leading factor in upholding a democratic regime. . . . In that activity, silver played an important part."[79]

Other influential figures in the cabinet supported a moderate response to Mexico. Secretary of the Interior Harold L. Ickes recorded his meeting with Sumner Welles about two weeks after the expropriations. Ickes told Welles:

> If bad feelings should result in Central and South America as the result of the oil situation that exists just now with Mexico, it would be more expensive for us than the cost of all the oil in Mexico. . . . Welles told me that very reassuring messages had come from President Cárdenas . . . that the Japanese have [not] effected a foothold in the Gulf of Lower California and . . . that it is the intention of Mexico to deny to Japan fishing rights in Mexican waters.[80]

Cárdenas' firm adherence to the expropriation decision, his reiterated statements about paying compensation, and his responsive orientation toward the United States on most other issues facilitated U.S. acceptance of the fait accompli while continuing to call for just and prompt compensation.

Mexico and Germany (1937–1940)

The United States' persistence in reaching a negotiated settlement of outstanding issues with Mexico was due primarily to U.S. desires to keep its southern neighbor friendly as war clouds gathered in Europe. Morgenthau, Ickes, and other U.S. leaders opposed harsh economic sanctions in the oil controversy as likely to force Mexico into the arms of Nazi Germany. Were these fears of Mexican-German rapprochement justified? Relations between Mexico and Germany in the late 1930s provide the answer.

Cárdenas and Hitler came from diametrically opposed ideological camps. The struggle between Axis and anti-Axis forces in world affairs was reflected in domestic Mexican politics. The Cárdenas government depended partly for its support on labor, Marxist-oriented, and other leftist groups, including such leaders as Vicente Lombardo Toledano. Strongly influenced by Soviet policies, these groups were the bitterest opponents of Mexican political parties on the Right, such as the Sinarquistas and their ally, the small Nazi party of Mexico.[81] The political philosophies and domestic policies of the Mexican and Nazi governments were antithetical.

In the international arena in the mid-1930s, Mexico, together with the Soviet Union, was one of the leaders of international efforts to check the expansionist tendencies of the Berlin-Rome-Tokyo axis. Mexico was a staunch supporter of the Spanish Loyalists with whose exiled government it continued to maintain diplomatic relations after Franco, with German and Italian assistance, gained control of Spain. Mexico was one of the few countries to protest publicly Germany's absorption of Austria into the Third Reich.

As a result, Germany's relations with Mexico during the 1930s were cool. The German Foreign Office was disturbed by the prevalence of anti-Nazi publications in Mexico and by Mexico's public opposition to Nazi foreign policies. Partly because of the Mexican government's express hostility, the German government advised German firms in Mexico to order from Germany only what could not be acquired elsewhere. Fearing Mexican transshipments to the Spanish Loyalists, Germany refused to sell Mexico munitions. The German minister reported that such munitions would go to the Spanish "Red" army.[82]

The two governments' conflicting domestic and international policies dampened the prospects for any form of collaboration that was likely to be viewed with concern in Washington. Not sanguine himself about such prospects, the German minister in Mexico reported to the Berlin Foreign Office in early 1938 that Mexico was "so definitely oriented against the authoritarian, or fascist countries . . . that in all probability even without pressure from the northern neighbor, the government would hardly be able to maintain a neutral attitude in case of armed conflict."[83]

The tension that arose between the United States and Mexico in the months following the Mexican seizure of the foreign oil properties in March 1938, however, created a new situation. Most of Mexico's former customers in Britain, France, and the United States, the main markets, did not buy Mexican oil. Mexican efforts to continue sales to customers in Britain and France were largely unsuccessful. The U.S. government refused to buy oil from Mexico, and the U.S. Navy boycotted Mexican oil as late as the fall of 1940.[84] Mexican exports of oil dropped 40 percent during the first year after the expropriation.[85] The refusal of British, French, and U.S. customers to buy oil forced Mexico to turn to the Axis.

The director general of the new Mexico oil export agency invited the German commercial attaché to his office on April 4, 1938, to inform him that Cárdenas had "agreed to oil sales to Germany as long, for domestic political reasons, as the negotiations could be conducted through Mexican or non-German firms."[86] Foreign policy considerations, namely U.S. concern about Germany, may explain why Cárdenas was unwilling to negotiate directly with the Germans.

When a Cárdenas representative asked Minister Rüdt whether Germany would be interested in Mexican oil and other agreements, Rüdt replied that this would depend on "the restoration of German confidence in the domestic political development of Mexico which had been disturbed by left radical agitation against Germany and above all by the government's position on the Austrian Anschluss."[87] Shortly thereafter Rüdt reported to the Foreign Office that the "present situation offers . . . great opportunities for Germany from a political [and] an economic point of view." In exchange for buying oil on acceptable terms, Rüdt suggested that Germany might "achieve a change in Mexico's political position towards Germany."[88]

Although the German minister's hopes for a political rapprochement were not realized, Germany bought about one-third of Mexican oil exports and Italy about eight percent in the year after the expropriation. The sales were mostly on a barter basis. Mexico received manufactured articles, structural members for bridges, and heavy equipment. Italy supplied three tankers with a 10,000 barrel capacity.[89] The sales to Germany were arranged through William Rhodes Davis, an American oil man and promoter who was heavily involved in politics in the United States and Mexico.

Meanwhile, Germany faced a dilemma with respect to domestic political conflicts within Mexico. In the tension following the oil expropriations, General Saturnino Cedillo prepared an armed revolt to overthrow Cárdenas. Cedillo was rumored to have the sympathy of Mexican Nazis and his leading military adviser was Colonel Ernesto von Merck whose descent was clearly German. In fact, it seems unlikely that von Merck had support from Germany.[90] Moreover, Minister Rüdt described Germany's dilemma thus: "On the one hand, Germany would welcome a movement against the left radicals, thus leading to the fall of the present government—yet, on the other, this might be accompanied by greater North American influences, and bring with it disorder in Mexico, which in the past has been unfavorable for German economic interest since this has been followed by American 'rule' under which German interests have been complicated if not threatened." He viewed the forceful overthrow of the Cárdenas government with "mistrust."[91]

The German minister was correct insofar as the foreign oil companies were conducting a critical press campaign against the Cárdenas government and, to that extent, encouraged Cedillo to revolt. No evidence was uncovered, however, that the oil companies actually financed the revolt.[92] President Roosevelt firmly opposed any official U.S. encouragement to Cedillo and warned pilots that they risked loss of their license if they enlisted in the Cedillo revolt. When an oil company representative tested the U.S. position with respect to the revolt, President Roosevelt passed the word that there would be no revolution in Mexico, a decisive though seemingly mild comment.[93]

In view of its sale of oil to Germany, the Cárdenas government was more circumspect publicly after the Nazi absorption of Czechoslovakia in the fall of 1938 than when Germany absorbed Austria earlier in the year.[94] Secretly, however, Cárdenas unsuccessfully proposed to President Roosevelt the establishment of an inter-American boycott against the aggressor nations.[95] Such a boycott would have cost Mexico her German market for oil but presumably would have facilitated the resumption of sales to other western nations. Meanwhile, Mexico made deliveries of oil to Germany from January to August 1939 and to Italy until the latter joined the war.[96] The Mexicans were quick to point out that the U.S. oil companies also sharply increased sales to Germany, Italy, and Japan during those years.[97]

Nazi Germany also had to define its position toward an opposition movement against Avila Camacho who was elected to succeed Cárdenas as president in 1940. A representative of General Juan Andreu Almazán, the opposition leader, requested military assistance from the Axis in the form of tanks, guns, and airplanes. Berlin replied that Almazán's movement was "without large support, its leader insignificant and a follower of the United States by whom he has apparently been bought." The message said the German minister in Mexico considered Avila Camacho "more advantageous for us," and ordered the refusal of assistance.[98] As indicated above, the Germans were as mistaken about U.S. ties with Almazán as with Cedillo.

Meanwhile, the United States and Mexico were gradually resolving their differences over the oil expropriation and tensions were declining. The prospect of Mexico disassociating itself from the United States or, less likely, moving into the German camp, became even more remote in December 1938 when Mexico gave Secretary Hull thoroughgoing support at the Lima conference for an unequivocal declaration of inter-American solidarity.[99] Mexico sold Germany some oil but otherwise kept it at arm's length, symbolized for example by its refusal to negotiate oil sales directly with the Germans. When France was falling in June 1940, the German minister reported that Mexico "can't do anything but follow what the United States prescribes" and expressed the view that it was "impossible" for Mexico to stay neutral in a war between the United States and Germany.[100]

Thus, the Mexican government rejected political collaboration with Nazi Germany not only because of opposition to Nazi policies and ideology but also because the United States was prepared to compromise its differences with Mexico, offer economic inducements, and collaborate politically. Apparently U.S.–Mexican relations were close enough during this period to convince the Nazi leaders that, for

German interests, Mexico offered insufficient opportunities to justify turning their attention from vital strategic and military problems in Europe.

Global Settlement

As the military conflict in Europe expanded into world war, Mexico and the United States moved toward reconciliation and collaboration in political and military affairs. At first unable to resolve the conflict over the oil seizures, Cárdenas moved toward a settlement of general claims and claims for seizures under the agrarian reform. Meanwhile, the two powers sought to reassure each other about their common interests with respect to the developing conflict in Europe. Mexico's sympathy for Britain and France and hostility toward Hitler were manifest in 1939 and 1940, and Mexico worked with most other American nations which shared its views.

After the 1940 elections the defeated candidate, General Almazán, hoped for support from the United States to overthrow Avila Camacho and approached the White House on the subject. After consulting the president and Secretary Hull, presidential assistant Marvin McIntyre wired an intermediary with respect to helping Almazán's counterrevolutionary activities: "My advice is Hands Off."[101] The appointment of Vice-President Henry Wallace to represent the United States at Avila Camacho's inauguration completely destroyed Almazán's hopes for effective U.S. support.

Moreover, the United States had little to gain and much to lose by opposing the established authorities in Mexico City. In June 1940 President Cárdenas agreed to send military representatives to Washington for the purpose of military collaboration and pledged the use of Mexican territory and naval bases for American forces if the United States was the object of an act of aggression. Meanwhile, too, Mexico had rejected an offer from Italy to send an aviation commission and other experts to Mexico City.[102] By mid-1941 Mexico and the United States had reached agreements on the control and export of strategic materials and on the reciprocal transit of military aircraft.[103]

On November 19, 1941, the United States and Mexico signed a general agreement, referred to as a "global settlement," on the issues in dispute between them. The term was apt in that the agreement settled not only a wide spectrum of strictly bilateral questions but also provided a basis for the collaboration of both nations in their relationships with the rest of the globe. Mexico agreed to provide specific sums to compensate for seized agrarian and oil properties and other claims. The United States agreed to establish a special fund to stabilize the Mexico peso, committed itself to silver purchases, and extended Mexico a long-term loan for the Pan American Highway. The U.S. credits facilitated and offset Mexican installment payments. For further details see chapter 4.

The Japanese attack on Pearl Harbor three weeks later occurred when relations between the United States and Mexico were probably better than at any other time in history. Mexico promptly announced on December 7 that the attack on Pearl Harbor was considered as aggression against her own sovereignty in accordance with the Havana Agreement of 1940 and broke diplomatic relations with Japan on December 8. Following Germany's and Italy's declarations of war on the United States, Mexico broke diplomatic relations with both countries on December 11. Throughout the balance of the war Mexico was a close and loyal ally of the United States.

Bolivia (1952–1964)

The Mexican and Bolivian revolutions were alike in that during their reformist phases both were treated with hostility by U.S. officials, as chapter 3 indicates. Madero suffered from the intrigues of Ambassador Henry Lane Wilson, and Villarroel was subjected to critical pressures from leaders in Washington as well as from U.S. representatives in Bolivia. After Madero's murder in 1913 and the revolution's turn to the Left, the Mexican revolutionaries were viewed sympathetically by the Wilson administration. Like Madero, Villarroel was murdered, but was followed by what could be termed "counterrevolutionary" governments from 1946 until 1952. When urban insurrections led to the deepening of the revolutionary process in 1952, Harry S Truman was still president and the Democratic party, which had so stubbornly opposed the participation of the Movimiento Revolucionario Nacionalista (MNR) in Villarroel's cabinet, was still in power. As will be shown below, a temporary accommodation was reached between the Truman administration and the MNR. The major responsibility for coping with the Bolivian Revolution devolved upon the new Republican administration under President Dwight D. Eisenhower since he assumed office in January 1953, nine months after the MNR gained control of the government and only weeks after the nationalization of the large tin mines. Although the Eisenhower administration did not have a record of hostility toward the MNR, there were none of the signs of presidential sympathy for the revolution that Woodrow Wilson had shown toward the Mexicans early in his own term. The Bolivian Revolution unfolded rapidly under a new U.S. administration whose response was scarcely predictable.

The causes of that revolutionary upheaval were profoundly domestic. In the 1930s and 1940s the economic base of the old social system was crumbling as the tin content of the ore gradually dropped lower and lower and Bolivia's share in the world tin market declined. The ailing tin mines and immobility in other economic sectors resulted in the deterioration of living conditions of the middle and working classes. Meanwhile, discontent grew among miners and other working class elements now being organized into trade unions.

New leaders who emerged in the late 1930s consolidated their political organizations and pressed harder their criticism of the old system which, since its defeat in the Chaco War in 1935, was increasingly discredited. Reform-minded military leaders, David Toro, Germán Busch, and Gualberto Villarroel, each having seized the presidency, moved against the traditional leaders. The fate of the last of these, Villarroel, is described in chapter 3. After his assassination, the rapid succession of

President Woodrow Wilson (center, front row) with his cabinet, including Secretary of State Robert Lansing (left, front row) and Secretary of the Navy Josephus Daniels (far left, back row), 1917. (Library of Congress)

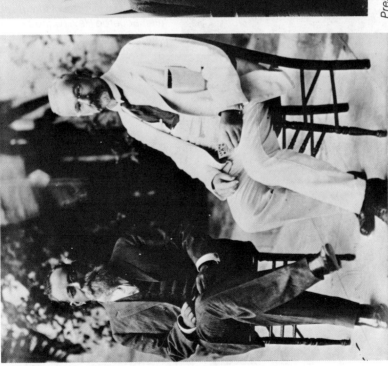

Venustiano Carranza, president of Mexico, 1915–1920 (left), with visiting U.S. journalist, G. F. Weeks. (Library of Congress)

Henry P. Fletcher, U.S. ambassador to Mexico, 1916–1920. (Department of State)

United States Ambassador Josephus Daniels (left) with Lázaro Cárdenas, president of Mexico, 1934–1940 (center), and the Mexican minister of foreign affairs, Eduardo Hay. (United Press International)

Víctor Paz Estenssoro, president of Bolivia, 1952–1956 and 1960–1964. (Organization of American States)

Víctor Andrade, Bolivian ambassador to the United States (right), presents an award to Milton Eisenhower, adviser to President Eisenhower, at Pennsylvania State University, April 1956. (Pennsylvania State University)

President Paz Estenssoro with President John F. Kennedy in Washington, D.C., October 1963. (John F. Kennedy Library)

presidents and cabinet ministers during the sexenio (1946–1952) was a symptom of the weaknesses of the traditional political parties and their growing lack of popularity in the cities. The decline of the ruling groups, growing discontent in the cities, and revolutionary turmoil in the mines all combined in the overthrow of the traditional parties in the 1952 insurrection and the deepening of the revolutionary process.

While domestic causes were the source of the social upheaval in Bolivia, they were still intimately linked in the public mind with foreign relations. Not only did Bolivia depend on foreign markets—often controlled by foreign governments—for the sale of tin, but the large tin magnates lived abroad as well, and profits flowed from the country to them. An aroused and frustrated nationalistic leadership found it convenient, if not always accurate, to attribute many of Bolivia's ills to foreign origins.

In the months preceding the April 1952 insurrection, Bolivia was once again faced with chronic economic crises, for the foreign demand for tin and the resultant high prices generated by the Korean War fell off. In 1951 negotiations between the Bolivian mining companies and Stuart Symington of the Reconstruction Finance Corporation (RFC) had reached an impasse. Bolivian ores began to pile up in Chilean and Peruvian ports in October 1951. The U.S. State Department, concerned about the political repercussions of the impasse, was reportedly hopeful that the RFC, which came under new leadership in early 1952, would soon reach an agreement with the Bolivians. The crisis continued and the economic impact on Bolivia by the following March was described as disastrous, further depressing the already low standards of living. Especially critical was the effect on the national diet since Bolivia used its tin revenues to buy agricultural products abroad. No agreement had yet been reached on April 9, 1952, when the insurrection occurred.

The breakdown in negotiations with the RFC on tin exports and the resultant popular discontent generated by the crisis facilitated the MNR's seizure of government, but the MNR was not inclined to have the revolution explained solely in terms of RFC intransigence on tin sales. Paz Estenssoro said that to assert that the revolution succeeded simply because negotiations with the RFC had broken down reflected a "shallow and superficial understanding of Bolivian problems."[104] The impasse over tin sales, however, did pose an extremely serious problem for the new MNR government since negotiations could not be resumed, even if agreement were possible, until the United States recognized the new regime.

Delayed Recognition

Prospects for a cordial relationship between Washington and the new men in La Paz were not good in April 1952. The MNR leaders were the same men tagged as Nazis during World War II and forced out of the Villarroel government in 1944. Party leaders, who made no secret of Marxist influence on their party program, were strongly critical of U.S. imperialism. Communists had also supported MNR candidates in the 1951 elections, with or without the candidates' consent. The MNR's vaguely leftist program, including proposals for the nationalization of the tin mines, disturbed conservative circles in Washington aroused by the anti-Communist campaigns of Senator Joseph McCarthy.

The MNR, however, did have some points in its favor. Paz Estenssoro, who had won a plurality in the 1951 elections, had a constitutional claim to the office. While strong on revolutionary rhetoric, the MNR, with its Right, Left, and Center factions, was not committed to a specific, detailed, and radical revolutionary program. The overthrow of the old regime in April 1952 was a primarily urban insurrection lasting only a few days and with relatively little loss of life; most of the revolutionary innovations were made many months later. The Bolivian Revolution had not yet taken place.

Having suffered through the ordeal of nonrecognition in 1944, the MNR leadership made a great effort from the very first moments after the insurrection triumphed on April 12, 1952, to calm U.S. fears and to pave the way for early recognition and, most important, continued U.S. purchases of tin. Within hours of becoming provisional president, Hernán Siles Suazo promised a peaceful government that would respect international agreements and private property.[105] On April 16 the new foreign minister, Wálter Guevara Arze, formally requested U.S. recognition in a note to the American embassy.[106] On his triumphant return from abroad after the MNR takeover, Paz Estenssoro assumed the presidency and reaffirmed the MNR's plans to nationalize the large tin mines. He was careful to point out that this would not be done hurriedly, expressing desire to reach an agreement about nationalization with the mine owners.[107] Siles was quoted early in May as saying that the MNR was the last bulwark against communism and was independent of Moscow, Buenos Aires, and Washington.[108] He went on to distinguish nationalization from confiscation and to express his desire for the friendship and understanding of the American government and people. At the same time he gave formal assurances that his government proposed to meet the international obligations contracted by Bolivia "in the fullest sense."[109]

Meanwhile, the MNR government was building its bridges abroad with the help of the United Nations technical assistance mission headed by Dr. Carter Goodrich of Columbia University, who had arrived the year before the April revolution when the mission was invited to Bolivia under an agreement negotiated with the pre-1952 government. Dr. Goodrich met secretly with Hernán Siles the February before the insurrection,[110] and the relationship established then facilitated the renegotiation of the UN mission's subsequent arrangements in Bolivia. Dr. Goodrich's willingness to work with the new government, his continued support of the mission's program at UN headquarters, and his persuasiveness with the new administration speeded the establishment of normal relations with the outside world. Meanwhile, too, the Latin American representative of the AFL, Serafino Romualdi, had changed his formerly critical view of the MNR and urged U.S. recognition at an AFL convention.[111]

The United States formally recognized the MNR government on June 2, 1952—some seven weeks after the MNR seized power—noting that the new government was in control of its national territory and had agreed to live up to its international obligations. Washington was quick to point out, however, that its recognition did not imply any judgment of Bolivian domestic problems;[112] but, in fact, the State Department agreed to recognize the MNR government only after it had been assured that compensation would be paid for the expropriated mining properties. Paz and Siles had already publicly expressed their intention to provide this compensation; moreover, it is likely that they privately made firm commitments to Washington in this regard. The sensitivity of the whole tin question was shown by Paz's announcement, only some twenty-four hours after the U.S. recognition, establishing a monopoly of all mineral exports. The government thereby took control of all foreign receipts for mineral exports.

The United States' grudging recognition of the Paz government eliminated a grave liability to the MNR regime and gave it a new lease on life. Formal communications between Bolivia and the United States were resumed, and, most important, the Bolivians were able to reopen their direct appeals for a long-term contract to sell tin at favorable prices. Ambassador Edward Sparks, a career foreign service officer, arrived in La Paz on June 3, 1952, the day after recognition was granted, and thereafter played an important role in strengthening U.S. ties with the new government. In September the United States bought up all available Bolivian tin not yet contracted for sale.

Communism and Expropriations

Recognition was essential to establishing formal channels of communication between the two governments and to facilitate trade relations. It did not, however, resolve profound issues that threatened to divide the new revolutionary Bolivian government and the United States. The first involved the ideological and international orientation of the new government, and the second, that government's treatment of foreign-owned property, particularly property belonging to North Americans. Resolution of these issues largely determined the initial U.S. response to the Bolivian Revolution.

The bitterest enemies of the new government charged the MNR with being Fascist and Communist, sometimes simultaneously. The charges of fascism first gained prominence in the "Nazi-putsch" episode described in chapter 3. As the years passed and the true record of the MNR became better known, these charges lost much of their force, even though the full facts with respect to the MNR and Germany did not become available until many years later. Washington attributed far less significance to charges of fascism in the 1950s than during the war when the Nazis dominated Western Europe.

Attempts to tag the MNR with the Communist label were a greater threat in the early 1950s when tension between the United States and the Soviet Union was great. Since Bolivia had virtually no direct political or economic relations with the USSR in 1952, about the only arena of possible Soviet influence was through the international

Communist movement. The charge of communism against the MNR was based partly on the vague intellectual influence that Marxism had exercised over the MNR's programs and the new government's moves toward the Left.

Making the charge of communism stick was difficult, however, because several different groups which identified with the international Communist movement had long maintained an identity distinct from the MNR and had, in fact, been bitterly hostile to it. The Communist movement in Bolivia had long been weak and divided. The strongest group initially was the Partido Obrero Revolucionario (POR) which, like other Trotskyite organizations, went into a steep decline in the 1940s. The Bolivian Stalinists were organized in the Partido de la Izquierda Revolucionaria (PIR), traditional rivals of the MNR. The MNR had offended the PIR in 1944 by refusing to admit its leader into Vallarroel's cabinet. The PIR retaliated by participating in the coup which overthrew Villarroel in 1946. From 1946 to 1952 PIR was associated with governments which suppressed the MNR. The PIR's policies became so unpopular that by the early 1950s the party was a shambles out of which emerged the new Bolivian Communist party. Around this time (1953) the U.S. Department of State estimated the number of Communists in all Bolivia at less than two thousand.[113] The Communists were not represented in the MNR command which led the uprising, and representatives of the Communist party as such did not hold any ministerial or comparable posts in the subsequent MNR governments. The Communists' candidate received only 12,000 votes in the 1956 presidential election as compared to more than 750,000 by MNR candidate Siles Suazo. The Communist party did not have its first national congress in Bolivia until 1959.[114]

The MNR government undertook to dispel U.S. fears about communism from the outset. Ambassador Andrade insisted, "[Our government] is not Communist. We give assurances that it is not dominated by a foreign government."[115] In interpreting the MNR–Communist relationship. Wálter Guevara, the MNR foreign minister, explained: "When the people of Bolivia were engaged in their final battle against the oligarchy of great mine owners and the feudal landholders, the Communists raised their voices with ours. They did us greater harm than good, but in a life-and-death struggle everyone who helps is good, as the Western powers proved during the Second World War when they enthusiastically welcomed Soviet Russia as an ally."[116] He maintained that international communism had "no true interest in stating and solving the problems of the country in which it operates . . . local organizations are like pawns in . . . world politics."[117]

In a surprisingly prophetic statement, Paz Estenssoro made his position on the Soviet-American conflict clear as early as 1944 when he said: "Especially in the case of nations like Bolivia international policy has to be formulated considering geographic and economic factors. In the event of a conflict of interest between the Anglo-American group and Russia, I believe that Bolivia will have to gravitate, necessarily, to the Anglo-American orbit."[118]

In his history of the MNR, Luis Peñaloza gives an authoritative summing up of his party's position on this issue. After criticizing the PIR for zigzagging with the

Soviet line, Peñaloza writes: "In contrast to [the PIR's] subordination to foreigners [lo extranjero], the Movimiento Nacionalista Revolucionario began its partisan activities claiming for the Bolivian people the right to direct their destiny . . . capturing attention not by being *for* or *against* the Reds or the Whites . . . but above all by claiming what seemed best for Bolivia."[119]

The MNR government succeeded in convincing the Eisenhower administration that it was not Fascist, Communist, or pro-Soviet. In his book, *The Wine Is Bitter*, Milton Eisenhower, who visited Bolivia as a representative of the president, dealt with this question directly. In fact, he used the Bolivian example to show how politicians, the mass media, and business leaders sometimes tag governments or political parties as Communist "in good faith but without essential knowledge." He added: "Sometimes men with selfish interests knowingly make false statements which poison the American mind and enrage Latin Americans. . . . It is harmful in our own country and devastatingly hurtful throughout Latin America for us to carelessly or maliciously label as 'Communist' any internal efforts to achieve changes for the benefit of the masses of the people. . . . We should not confuse each move in Latin America toward socialization with Marxism, land reform with Communists, or even anti-Yankeeism with pro-Sovietism."

Dr. Eisenhower explained that Paz Estenssoro's government "may have been inexperienced, sometimes critical of us, and more inclined toward socialism than Americans generally prefer. . . . But they were not Communists." And he stoutly denied that the Bolivian land reform was Communist-inspired: "Feudalism is far closer to Communism than the system of owner operated farms installed by the Paz Estenssoro government. Why we should call land reform under such circumstances Communism is beyond me." In fact, he went on to argue that "rapid peaceful social change is the only way to avert violent revolution in Bolivia; physical strife would be the surest way of giving the Communists control."[120]

The second major issue, the treatment of foreign-owned property, dramatically came to public attention when the MNR government nationalized the three large tin mining companies in October 1952. Nationalization was a dangerous step since it jeopardized Bolivia's sales of tin abroad—the nation's largest single source of foreign exchange to cover food imports. Such imports constituted about one-quarter of the national diet. The crisis was further aggravated by a precipitous drop in tin prices.

As chapter 4 indicates in greater detail, the MNR leaders committed the government to paying compensation for the expropriated mines and time and again reassured Washington that the nationalization decree was not directed against private property in general nor against foreign holders in particular. Agreements were reached with all three mining companies providing for compensation, the first with the Patiño company in June 1953. As a gesture of its faith in private foreign investment, the MNR government subsequently entered into agreement with foreign companies such as that of Glen McCarthy to develop sulfur deposits and with Gulf and other companies to exploit oil deposits.

Dr. Eisenhower described how he "listened for hours to explanations of the

Bolivian tin mine expropriation in conversations with President Paz Estenssoro, his Foreign Minister, and his able Ambassador in Washington. I recall distinctly spending most of one day at a small military school down a mountain." Dr. Eisenhower also talked with the former mine owners and other bitter critics of the expropriation so that he admitted to not having learned where the "full truth lies." But he did express his firm conviction that the MNR's "officials were honestly convinced that the expropriation with compensation was in the long-time interest of the nation."[121]

Emergency Assistance (1953–1956)

The MNR government's convincing reassurance on the Communist issue and nationalization laid a good foundation for collaboration but placed the U.S. government in a dilemma. The strategic U.S. stockpile of tin had grown large and the United States sought both to economize on the price and to lower the volume of minerals purchased. United States officials were also disinclined to keep open indefinitely the government-owned tin smelter built in Texas during World War II, which was especially equipped to refine Bolivia's low-grade ores. Yet Bolivia had cooperated with the United States during World War II when tin was in such short supply, and it continued to be the only reliable, although costly, source of tin in the Western Hemisphere. Bolivia was desperately dependent on the United States to buy a large part of its product, particularly those low-grade ores which could not be easily processed in European smelters. Low prices on the world market, in addition to U.S. reluctance to continue purchasing ore at earlier levels, were having a disastrous impact on the Bolivian economy. It appeared unlikely that the existing government could survive if relief were not forthcoming. In May 1953 Assistant Secretary John Moors Cabot told a congressional committee, "Bolivia is in a very serious economic state, and at the same time, we have stockpiled so much tin, we do not want any more, and I am trying to figure that one out."[122]

The Bolivian government's announcement of the agreement with the Patiño interests in June 1953 set the stage for U.S. action. The *New York Times* praised the Bolivian government for the settlement, for having resisted the blandishments of Perón, and for having kept "the Reds in check."[123] The editorial urged that the United States not permit the government to collapse in spite of the size of the U.S. stockpile and favored a long-term tin contract for "political" reasons.

The response of the Department of State was not long in coming. In a press release on July 6, the department offered the Bolivians a one-year contract to buy tin ores at the world market price at the time of delivery.[124] In addition, the department committed itself to doubling the amount of technical assistance and undertaking studies of possible joint efforts to solve the country's economic problems—a broad hint of economic assistance to come. The announcement came at a crucial time, on the eve of the arrival in La Paz of the president's brother, Milton Eisenhower, on his first official fact-finding trip to Latin America. The significance of the Milton Eisenhower visit was not that he set a new policy, but that he provided authoritative and influential confirmation of the department's earlier policy reflected in the July 6 press release and initiated action to implement that policy.

What Dr. Eisenhower saw and learned in Bolivia disposed him favorably toward the MNR government, and his personal assessment of the situation and his influence in the U.S. administration appear to have played a vital role in implementing a large, long-term program of U.S. economic assistance to Bolivia: "Bolivia was in real trouble when I arrived. The price of tin had fallen sharply and people were starving. President Paz Estenssoro urged me to have the United States send emergency food supplies. In response, I made my first call home and spoke to Secretary Dulles, asked him to ship surplus food to Bolivia if possible. We did."[125] One of the top leaders of the MNR who dealt personally with Dr. Eisenhower has said that the United States came to the aid of Bolivia at this time because Milton Eisenhower, an agriculturist by training, fell in love (se apasionó) with the agrarian reform.[126]

The U.S. emergency assistance to Bolivia was formalized in an exchange of letters between Presidents Paz Estenssoro and Eisenhower on October 1 and October 14, 1953, respectively. President Eisenhower authorized the following emergency assistance:

1. To make available $5 million of agricultural products from Commodity Credit Corporation Stocks under the Famine Relief Act
2. To provide $4 million from Mutual Security Act funds for other essential commodities
3. To more than double the technical assistance program

President Eisenhower also referred to an earlier decision to purchase tin "at a time when his country [had] no immediate need for additional tin,"[127] because of the traditional U.S. friendship with Bolivia and an awareness of the security threat to the free world when free men suffered from hunger or other severe misfortunes. Both presidents emphasized the emergency and humanitarian nature of the assistance but linked it to the development of Bolivian agriculture and the diversification of the economy, heretofore excessively dependent on tin exports. Counterpart funds generated by the sale of agricultural and other commodities were to be used in implementing Bolivia's diversification program. As Assistant Secretary Cabot's statements quoted in chapter 4 show, the United States insisted as a condition of granting economic assistance that the MNR government reach an agreement with the former owners of the tin mines regarding compensation.

Cabot was more explicit than the president about the security factors bearing on the U.S. decision. Not only did he express his belief in the sincerity of the MNR government's opposition to "Communist imperialism," but he went on to describe the "implacable challenge of Communism" in the hemisphere:

The true test of hemispheric solidarity, upon which our security so importantly depends, is our willingness to sink our differences and to cooperate with regimes pursuing a different course from ours to achieve common goals. . . .
We are therefore cooperating with it, for history has often described the fate of those who have quarreled over nonessentials in the face of mortal peril.[128]

No clearer statement than this is needed to show that the United States did not extend assistance to Bolivia solely as a humanitarian gesture toward a people faced with famine—such assistance was also justified as a means of contributing to the security of the United States.

The crucial decision to come to the assistance of the new revolutionary government was much facilitated by the work of the Bolivian ambassador in Washington, Víctor Andrade. Andrade had been trained in an American school in La Paz. As ambassador to the United States for Villarroel, he became well acquainted with Nelson Rockefeller and learned his way around Washington. In the early 1950s Andrade worked for the Rockefellers' International Basic Economy Corporation in Guayaquil, Ecuador.

Returning to the United States as ambassador in the 1950s, he developed a personal relationship with Milton Eisenhower before the latter went to Bolivia on his first official visit, briefing him thoroughly on the MNR as well as on the oppositions' positions. Andrade played golf with President Eisenhower from time to time at the Burning Tree Golf Club, an informal access to the president denied most ambassadors. According to Andrade, his most effective argument with the president was that aid to Bolivia would show the world that Eisenhower was not a reactionary inflexible Republican and could support a revolution.[129]

An interesting sequel to the decision on emergency assistance was a visit of a congressional committee to Bolivia just a few weeks later on November 8 to 11, 1953. The leader of the congressional delegation was Senator Homer Capehart of Indiana and one of its other members was Senator John Bricker of Ohio, both of the conservative wing of the Republican party. Their published report of the visit was a technical, notably unpolemical account of economic conditions in Bolivia; and their conclusions, though restrained, were not unfavorable to the MNR government. For example, the report noted that the "committee was impressed with the fact that the Bolivians have a full realization of the problems confronting them and a desire to overcome them."[130]

The United States continued to provide emergency economic and other assistance to Bolivia within the framework of the policies established in July 1953 and continued to buy Bolivian tin at world market prices until 1957, when the U.S. government divested itself of its uneconomical tin smelter in Texas City. Meanwhile, the United States increased economic assistance from the $11 million authorized in 1953 to about $20 million in each of the following two years, making Bolivia one of only three Latin American countries to receive outright grants, as opposed to loans (see figure 1). These three countries, Bolivia, Guatemala, and Haiti, received this special treatment because each faced emergency economic and political problems. The post-Arbenz regime in Guatemala received assistance to offset the alleged setbacks the country had suffered under Arbenz and to provide U.S. support for the new anti-Communist government. Grant aid was rushed to Haiti and Bolivia to prevent famine and chaos.

The tendency to justify U.S. emergency assistance in Bolivia as support of a

FIGURE 1

U.S. ECONOMIC AND MILITARY ASSISTANCE TO BOLIVIA, 1952–1968

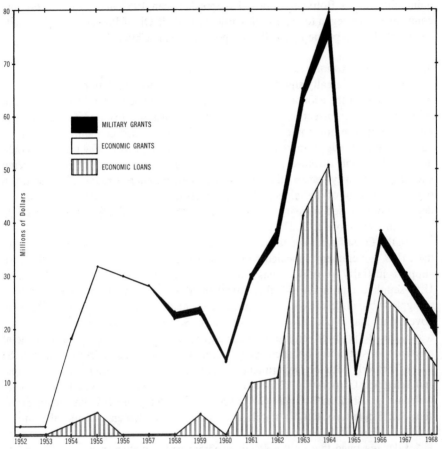

SOURCE: *U.S. Overseas Loans and Grants and Assistance from International Organizations: Obligations and Loan Authorization, July 1, 1945–June 30, 1969* (Washington, D.C., 1969)

government "showing courage and resourcefulness in combating the Communist problem" were intensified. Henry Holland, then Assistant Secretary for Inter-American Affairs, defended the expenditure as a way of helping the Bolivian government "to counteract Communist pressure."[131]

One result of U.S.–Bolivian collaboration was that it encouraged foreign interests to invest in Bolivia. Of special significance was the signing of an investment agreement by the two governments in La Paz on September 23, 1955. By June 30, 1964, some $20 million in foreign investment was insured against expropriation under the program and over 80 percent of this amount was in oil. Drawn up with the assistance of U.S. experts, a new petroleum code was promulgated on October 26,

1955, that attracted more than a dozen foreign oil companies to undertake exploration in Bolivia. Foreign interest was further stimulated by the government corporation's quintupling of its Bolivian crude oil output between 1952 and 1961.[132] Foreign companies later began to export oil, particularly Gulf Oil of Pittsburgh which made shipments by a pipeline to the Pacific port of Arica, Chile.

Monetary Stabilization (1956–1960)

The next politically significant phase in U.S.–Bolivian relations was the political struggle over the economic stabilization program announced in December 1956. After the 1952 insurrection the government increasingly resorted to the printing presses to finance governmental operations, publicly owned economic enterprises, and to meet demands of groups on which it relied for support.[133] The tin mines could not provide taxable surpluses, partly because of the declining yields of tin and foreign exchange and partly because the politically powerful miners' organization had taken over management of the mines, where featherbedding, high government subsidies, declining output, and wage increases prevailed. The cost-of-living index, with a base of 100 in 1952, rose to 2,270 in 1956.[134]

In the face of what appeared to be impending political and economic collapse, the MNR government appealed to the United States for assistance, but the cash support initially provided was swallowed up in government deficits, and U.S.-supplied commodities either found their way to the black market or were smuggled abroad. In the end, the United States made it clear that either the Bolivian government had to put its house in order or U.S. assistance would be cut off. As a result, the Bolivian government requested that the United States send a financial mission to assist in this housecleaning operation, and George Jackson Eder, a U.S. lawyer formerly with the Department of Commerce and the International Telephone and Telegraph Corporation, came to Bolivia in June 1956 as "an invited, but scarcely welcome, guest of the Bolivian Government."[135] Eder's studies began under President Paz Estenssoro, but his stabilization plan was implemented under the latter's successor, Hernán Siles Suazo.

Eder reasoned that only a drastic program had any chance of success, and he recommended that a surgical operation be put into effect. The major elements of the new program were:

1. The establishment of a realistic single exchange rate with fixed compensation for the miners and others to compensate for the proposed elimination of food and other supplies subsidized at artificially low prices
2. Consolidation of all government budgets and the achievement of an overall balance to eliminate further borrowing from the central bank
3. The simultaneous elimination of state subsidies and restrictions and controls on foreign exchange transactions (except customs duties) and on prices (except rents)[136]

The International Monetary Fund, the U.S. Treasury, and the International Cooperation Administration established a $25 million fund to stabilize the exchange rate of the boliviano.

One of the most significant aspects of the stabilization program with regard to U.S.-Bolivian relations was that the program itself, sponsored and in a sense imposed by the United States, became the single most important political issue in the administration of President Siles. Eder appears not only to have provided the diagnosis and the remedy of Bolivia's inflationary ills but also to have been one of the president's major advisers and supporters in the implementation of the stabilization plan. According to Eder, he made every effort on his arrival in Bolivia to secure widespread participation of cabinet officers, including Juan Lechín, in drafting and carrying out the program. Eder cites several instances of Lechín's participation in planning the program as well as his early publicly expressed support for it.[137] Yet Lechín and the vice-president, Ñuflo Chavez, led opposition to the plan on political and ideological as well as economic grounds. They charged that the program failed to promote Bolivia's economic development, bore more heavily on the poor than the rich, damaged public welfare on behalf of private interests, and constituted a renunciation of the MNR's revolutionary position.[138] Lechín sought to circumvent the line on wages by securing increases for his miners.

The struggle over stabilization concerned more than the additional burden of checking inflation; it became a struggle for control of the MNR. The crisis was intense, with President Siles wondering whether he might end up like ex-President Villarroel, hanging from a lamppost in the Plaza Murillo,[139] and Eder's insistence that U.S. aid would be cut off if the stabilization plan were not carried through.

In the face of U.S. pressure and apparently convinced of the validity of the plan, President Siles dramatically defended stabilization, first by going on a hunger strike in La Paz and later, by a courageous visit to the mines to confront personally the miners whose wages Lechín sought to raise. Meanwhile Lechín leveled an attack against Eder's "colonial attitudes."[140]

By August 1957 President Siles had broken the opposition to the stabilization program, and from that time and through the 1960s Bolivia has had one of the most stable currencies in South America. In an address to the Bolivian congress in August, President Siles said that the country had been "on the brink of civil war" and that the stabilization program "saved the country from disaster."[141] As a result of this episode, U.S. policy became even more clearly identified with the right wing of the MNR.

The implications of monetary stabilization were profoundly ideological, or at least, they were so conceived by George Jackson Eder whose proud and personal dedication to a free market economy seemed indisputable. The conditions which the Bolivians were required to fulfill in order to qualify for the loan reflect his well-known support for the laws of private property and free enterprise. He told the Bolivians, for example, that the U.S. State Department, Treasury Department, and

International Cooperation Administration required, among other things, "satisfactory arrangements for resumption of payment on the foreign debt;[142] a mutually acceptable agreement on compensation for the Patiño interests; legislation providing prompt, adequate and effective compensation for expropriated private property; [and] fair mining and investment codes."[143]

The leitmotiv of Eder's approach to the stabilization program was his suspicion and disapproval of Keynesian economics and his dedication to the free market economy as exemplified by Ludwig Erhard and the West German economic miracle. On the latter point, Eder wrote: "The essence of the stabilization program was a return to a free market economy, at least in the matter of freedom from price controls, foreign exchange controls, and controls on imports and exports. It was a constant battle, however, and one that had to be waged continually against those who could not conceive of any economic system not controlled by the government."[144] However one judges Eder's views, the stabilization program checked Bolivia's inflation, as the statistics so eloquently prove.[145] It also directed the country toward a free market economy despite the socialist and statist orientation of many of its political leaders.

Eder's interpretation of the stabilization program, the main source now available, should be tempered with different perspectives when archival and other materials become available. After Eder completed his controversial assignment, the International Monetary Fund[146] and the U.S. embassy, headed by Ambassador Philip Bonsal, played crucial roles in carrying the program forward. United States economic assistance in the 1950s, mainly in grants, rose to a peak of $34 million in 1955 and dropped to $25 million in 1959.

Economic Development (1960–1964)

The MNR leadership was so deeply involved in the revolutionary changes introduced after the 1952 insurrection and in conducting defensive economic policies that it was not feasible to mount an economic development drive until the early 1960s. Economic development became the major objective of Paz Estenssoro during his second term (1960–1964). This corresponded with the presidency of John F. Kennedy and the beginning of the Alliance for Progress.

After the 1952 insurrection the tin mines, which were still Bolivia's principal industry and the major source of foreign exchange, were looked to as a means of financing capital imports for economic development. Tin seemed to hold the key to Bolivia's economic development, but as production plummeted, revenues from tin sales sank. Low yields of ore, the deterioration of mining equipment, and inefficient management and labor practices meant that the cost of production frequently exceeded the price tin brought on the world market. Rehabilitation of the tin industry required a two-pronged approach: (1) the revitalization of the industry through extensive capital investments, and (2) reforms in the organization and operations of the government-owned mining corporation, COMIBOL.

But the type of reforms which foreign experts felt were necessary in management-labor relations and labor practices constituted political dynamite. Because labor had control of management in the tin mines, many experts estimated that several thousand surplus workers were featherbedding. Employment in the big three tin mines rose from 24,000 miners in 1951 to 36,500 in 1956 and dropped to 27,000 in 1961. The mines produced, however, only 15,000 tons in 1961 as compared with 34,600 tons in 1949, produced by only slightly fewer workers (26,000).[147] The miners also traditionally received subsidies in the sense that commissary stores provided food and other items to the miners at below market prices. In addition, theft was common in the mines and infractions of labor discipline were widespread. Measures to correct these practices faced the stolid opposition of the tin miners, the very group which had been a major element in the insurrection bringing the MNR to power and which was perhaps the largest organized group behind the MNR.

Despite the need for heavy investments in mining equipment, the United States had refrained from providing economic assistance to publicly owned and managed mining and industrial activities. The impact of U.S. economic assistance was strictly limited because of the unwillingness to grant aid to the nationalized industries, tin and oil, which provided a major share of GNP and export earnings. Economic assistance for education, health, and agriculture was politically less controversial in the United States than the provision of funds from U.S. tax sources to support nationalized industries.

The connection between reforms in the tin mines and economic development came sharply into focus just as the United States and Latin America were coming to a political crossroads. In the last year or two of the Eisenhower administration greater attention and resources were devoted to Latin America's needs generally, although there was greater skepticism about Bolivia. Attention to Latin America was intensified after the election of John F. Kennedy to the presidency in 1960 and the announcement of the Alliance for Progress in early 1961.

Paz Estenssoro returned to Bolivia from his diplomatic post in London in the late 1950s and was elected president for a four-year term in 1960. Early in his term he tried to lead Bolivia out of economic stagnation and showed a willingness to assume the political risks that rapid economic development would entail. He sought the economic and social objectives for Bolivia which had been denied the MNR earlier, capitalizing on the new, more liberal economic assistance policy of the Alliance for Progress and the Kennedy administration. In a sense, the MNR's revolution had adopted objectives as early as 1952 which were very similar to those of the Alliance for Progress a decade later. Kennedy looked to Bolivia as a kind of model, and Paz counted on Kennedy for personal and official support.

In the meantime, the USSR had developed interest in Bolivia, and during his visit to the United Nations in 1960, Khrushchev dramatically offered Bolivia the funds for constructing its own tin smelter so the nation would no longer have to depend on U.S. and European smelters. In December of the same year a delegation from the Supreme Soviet visited La Paz and announced a Soviet offer of credits in the amount of $150 million for the government-owned petroleum corporation, road building, railroads, and other public works, as well as the smelter; but, despite pressure from the miners and other leftist groups, the government postponed a decision. The United States opposed acceptance of the Soviet offer; therefore, President Paz considered the Bolivian choice clear—partly because prospective U.S. assistance was far more than he expected from the Soviets.[148] Faced with the Soviet bid, the United States overcame its reluctance to support the government-controlled mining corporation, COMIBOL, and the Plan Triangular was presented as the U.S. answer to the Soviet offer.

Formulated in early 1961 and implemented over the course of the succeeding years, the Plan Triangular was the initial motivating force of Bolivia's economic development plan for the 1960s. But achieving rapid economic development meant facing up to the tin problem and the political implications its solution involved. The plan sought to rehabilitate the tin mines by providing funds for investing in the exploration of new mineral deposits, for metallurgical work to increase the recovery rate, for replacement of materials and equipment, and for commissary supplies, elimination of surplus labor, and technical assistance.

All this involved administrative changes in COMIBOL, greater labor discipline in the mines, and other politically sensitive issues. The United States, the Federal Republic of Germany, and the Inter-American Bank together pledged more than $37 million to the plan under conditions specified in the agreement with the Bolivian government. Like the earlier stabilization program, the Plan Triangular linked the United States once again into direct conflict with the tin miners' union and their leader, Juan Lechín.

Not surprisingly, the tin miners bitterly resisted the required layoffs of thousands of excess workers, and Paz faced a crisis and confrontation with the miners led by Juan Lechín similar to that of former President Siles in the stabilization controversy. He rose to the occasion, as Siles had, meeting the strikes, demonstrations, and other agitation with persuasion and coercive countermeasures. President Paz temporarily managed to survive the crisis over mine reform, but the miners' unrest continued, and his conflict with Lechín as well as other issues ultimately led to a serious split in the MNR.

Meanwhile, U.S. commitments to Bolivia rose slightly above the average of the late 1950s through 1961 and mounted sharply to more than double the earlier level in fiscal year 1964. Obligations in that year amounted to nearly $60 million under AID programs.

The U.S. Impact

The United States and Bolivia not only reconciled their most profound conflicts and maintained friendly relations after the 1952 revolution but worked more closely together than almost any two countries in the hemisphere. The United States became intimately involved not only in the formulation of Bolivian policy but in its implementation as well.

Some of the most authoritative and convincing evidence of the deep U.S. involvement in Bolivian domestic affairs is contained in George Jackson Eder's account of the stabilization program. Eder, for example, drafted domestic legislation:

I was forced to take charge of the long process of a complete revision of customs tariffs and devoted considerable time to the elimination of nuisance taxes and to the question of social security taxes, matters that [Roger] Freeman could have handled more effectively had he been fluent in Spanish. A much needed reform in the real property tax system, proposed by me, and an effective income tax, proposed by Freeman, went by the board solely because there was no one who had the time, the fluency in Spanish, and the persuasiveness to put the measures across. This was unfortunate, as it would have been simpler to reorganize the tax laws and administration under the temporary emergency powers of the monetary stabilization program than at any other time, before or since, in Bolivia's history.[149]

In addition, Eder was deeply involved in Bolivia's domestic politics and had great influence over President Siles in the stabilization controversies and the struggle with Lechín. For example, Eder drafted the president's reply to Lechín's critique of the stabilization program,[150] and his assertiveness and dogmatism caused friction and resentment. Indignant about Eder's interference, Lechín criticized his "paternalistic effrontery."[151] Nonetheless, the stabilization program achieved its objective of stabilizing the currency, and Eder's participation appears to have been an indispensable element in its conception and implementation.

In the later years of the MNR governments, the United States had immense influence in Bolivia. Ambassadors Stephansky and Anderson traveled with President Paz and were widely acclaimed throughout the country. The U.S. official missions in Bolivia were huge. In 1959 the economic assistance mission reached a peak of 118 professional employees and then stabilized at about 70 persons in the early 1960s. United States missions were about half that size in larger countries like Chile and Colombia, and Brazil, which literally dwarfs Bolivia, had only a slightly larger economic mission. The U.S. aid program was involved in almost all major aspects of Bolivian life including agriculture, education, health, industry, and public administration. The United States provided a direct subsidy for almost one-third of the Bolivian central government's budget in 1957 and continued to do so at gradually declining levels for the MNR governments thereafter. Consider how much influence U.S. officials whose government was meeting part of the Bolivian payroll had!

From the beginning the U.S. influence tended to check the nature and extent of revolutionary change. United States insistence on compensation for expropriated mining properties and support of private ownership and control served to prevent nationalization beyond the three major tin mining groups. United States policies consistently sought to limit or decrease government participation in the economy, such as control over foreign exchange and management of extractive industries, and to promote expansion of the private sector.[152] Enacted under U.S. influence, the petroleum code, the mining code, and other measures helped to improve the investment climate for foreign capital.

Stabilization in 1957 and the Plan Triangular in 1961, both conceived and implemented with U.S. support, brought the MNR government into head-on conflict with organized labor, especially with the tin miners. Although U.S. representatives may not have felt politically or personally friendly to the tin miners, it would be difficult to prove that U.S. policies were directed against organized labor as such. Even so, the effect of U.S. influence was to make the United States an ally of the MNR Center and Right and the enemy of the labor Left. Thus, the effort of U.S. policy was to bolster the position of the Bolivian middle classes against organized labor as reflected in the well-known and persisting U.S. antagonism toward Juan Lechín.

In fact, that antagonism was sufficiently great as to have been an important factor in Paz Estenssoro's decision to amend the constitution to permit him to run for reelection in 1964. As one of the top three or four leaders of the MNR, Juan Lechín was to have his "turn" at the presidency in 1964, or so at least ran much talk within the MNR. Aware that he had long been considered in the United States as the bête noire of the Bolivian Revolution, Lechín sought to establish himself in the good graces of the United States. He visited the United States and later paid a formal call on Chiang Kai-shek in Formosa. When Lechín failed to win U.S. support, Paz concluded that the only way to insure the continued flow of needed external resources from the United States and from the international agencies was to run for the presidency himself as the only candidate who could beat Lechín.[153] Not unexpectedly, evidence that the United States actually said no to Lechín's candidacy is not available, but an explicit statement to that effect was probably unnecessary anyway since U.S. antagonism to Lechín had long been widely accepted as fact. The charge that Paz may have wanted to remain as president for selfish reasons does not deprive his argument of plausibility.

United States per capita economic assistance to Bolivia from 1952 to 1964 averaged more than to any other country in the world.[154] After the emergency assistance was granted, President Paz testified that his government "would not have lasted without North American aid."[155] President Siles later said that the stabilization program saved Bolivia from "disaster."[156]

The United States appears at times to have influenced Bolivian foreign policy in its favor. For example, while having its own rationale, Bolivia supported Secretary Dulles' anti-Communist resolution at Caracas in 1954 and broke relations with Cuba in 1964 to help insure continued U.S. support. Bolivia, however, also successfully sustained positions counter to U.S. policy such as voting against the expulsion of the Cuban government from the OAS in 1962 and initially refusing to break relations with Cuba in August 1963.[157] Bolivia maintained diplomatic relations with the eastern European socialist countries such as Czechoslovakia, Hungary, and Yugoslavia.

Military assistance from the United States had also been important in the development of domestic politics in the late 1950s and 1960s. In order to counter the opposition of armed miners in the stabilization controversy, President Siles began rebuilding the armed forces in 1958 with U.S. military assistance. Paz Estenssoro intensified this process in the 1960s as internal opposition to him grew as well. It appeared that he was relying increasingly on the military to strengthen his hand in dealings with Juan Lechín who· broke with him in his second term. In fact, the Bolivian armed forces with U.S. military assistance and increased influence through U.S.-sponsored civic action programs, became so powerful that they were able to overthrow Paz in November 1964.

Certain U.S. military officers were close to the leaders of the coup and the Pentagon and State Department may have been at odds over the issue. President Paz deeply felt the loss of President Kennedy at the time of his assassination and felt his relations with Washington were never the same again. However, the official U.S. position, as represented by Ambassador Douglas Henderson and the American embassy, supported Paz. Henderson appears to have done his best to bolster Paz as the head of a government which was heavily supported under the Alliance for Progress. In any case, the coup against Paz, and the fall of the MNR government to the military under the leadership of the vice-president, General René Barrientos Ortuño, appear to have been primarily domestic matters.[158]

Reconciliation: How and Why

Continuing tensions between the United States and the revolutionary regimes in Latin America make the lessons learned in the Mexican and Bolivian cases especially valuable. Why were the opposing sides able to reconcile their conflicting interests in these two cases and not in others, most notably the Guatemalan and Cuban cases described in the next chapter? What can be learned from the Mexican and Bolivian cases which would contribute to reconciling the interests of the United States and Latin American revolutionary regimes in the future? For one thing, *both* sides helped make reconciliation possible. In retrospect, mutual goodwill was essential to negotiated settlements.

Mexican and Bolivian Perspectives

Most Mexican and Bolivian revolutionary leaders had a fairly good understanding of U.S. policies and a healthy respect for U.S. power. Presidents Carranza and Cárdenas, Paz Estenssoro and Siles Suazo seemed to understand why the United States acted as it did and oriented their policies vis-à-vis the United States to suit the national interests as they saw them.

These Latin American presidents' recognition of the realities of U.S. power was reflected time and again in their own conduct. First, all established early contact with the U.S. government and kept communications open in times of great stress. Carranza had a representative in Washington and received a presidential agent at his own headquarters long before he was recognized. Benefiting from experience under Villarroel, Paz Estenssoro devised a shrewd and successful strategy to secure U.S. recognition in 1952. These governments usually sent able representatives to Washington and cultivated close personal relationships with U.S. ambassadors. Cárdenas and Paz made friends of Presidents Roosevelt and Kennedy.

The presidents of these revolutionary governments were so dependent on U.S. markets for their exports and on U.S. sources of credit, capital, arms, and technology that they were willing to make adjustments in public policy to meet the importunities of U.S. leaders about the protection of private American interests. The high point of Mexican concessions to private interests was the Bucareli agreements of 1923 which largely confirmed the position of U.S. and other foreign oil companies in Mexico without openly abrogating provisions in the Mexican constitution reserving rights in the subsoil to the nation. The Mexicans and Bolivians usually acknowledged promptly an obligation to compensate for nationalized property, even without having the capacity to pay. Such commitments to principle went a long way toward disarming Americans incensed by official seizures. The Mexicans made substantial compensation for expropriated property under intergovernmental agreements and paid damages to Americans caught in revolutionary violence. The Bolivians agreed to compensate the former owners of nationalized tin mines under arrangements initiated in 1953. Both governments opened their countries to foreign investment, the Mexicans primarily in manufacturing, the Bolivians in oil.

The willingness of the Mexican and Bolivian revolutionaries to compromise with the United States appears to have moderated the movements' revolutionary policies. The Mexican revolutionaries' fiscal difficulties, need for foreign loans, and vulnerability to foreign interference forced them to compromise on domestic policies, especially with respect to the Constitution of 1917. There is little doubt that Carranza and Obregón would have carried nationalization, perhaps socialization, further in the absence of such persistent counter pressures from abroad. Similarly, U.S. strictures about private property in Bolivia in the early 1950s, George Jackson Eder's influential efforts on behalf of a free market economy in the late 1950s, and the American ambassadors' deep involvement in Bolivian affairs in the early 1960s had an indisputable impact on the course of the revolution. In both Mexico and Bolivia the result of the revolutionaries' willingness to compromise meant that the United States was able to exert a deradicalizing influence.

At the same time, the United States helped sustain the revolutionary governments in power. Foreign support often steadied the revolutionaries' shaky grips on the reins of power. In Mexico the United States used recognition and, sometimes more importantly, its capacity to sell or withhold arms from competing Mexican factions in support of incumbent revolutionary governments. Time after time the United States refused to give encouragement to opposition groups in Mexico seeking to interfere with the succession. Both Presidents Paz and Siles testified that U.S. economic assistance saved the Bolivian Revolution in its earlier years.

It is well to note, however, that the Mexicans' and the Bolivians' capacity to compromise was by no means synonymous with capitulation. The revolutionary governments stood their ground and many times refused to accept what they described as interference in their internal affairs. Such a stance was essential not only to defend the national interest, but also to defend their political lives. Any Mexican or Bolivian government which obviously capitulated to U.S. pressure risked popular wrath and ultimately its own destruction. Political and military advisers from the United States were playing such a huge role in Bolivian affairs at the end of Paz Estenssoro's last government that they had, in a sense, displaced part of his Bolivian following.

The Mexican and Bolivian revolutionaries skillfully used Great Power rivalries to their own advantage in dealing with the United States. In World War I, Carranza played up to imperial Germany enough so that the latter served as a real counterweight to U.S. influence in Mexico. Fear of Mexican-German rapprochement was the major reason Wilson withdrew the Pershing military expedition from Mexico. Because Carranza allowed the Germans sufficient espionage and propaganda facilities, the Germans, to avoid sacrificing their relationship with Mexico, decided against sabotaging the rich Mexican oil fields. This action could have seriously damaged both Mexico and the Entente powers. Cárdenas dealt with both the United States and Germany without falling under the domination of either. The fact that there was no important European counterweight to U.S. influence in the Americas in the 1920s partly explains why Mexico went to such great lengths in the Bucareli agreements to secure U.S. recognition. In the 1930s Cárdenas was supportive of collective security measures against the Axis but not to the point where the possibility of Mexican links with Germany, Italy, and Japan were excluded from U.S. official considerations.

Similarly, the Bolivians profited from the rivalries of the United States and the Soviet Union in the 1950s. Emergency assistance in 1953 was justified largely as an anti-Communist measure and the large resources mobilized behind the Plan Triangular in the 1960s were an answer to Khrushchev's offer of long-term credits to Bolivia. Bolivian leaders led Americans to fear that failure to support them might result in the rapid growth of Communist or Soviet influence in Bolivia, but did not do so blatantly as to antagonize their benefactor.

U.S. Perspectives

United States considerations about Great Power rivals are vital to understanding its reconciliation with these two revolutions. The first climactic moment in Mexico came in early 1917 when the United States withdrew the Pershing expedition. In this episode, Wilson rightly decided that Pershing had to be withdrawn to prevent the outbreak of hostilities with Mexico and a deal between Mexico and Germany. The German archives show that the Mexicans had already tentatively turned to the Germans. Carranza's subsequent coolness to German responsiveness appears to have been directly related to the resolution of the military crisis with the United States. In the United States, Pershing's return home was widely viewed as a kind of capitulation since the Mexicans refused to meet Wilson's conditions for withdrawal. Nevertheless, Wilson withdrew the troops, absorbing this "defeat" in order to make the U.S. flank secure for the coming hostilities with Germany.

The second climactic moment in Mexico came after the seizure of the oil fields in March 1938. In spite of the clamor in the United States for strong action against

Mexico, the moderate counsels of Roosevelt and his advisers, Morgenthau and Ickes, prevailed. Ambassador Daniels in Mexico City blunted the force of a strong protest and the United States did not try to bring Mexico to her knees through military or economic sanctions. Although Mexico did increase oil sales to the Axis, these were not accompanied by political rapprochement. While insisting on compensation, the United States made payment easier by making large silver purchases and long-term loans to Mexico. Amicable settlement of the disputes over oil and land made possible political and military collaboration during World War II.

The climactic moment in Bolivia came in 1953 when the MNR government was near collapse. Despite the nationalization of the tin mines and plans for land reform, the United States provided emergency economic assistance to Bolivia that made it possible for the Paz Estenssoro government to survive. The United States' economic and military assistance also played a generally supportive role in most subsequent crises of the revolutionary government. The major justification for economic assistance to Bolivia was to prevent the country from going Communist, the explicit explanation given in 1953. Much subsequent assistance was justified, in roughly the same Cold War terms, as a counter to possible Communist or Soviet influence in Bolivia. Communist and Soviet influence in Bolivia in those years was small and, of course, the extent of the presumed "threat" is a speculative question—nor do we know how seriously U.S. officials took it. Nonetheless, the potential for Soviet intrigue in the area was the rationale behind U.S. economic and military assistance to the revolutionary governments. Thus, security considerations, that is, U.S. calculations about the implications of the Mexican and Bolivian revolutions in their relations with Great Powers, were the dominant considerations defining the U.S. response.

Germany and the USSR

The persuasiveness of this hypothesis should not lead to an exaggerated conception of the capacity Germany and the Soviet Union had to influence the course of the two revolutions. The Western Allies' control of the Atlantic during both world wars ruled out Mexico as a source of supply for Germany and prevented Germany from making large deliveries to Mexico. Carranza and Cárdenas were both skeptical about the economic benefits to be gained from a closer relationship with Germany. Carranza approached Germany only *in extremis*, that is, when Pershing's occupation of northern Mexico posed the threat of political domination and war. When Pershing withdrew, Carranza cooled toward Germany and refused to commit himself to Zimmermann's proposals. Similarly, Cárdenas had long held a dim view of Hitler, trade relations had not been great, and Mexico's sale of oil to Germany jumped only after Mexico was prevented from selling to its usual customers.

Mexico did not have closer relations with Germany partly because of the latter's limitations mentioned above, but also because of the ineptness of German policies. Imperial Germany and the Nazis devoted most of their efforts to building connections with the counterrevolutionary opposition in Mexico, backing losing horses. Only when this strategy failed did the Germans turn to Carranza and Cárdenas as a last resort. These last-minute switches so obviously appeared to be designed to promote Germany's advantage at the expense of Mexico that Germany commanded little credibility or respect with the Cárdenas government.

The Soviet potential for influence in Bolivia, especially in the 1950s, was probably relatively less than the German in Mexico. The Bolivian Revolution broke out during Stalin's last days and was consolidated during the years when the struggle for the Soviet succession was at its height. As a result, the Soviets were so heavily engaged at home in reviving the economy and resolving internal political conflict that there was little time or interest for a country as remote and obscure as Bolivia. When Khrushchev consolidated his power at home and began to take a personal interest in Bolivia in 1960, Bolivia's ties with the United States were already strong. In the showdown, the Americans outbid the Russians and led the Bolivians to believe that they could not receive both U.S. and Soviet assistance. Not unexpectedly, the Bolivians chose the Americans.

The other major vehicle for Soviet influence, the Bolivian Communist party, had long been weak, partly a coincidence since the Trotskyites had done relatively far better in Bolivia than in most other countries. The Communist party did not really get under way as an operating entity—and a small one at that—until the late 1950s. Thus, the potential dangers Germany posed in Mexico in World Wars I and II were real and substantially greater than the perceived dangers the USSR posed in Bolivia in the 1950s and early 1960s.

Extra- and Intra-Governmental Bargaining

Emphasis on national security considerations in explaining the U.S. reconciliation with the Mexican and Bolivian revolutions may trouble those who conceive of U.S. policy as primarily designed to protect and promote private business interests in Latin America. Yet U.S. presidents have given priority to national over private interests.[159] Wilson's de facto recognition of Carranza in 1915, his withdrawal of Pershing in 1917, and de jure recognition of Carranza in 1917 were all done for security reasons over the objection of business interests hostile to the revolutionaries. When economic and business considerations clearly appeared dominant in the Bucareli agreements, the Americas were largely isolated from Great Power rivalries. Roosevelt's refusal to invoke harsher sanctions against Mexico over the oil expropriations overrode the opposition of the U.S. oil companies.

Since little U.S. investment was affected by the Bolivian Revolution, criticism of it in the United States was due more to political or ideological considerations than to business considerations. The U.S. groups exerting the strongest influence over U.S. policy were U.S. economic assistance, diplomatic, and military officials. Many of them were dedicated professionals in economic and social development who identified closely with the goals of the Bolivian Revolution. Their jobs depended on the program, and they had a vested interest in its success. The satisfaction from mobilizing resources to do their jobs well was accompanied by the psychic payoffs of exercising political influence and power.

Other reasons, however, were advanced to persuade Congress to appropriate funds for Bolivia. The emergency assistance authorized in 1953 was justified as a means of preventing Bolivia from going Communist, the Plan Triangular of 1961 was an answer to Khrushchev's offer of a tin smelter, and the large grants and loans made thereafter were part of the larger strategy of the Alliance for Progress.[160] United States officials offered these reasons to justify the U..S. assistance, but they also believed in the validity of their Cold War rationale.

In the complex relations between these governments, there were conflicts *within* governments and societies as well as *between* them. Groups favoring reconciliation achieved dominance on both sides. In Mexico and Bolivia the leaders who emerged victorious managed to defeat revolutionary rivals who appeared bent on extremist policies either of capitulation or intransigence with respect to the United States. Within the United States, there were groups who competed to influence U.S. policy toward Mexico: Roman Catholics who were bitterly hostile to the Mexican Revolution largely because of its anticlerical policies; U.S. military forces who were bent on maintaining order along the border and defending U.S. honor at the risk of hostilities; oil, agricultural and financial interests seeking to protect access to lands and other profit opportunities; and presidents and secretaries of state who were primarily concerned with avoiding war with Mexico in order to strengthen their hand in dealing with German threats to Europe. Conflict over U.S. policy toward Bolivia within the United States was less intense because few U.S. private interests were at stake, and counterrevolutionary groups had to make their appeals primarily on ideological grounds.

In the end, U.S. leaders favored reconciliation since both revolutionary governments preferred compromise and since such compromises suited U.S. strategic objectives.

6 Guatemala and Cuba: Paramilitary Expeditions

The Eisenhower administration's strategy for coping with the Guatemalan and Cuban revolutions was the antithesis of its own policy toward Bolivia and of Franklin Roosevelt's earlier policies toward Mexico. Whereas reconciliation became the aim and the result of U.S. policies toward Mexico and Bolivia, the Guatemalan and Cuban revolutions culminated in U.S.-sponsored armed invasions. This chapter explains why the United States responded with force in these two cases.

Relations with Guatemala and Cuba were, probably, the two most important aspects of Eisenhower's Latin American policies. "Communism" in Guatemala was a major issue during his first two years in office and "communism" in Cuba during his last two years. Considered a success at the time, policies toward Guatemala in 1954 shaped policies toward Cuba in 1960–1961. The consequences of both have cast a long shadow over relations with Latin America ever since.

Two men provided the principal continuity of these policies: President Dwight D. Eisenhower and Director of the Central Intelligence Agency (CIA) Allen W. Dulles. The same continuity was not found in the Department of State. Secretary John Foster Dulles and his undersecretary, Walter Bedell Smith, who had previously been director of the CIA, were the senior officials during the Guatemalan episode. By the time the crisis with Castro reached its height, the leadership of the Department of State had been assumed by Christian Herter and C. Douglas Dillon.

The Guatemalan experience also shaped Castro's military plans and strategy toward the United States. Che Guevara had witnessed firsthand the revolution in Guatemala, fleeing the country when Arbenz was deposed. Castro, noting that Arbenz did not eliminate the Guatemalan army which overthrew him, resolved to destroy the Cuban army.

Jacobo Arbenz (1951–1954)

Arbenz took office in March 1951 under less happy circumstances than his predecessor, Juan José Arévalo.[1] Two episodes cast a cloud over his tenure as constitutional president.

The first involved the mysterious circumstances surrounding the death of his chief political rival and fellow army officer, Francisco Javier Arana. Arana and Arbenz were members of the three-man junta that assumed control of Guatemala from the successful overthrow of General Federico Ponce Vaides on October 20, 1944, until Arévalo took office as president in 1945. Arana became chief of the armed forces and Arbenz minister of defense. As the strong man in the army, Arana attracted conservative forces within and without the revolutionary movement that favored his candidacy in the next presidential election. His political influence also made him simultaneously best able to protect or endanger Arévalo's hold on the presidency. Meanwhile, the forces of the Left began to group behind Arana's rival, Jacobo Arbenz.

Arana was ambushed and assassinated on July 18, 1949, near Guatemala City. Although satisfactory explanations of his death have never been made, Arbenz's chauffeur appears to have been involved in the attack as was another close Arbenz associate, Alfonso Martínez Estévez.[2] Arana's death eliminated Arbenz's major competition in the 1950 presidential elections and intensified political polarization.

The second episode was the 1950 presidential election itself. Two of Arbenz's opponents, General Ydígoras Fuentes and Colonel Miguel Angel Mendoza, were forced into hiding, and mobs interfered with the campaign of Jorge García Granados. Observers widely suspected multiple voting and other fraud.[3] When the votes were counted, Arbenz received far more votes than his nearest competitor. Even though Arbenz may well have had more popular support than other candidates, the manner in which the elections were conducted and the fact that the government threw its weight behind Arbenz clouded his victory.

Revolutionary Change and U.S. Interests

When Arbenz became president, the pace of social change accelerated. Attitudes and social relations were affected mainly in the cities; rural areas responded far more slowly. Arbenz sought to break the economic and political power of the traditional groups which controlled the countryside and the foreign interests which owned and operated the nation's largest public utilities and agricultural properties. Arbenz moved to regulate and check their political influence in the name of Guatemalan urban and rural workers. In announcing his government's program, Arbenz said:

> We are going to promote the economic development of Guatemala in accordance with three fundamental objectives: first, to convert our country from a dependent nation and semi-colonial country into an economically independent country; second, to transform our nation from a backward country and a predominantly feudal economy into a modern capitalist country; and third, to effect this transformation so that it is accompanied by the greatest possible increase in the living standards of the large masses of the people.[4]

Land reform became the major plank in Arbenz's program. After extensive discussions in the congress and among different social groups, Arbenz promulgated the Agrarian Reform Law on June 17, 1952. The law provided for the expropriation of uncultivated land above a specified size with compensation in agrarian bonds. Rural workers were to receive land in their own names or for use (without title), upon the payment of a percentage of the crop. The law was generally viewed as moderate, and specifically provided for compensation in contrast to early drafts supported by the Guatemalan Communists which had not. Difficulties in interpreting the provisions of the law and the manner of its implementation, with restrictions on the right of judicial appeal, frightened many landowners. Moreover, members of the Communist party were heavily represented in the agrarian reform agency and strong-arm methods and other excesses occurred, particularly in the department of Escuintla. About 1.5 million acres of land belonging to about one thousand plantations were expropriated with bonds worth about $8.4 million.[5]

Easily the company most affected was United Fruit with 83,029 of its 188,399 hectares expropriated.[6] In order to have some idea of the relative economic strength of the contending parties in the land reform dispute, one should know that the annual sales of United Fruit in the six Central American countries were more than double the ordinary revenues of the Guatemalan government.[7]

The land reform not only created tensions with United Fruit but also became a source of friction with the Department of State as well. Less than a month after the first expropriation of United Fruit property, that is, on March 25, 1953, the Department of State lodged a formal protest making expropriation an issue between the two governments (see chapter 4).

Another dramatic aspect of Arbenz's program was his effort to end monopoly control by the United Fruit Company and other U.S. interests of Guatemala's central public services. Most of Guatemala's exports and imports were carried by the International Railway of Central America (IRCA)—controlled by the United Fruit Company—to the Atlantic port of Puerto Barrios. Docking facilities there belonged to the United Fruit Company, as did the Great White Fleet which used them. In the absence of any other overland connection and to break the monopoly responsible for freight rates which the government considered excessive, Arbenz initiated the construction of the highway to the Atlantic on July 2, 1951. Meanwhile, Guatemala was continuing on its own the construction of the Pan American, or Franklin D. Roosevelt, Highway through Central America, contributions to which the United States ceased to make in July 1951. It was not until more than two years later that Guatemala was able to finance and, under a contract with a U.S. private firm, begin construction of a new port at Santo Tomás. The latter provided an alternative to the nearby United Fruit port at the terminus of the new highway route.. The new highway and port thus posed a direct challenge to the United Fruit Company's long-established control of Guatemala's central transportation network.

Similarly the major source of electric power in and around Guatemala City was a U.S.-controlled power plant. Arbenz arranged financing and initiated construction of additional electric power facilities to break this other foreign-controlled monopoly of public services. In addition, the government took over its management from July to November 1953 in order to maintain services during a management-labor dispute.

The government thereby challenged and interfered with another long-established U.S. private interest.

Whereas Arbenz's plans for land reform and the development of public services created grave friction with powerful private interests in the United States, his independent foreign policies troubled the Department of State. After the outbreak of the Korean War, Guatemala had taken the leadership in the United Nations General Assembly insisting that the provision of troops for the United Nations' efforts in Korea be optional. Similarly, when the foreign ministers of the Organization of American States (OAS) met in Washington at the end of March 1951 to consider military support for United Nations forces in Korea, Guatemala together with Argentina maintained that each state should decide for itself whether to send troops. Shortly thereafter the foreign minister announced that Guatemala would not send troops to Korea and would focus all its efforts on its own development.[8]

The Communist Issue

As relations became increasingly tense, U.S. spokesmen focused attention not so much on land reform and the expropriation of United Fruit as on allegations that the international Communist movement had established a beachhead in Guatemala. Although the Department of State did not make fine distinctions, there are several aspects to this question: first, the nature and extent of the influence of Guatemalan Communists on the Arbenz government; and second, the nature and extent of the influence of the international Communist movement, particularly the Soviet Union, on the Guatemalan Communists and the Arbenz government.

Under the Ubico dictatorship (1931–1944), Communists had little opportunity to expand their influence and activities and thus got a relatively late start in Guatemala. The revolution took place in 1944 at a time favorable to the Communists during the height of Soviet-American collaboration against the Axis. Guatemala had not experienced firsthand the sobering experience of Communist maneuverings in domestic politics before World War II as had Chile and Cuba.

Arévalo held that communism, as a doctrine, was antidemocratic and that the international movement was an enemy of democracy and of the people of Latin America.[9] Arévalo banned the Communist party and deported Communist leaders for illegal activities early in his administration. Yet he insisted that the civil rights of all citizens, including Communists who did not violate the law, be protected. As a result, Communist leaders did have an opportunity to air their beliefs and programs, and popular support for them grew under Arévalo. Communists from abroad were allowed to visit the country and local Communists held posts in his administration. The assassination of the strongest anti-Communist in his cabinet, Colonel Arana, described above, made Arévalo increasingly dependent on Arbenz and the Left in his final two years in the presidency.

Arbenz was a professional military officer who knew little about Marxist ideology and had little contact with the Communists until the end of Arévalo's administration. Gradually, he learned something of Marxism-Leninism and maintained close personal relations with many of Guatemala's leading Communists. Arbenz's wife, María, from a well-known Salvadorean family of means, was sympathetic to many causes enjoying Communist support. Two of her closest friends, who acted at various times as her private secretaries, were the Chilean Communist, Virginia Bravo Letelier, and the Salvadorean Communist, Matilde Elena Lopez. Guatemalan Communists were among Arbenz's earliest supporters for the presidency and were active in his election in 1950. As his presidential term wore on, Communist leaders had free access to Arbenz who consulted them on state policies.[10]

The Communists' influence was based first and foremost on their control of organized labor. Anti-Communist labor leaders failed to break their control in Guatemala unlike in most other Latin American countries at the end of the 1940s.[11] A key to the Communists' success was the Federación Sindical de Guatemala (FSG)—organized in 1946 and initially opposed to Communist control—which eventually agreed to join with the Communists in a national labor confederation. Labor unity was achieved in October 1951 with the Communists dominant. The Confederación General de Trabajadores de Guatemala (CGTG), as the unified national organization was known, affiliated with the Confederación de Trabajadores de América Latina (CTAL) and the World Federation of Trade Unions (WFTU). The Communist labor leaders' success in Guatemala was a major defeat for anti-Communist labor groups in Latin America.

Another Communist victory in the labor field was the rapid expansion of membership in the national peasant union, Confederación Nacional Campesina de Guatemala (CNCG). The latter expanded rapidly under Arbenz to a claimed membership of some 400,000 peasants whose organization was under Communist influence and control. Its leader, Leonardo Castillo Flores, whose early organizational efforts were independent of the Communists, worked ever closer to the CGTG and eventually affiliated the CNCG with the CTAL and the WFTU.[12]

Communist control of labor organizations, industrial and agricultural, gave the party links with a mass base and influence in national politics and government.

The Communists did not operate openly as a political party under Arévalo because he held that the international connection was incompatible with the Guatemalan constitution. As a result, the Communists organized secretly as the Vanguardia Democrática Guatemalteca within a recognized political party, the Partido de Acción Revolucionario (PAR). The Vanguardia, incidentally, was not established until September 1947, surprisingly late when one considers the much longer established Communist parties in many other Latin American countries.[13] The Communists thereafter were organized under various names, sometimes in conflicting and separate organizations. After Arana's assassination, one Communist group openly took the name, Partido Comunista de Guatemala (PCG), which was changed in 1952 largely as a matter of window dressing to the Partido Guatemalteco de Trabajo (PGT). From about forty members in 1949 the party grew to some 4,000 in 1954.[14]

Under Arbenz the Communist influence in governmental affairs grew. Although only four of the fifty-six members of congress were Communists, Communist deputies had seats on all major committees, were among the acknowledged leaders of the congress, and enjoyed enhanced influence on legislative matters in view of their recognized ties with the president. Communists held posts in the ministry of education, the national agrarian department, the press and propaganda offices, and other government agencies. In government agencies for the implementation of the agrarian reform communists were, perhaps, the most important single political group represented.

The foregoing description probably leaves an exaggerated impression of the Communists' influence. Any balanced appraisal of the influence of various political groups would require describing the positions of each in the executive and legislative branches of the government. When the whole political spectrum is considered, the Communists seem much less prominent than when attention is focused solely on them. The positions they did *not* hold were, of course, much more numerous than those they held. For example, none of the Arbenz cabinet ministers were Communists.

In his last annual report to the congress in March 1954, President Arbenz discussed communism and its alleged threat to the solidarity of the western Hemisphere. His theme was that the workers' and peasants' movement and the Guatemalan Revolution itself were being attacked on the pretext of anticommunism. Foreign companies and "monopoly capital," he charged, were speaking in the name of democracy and the defense of the Western Hemisphere while in fact attempting to divide the forces of democracy by placing Communists and others called Communists in quarantine. He insisted that his administration would respect the civil rights of Communists and would not sacrifice the democratic and revolutionary movement to the so-called danger of communism.[15]

The Guatemalan Communists remained in more or less close contact with their fellows elsewhere in the world. Party leaders traveled frequently to the Communist countries. According to Schneider, 130 Guatemalans traveled to such countries while Arbenz was president.[16] Many leading Latin American Communists visited or resided in Guatemala in support of various Communist causes. Communist writings and the Communist press reflected the ideological and political positions of the international Communist movement, dominated much more then than now by Soviet leaders. Similarly, the Communist leaders of the Guatemalan labor movement remained in close and frequent contact with other Communist labor leaders in Latin America as well as with the Communist labor leadership in Europe and elsewhere. The practices of the Guatemalan Communists in these respects were essentially the same as those of Communists elsewhere.

All the foregoing evidence leaves no doubt that Guatemalan Communists had made substantial political gains in a half dozen years. They dominated the Guatemalan labor movement and had relatively free access to and influence with the president. Influence is one thing; control another. It would be difficult to determine by quantitative methods whether the Communists "controlled" or "dominated" the Guatemalan government. As events so dramatically showed later, the Communists most emphatically did *not* control the most powerful organization in the country—the armed forces. And the weight of the evidence would seem to show that, lacking a single cabinet post, they could scarcely have controlled the government as a whole. What would, no doubt, be fairer to say is that the groups which controlled Guatemala under Arbenz had interests and policies established independently of the Communists which the Communists supported. As a result of domestic and foreign developments, the government's and the Communists' policies overlapped in many areas. For reasons which will be discussed later, President Arbenz found Communist support useful. As he grew weaker, he needed that support even more.

United States officials have frequently railed against "international communism" without making clear the definition of that term. One aspect of international communism is ideological, that is, the spread of Marxist-Leninist doctrines. Clearly, the Guatemalan Communists were engaged in that activity as were Communists elsewhere in the world. The Guatemalans tended to follow the Soviet interpretations and applications of these doctrines, though even within that movement there have been many differing views and ideological conflicts. Yet the United States has often hesitated to push its attack on Communist propaganda too far since presumably the U.S. Constitution and traditions require freedom of thought and freedom of expression, even for Marxist-Leninists.

Another aspect of international communism relates to the foreign ties of the Guatemalan Communist party whose membership in Guatemala at its height in 1954 numbered about four thousand. That party proved no match for traditional elements within Guatemala, much less for the United States, for which such a group alone could hardly be taken seriously as a physical threat.

About the only way the activities of Guatemalan Communists could seriously endanger the United States was through their connection with the Soviet Union. The latter's military, economic, and other power could threaten the United States. To make that threat credible with respect to Guatemala, it was convenient to allege not only that the Guatemalan Communists took orders from Moscow but also that Soviet or Guatemalan Communists controlled the Arbenz government.

No doubt Soviet officials exercized influence over the Guatemalan Communists, as they did over others geographically remote from Moscow. Soviet and Guatemalan Communists held many common political views and sought similar social changes in Guatemala; their political and material interests converged at many points. The Soviet Union or organizations it sponsored were the major source of the Guatemalan Communists' external financial, political, and moral support. International Communist organizations footed travel bills and subsidized publications. The Soviet Communists used and were used by the Guatemalan Communists.

The main purposes of the Guatemalan Communists, however, could only be served in a very marginal sense from without. Their work was primarily political, that is, organizing large numbers of people behind specific programs and political organizations. Non-Guatemalans were hardly suitable for much of that work, and there were limits not only to the money the international Communist movement could provide but to the extent to which money could be substituted for political conviction and political commitment. The men Soviet rubles might have bought were not likely to produce reliable political support in the long term. Jaime Díaz Rozzotto has written an analysis of the Guatemalan Revolution from the Marxist-Leninist perspective which implicitly clarifies how peripheral external support was to the real problems with which the Communists were concerned.[17] His critical analysis shows the ideological and political weaknesses of the Communist party and, despite its strong and prominent support for Arbenz, its limited influence in the body politic. Leading Soviet scholars also carefully distinguish between Arbenz and the Communist party. They characterize him as representing the interests of "petty bourgeois democrats."[18]

Díaz Rozzotto also unintentionally shows the limits of the Guatemalan Communists' influence on the Arbenz government. The Communists supported Arbenz's efforts on behalf of economic independence, especially with respect to United Fruit interests, favored the "bourgeois-democratic" reforms he was introducing, and supported his efforts to resist various forms of U.S. pressure. Arbenz needed the political support the Communists supplied, and they for their part were able to expand their influence in government and their local following while helping him. All this substantiates their influence but does not prove their "control."

Another question relates to the extent of direct Soviet influence on the Arbenz government. Guatemala and the Soviet Union formally announced the establishment of diplomatic relations in April 1945 but neither country sent resident diplomatic missions to the other's capital. Arbenz carried on extended conversations with the Czech commercial attaché from Mexico in March 1953 and a Czechoslovak minister presented credentials to Arbenz in January 1954. In October 1953 the Soviet commercial attaché from Mexico had a three-hour interview with Arbenz.[19] Ronald Schneider who has studied a mass of documents from the Arbenz government and the Guatemalan Communist organizations presents little or no other evidence of direct official Soviet contact with Arbenz. (The arms shipment from Szczecin is discussed below.) There is no question that the Soviet Union could have been in contact with the Arbenz government through its own or East European government agents, unmonitored. I have, however, found no convincing evidence of the exercise of direct control over the Arbenz government or for that matter much evidence of direct Soviet contact.[20]

The foregoing discussion does not bear out the extreme position of the U.S. government. The latter made a strong case for Soviet influence over the Guatemalan Communist party and for Communist influence on Arbenz but did not conclusively establish that the Arbenz government was Communist or Soviet controlled.[21]

Central American Conflict

The revolutionary changes introduced under Arbenz had some of their first negative repercussions among Guatemala's neighbors in Central America. Political groups in one Central American country frequently have helped like-minded groups in other countries to overthrow a dictator or a democratic president, as the case may be. Arbenz's policies disturbed regimes committed to the status quo, particularly in Nicaragua and El Salvador. By late 1952 leaders in some of these countries began to talk to other Central American countries about the threat of communism in Guatemala.

The political dispute within Central America caused a crisis in the newly formed Organization of Central American States (ODECA). This most recent expression of long-standing sentiments in favor of Central American unity had come about in no small measure because of the goodwill and idealism of the Arbenz government and particularly its first foreign minister, Manuel Galich. As a kind of personal project of his own, Galich had persuaded Arbenz to resume diplomatic relations with the Nicaraguan dictatorship, suspended partly for ideological reasons under Arévalo and an obstacle to Central American unity.[22] ODECA came into existence in early 1952 after ratification of the Charter of San Salvador.

Tension developed within ODECA when the Salvadorean foreign minister began to urge the other members to join together in an anti-Communist front "to oppose the subversive action of international Communism in Central America."[23] Military leaders of four of the five countries, excluding Guatemala, met in Managua to consider appropriate military measures.[24] The Salvadorean proposals, calling for what really constituted the formation of an anti-Guatemalan bloc within Central America, angered the Arbenz government. Arbenz could not expect to have continued Communist support at home if he supported decisions within ODECA to repudiate international communism. Moreover, Guatemala's neighbors appeared to favor anti-Communist organizations in Guatemala. One such organization attempted to overthrow the Arbenz government in an armed uprising at Salamá on March 29, 1953. Arbenz crushed the revolt but found that the rebels had received foreign assistance, probably from a neighboring Central American country. On April 4, 1953, Guatemala withdrew from membership in ODECA, charged that other member governments had conspired to form a political military pact against Guatemala and that Central American groups were linking up with Guatemalans hostile to Arbenz for the purpose of intervening in Guatemalan politics.[25]

The Counterrevolutionary Movement

Relations between Guatemala and the United States continued to deteriorate when the Eisenhower administration came into office in 1953. Unfriendly governments in Central America had already discussed seeking U.S. assistance against Arbenz, and the appointment of John Foster Dulles as secretary of state was interpreted as a bad omen.[26] Dulles had reportedly served as the attorney of the United Fruit Company many years previously. Opposition to Arbenz within Guatemala was intensifying, and there was talk among foreign interests there of economic sanctions against the Arbenz regime.[27] In a speech at Dartmouth College on March 12, 1953, the former assistant secretary of state, Spruille Braden, said that the suppression of communism, even by force, in an American country would not constitute intervention in its internal affairs.[28] In that talk Braden had also criticized the Agrarian Reform Law and its enforcement against the United Fruit Company. Braden, incidentally, a friend and associate of Kenneth Redmond who headed United Fruit, served as a consultant to the company in the 1950s.[29]

At the end of April 1953, John Moors Cabot, assistant secretary for American republic affairs, arrived in Guatemala in an apparent effort to settle issues dividing the two countries. According to the then foreign minister, Raúl Osegueda, Cabot sought to quiet press and radio criticism of the United States, called attention to the activities of Communists in government and labor organizations, and supported claims of the United Fruit Company. Osegueda describes his reply as indicating that the government did not control Guatemala's free press, some of the men named had already left their jobs, others were not Communists, etc., and that the government would not discriminate against local firms in favor of the United Fruit Company. The two men reportedly parted on cordial terms without having reached a meeting of the minds.[30]

Official U.S. concern over the situation in Guatemala began to mount rapidly in October 1953 when Cabot publicly charged that "the international Communist conspiracy to destroy free governments" was prejudicing the independence of Guatemala. He added, "When we are resisting Communist aggression and subversion all over the world, no regime which is openly playing the Communist game can expect from us . . . positive cooperation."[31] Senator Alexander Wiley followed up shortly thereafter in a reference to Guatemala as a Communist "beachhead" in the Americas and there was talk in the Department of State about "joint action" with other American republics, possibly at the next inter-American conference.[32]

As U.S. opposition to the Arbenz government hardened, Guatemalans within and outside intensified plans for his overthrow. The man who proved the most effective opposition leader was an army officer, Carlos Castillo Armas, who had led an abortive coup attempt in November 1950 and made a dramatic escape in July 1951 from a prison in Guatemala City. Not long after that escape, he began preparations to overthrow Arbenz, linking his fortunes to a senior army officer, General Miguel Ydígoras Fuentes. The two officers signed a "gentlemen's agreement" on March 31, 1952, in San Salvador in which Castillo Armas assumed supreme command of the counterrevolutionary forces and was to serve later as provisional president, while Ydígoras was to be the candidate in the elections after Arbenz's fall.[33]

The hostility of neighboring countries first toward Arévalo and later toward Arbenz facilitated Castillo Armas' efforts to recruit financial and logistical support from neighboring governments. President Rafael Leonidas Trujillo of the Dominican Republic was a likely prospect for such support because of his running feud with the Guatemalans since Ubico's fall. In fact, Guatemala had served as the base for the ill-fated effort to overthrow Trujillo at Luperón in 1949. Although Castillo Armas apparently was not Trujillo's first choice to lead the movement, Trujillo provided him assistance nonetheless.[34] Trujillo's choice appears to have been Roberto Barrios Peña, a conservative and former collaborator with Ubico.

An even more important supporter of Castillo Armas was the long-time president of Nicaragua, Anastasio Somoza. Remembering Arévalo's earlier support for his Costa Rican antagonist, José Figueres, Somoza appears to have provided initial material aid to Castillo Armas before the United States had reached a decision about its own covert assistance. In July 1953, for example, Somoza's son, young Anastasio, provided Castillo Armas with copies of written offers for the sale of arms, ammunition, and other military equipment and supplies from an arms dealer in Hamburg, Germany.[35]

Although Trujillo and the Somozas provided assistance early, the U.S. Central Intelligence Agency was the organization whose approval was essential for Castillo Armas to exercise leadership.[36] Although there has never been explicit official acknowledgment of the CIA's support for Castillo, the evidence is overwhelming and virtually irrefutable.

Strong evidence in this respect is located in the letters of Castillo Armas himself, letters which one of his intermediaries, Jorge Isaac Delgado, sold to Arbenz and which were made public on January 29, 1954.[37] In a letter to President Anastasio Somoza of Nicaragua on September 20, 1953, Castillo reported the following:

I have been informed by our friends here that the government of the North, recognizing the impossibility of finding another solution to the grave problem of my country, has taken the decision to permit us to develop our plans.
Because of the importance of this basic decision, I immediately sent confidential messages so that it could be confirmed to me directly. Nevertheless, up to now I have not received any reply which apparently can be interpreted as confirming the foregoing.[38]

A letter of October 15, 1953, to Somoza's son confirmed the earlier news: "Our work with our friends from the North has ended in complete triumph in our favor and . . . shortly we will enter into a very active plan which will inevitably end with the victorious result which we all desire."[39]

In an interview with the author in Guatemala City on July 15, 1969, Eduardo Taracena de la Cerda, one of Castillo's chief lieutenants in the Liberation Movement, gave at length the nature and scope of the CIA's involvement which he described as providing most of the support to Castillo Armas. In another interview in Guatemala City on July 18, 1969, Arbenz's ambassador in Honduras, Colonel Amadeo Chinchilla, openly discussed CIA support to the Liberation Movement and described how he pleaded with the American ambassador in Tegucigalpa to have his government hold back the invasion to permit the Guatemalans to deal with the Communist problem themselves.

The American ambassador in Tegucigalpa, Whiting Willauer, told a Senate committee in 1961 about the CIA's involvement, excerpts from which testimony follow:

MR. SOURWINE: By 1954, Guatemala had become controlled by international Communism, had it not?

MR. WILLAUER: There was no doubt about it.

MR. SOURWINE: There was then in existence an anti-Communist revolutionary movement?

MR. WILLAUER: Yes, and it was largely based in Honduras.

MR. SOURWINE: And it was part of your job to assist that movement?

MR. WILLAUER: Yes, it was. In fact, after the revolution was successful, I received a telegram from Allen Dulles in which he stated in effect that the revolution could not have succeeded but for what I did. I am very proud of that telegram. I also received a telegram from Secretary Dulles, which was in more general language, complimenting me on my work. . . .

MR. SOURWINE: Jack Peurifoy was down there?

MR. WILLAUER: Yes, Jack was on the team over in Guatemala; that is the principal man, and we had Bob Hill, Ambassador Robert Hill, in Costa Rica, where there was [sic] certain side effects. And we had Ambassador Tom Whelan in Nicaragua, where a lot of activities were going. And, of course, there were a number of CIA operatives in the picture.

MR. SOURWINE: What was Mr. Dulles' involvement in that area?

MR. WILLAUER: Mr. Allen Dulles?

MR. SOURWINE: Yes.

MR. WILLAUER: Well, the CIA was helping to equip and train the anti-Communist revolutionary forces.[40]

The memoirs of the principal participants on the U.S. side tend to corroborate, though in less specific terms, the foregoing evidence. President Eisenhower recalled:

[On June 22, 1954] Allen Dulles reported to me that Castillo had lost two of the three old bombers with which he was supporting his "invasion." . . . The country which had originally supplied this equipment to Castillo was willing now to supply him two P-51 fighter-bombers if the United States would agree to replace them. . . . our proper course of action—indeed my duty—was clear to me. We would replace them. . . . Delivery was prompt and Castillo successfully resumed his progress.[41]

In his book *The Craft of Intelligence*, Allen Dulles stated that when Arbenz sought to create a Communist state in Guatemala, "support from outside was given to loyal anti-Communist elements."[42]

Robert Murphy, then deputy undersecretary of state, wrote in his memoirs that "we had given whatever assistance we legitimately could to Castillo Armas and his fellow exiles,"[43] without explaining what assistance was given or how any assistance likely to be of use to a counterrevolutionary movement against a government with which the United States maintained diplomatic relations could be "legitimate."

Leaders of the Arbenz government on many occasions have accused the United Fruit Company of having helped finance Castillo Armas, and the circumstances leave little doubt about United Fruit's involvement, at least initially. It will be recalled that Spruille Braden, whose association with the United Fruit Company is a matter of public record (see note 29), was one of the first prominent public figures to propose an end to the Arbenz government. Former President Ydígoras Fuentes describes how a former executive of the United Fruit Company, Walter Trumbull, and two other men, introduced as representatives of the CIA, tried to interest him in leading a revolt against Arbenz. Ydígoras refused.[44] Toriello has also pointed out that the Castillo Armas forces crossed into Guatemalan territory on United Fruit properties.[45] In any case, the hostility of the United Fruit Company to the Arbenz government was well known, and there is little doubt that the company hoped for and sought his political defeat. The lengths to which the company went against him must remain, however, an open question. Once influential Americans had helped persuade the U.S. government to supply a counterrevolutionary force, it is doubtful that a private company would have been willing to use its funds for this purpose.[46]

In retrospect, U.S. support for Castillo Armas appears to have been the result of a convergence of forces following Eisenhower's assumption of the presidency in January 1953. Arbenz had already defined and was rapidly implementing his program on behalf of "economic independence" and the welfare of poorer sectors of the population. At that time Castillo Armas was committed to leading a revolt against Arbenz. The United Fruit Company and other foreign interests were alerting the Department of State and influential senators and representatives to the "Communist menace" in Guatemala. John Foster Dulles had taken a strong anti-Communist line in the 1952 campaign. If the liberation of Eastern Europe which he had called for was too dangerous to undertake, nearby Guatemala provided him a much safer and more convenient country to "save" from communism.

In the spring of 1953 tensions mounted as Spruille Braden called for forceful action against Guatemala, conservative elements failed in their March insurrection, and the other Central American governments appeared bent on the formation of an anti-Communist, anti-Arbenz bloc. Walter Bedell Smith, Eisenhower's chief of staff in Europe in World War II and later director of central intelligence under Truman, moved over to the Department of State as Dulles' undersecretary when Eisenhower became president. Smith was thus in an ideal position to oversee and help coordinate the activities of the CIA and the Department of State in the Guatemalan affair. Meanwhile, Castillo Armas was receiving encouragement and, no doubt, funds from Presidents Trujillo and Somoza.

According to Spruille Braden, several Latin American ambassadors representing governments ill-disposed toward Arbenz called on Smith and urged U.S. assistance to Castillo Armas since the United States was being blamed for supporting Castillo anyway.[47] Castillo's correspondence with Somoza cited above indicates that the U.S. decision was taken in early fall 1953. A correct and reserved career diplomat of the old school, Ambassador Rudolph Schoenfeld, who got along fairly well with

Arbenz was replaced by John Peurifoy, a former military officer who worked his way up in the Department of State rather than in the Foreign Service. Peurifoy arrived in Guatemala not long after Assistant Secretary Cabot had openly attacked the Arbenz government at a public meeting in Washington, D.C. Early in the new year, *Time* magazine ran an article purporting to quote Peurifoy that "public opinion could force us to take measures to prevent Guatemala from falling into the lap of international Communism. We cannot permit the organization of a Soviet republic between Texas and the Panama Canal."[48] Only Peurifoy's prompt and personal denial of the statement appears to have prevented his being asked to leave the country.[49]

In January 1954 Jorge Isaac Delgado, the intermediary between Castillo Armas and Anastasio Somoza, Jr., sold photostatic copies of the Liberation Movement's documents to the Arbenz government, which subsequently published them.[50] The Department of State called the charges that the U.S. government had acquiesced in a plot by other nations against Guatemala "ridiculous and false."[51]

These revelations hastened the tempo of Castillo Armas' preparation. His forces were trained and equipped in Nicaragua, as the extensive documents involving the Somozas substantiate. Later Castillo's force of some 168 men moved to Honduras which has a common border with Guatemala.

Public Versus Private Interests

Before examining Arbenz's climactic ouster, his government's charges with respect to the United Fruit Company, Secretary Dulles, and Assistant Secretary John Moors Cabot require discussion. The Guatemalans maintained that Sullivan and Cromwell, the law firm which Dulles headed, had long been the attorneys for the United Fruit Company and that Dulles himself had actually drafted the United Fruit contracts with the Ubico government in 1930 and 1936. Moreover, they maintained that the Cabot family had long been intimately linked with the United Fruit Company as shareholders. In addition, Henry Cabot Lodge, the ambassador to the UN, from another old Boston family, was mentioned in the same connection. The Guatemalans were clearly acting on the assumption that Dulles and Cabot had vested interests in the United Fruit Company which conflicted with their official duties.[52]

Before leaving the Washington embassy to become foreign minister, Toriello discussed these matters at length with Undersecretary of State Walter Bedell Smith and President Eisenhower himself. Toriello describes his interview of January 14, 1954, with Smith:

> I found Bedell Smith . . . misinformed about Guatemalan realities. . . .
> After an hour and a half interview in which I made a detailed
> presentation . . . , the attitude of Mr. Smith changed completely. He shared
> the sense of gravity of the situation . . . and was in agreement that a change
> in the condition of operations of the United Fruit was necessary . . . and
> took interest in arranging my interview with the president.[53]

Two days later Toriello met with President Eisenhower:

> If Bedell Smith was little informed of Guatemalan realities, the president was
> even less. All he knew was "the Communist danger for the Continent," the
> "red menace" which Guatemala constituted. He was greatly surprised when I
> revealed to him the panorama of economic subjugation in which foreign
> monopolies held us and the conspiratorial activities in which they were en-
> gaged to crush the democratic movement, . . . [and] which made us appear
> as Communists. He could hardly believe the exaggerated privileges which
> these firms have enjoyed, as well as the connections between the United
> Fruit and the Department of State. It was difficult for him to believe that
> these same firms did not pay taxes and that some of their contracts were valid
> until the next century. With frightening ingenuousness he suggested to me
> that on my return to Guatemala I discuss possible solutions with Ambassador
> Peurifoy. Naturally, at least this was my impression—the president knew
> nothing of "Operation Guatemala" in which his own Department of State
> and his ambassador in my country were participating.
>
> I was forced to express my extreme skepticism about this prospect point-
> ing out discretely that Mr. Dulles was a member, no less, of the law firm of
> the United Fruit Company and that Mr. Moors Cabot (there present) and his
> family were stockholders of the same company. The president must have
> found my reasoning worth considering because he proposed that an impartial,
> mixed commission of Guatemalans and U.S. citizens . . . be formed to dis-
> cuss at the highest level the problem of monopolistic firms in Guatemala and
> all other subjects which had occasioned friction between the two
> countries. . . . Unfortunately . . . the good intentions of the president were
> this and nothing more . . . [and were] incapable of checking the aggression
> which was under way.[54]

The problem of conflict of interest deserves consideration because it was a
source of grave misunderstanding on both sides. First is the question of fact, whether
the firm of Sullivan and Cromwell was the United Fruit counsel and whether
Secretary Dulles had himself worked on their case. I have read the testimony of one of
Mr. Dulles' associates that he did in fact serve the International Railways of Central
America, a company long controlled by United Fruit, but I am not at liberty to give
the source of that testimony. Former Foreign Minister Osegueda reports that Mr.
Cabot told him on a visit to Guatemala that Sullivan and Cromwell were attorneys for
United Fruit and that Cabot's daughter was a stockholder in the United Fruit
Company.[55] Furthermore, it would not be surprising that as rich and influential a
family as the Cabots would have stock in as old a Boston firm as United Fruit.

My opinion is that by the nature of their upbringing, associations, and private
interests, Secretaries Dulles and Cabot would tend to give a sympathetic initial

hearing to any presentation of the United Fruit Company's point of view. Perhaps the best piece of evidence of probable bias in favor of the United Fruit Company in the Department of State is its note of August 28, 1953,[56] protesting the treatment of the United Fruit Company under the Guatemalan agrarian reform. The note reads more like a legal brief for the United Fruit Company than an intergovernmental note and is in sharp contrast, in this respect, to other such protests since the announcement of the Good Neighbor Policy in 1933.

In spite of the foregoing, I believe that the Arbenz government greatly misunderstood Dulles and Cabot and the U.S. government in this respect. The Guatemalan properties of the United Fruit Company represented only a fractional part of the company's total interests and the Arbenz measures were likely to have an adverse impact on profits in Guatemala, but it was not clear to what extent since only fallow land was directly affected. And even if the value of United Fruit stock fell sharply as a result of Arbenz's measures—which was not all that likely—it is most improbable that it would have had any substantial effect on the personal fortune of either Dulles or Cabot. Moreover, whatever may have been their shortcomings with regard to policy decisions, I have discovered nothing on the public record or in their reputations reflecting adversely on their financial integrity. No doubt, too, they were wiser than to risk their reputations and the verdict of history on behalf of United Fruit profits.

One curious aspect of the Eisenhower administration's policy was the Department of Justice's antitrust suit against the United Fruit Company filed on July 2, 1954.[57] Apparently, federal attorneys had rushed to make this legal action public less than a week after Arbenz's political demise. Their haste suggests that the Department of State thereby sought to give the lie to Latin American critics' allegations about U.S. motives in the Guatemalan affair. No doubt partly for reasons unrelated to U.S.–Guatemalan relations per se, the U.S. government continued to press its suit against United Fruit until 1958 when the company agreed to reform its structure and operations.[58]

Although not unreasonable under the circumstances, the Arbenz government's suspicions about U.S. collusion with United Fruit led to exaggerations of the importance of the protection of the United Fruit Company as a motive for U.S. policymakers and to an underestimation of U.S. fears and concern for the "Communist threat." Convinced of the probity of Dulles and Cabot, U.S. policymakers were offended by the Guatemalan charges which seemed to them preposterous, thereby making it hard to take the Guatemalans seriously on other issues.

Toriello's report of his conversations with Bedell Smith and the president offer further confirmation of the abysmal ignorance of Guatemala of the top officials in the Eisenhower administration. That ignorance comes as no great surprise but is tragic nonetheless. No doubt Eisenhower and Smith both had second thoughts on policy toward Guatemala, thoughts which probably never had a chance in the face of the momentum of the CIA operation and John Foster Dulles' single-minded obsession to secure a victory over communism in the Americas. The latter considerations were coupled with immense pressures created in Congress by the United Fruit and other interests. An influential constituency that called for Arbenz's demise existed in the United States; there were few spokesmen for reconciliation and compromise. Nothing came of talk about a joint commission to settle differences or about a face-to-face meeting between Presidents Eisenhower and Arbenz.

The Conflict Without: Dulles' Role

The closing months of the Arbenz government were marked by two parallel conflicts: one in the international and the other in the national arena. The external conflict was the struggle between the U.S. and Guatemalan governments to marshal support for their respective positions with other governments in Latin America and Europe. Secretary of State John Foster Dulles succeeded in dominating that struggle with the assistance of the U.S. ambassador at the United Nations, Henry Cabot Lodge. The internal struggle focused on attempts to overthrow the Arbenz government and establish the succession. Ambassador John E. Peurifoy and Colonel Castillo Armas won that contest.

The external struggle commanded international attention first at the Tenth Inter-American Conference in Caracas, Venezuela, on March 1, 1954. The conference was called partly on the initiative of the U.S. Department of State, whose leaders were concerned by internal developments in Guatemala and foreign reaction to them. Secretary Dulles wished the conference to provide a stronger political and juridical basis for unilateral or collective action against the Arbenz government. Dulles needed international support for his policies, particularly to counteract the likely international repercussions if U.S. involvement in the armed revolt against Arbenz became widely known. The United States proposed a draft declaration, excerpts from which follow:

> That the domination or control of the political institutions of any American State by the international Communist movement, extending to this hemisphere the political system of an extra-continental power, would constitute a threat to the sovereignty and political independence of the American States, endangering the peace of America, and would call for appropriate action in accordance with existing treaties.[59]

The resolution clearly provided a juridical basis for action against Guatemala, although the latter was not mentioned by name.

The Guatemalan foreign minister denied that his government was Communist, that he had any intention of defending international communism, and asserted that Guatemalans would rise up "as one man" to defend the continent against any external attack.[60] But he insisted that the alleged threat of international communism should not be used as a pretext for interfering in Guatemala's internal affairs, nor as a means for "the armed suppression of every effort for the political and economic liberation . . . of the oppressed peoples of Latin America."[61] Several countries expressed concern about the resolution being a cloak for intervention. Secretary

Dulles accepted amendments to the above draft calling for a meeting of consultation to consider appropriate measures, thus allaying Latin American concern about possible unilateral U.S. action. He also accepted a paragraph specifying that the resolution was designed to protect, not impair, the right of each American state freely to choose its own form of government. Despite the reluctance of many of the Latin Americans present, the resolution passed seventeen votes to one. Guatemala cast the single negative vote and Mexico and Argentina abstained. In the course of the debate, at which very time Castillo Armas was completing preparations for the attack with arms provided by the CIA, Mr. Dulles said, "I believe that there is not a single American state which would practice intervention against another American state."[62]

The substance of the Caracas resolution was not new. Article 6 of the Rio Treaty of 1947 provided for consultation on measures to counter, for example, threats to the political independence of an American state. Following the riots in Bogotá in 1948 at the Ninth Inter-American Conference, the member states resolved that the "anti-democratic nature" and "interventionist tendency" of international communism were incompatible with the American conception of liberty. Again, the foreign ministers' meeting in Washington in 1951 condemned "the aggressive activities of international Communism."[63] The significance, then, of the Caracas resolution of 1954 was not so much its content as its context, namely that it was passed with an eye to its possible application in Guatemala over the express opposition of the Guatemalan government. The reluctant acceptance of the resolution by many Latin American governments reasssured the Eisenhower administration in its plans to promote Arbenz's fall and made Latin American opposition to U.S. involvement in the revolt even less effective than before.

The precipitant, or better the pretext, for foreign authorization of the counter-revolutionary attack was the delivery to Guatemala of about two thousand tons of Czech-manufactured light arms and ammunition aboard the S.S. *Alfhem* which was chartered by a Swedish company from an English firm. The arms were loaded aboard the *Alfhem* at the Polish port of Szczecin in the Baltic Séa, and once it was made public, the shipment raised a stir in the world press.

The United States and other groups critical of Arbenz seized on the shipment as clear proof of Soviet intervention in the Western Hemisphere and as partial grounds for implementation of the Rio pact. Yet this event can only be fully understood in the light of its historical background.

The United States refused to sell Guatemala arms beginning in 1948. While still president, Arévalo had almost completed the purchase of arms from Denmark when his order was cancelled at the last minute, according to him "by North American espionage agents."[64] The United States, with Great Britain in collaboration, prevented sales by third parties to Guatemala.[65] Ex-President Arévalo has described Arbenz's unsuccessful efforts to secure arms in Mexico, Cuba, and Argentina and finally his turning to Europe, initially to Switzerland. A shipment from that country was impounded by U.S. officials as it was being transhipped through the New York harbor. Herbert Fauntleroy Julian, the "Black Eagle of Harlem," has described the U.S. boycott on arms sales to Guatemala and the latter's wish to avoid purchases in Eastern Europe "regardless of the price."[66] Thus, it appears that the 1954 purchase from Szczecin was a kind of last resort after a series of abortive efforts to secure arms from other western countries. Arbenz felt a pressing need for arms to defend his government from internal revolt (such as that at Salamá, March 1953) and from external attack, knowing as he did about Castillo Armas' invasion plans.

Meanwhile, tensions were rising between Guatemala and Honduras from which Castillo Armas intended to launch his attack. The latter country was beset in May by a general strike, the leaders of which may have been sympathetic to the Guatemalan Revolution and have received financial support from the Arbenz government.[67]

As external pressures and the anxiety of the Arbenz government about the impending revolt increased, security measures were tightened and plotters against the government discovered. Government arrests mounted and, according to the accounts of its critics later, the Arbenz government unleashed a reign of terror involving night arrests, interrogations, murders, and torture.[68] The Arbenz government was fighting for its life and had difficulty preventing inhuman excesses. These actions further increased apprehension abroad and were used to discredit Arbenz.

At the end of May and well into June, political conditions reached the boiling point while Castillo Armas was poised for his armed attack in the northeast. (Both of these developments, and U.S. involvement therein, are described in the immediately following section.) Castillo Armas launched his attacks on June 18, 1954.

On that day the foreign minister of Guatemala cabled the president of the Security Council for that month, Henry Cabot Lodge, requesting that he convene the council immediately to take measures to stop the aggression against Guatemala.[69] In his request Foreign Minister Toriello reviewed how, after concluding military assistance agreements with the United States, Nicaragua broke diplomatic relations with Guatemala at the end of May. He also described violations of Guatemalan airspace on several specific dates and his pleas to the Honduran government to contain the military forces hostile to Arbenz within its borders.

Ambassador Lodge convened the Security Council on June 20 to hear the Guatemalan complaint. The Guatemalan ambassador charged that his country "had been invaded by expeditionary forces forming part of an unlawful international aggression," and that it was the victim of a campaign "to prepare the way for open intervention in the domestic affairs of our country . . . set on foot by the United Fruit Company . . . and encouraged by the United States State Department [which] has sought to represent Guatemala as an outpost of Soviet Communism on the American continent, a tool of Moscow and a spearhead of the Soviet Union against the United States."[70] He then reviewed the evidence made public in January to show Nicaraguan and U.S. complicity in the "aggression." He urged that the Security Council send a mission to investigate his charges as quickly as possible.

Ambassador Lodge said that his information "strongly suggests that the situation does not involve aggression but is a revolt of Guatemalans against Guatemalans." He denied that the Guatemalans had produced any information showing that the State Department has "ever acted in an improper manner," and said that Soviet charges that the United States prepared this armed intervention were "flatly untrue."[71]

Opposition to the Guatemalan request took the form of a proposal to refer the complaint to the Organization of American States, which proposal was made by representatives of the Brazilian government under General Getulio Vargas and the Colombian government under General Gustavo Rojas Pinilla. All the members favored the proposal except Guatemala and the Soviet Union which preferred that the Security Council itself take action to halt the "aggression" against Guatemala.

When the Soviet Union vetoed the Brazilian and Colombian motion, the Security Council unanimously agreed to accept a French proposal calling for the "termination of any action likely to cause further bloodshed."[72] This resolution did not prevent the OAS from assuming jurisdiction over the case. In the meantime, the Guatemalan government's initial appeal to the Inter-American Peace Committee to investigate the complaint was withdrawn in hopes of exclusive United Nations jurisdiction. The effect of the Guatemalan withdrawal of the case from the Peace Committee and the Security Council's unwillingness to investigate the case temporarily ruled out an investigation of developments on the spot.

Meanwhile, two of Castillo Armas' three attack units were badly mauled. The attack overland against Chiquimula, however, met with success partly because the regular Guatemalan army forces decided to stay well back from the border to avoid providing any pretext for charging the Arbenz government with aggression and for U.S.-supported retaliation. On June 22, in the air battle, Castillo Armas lost two of the three old bombers with which he was supporting his invasion. On that afternoon President Eisenhower authorized Allen Dulles, the CIA chief, to provide two P-51 fighter bombers for transfer to a "third country" which in turn would provide aircraft to Castillo Armas.[73]

On that same day, June 22, the Guatemalan representative reported that the Security Council resolution of June 20 had not had the desired effect, that is, the aggression against his country continued, and requested that the Security Council convene immediately to deal with the case. Toriello also cabled Foreign Minister Molotov in Moscow appealing for his support in the implementation of the Security Council's resolution of June 20. Molotov replied expressing his sympathy with Toriello's requests and indicating that the Soviet representative had been instructed to do all in his power to that end.[74] The two messages were a formal exchange between two members of the United Nations dealing with the implementation of a resolution passed unanimously by the Security Council. Nevertheless, Secretary Dulles in a radio address about one week later, and without specifying any other Soviet-Guatemalan contact, charged that Toriello had "openly connived" with Molotov and that the two were in "open correspondence and ill-concealed privity."[75]

As president of the council, Ambassador Lodge convened the Security Council on June 25, 1954, to consider whether the council should again hear the Guatemalan complaint. First, he led the opposition to inviting the Guatemalan, Honduran, and Nicaraguan representatives to join in the deliberations until the council had formally placed the Guatemalan complaint on the agenda. Over the objection of the Soviet representative, the majority refused to invite the three powers to participate. Then Ambassador Lodge opposed formally taking up the Guatemalan complaint on the agenda at that time on the grounds that it was in the hands of the OAS. The U.S. position was generally supported by Brazil, China, Colombia, and Turkey, together making five of the council's eleven members.[76]

The Soviet Union favored including the Guatemalan complaint on the agenda for the same reasons as earlier. More interesting was the fact that Denmark, Lebanon, and New Zealand also favored the agenda item, largely because they wished to give Guatemala another hearing, not because they sought to deprive the OAS of any jurisdiction.

Crucial to the decision was the vote of the United Kingdom and France. The very morning of the vote Sir Anthony Eden, in the company of Prime Minister Churchill, arrived in Washington. Secretary Dulles asked Eden for British support on the issue as they rode into the city from the airport. Mr. Eden preferred to include the item on the agenda, but Mr. Dulles feared that then "we should be in danger of losing control of the proceedings."[77] As a result, Mr. Eden instructed the British delegate to abstain in the vote, and when France joined Britain in abstention, there were insufficient votes to place the Guatemalan complaint on the agenda. The meeting, therefore, adjourned forthwith, presumably with the OAS seized of the matter. In this way, the United States was able to prevent further action by the United Nations at that time and limited consideration to the OAS.

Faced with the refusal of the Security Council to take further action, the Guatemalan government reversed itself, requesting the Peace Committee to investigate the charges firsthand. The latter under the chairmanship of the Mexican diplomat, Luis Quintanilla, prepared to depart Washington for Central America. The Peace Committee's action, however, was precluded by Arbenz's overthrow, described in the following section, which led to the cancellation of their trip.

Several days after Arbenz's resignation, Secretary Dulles reviewed the Guatemalan episode in a radio and television report to the American people, excerpts from which follow:

Dramatic events [in Guatemala] expose the evil purpose of the Kremlin to destroy the inter-American system. . . . The intrusion of Soviet despotism was, of course, a direct challenge to the Monroe Doctrine. . . . The Communists seized on [the Guatemalan Revolution] not as an opportunity for real reforms, but as a chance to gain political power. . . . The master plan of international communism is to gain a solid political base in this hemisphere [which] can be used to extend Communist penetration to other people of the American governments. . . . The Foreign Minister of Guatemala openly connived [in the United Nations deliberations] with the Foreign Minister of the Soviet Union. The two were in open correspondence and ill-concealed privity. . . . Patriots arose in Guatemala to challenge the Communist leadership and change it. Thus, the situation is being cured by the Guatemalans themselves. . . . The events of recent months and days add a new and glorious chapter to the already great tradition of the American states. . . . Need for vigilance is not past. Communism is still a menace everywhere.[78]

The Conflict Within: Peurifoy's Role

In his final days in office President Arbenz faced Guatemalan enemies on two fronts. The first, and better known, were the armed attacks staged in eastern Guatemala by the Liberation Movement headed by Castillo Armas. Castillo's original forces comprised some 400 émigrés who after selection and training were reduced to 300 men. About half of these were designated "instructors" who were to return clandestinely to Guatemala to lead internal revolts, receive and distribute airdrops of arms and supplies, conduct sabotage, and support anti-Communist political organizations within the country. Only about a third of these, that is fifty, made successful border crossings and almost all of those were arrested or killed. The lucky few who escaped reincorporated themselves into the other wing of Castillo Armas' forces.[79]

That wing was the attack force of some 150 men. Part of that group was assigned the task of taking Puerto Barrios by both land and sea to prevent reinforcements from being sent southeast to Zacapa. The latter town was the objective of the other major column which, however, was largely wiped out by regular Guatemalan army forces. Two other smaller operations, with remnants from the two major columns, did converge and on June 24 took by force the departmental seat, Chiquimula, which was proclaimed the headquarters of the new "provisional government."[80]

In his account from the perspective of Guatemala City, Foreign Minister Toriello characterized the "liberation" as a failure. Such success as Castillo Armas had, Toriello attributed to the Arbenz government's decision not to resist the invasion in the frontier zone because "the United States would capitalize on the most insignificant opportunity, such as a frontier incident, to proclaim Guatemalan aggression against Honduras."[81]

In fact, it appears that air attacks in and around Guatemala City were among the most psychologically influential of Castillo Armas' military measures. Toriello describes these attacks as "the only effective element of the invasion" due on the one hand to the U.S. boycott which denied airplanes to the Arbenz government, thereby permitting "the U.S. bombadiers loaned to Castillo Armas" to carry out "their work of destruction and death" with impunity.[82] It will be recalled that President Eisenhower reported that on June 22 the Liberation forces lost two of the three old bombers, which Eisenhower scrupulously described as "presumably" under Castillo Armas' direction.[83] Incidentally, these were the bombers which Eisenhower sought to have replaced through a third government (no doubt the Nicaraguan or Honduran). On June 27, the day of Arbenz's resignation, the Liberation Movement reported that to date five of its men had been killed and two wounded, while the regular forces had lost fifteen men, with twenty-five wounded and thirty taken prisoner.[84]

The more serious threat to the Arbenz government on the home front was his own rebellious military forces. Opposition to Arbenz's associations with leading Communists had long been a source of concern to the military and particularly to Colonel Elfego Monzón, minister-without-portfolio, whose presence in the cabinet and reputation of opposition to the Communists had helped neutralize non-Communist criticism. In the spring of 1954 many professional military officers were upset by trends in Guatemalan foreign policy and growing hostility with the United States. In addition, they were concerned by the agitational and organizational activities of leftists with administrative responsibilities in the government.

These concerns came to the surface in a meeting between Arbenz and his leading military officers on June 3, 1954, at which time Arbenz's statement about land reform, imperialism, and communism aroused concern. In order to clarify possible misunderstandings about Guatemalan foreign policy and Arbenz's relations with the Communists, Arbenz invited the military to present a questionnaire to which he would undertake to make replies.

The questionnaire submitted on June 8 made very clear the desire of many of the military that Arbenz discharge some of the leading Communists and leftists from the government and "rely solely on the National Army" rather than on political groups who sought "selfish ends" in exchange for their support in the elections.[85] The officers also expressed concern about the Communists' demand that popular militias, that is, armed members of industrial and peasant unions, supplement the army. These issues remained unresolved until Arbenz fell.

Arbenz's own account of those final days is revealing:

On Wednesday, June 23, it was clear to everybody that the military situation had been dominated, the aggression defeated . . . Castillo Armas had only 1,500 [sic] men against our army of more than 5,000 relatively well-equipped soldiers. . . . On Thursday the 24th, worker and union leaders informed me that something was wrong in the army. The military chiefs refused to accept the people's collaboration in defense, and news from the front created suppositions about the existence of a conspiracy within the armed forces. . . . The troops commanded by my best . . . officers, were . . . at the front. . . . I never imagined that in a case of foreign aggression in which the liberty of our country, its honor and independence were at stake, the army could betray us. . . .

The specific case is that on Friday, June 25, these same troops, commanded by officers with my complete confidence, sent me an ultimatum from the front: I should resign or they would come to an agreement with the invaders. . . . To "convince" the high officials . . . the excellent offer of the United States ambassador was sufficient.

As soon as I received the ultimatum, I gave the order to the chief of the armed forces Colonel Díaz to distribute arms to the people's organizations and the political parties. . . . We knew that with the people armed, we could fight perfectly well not only against the invaders but also against our own treacherous army.

Nevertheless these orders were never carried out by the army. Colonel Díaz himself told me that I did not have the obedience of the chiefs of the troops and on Sunday morning he told me that the military chiefs had delivered to him for me a final ultimatum and that they had invited him to a meeting which was taking place in the American embassy that very morning to negotiate the conditions of the betrayal.[86]

Meanwhile, Ambassador Peurifoy appears to have been working for Arbenz's overthrow. As Arbenz's statements indicate, he was not only deeply involved in the successful palace coup which led to Arbenz's resignation on June 27, but continued to play a leading role in the events which culminated in the assumption of the provisional presidency by Carlos Castillo Armas ten days later on July 7, 1954. In fact, available evidence suggests that the ambassador played a decisive role in these events and succeeded in arranging that the Guatemalan leader favored by the United States and whom the CIA had supported should become provisional president. Four men controlled the presidency during these ten days and the ambassador appears to have been a determining factor in the fate that befell each.

The first, Arbenz, was forced to resign under duress by the ranking members of the armed forces, as we have seen. Arbenz has described the role of the American ambassador in these events, showing how Colonel Carlos Enrique Díaz had delivered the chiefs' ultimatum and then met with them and the ambassador at the American embassy to arrange the terms of his overthrow:

The work of the United States ambassador was sufficiently correct and subtle so that none of the members of the government, I among them, realized his game before the aggression. Naturally, we all knew what the position of the embassy was, and Mr. Peurifoy had sufficient antecedents against him from other countries. But we never had a concrete ground on which to accuse him. But once the invasion began, the ambassador took off his mask and much came to the light.

After returning from the meeting [in the American embassy], Colonel Díaz told me it was decided to present me with a final ultimatum: I had until 4 P.M. to leave the Presidential Palace; I must turn over command to a military junta . . . and the first acts of that junta would be to outlaw the Communist party and discharge the chiefs of the judicial police and the civil police. . . . Immediately thereafter the Presidential Palace was occupied by officers armed with machine guns . . . and we were completely disarmed.[87]

Arbenz explained in exile that the popular militias had not yet received sufficient arms to resist and that to have done so against the vastly superior armed forces would have resulted in a bloodbath.[88] In his radio speech of resignation he also expressed indignation against the "cowardly attacks of mercenary North American aviators."[89] He therefore agreed to resign on the condition that the lives of himself and his followers be spared and that the struggle against the Castillo Armas forces continue. The man whom he trusted most to carry out these conditions was Colonel Díaz in whose favor he resigned that very evening after denouncing the United Fruit Company and "North American governing circles" as responsible. Díaz thereupon assumed the provisional presidency and announced the outlawing of the Guatemalan labor party, that is the Communist party. These were the arrangements, Arbenz explained, reached between the military chiefs and the United States.[90] Arbenz took political asylum in a foreign embassy and later was given safe conduct to leave the country.

The second man in the presidency, Carlos Enrique Díaz, was allowed to serve as provisional president for only a few hours. It appears that Díaz, the person Arbenz most trusted to carry out the conditions of his resignation, was chosen as leader of the three-man military junta which succeeded Arbenz mainly to facilitate Arbenz's resignation. In fact, the military opposition and Peurifoy insisted shortly thereafter on sweeping the slate clean of leaders from the Arbenz government. Arbenz's foreign minister, Guillermo Toriello, reported that after the principal leaders of the Guatemalan Labor party and of some unions had already been arrested and Díaz had been performing his functions for only a few hours, Peurifoy arrived in his office at the headquarters of the Armed Forces. Toriello gave the following summary of this interview as related to him by Díaz himself:

> Peurifoy waved a long list of names of some leaders. He was going to require Díaz to shoot those who were on that list within twenty-four hours. "That's all, but why?" Díaz asked. "Because they're Communists," replied Peurifoy. Díaz refused absolutely to soil his hands and soul with this repugnant crime and rejected the pretensions of Peurifoy to come and give him orders. "It would be better, in that case," he went so far as to tell him, "that you actually sit on the presidential chair and that the stars and stripes fly over the Palace." Saying too bad for you, Peurifoy left.[91]

Since this is the only detailed version I have of this meeting, the statements attributed to Peurifoy, particularly with respect to shooting Communists, should be viewed with caution. I have no doubt, however, that Díaz and Peurifoy reached an impasse regarding some aspect of Díaz's functions and that Peurifoy thereafter sought his removal.

The *New York Times* described Peurifoy's efforts to remove Díaz:

> President Arbenz resigned Sunday and the Díaz junta took over. Its members called on Mr. Peurifoy at 4 A.M. Monday to ask that the Ambassador make contact with Colonel Castillo Armas for a cease-fire. Mr. Peurifoy said the

United States had no direct contact with the rebels, but, under urging, agreed to see what he could do.

That night Mr. Peurifoy got in touch with Colonel Díaz and Col. José Angel Sanchez, a second member of the three-man junta, to report on his efforts. The third member of the government, Col. Elfego Monzón, was located at 4 A.M. Tuesday. He agreed to go to Colonel Díaz's home where the others were meeting with Mr. Peurifoy.

In the dramatic climax of the negotiations Colonel Díaz announced he and Colonel Sanchez were resigning for the peace of the country. Colonel Monzón and two other army officers strode in.

The situation was tense. According to eyewitnesses, Mr. Peurifoy leaned back and crossed his arms over his chest—where he had a shoulder holster. A United States Marine aide in civilian clothes edged nearer the envoy, fearing bullets might fly.

Colonel Monzón announced the formation of a new Junta, with himself as president.[92]

The days of Monzón, the third man in the presidential chair, were also numbered. Peurifoy, it seems, wanted to end the fighting and urged President Osorio through the American ambassador in San Salvador, Michael McDermott, to mediate between Colonels Monzón and Castillo Armas. The two colonels met in San Salvador on June 30, reaching an impasse after many hours of discussion. The major issues were control of the provisional presidency and arrangements for Castillo Armas' triumphal reception in Guatemala City. The two colonels were on the point of returning to their troops under threat of continuing the struggle when President Osorio urged Ambassador Peurifoy to fly into El Salvador from Guatemala City to save the situation. He came that afternoon and, after further discussion, the two colonels agreed that: (1) Monzón would continue temporarily as provisional president with the three-man junta expanded to five men, Castillo Armas and one of his trusted followers, (2) that the provisional presidency would be determined definitively within fifteen days, and (3) that Castillo Armas would be able to return to Guatemala at the head of his forces.[93]

After further arrangements, Ambassador Peurifoy and the two colonels returned with their parties to Guatemala City in the U.S. embassy airplane. Castillo Armas drove into the center of the city as a returning hero at the head of a triumphal procession. The junta members convened on July 7 and elected Castillo Armas provisional president, and the two original members of the Monzón junta resigned leaving Castillo Armas in control of the remaining three-man junta.

It is not entirely clear whether agreement for Castillo Armas' takeover was secretly reached in the negotiations begun on June 30 or in later negotiations. According to some accounts, there was a "secret" pact providing that the two other members of the three-man junta "would resign to take diplomatic posts on the payment of a certain sum of money."[94] In any case, there is no doubt that the U.S.

Jacobo Arbenz, president of Guatemala, 1951–1954. (Organization of American States)

John E. Peurifoy, U.S. ambassador to Guatemala, 1953–1954. (Department of State)

John Foster Dulles, U.S. secretary of state (right), condemns "international communism" in the presence of the Guatemalan minister of foreign affairs, Guillermo Toriello (far left), at the Inter-American Conference in Caracas, Venezuela, March 1954. (United Press International)

Representatives meeting on the Guatemalan situation in San Salvador in July 1954. From left to right, John E. Peurifoy, U.S. ambassador to Guatemala; Msgr. Genaro Verolino; Col. Elfego Monzón; Col. Oscar Osorio; Gen. Carlos Castillo Armas, president of El Salvador; José María Peralta, president of the Congress of El Salvador; and Michael McDermont, U.S. ambassador to El Salvador. (United Press International)

Fidel Castro with U.S. Ambassador to Cuba Philip W. Bonsal, Havana, March 1959. (Wide World Photos)

Fidel Castro with Vice-President Richard M. Nixon, Washington, D.C., April 1959. (Wide World Photos)

Fidel Castro with Soviet Premier Nikita Khrushchev at the United Nations, New York, September 1960. (Organization of American States)

government and Ambassador Peurifoy were pleased by Castillo Armas' assumption of the presidency and his election to that office later in the year, satisfaction demonstrated by prompt recognition of his government on July 13 and the large amounts of economic and military assistance extended to him thereafter.

Denouement

The Castillo Armas government suppressed the unions and political parties which had collaborated with Arbenz. Thousands of his supporters were pursued and arrested as a form of revenge for the Arbenz government's attempts to suppress revolt during its final days and to purge the enemies of the new government. The right to vote was restricted to the literate citizenry, thereby disenfranchising the vast majority of the Guatemalan population.[95]

The lands under the Arbenz agrarian reform were returned. The United Fruit Company got its lands back and then, in turn, transferred smaller amounts of land back to the government for distribution to the peasants. Reversing Arévalo and Arbenz's prohibitions on oil concessions, Castillo Armas opened the country to foreign concessions.[96]

The United States undertook not only programs of technical assistance but also extended development assistance to Guatemala which, with Bolivia and Haiti, was the only Latin American country to receive the latter type of assistance at that time. At the end of 1954 the United States promptly made a grant of over $6 million for public works to relieve unemployment. Much was used for work on the inter-American and Pacific coastal highways. Technical assistance was also granted. Meanwhile, the Guatemalan government proceeded with the construction of the highway to the Atlantic and the port of Santo Tomás. Development assistance in the amount of $5 million was requested for expenditures beginning in the summer of 1955.[97]

In the United States, the Eisenhower administration regarded the fall of Arbenz as one of its major achievements. In speeches in the late summer and fall of 1954 preceding the elections to Congress, President Eisenhower referred many times to the Guatemalan episode, usually as having rid the hemisphere of a "beachhead of international Communism."[98] Similarly, in the months preceding the 1956 presidential elections, the president referred frequently to Guatemala as a victory in the Cold War.[99]

The conclusions to be drawn from these events will be discussed in the final section of this chapter.

Fidel Castro (1959–1961)

The demise of the Arbenz government in 1954 was one of the major historical experiences shaping Fidel Castro's policy toward the United States and the latter's response to him in the years 1959 to 1961.[100] Che Guevara was a human link between the Guatemalan and Cuban revolutions.

After completing medical school in Argentina, Guevara set out to work his way around Latin America. He arrived in Guatemala in January 1954 as the events leading to Arbenz's fall were reaching a climax. In need of funds, he was befriended by the former foreign minister, Raúl Osegueda, and other Guatemalans. Openly committed to revolution, he held the mild measures of the Arbenz government in contempt. He appears to have taken no formal part in the revolutionary movement nor to have served the government in any political capacity. Most of his time he required for earning his keep; much of the rest was spent with exiles from other Latin American countries and in the company of the woman he later married, Hilda Gadea. When Arbenz began to totter and U.S. hostility was manifest, Guevara briefly began to organize resistance groups. When Arbenz resigned a few days later, Guevara ceased his organizational activities on the advice of an official from the American embassy, took refuge in the Argentine embassy, and later traveled to Mexico under a safe conduct.[101]

Guevara learned in Guatemala that armed forces inherited from the old regime and not fully controlled can destroy a revolutionary government. On his arrival in Havana five years later, Guevara reportedly insisted: "We cannot guarantee the Revolution before cleansing the Armed Forces. It is necessary to remove everyone who might be a danger. But it is necessary to do it rapidly, right now."[102] As it turned out, Castro eliminated the old army leadership early in 1959.[103]

Readers may recall that Cuba was not represented in chapter 3 dealing with U.S. relations toward the reformist governments emerging from revolutionary movements. Cuba's first government in this century aimed at a sharp break with the past was that of Ramón Grau San Martín following the overthrow of the dictatorship of Gerardo Machado in 1933.[104] Grau introduced a number of important measures of economic and social reform, but lasted only four months, as described briefly in chapter 3. Some of these reforms were adopted by subsequent governments dominated by Fulgencio Batista, a member of Grau's junta in 1933. The governments emerging from the 1933 revolutionary movement were Grau's (1944–1948) and his constitutional successor's, Carlos Prío Socorrás (1948–1952).

The Grau and Prío governments widened the distribution of income, especially among sugar workers, introduced new social legislation, built new public works, and strengthened public education; under them the Cuban economy was relatively prosperous. The two governments took strong measures against the Communist party and arranged to break Communist control of organized labor. At the same time, under their administrations Cuba was beset with corruption and gangsterism.[105]

Although less oriented toward reform, Grau and Prío were, roughly speaking, the Cuban counterparts of Madero in Mexico, Villarroel and Paz Estenssoro in Bolivia, and Arévalo in Guatemala. Yet the revolutionary governments and leaders which eventually succeeded them in countries other than Cuba were heirs and part of the same revolutionary movement. In Cuba, on the contrary, Castro had broken with the mainstream of that movement and established his own political organization, the 26th of July Movement. Partly for this reason, an examination will not be made here of the U.S. response to the Grau and Prío governments. Moreover, their policies toward the United States and the latter's response largely conformed to established patterns of U.S.–Cuban relations.

Castro followed what was essentially a reformist model during the first few months of 1959. The symbol of his adhesion to reformism was his formal commitment to the Constitution of 1940. His first major step toward a radical transformation of Cuban society was, perhaps, the land reform decree of May 17, 1959. For convenience sake, the discussion below will focus on the U.S. response to Castro from his takeover at the beginning of 1959 and continuing as revolutionary changes were introduced into Cuban society.

Castro's Early Strategies

Batista's flight led to popular rejoicing throughout the island and Castro, the symbol of forceful resistance against Batista, became the undisputed hero of the moment. Castro capitalized on the popular euphoria by receiving the plaudits of the populace in an overland procession to Havana which lasted the better part of a week. The Department of State, despite its misgivings and lingering doubts, decided to make the best of the fait accompli. Besides, Castro had committed himself squarely to the implementation of the Cuban Constitution of 1940, had denied any plans for expropriating foreign property, and had said little for or against the United States. As a result, the United States promptly recognized the new government, headed by Castro's designee, Manuel Urrutia, and recalled Ambassador Smith whose antipathy for Castro was already well known. Philip W. Bonsal, then U.S. ambassador to Bolivia, was promptly selected to succeed him.

The insurrectional phase of the revolution ended with Batista's flight. At that time Castro had several vital assets, the most important of which was control of an effective, though relatively small, guerrilla force. (Castro's armed units numbered only a few hundred men until the concluding months of the resistance.[106] And even toward the end, when their numbers mushroomed as Cubans rushed to Castro's bandwagon, the regular army was still far larger.) Also, Castro was widely recognized as the leader of the armed resistance against Batista. He had achieved this position by his astute use of the foreign press and through the resistance radio, "Radio Rebelde," as much as through the guerrilla action against Batista. No other person enjoyed his immense personal prestige.

However, Castro was weak in many respects. In the first place, he had never controlled the Cuban resistance, particularly in the cities and in rural areas other than those occupied by his own forces at the eastern end of the island. Secondly, he did not control a political party as such. Several of the anti-Batista political parties, the students, and even organized labor had larger and more firmly established organizations. Castro lacked a clearly defined base of popular support in the sense of a political program tied to the interests of specific Cuban groups. Toppling Batista was one thing; gaining control of the government and establishing his political authority in Cuba were quite another.

It is doubtful that Castro had initially planned any grand domestic political strategy. In fact hindsight suggests that he developed his strategy incrementally during the early months of 1959. In any case, the strategy he developed placed important limits on the nature of his relations with the United States, not to mention the domestic course of the revolution.

First, Castro sought to secure control of the armed forces and to destroy the remnants of Batista's influence in Cuba. The rebel army arrested General Cantillo whom Batista had left in charge of the armed forces. Colonel Ramón Barquín took charge briefly. He was a former Batista official who had been imprisoned after an unsuccessful military coup to depose the dictator, and a man the United States had once considered as a possible alternative to Castro. Castro ordered Camilo Cienfuegos, his representative, to take over from Barquín. In the next few weeks, Castro's forces conducted a series of spectacular trials leading to the imprisonment or execution of hundreds of persons charged with crimes under Batista. Widespread popular revulsion toward Batista and the euphoria following his flight made the political elimination of the "Batistianos" relatively easy. The procedures used in the public trials, conducted in the heat of national emotion, were widely criticized in the United States. In fact, the trials were among the first important sources of friction in official relations with the United States, and Castro demonstrated great sensitivity to criticism of the trials by U.S. journalists and politicians.

Much more difficult was establishing his primacy over other groups. By using his immense personal prestige and the rebel army and by skillfully manipulating the public media, Castro faced down other armed units, including those of the Student Revolutionary Directorate. Many of the leaders of the political opposition to Batista who were not part of the July 26 movement were needed and quite naturally took over posts in the government in early 1959. At first, Castro's strategy was to remain outside the civilian government and exercise power as head of the armed forces. However, early in February a decree concentrated legislative and executive power in the cabinet, and Castro took over as prime minister on February 16. During the course of the year, he discredited and separated potential opposition leaders from their bases of popular support one by one. By the end of the year, the once independent student and labor movements were bent to his will. Many of the eliminated leaders had close ties with the United States.

Castro gained control of the government without recourse to free elections. Few people have doubted that Castro could have been elected by an overwhelming majority of Cubans, at least initially. However, Castro may have reasoned that to follow such a course would have meant a return to the corrupt politicking of the past and would have established his dependence on the traditional electoral and legislative process—a dependence he was not prepared to accept. In order to carry through his audacious challenge to the old system and to other groups of the political Center and Left, he needed to develop other sources of popular support. Identifying with the needs and aspirations of the rural and urban poor, Castro put through a series of economic measures at the expense of the middle class. In addition, he moved closer to and made use of the Partido Socialista Popular (PSP—the Cuban Communist party), at that time one of the best-organized parties in the country though with limited popular support.

All of the above developments were viewed first with concern and later with alarm in the United States. The public trials and executions of the so-called "Batistianos" shocked Americans whose historical traditions and personal experience made it difficult for them to understand the passionate and violent forces unleashed by a social revolution. Many of the leaders of government in 1959 who became the political victims of Castro's maneuvers were the very persons on whom U.S. leaders had counted for cooperation. Castro's cavalier postponement of his pledge to hold free elections flew in the face of U.S. political ideals. And his willingness to collaborate with the Cuban Communists alarmed public opinion in the United States where the Cold War psychology prevailed.

In April 1959, Castro first visited the United States as Cuba's undisputed leader. This came about in an unusual way. The American Society of Newspaper Editors asked him to give a luncheon address without discussing their invitation with officials in the Department of State. The visit might have gone smoothly if Castro had simply come to Washington for the day, given the luncheon address, and then returned home. Instead, he brought with him a planeload of high-ranking officials, particularly those concerned with financial and economic matters, and remained for several days, thus giving the impression of an official visit. The Department of State did not have much time to prepare for the visit nor did it have the opportunity to pick its own date for a meeting, as is usually the case when one country plays host to the head of another government. President Eisenhower was irritated over the invitation and was out of town when Castro was in Washington. Nevertheless, the Department of State arranged several meetings at which opportunities were provided to discuss substantive issues of mutual interest.

There was much speculation in Cuba about whether the visit would result in a U.S. program of economic assistance for Cuba, since the issue would serve as an indicator of future relations between the two countries. Cuban Minister of Finance Rufo López-Fresquet hoped to arrange for economic assistance and was encouraged when he and other officials with economic responsibilities were asked to make the trip. However, on the way to the United States, Castro dampened his hopes about any immediate results when he told him: "Look Rufo, I don't want this trip to be like that of other new Latin American leaders who always come to the U.S. to ask for money. I want this to be a good-will trip. Besides, the Americans will be surprised. And when we go back to Cuba, they will offer us aid without our asking for it. Consequently, we will be in a better bargaining position."[107]

In any case, as López-Fresquet recounted later, Assistant Secretary of State Roy R. Rubottom "offered to help us carry out our economic plans," but "not being able to say anything else, I told him we had already solved our immediate problems and we preferred to wait until we made our long-term plans before making a presentation of needs."[108] Apparently, the United States did not push the matter further and neither did the Cubans. (On his visit to Buenos Aires shortly thereafter, Castro publicly proposed a U.S. economic assistance plan of $30 billion to Latin America, but without specific reference to aid for Cuba.)

Actually, during Castro's visit Vice-President Richard Nixon had a three-hour talk with Castro on Capitol Hill and wrote a confidential memorandum asserting that Castro was "either incredibly naive about Communism or under Communist discipline." At that time, however, Nixon believed that his view was a minority of one within the administration and, particularly, within the Latin American branch of the Department of State.[109] In any event, the Department of State's willingness to talk about economic assistance was one thing, and the granting of authorization for aid was another. United States suspicion and distrust of Castro during his resistance years lingered on and was heightened by the events of early 1959. The United States may well have been prepared to consider seriously large-scale aid to Cuba at this time, but no doubt only after a clarification of a number of pending issues and receiving guarantees regarding Castro's political direction.

The issue of aid is purely academic since the two parties never sat down to serious negotiations on this point. For his part, Castro could hardly have been oblivious to U.S. suspicions, given his pre-1959 experience and the interview with Vice-President Nixon. And, surely, he must have suspected that certain conditions would have to be fulfilled before large-scale aid would be extended.[110] Nevertheless, it is difficult to find conclusive evidence to bear out the conclusion expressed by López-Fresquet that Castro never intended to ask for U.S. aid. It would be interesting to know just when Castro decided that close political relations with the United States, a sine qua non of extensive economic assistance, were incompatible with his revolutionary objectives.[111] It is possible that when Castro decided to postpone indefinitely the promised elections, a decision announced during his visit to the United States, he also ruled out economic assistance from the United States.

The United States: Obstacle to Castro's Revolutionary Goals?

Castro's objectives for Cuba, that is, the shape he hoped Cuban society would take after Batista's fall, were vague not only before 1959 but during the early months of the new regime as well. In fact, the Castro regime developed less from advance blueprints than through day-to-day accretion. Nevertheless, by the end of 1959, Tad Szulc of *The New York Times* was able to report:

> In the year since the demise of the Batista dictatorship, Cuba has become a full-fledged revolutionary state whose regime is determined to refashion the country in a new image as speedily as possible. . . . The Cuban revolution addressed itself . . . to the task of initiating sweeping economic and social changes at the expense of the restoration of democratic institutions battered by the Batista dictatorship.[112]

As Castro admitted later, his early political ideas were not truly Marxist and his position in coming to power was still somewhat "idealistic" and "utopian." He did not announce in early 1959 the revolutionary reforms introduced later, probably because they had not yet crystallized in his mind. And in any case he believed, and it appears correctly, that it was politically astute not to elaborate his ideas at that time. Yet it was already clear that Castro's vague objectives vaulted high and that he would not be content with the gradual reform of traditional Cuban institutions. Instead, he sought to establish a commanding place in Cuban history through a comprehensive social transformation. Some sense of his aspirations comes through in his claim to the multitudes who assembled in Central Park during his visit to the United States in April 1959, "The Cuban Revolution has been, in our opinion, the most generous and the purest revolution which has been carried out in the history of the world."[113]

Any comprehensive transformation of Cuban society faced not only the opposition of entrenched Cuban interests, but U.S. vested interests as well. Castro gave his own slant to this matter in August 1959: "The campaigns in the U.S. and the constant charge of communism form part of a grand conspiracy of vested interests against the effort of a nation to move ahead, to achieve its economic independence and political stability."[114]

Whether the Castro version was correct or not, few would deny that U.S.–Cuban relations for more than half a century had resulted in closely interlocking social structures. The two societies were intimately related, especially in trade and investment. In a sense, U.S. interests occupied, to use a Soviet expression, the "commanding heights" of the Cuban economy. The United States bought about two-thirds of Cuba's exports and paid, under the quota system, large premiums, sometimes approaching nearly twice the world market price for Cuban sugar. In exchange, Cuba offered the United States tariff preferences, which was only one of several reasons why the United States sold Cuba nearly 70 percent of its imports. United States interests controlled a declining, but still large, percentage (about 40 percent) of raw sugar production, 90 percent of telephone and electric services and 50 percent of public service railroads. In addition, U.S. banks had about 25 percent of all Cuban bank deposits.[115] Clearly, these powerful U.S. interests stood in the way of any comprehensive economic transformation undertaken at their expense with the full weight of tradition, law, and U.S. policies to back them up.

It gradually became clear that Castro was seeking a fundamental transformation not only of Cuban society but also of the character of that society's relationship with the United States. For reasons of its historical origins, its propinquity to the United States, and the nature of its economy, Cuba had fallen under U.S. influence more than almost any other Latin American country, with the possible exception of Panama. Cuba had grown so dependent on the United States as to raise doubts about the long-term stability of the arrangement in a world of rising nationalist sentiment.

Take, for example, the special relationship created under the sugar quota. In the 1950s the United States consistently took the largest share of the Cuban sugar crop, ordinarily at prices above those of the world market. The U.S. government fixed this quota from year to year in accordance with the law, and the amount purchased and the price paid had an immense impact on the Cuban economy. During the 1950s, except during the Korean and Suez crises, Cuban exporters benefited from the price differential. The benefit to Cuban exporters of quota price arrangements often totaled $100 million a year and rose to $153 million in 1959.[116] The political power that the United States wielded on the quota issue put the Cuban government at the mercy of the U.S. authorities. The U.S. government secured this negotiating advantage partly through this "subsidy" paid by the North American consumer to the Cuban sugar industry. Furthermore, the quota system had several aspects: one was that the quota assigned to domestic U.S. producers and the tariff barrier protected high-cost producers in the United States. Also, the premium prices paid Cuban sugar producers went, in part, to U.S.-owned sugar companies in Cuba, which accounted for about 40 percent of Cuba's raw sugar production.

In the early negotiations, the United States secured, as a concession from the Cubans for the quota and premium price arrangements, preferential entry of U.S. goods in the Cuban market. The results of this arrangement, and more importantly, the U.S. competitive advantage in many products, even in the absence of tariff protection, were Cuban dependence on U.S. manufacturers and limited development of domestic industry in the face of U.S. competition.

The United States exercised an overriding political influence in Cuba from the time of the Spanish-American War up to January 1, 1959, when President Batista fled the island. General Leonard Wood, the U.S. commander in the occupation of Cuba after the Spanish-American War, presided at the first session of the Cuban constitutional convention, and the U.S. government forced the delegates to include the so-called Platt Amendment as part of their constitution by convincing them that refusal to accept American demands insured the continuation of the American occupation.[117] The Platt Amendment made Cuba a protectorate of the United States by limiting Cuba's treaty-making and fiscal powers, and gave the United States "the right to intervene for the preservation of Cuban independence, the maintenance of government adequate for the protection of life, property, and individual liberty."

The United States exercised these rights through military intervention, military and civilian advisers, or through the U.S. ambassador from 1902 until 1934 when the Platt Amendment was officially abrogated. The United States made and unmade Cuban governments up to 1934. The unwillingness of the United States to recognize the Grau San Martín government in 1933 and early 1934 was an important reason for its downfall, and the U.S. ambassador contributed to Fulgencio Batista's rise to political dominance in the mid-1930s.[118] The U.S. ambassador continued to be regarded, by many at least, as the "second most important man in Cuba," and the last U.S. ambassador to Cuba before Castro made a formal call on President Batista to request his resignation.[119]

In view of the above, is it any wonder that Castro aspired to a fundamental change in U.S. relations with Cuba? Observers of many different political persuasions believe that the U.S.–Cuban relationship before 1959 was fundamentally inequitable. But, whether it was is less significant than the fact that many Cubans, including Castro, passionately believed it was. Castro put the Cuban nationalist attitude in a nutshell during a visit to the United States in 1959, "In economic and political matters relations have been solely unilateral . . . one party [the United States] has decided our political principles and . . . solved economic problems for us."[120]

Castro perceived the United States as a potential threat to his revolutionary aspirations in a more ominous sense. After Batista's fall and the prompt dispatch of his followers through execution, imprisonment, and exile, the major initial threats to Castro were the leaders of other groups in opposition to Batista. Within a year, Castro had largely subjected them to his will or eliminated them from influence in the government or politics. Yet, these elements still represented a potential threat in the event of serious political or economic difficulties. And this threat would be magnified should such groups secure the support of the United States and attempt to overthrow Castro by force.

A U.S. journalist who interviewed Castro in mid-July 1959 has reported that the latter sat up all night expounding the theory that "the United States simply *had* to fight his revolution, then rationaliz[ing] his decision to cancel the promised elections."[121] Castro explained that the revolution, faced with such a formidable adversary, could not afford the luxury of the democratic process.

Castro soon developed what appeared in the United States to be almost a paranoiac fear of enemies at home and abroad. As time progressed, he described the threats to Cuba in increasingly strident and dramatic tones, lashing back at his opponents frequently and with vehemence. When asked by a journalist in January 1960 why Cuba had introduced militias, Castro replied, "because of the obvious international conspiracy against Cuba, the insolent threats, the plans of the monopolists, war criminals and the international oligarchy to approach and destroy us."[122] Castro stressed that militias were needed not simply to deal with domestic oppositions: "The large landowners and war criminals do not have sufficient strength . . . to threaten danger, . . . the only hope is to mobilize . . . foreign resources."[123]

Castro was well aware of the threat the United States could pose, as demonstrated by U.S. support of counterrevolutionaries in Guatemala in 1953 and 1954. It must be remembered, too, that Castro had struck out on an audacious and risky course in the face of much opposition within the Cuban middle classes that formed the traditional cadres of Cuban government and politics. Also, his political and economic measures put him under immense personal and political pressures. All this helps to explain his extreme sensitivity to criticism from U.S. politicians, journalists, and others.

Nor were the attacks on his regime purely verbal. Mounting opposition among émigrés took the form of incursions on Cuban territory and anti-Castro propaganda, which paralleled the crystallization of the opposition in Cuba. Castro played up these incidents in order to mobilize support at home. In response to Castro's accusations, the United States argued in a lengthy press statement on October 27, 1959, that extensive efforts had been made to enforce the neutrality act and deal with specific Cuban charges, including the question of air incursions. On November 2, 1959, the

Department of Justice announced that special measures were being undertaken to enforce these laws. In late October and early November 1959, the Departments of State and Justice arranged to tighten up the enforcement of U.S. laws to prevent aliens from using U.S. territory as a "base of operations for starting or furthering civil strife in Cuba."[124] And yet Castro remained skeptical about U.S. intentions with regard to forays from the mainland. Having once mounted a revolutionary expedition against Batista himself, he was well aware of his own vulnerability in this respect. In fact, Castro contrasted his own isolation in organizing the expedition to Cuba from Mexico with the immense resources that he believed lay at the disposal of the rapidly growing Cuban opposition.

An analysis of Castro's position in terms of the balance of international and national forces, after he had overthrown Batista and subdued his rivals, shows that a hostile United States could pose the greatest potential threat to Castro. Other Latin American countries were either unwilling to oppose Castro or, as in the case of Trujillo in the Dominican Republic, lacked the capacity. And the United States could make sure that no other western power would do so. So the United States loomed as the main enemy against which Castro could rally and unite the Cuban people as he had earlier against Batista.

The fact that the United States posed the greatest *potential* threat to Castro through its links with his domestic opposition as well as the external pressures it was capable of exerting does not mean that the United States actually did threaten Castro or use these pressures in 1959 and early 1960. There were many critical voices in Washington during these months but the U.S. government was relatively accommodating, certainly in comparison with the policies inaugurated in March 1960 (see below). As a result, Castro's concern during this early period was based not so much on what the United States had done, as on what he feared it was doing or could do. Castro surely knew better than Washington how far he wanted to change Cuba and he estimated, correctly as it turned out, that his policies would encounter stubborn resistance. In a way, he was already responding to what the United States would do, not to what it had done in 1959, thereby helping to fulfill his own dire prophecies.

Castro's opposition at home also anticipated strong U.S. opposition to Castro's revolutionary innovations. Like Castro, his opponents overestimated U.S. effectiveness in opposing the revolutionary drive. Both sides expected more of the United States than the bankrupt policies that ended in the Bay of Pigs fiasco. As Ambassador Bonsal has put it, "A conviction that the United States would take care of the situation sapped the activism of much of the opposition."[125] Mr. Bonsal believes that this fact helps explain why Castro was able to "revolutionize" Cuban society with so little domestic resistance.

Castro's Independent Course

Castro inherited the complex and intimately related web of interests and practices that constituted the U.S.–Cuban relationship. United States interests stood in the way, so to speak, of changes Castro wanted to make in Cuba. Castro did not hesitate to oppose these interests to achieve his domestic objectives. Besides, he found the nature of the U.S.–Cuban relationship unacceptable. It was Castro, not the United States, who first sought to change it. He had several ways to achieve his domestic objectives which simultaneously served as attacks on what he believed was unwarranted U.S. domination.

The first was his capacity to regulate and seize U.S. private investments in Cuba. According to his count, these were worth some $800 million, and according to U.S. figures about $1 billion.[126] United States investments in Cuba were at Castro's mercy—hostages so to speak. The second major weapon was his potential for getting extrahemispheric support, that is, for bringing Soviet economic, political, and military power into play against the United States. The following pages deal with Castro's implementation of these two means of opposition to the United States.

There are some observers who believe that fomenting social revolution and guerrilla wars in other Latin American countries was another means Castro had of resisting the United States. Be that as it may, Castro has actually had little success fomenting revolutions elsewhere in Latin America.[127]

Seizing U.S. Investments. The seizures of property in 1959 and early 1960 were not directed primarily against U.S. interests. The first Agrarian Reform Law of May 17, 1959, was aimed at improving the lot of tenant farmers and agricultural wage laborers and attracting their political support as part of a broad program of social reform. North American property owners suffered, but Cuban owners did too.

Seizures of land under the Agrarian Reform Law constituted some of the first serious damages to U.S. private interests. Many large American-owned properties were seized by the Cuban authorities and no compensation was paid. The burden of the U.S. case was not to deny the Cuban government the right of expropriation, but to insist on "prompt, adequate, and effective" compensation (see chapter 4).

Actions against U.S.-owned property were not confined to agriculture. The Cuban government took over the management of the Cuban Telephone Company on March 3, 1959, and revoked a rate increase authorized toward the end of Batista's government. The Cuban government later lowered the rates for electric power charged to rural consumers by the U.S.-owned Cuban Electric Company. The lowering of the rates was aimed at supplying cheaper services to the less affluent in the cities and the countryside. The fact that Castro may have taken a nationalist's satisfaction in depriving U.S. interests of control of the rates of these public services does not mean that anti-American action was his fundamental purpose at that time.

One year later, March 9, 1960, Castro took over ("intervened") the management of the Moa Bay Mining Company, a subsidiary of the Freeport Sulphur Company. On June 10 four hotels in Havana (the Hilton, Capri, National, and Havana Riviera) in which U.S. citizens or corporations had interests were nationalized also. The takeovers of the mining company and the hotels were designed primarily to keep these businesses running, since all were having serious operating or financial problems in the chaotic economic situation that developed after Castro's takeover.

Seeking Extrahemispheric Support. In view of Cuba's political, strategic, and economic vulnerability, and Castro's ambitious social and national objectives, it is no wonder that he sought an extrahemispheric counterweight to U.S. influence. What is surprising is that he did not cultivate relations with the USSR, or the latter with him, earlier. Although the USSR announced recognition of the revolutionary government on January 10, 1959, the first official Soviet representative in residence, a Tass correspondent, did not come to Cuba until that December. Diplomatic relations —broken by Batista in early 1952—were not formally restored until May 1960, nearly a year and a half after Castro's march into Havana.

Castro needed arms to realize his larger purposes, one of which was to protect himself against domestic opposition and possible foreign intervention as the revolution deepened. Castro also wanted arms to support revolutionary forces in the Caribbean against traditional military dictatorships, and to mount expeditionary forces against neighboring governments. Early expeditions, such as that against the Dominican Republic in mid-1959, became a heightening source of friction with the United States.

Castro opened negotiations for arms in Europe in the early spring of 1959 and with the United States shortly thereafter.[128] In fact, he wished to spend some $9 million to purchase U.S. destroyers and other military equipment. The United States, however, insisted on keeping the arms embargo (introduced under Batista) in full effect. In a press statement on October 27, 1959, the Department of State explained why it had introduced and continued to maintain in force the embargo of March 1958 against the shipment of arms to Cuba, "Armed expeditions were organized and launched against various countries, an armament race appeared imminent, and armed civil strife and terrorism continued. . . . This policy was made known to allied and friendly governments."[129]

Although accepting an embargo on U.S. arms, Castro complained bitterly about U.S. efforts to prevent Cuba from buying arms in Western Europe in a speech on March 5, 1960, the day after the French merchant ship, *La Coubre*, carrying a cargo of munitions, blew up at a Havana dock (the Cubans estimating some seventy-five dead and twice that number injured). While admitting the absence of conclusive evidence, Castro charged U.S. sabotage. Castro said that the British, referring to U.S. statements on the subject, had refused to sell him arms, and that a U.S. consul and military attaché had tried unsuccessfully to persuade an arms dealer in Belgium not to sell to Cuba. Then he warned that Cuba would buy arms where it thought best, an only slightly veiled allusion to later purchases of Soviet arms.[130]

The Department of State sharply repudiated Castro's "irresponsible" charges of U.S. participation in the *La Coubre* explosion, and tempers flared in a meeting between Secretary of State Christian Herter and the Cuban chargé d'affaires. The *New York Times* featured a report in Washington from "reliable sources" in Havana that Castro had spent more than $120 million for arms in 1959.[131]

Dependence on foreign supplies of arms was not Castro's only strategic liability. Cuba imported most of its oil since island production only covered a small fraction of domestic consumption. U.S. and Anglo-Dutch refineries in Cuba were supplying Cuba's needs with crude oil from Venezuela and elsewhere. Cuba was falling behind in foreign exchange payments to cover these purchases. On April 19, 1960, a shipment of Soviet crude oil in exchange for Cuban products arrived[132]—the first time Cuba had established an alternative to western petroleum suppliers.

Finally, Castro sought to lessen Cuba's extreme dependence on U.S. sugar purchases and to diversify her sugar markets. Talk in the United States about cutting the sugar quota made finding new markets more urgent. President Eisenhower indicates in his memoirs that cutting the quota came under consideration late in 1959.[133] In a news conference on December 10, Secretary Herter declined to discuss "punitive action" against Cuba but left no doubt that this was a possibility. One result was that Castro complained about "daily threats" to cut the sugar quota in January.[134]

During December and January arrangements were made for the Soviet trade exhibitions in Havana. The arrival of Soviet First Deputy Chairman Mikoyan on February 4, 1960, set the stage for Castro's negotiations with the USSR. On February 13, the two countries announced the conclusion of a trade agreement including a five-year contract by which Cuba would sell to the Soviet Union 425,000 tons of sugar in 1960 and one million tons a year from 1961 to 1964. The Soviets also granted a credit of $100 million to Cuba for the purchase of plants, machinery, materials, and technical assistance. Agreements followed with East Germany in February and Poland in March.

In a television interview on March 28, Castro publicly repudiated Cuba's obligation under the Rio Treaty of 1947, a hemispheric agreement designed in part to protect the Americas from external aggression. Since the Rio Treaty has been considered the cornerstone of U.S. security arrangements in the Western Hemisphere, adherence to it, from the U.S. point of view, has been the principal test of a Latin American government's commitment to the inter-American system. Castro's overt flaunting of that agreement cut the United States to the quick, as the Department of State indicated in a press release of March 30, 1960. A few weeks later, Cuba reestablished diplomatic relations with the USSR, broken by Batista soon after his coup d'etat in 1952.

From a purely Cuban and nationalistic point of view, Castro had grounds for seeking to strengthen his hand vis-à-vis the United States with extracontinental support. Other Latin American leaders have strengthened their ties with extracontinental powers in order to lessen their economic and political dependence on the United States. In view of the overwhelming power of the United States, the issue posed to Cubans was not so much whether this might be a useful political ploy in the abstract, but whether Castro or Cuba could or should pay the price that challenging traditional U.S.–Cuban relationships might entail.

The U.S. Response to Castro's Actions

Throughout 1959 and early 1960 the Department of State remained largely passive, responding through established channels to Castro's various moves, often with diplomatic protests.[135] It was not then disposed to take harsh measures against Cuba. This was demonstrated at a regional meeting of U.S. ambassadors in San Salvador in April 1959 when U.S.–Cuban policy became the subject of heated discussion. Those who favored a moderate response at that meeting defeated a proposal of Robert C. Hill, then U.S. ambassador to Mexico, to make a strong public statement critical of Castro.[136]

In spite of opposition inside and outside the government, forbearance continued to characterize official policy into 1960 when on January 26, President Eisenhower issued a public statement, which Ambassador Philip W. Bonsal has described as one of "continued moderation and restraint on our part, denying Castro the chance to make political capital out of alleged American economic aggression."[137] The statement expressed U.S. determination to do its best to enforce the laws against anti-Castro exiles and to show its sympathy with the aspirations of the Cuban people for social reform, its continuing interest in the rights of its citizens under international law, and its willingness to resolve any conflicts in this respect through negotiations. Above all, the statement led off with a short but unequivocal reaffirmation of the policy of nonintervention in Cuban domestic affairs.

With regard to the Agrarian Reform Law of 1959, the Department of State's protests were lodged not primarily against the law itself but against arbitrary seizures without payment. Dispossession of land from owners was made purportedly under the authority of the law whereas, in practice, the provisions of the law regarding the procedures for seizure and compensation were flaunted. The Department of State did not insist, as Castro charged in his 1960 speech at the United Nations, on immediate cash payments in full at a U.S. evaluation, but rather sought to negotiate arrangements for compensation. The two governments never achieved sufficient mutual understanding to begin serious negotiations. As it turned out, the Castro government did not begin payments to either U.S. or Cuban owners under the provisions of the 1959 law. (A second Agrarian Reform Law was issued in 1963, and most confiscated lands ended up as part of large state-owned and operated farms.)

The policy of forbearance in late 1959 and early 1960 lasted only a few months. In February and March 1960, the following significant events had already taken place: the conclusion of trade agreements between Cuba and the USSR and other Eastern European countries; Castro's warning that he would buy weapons from any country, implying Communist sources; the expropriation or intervention of some U.S.-owned businesses; and greater domestic alignment of Castro with the Cuban Communists.

The furor was at its height in Cuba and the United States when President Eisenhower returned from his trip to South America in March. Castro's bitter denunciation of the U.S. government as responsible for blowing up a French munitions ship in Havana harbor on March 4 may have been the last straw, convincing the president to abandon nonintervention. Nor had steps been taken to meet the protests of Americans deprived of their property under the agrarian reform. The administration's moderate policies also were becoming a political liability as electoral politics were heating up for the 1960 presidential elections. Eisenhower thus began to ready important measures for "bringing Castro into line." Taken together, these measures constituted what was, in effect, a policy designed to overthrow Castro by all means available to the United States short of the open employment of American armed forces in Cuba.[138]

Training a Counterrevolutionary Force. The CIA began to recruit anti-Castro exiles in December 1959, if not earlier. On December 14, Americans from the U.S. embassy in Cuba engineered the departure of Manuel Artime, who later became one of the leaders of the abortive Bay of Pigs invasion.[139] The actual decision, however, to organize a counterrevolutionary force under the auspices of the CIA was not taken until March 17, 1960. At this time, President Eisenhower gave orders "to begin to organize the training of Cuban exiles, mainly in Guatemala, against a possible future day when they might return to their homeland."[140]

How President Eisenhower came to make this sharp reversal in his policy toward Cuba has not been revealed to the public as yet, and his memoirs are not very illuminating. Ambassador Bonsal, a strong advocate of the earlier policy and critic of the latter, was not consulted in advance of the change. Vice-President Nixon, who had warned President Eisenhower about Castro during the latter's visit to the United States, claims to have been in the "minority" within the administration in opposing the initial policy of forbearance. In *Six Crises* Nixon explains, "Early in 1960, the position I had been advocating for nine months finally prevailed, and the CIA was given instructions to provide arms, ammunition, and training for Cubans who had fled the Castro regime."[141] The information available to the public, however, probably tells only a small part of the story. Little is known about how this decision was reached, partly because it involved intelligence operations that are ordinarily "held close" with limitations on coordination with other government agencies. The U.S. president apparently did not consider his decision to arm exiles an irrevocable commitment, but the U.S. government may not have fully appreciated the impact the knowledge of official U.S. involvement would have on Castro and his policies nor the high political costs of disbanding such an effort once launched.

The Refusal of the Oil Companies. Cuba was dependent on two U.S. companies, Esso and Texaco, and one Anglo-Dutch company, Shell, for petroleum—the refining capacity for which had been sharply increased during Batista's last administration. Under the provisions of the February 1960 trade agreement with the USSR, Soviet crude oil was one of the Soviet products that could be exchanged for Cuban sugar. Shipments of Soviet crude oil began arriving in Cuba in April. The Cuban government insisted in May that the companies refine future shipments. Representatives of the American companies met with secretary of the treasury, Robert Anderson, who urged the companies to refuse.[142] Early in June, the three companies communicated their refusal to refine Soviet oil to the Cuban government. That refusal posed an unprecedented challenge to the Castro government, not only with regard to its foreign exchange and commercial policies, but on strategic grounds as well.

Cutting the Sugar Quota.   Pressure mounted within the United States during 1960 to cut the Cuban sugar quota. The argument ran that Cuba should no longer enjoy preferential treatment in the purchase of sugar and, particularly, the benefit of the quota premium, which amounted to $150 million in 1959, while the Cuban government was seizing or "intervening" U.S.-owned property and otherwise damaging U.S. private business interests. Draft legislation authorizing the U.S. president to cut the sugar quota was formally presented to the Congress early in March.

Late in June 1960, the Eisenhower administration pressed the Congress hard for authority to reduce the Cuban sugar quota for 1960. A hearing of the House Committee on Agriculture on June 22, 1960, together with the debates in the House and the Senate about a week later, throw much light on the purposes underlying the government's decision.

In his testimony on June 22, Secretary Herter said that a primary purpose of the administration's request "was to safeguard consumers in this country from possible interruptions in supply and fluctuations in price," and the administration reiterated this contention time and again to answer charges that the cut was a form of economic sanction, or as the Cubans charged, "economic aggression."[143] In fact, the administration's justification was neither internally consistent nor convincing. The immediate problem was not to protect the United States from domestic shortages, and the administration, as congressional debate showed, was trying to rush through the legislation to prevent Castro from completing stepped-up deliveries under the quota arrangements. One of the major impulses behind the quota cut was the clamor of various foreign and domestic interests for part of the Cuban quota. Castro's interest was to sell as much sugar as he could for high prices, and the United States continued to be a prime market. Eventually, as Cuba developed other markets including those in Communist countries, Cuba might decline to sell the United States as much sugar as the latter might want. But this eventual possibility could hardly justify eliminating all purchases in Cuba, accomplished by administrative decision in less than a year, and was the kind of abrupt and emergency adjustment this act presumably sought to avoid.

The debate in both the House and Senate was carried out in an atmosphere of urgency, haste, and high emotion. In spite of its immense foreign policy implications, the bill was not considered by the Senate Foreign Relations Committee. Much of the pressure for enactment of the bill came from members of the House Committee on Agriculture and other congressmen with ties to sugar interests. The chairman of the committee, Congressman Cooley, in the following statements gives some idea of the atmosphere in which the bill was considered: "I have been on this committee 26 years . . . more or less grown up with the sugar law . . . and I can truthfully say that never before in more than 25 years, has this legislation become involved in partisan politics."[144] One congressman appeared to be more concerned that his vote on the issue would be interpreted as a "vote for communism" than with its effect on the national interest.

Powerful vested interests in the United States and in some Latin American countries hoped to profit from Cuba's political difficulties and get part of the Cuban quota. President Eisenhower was aware of these influences and explicitly disassociated himself from the decision to give part of the Cuban quota to the Dominican Republic.[145] There seems little doubt that other sugar interests capitalized on Cuba's difficulties and contributed to the pressures on the Congress and the president to cut the quota for reasons not related exclusively to public interests.

Whatever may have been the administration's motives, the congressmen who backed the legislation gave forthright explanations of their positions. Congressman Rivers said: "Think of what is happening—Castro and Communism—both must be destroyed. . . . Let us take a little of the Rivers' backbone. . . . God Save America."[146] Congressman Haley said, "The time has come to deal with Castro where it hurts: in the pocketbook."[147] Congressman McDowell said, "It is high time that the bluff of the Cuban Prime Minister and his colleagues was called."[148] Congressman Conte said: "I am a patient man, but I am also an American. I cannot allow my country to continue to suffer the constant humiliations and opprobrium heaped upon her in an irresponsible manner. . . . We are, in fact, supporting the rapid growth of international communism at our very door step."[149]

The bill was passed overwhelmingly in the House, 396 yeas, no nays, and 36 not voting. The bill had more difficulty in the Senate, but the conference report passed easily: 32 to 24, with 44 not voting. Congressman Cooley and Senator Morse frequently expressed their concern about the implications of the bill, the latter primarily on the grounds that it would immensely complicate our relations with many friendly Latin American countries. One member of the House expressed concern that the bill might make a martyr out of Castro.

The administration could have ended the favored treatment which Cuban sugar enjoyed by eliminating the quota premium while continuing to purchase Cuban sugar at world market prices. William Wieland, the Cuban desk officer, favored such a course in connection with a negotiated general settlement, reserving the savings as premiums in a special fund to compensate owners of expropriated property.[150] Instead the president proceeded to terminate all U.S. purchases, constituting half the Cuban sugar crop, the bulk of its exports, and the main contributor to its gross domestic product.

Armed with authority from Congress, President Eisenhower cut the Cuban sugar quota by 700,000 tons on July 6 for the balance of 1960, permitting new authorization of only 39,752 short tons. On December 16, 1960, the president fixed the Cuban quota at zero for the first quarter of 1961, thus establishing the policy of eliminating the Cuban quota entirely, a policy that was confirmed by the Kennedy administration.

Some observers have mistakenly attributed the sugar quota cut to the large-scale nationalizations that took place thereafter, partly because authority for the two actions was given and announced almost simultaneously in early July. Actually, most of the nationalizations, which were not effected until August, were a response to, not a cause of, the sugar quota cut. On the other hand, it would be a serious error to assert that Castro did not make major moves against U.S. private interests prior to the sugar quota cut. The Department of State estimated, for example, that prior to the cut Castro had seized about half the U.S.-owned properties, mainly in agriculture, mining, public utilities, and tourist facilities.[151] Seizures of most U.S. investments in manufacturing, commerce, finance, and transportation were not made until August and September.

I have been able to find no instance in the hearings or in the debate where a congressman anticipated that cutting the Cuban sugar quota might have an effect diametrically opposite to the intended effect: that rather than combatting communism in Cuba, the cut would help strengthen Soviet influence there. If such a concern existed, it did not seem to receive attention. Several congressmen appeared to believe that Castro would have difficulty surviving the quota cut. Congressman McDowell said, "If Cuba's splendid people understand that they must sell their sugar or their economy will be destroyed, they will themselves find a way to deal with the present misleaders and fomenters of hatred." He was then prepared to let the Cubans sell their sugar elsewhere, but expressed the belief that the Russians would "not find Cuban sugar sufficiently important to them or their economy to take the place of the United States as the largest consumer of Cuban sugar in the world."[152]

Why did President Eisenhower take such severe measures against Cuba with all the risks these entailed? As suggested above, there were a number of pressures at work in the Congress not directly related to U.S.–Cuban bilateral relations per se. As for the administration, Castro's seizures of U.S. property were an important element, as well as the growing totalitarian and socialist nature of the new Cuban regime. But perhaps what convinced Eisenhower was not primarily that Castro threatened U.S. private interests and the traditional Cuban political structure, but that Castro was becoming a channel for the introduction of Soviet political and military influence into the western hemisphere.

As will be shown below, Castro had already made arrangements in June or earlier to receive large shipments of arms from socialist countries. In the debate on the sugar quota issue on the floor of the House of Representatives, Congressman Brook expressed his great apprehension of Soviet activities in Cuba, "Arms are being purchased by the Castro government, airports are being built by the Soviets and I have read of submarine activities unloading arms and munitions of war."[153] It would be interesting to know, too, whether the confidential part of Secretary Herter's testimony before the Committee on Agriculture in late June mentioned Cuban purchases of arms from Eastern Europe. In any case, the preceding evidence is sufficient in the light of all the pertinent circumstances to justify the inference that the Department of State was already deeply concerned about Castro's strategic and military ties with Communist countries on the eve of the sugar quota cut. These considerations, coupled with Castro's open and belligerent defiance of U.S. political primacy in the hemisphere, caused the president to take this economic measure which was apparently designed to eliminate Castro politically.

Whether the decision to arm anti-Castro exiles and stop buying Cuban sugar helped or hindered the achievement of the administration's objectives is an entirely different question indeed. This subject, together with a consideration of the broader causes for the U.S.-Cuban split will be taken up in the conclusions. First, let us examine the immediate repercussions of the president's anti-Castro measures.

The Elimination of U.S. Influence

Any one of the Eisenhower administration's anti-Castro measures—the counterrevolutionary force, the refusal to refine Soviet crude oil, the cut in the sugar quota—might have led to the fall of the Castro government. Castro reasoned, not implausibly, that he was in mortal peril. In his reflex reaction to protect himself, he turned first to the Soviet Union and other socialist countries for the means to counter Eisenhower's punitive policies. Once Soviet help was assured, he was then able to strike back against the United States.

Castro feared U.S. armed intervention long before Eisenhower reached his decision in March 1960 to arm a counterrevolutionary force, and Castro had been seeking, sometimes with bitter frustration, to buy arms to protect himself as well as for armed attacks against other Caribbean countries such as Trujillo's regime nearby. Acquisition of arms became doubly urgent when he learned about Eisenhower's decision. It is difficult to pinpoint that date, but Castro said on May 1, 1960, nearly one year before the Bay of Pigs invasion, "We have reports that the foreign office of the United States is preparing an aggression against Cuba through the Government of Guatemala."[154] Apparently, the first group of Cuban exiles arrived at the Retalhuleu Base in Guatemala in May 1960, and arrangements to set up that base had to have been made sometime before.[155] Therefore, it seems reasonable to assume that Castro had knowledge of the CIA's operations in May and acted on the basis of that knowledge.

No doubt, Castro intensified his efforts to secure arms from the Communist countries and could cite the CIA's Guatemalan operations to strengthen his case. Castro stated publicly on July 8, 1960, that the arrival of an arms shipment was imminent and confirmed later that it had arrived by July 26. Thus, Suárez's suggestion that the Castro government had already arranged for the purchase of arms from Czechoslovakia and possibly the USSR no later than June, if not sooner, is plausible.[156] A report of the Department of State made public on November 18 described how Castro had built up an army "ten times" the size of Batista's and listed the number of rifles, submachine guns, mortars, tanks, helicopters, etc., received from Communist countries, most beginning in July.[157] Thus, by mid-1960 Castro had arranged for a source of arms and munitions independent of U.S. controls and was rapidly bolstering his capacity to resist an armed attack. To do this, however, Cuba became militarily and strategically dependent on the Communist countries.

Castro followed a similar strategy with regard to the oil companies' refusal in early June, under official U.S. encouragement, to refine Soviet crude oil. No doubt after assuring himself that he could count on the Communist countries as a regular source of supply, Castro took over the American and Anglo-Dutch refineries (Texaco, Esso, and Shell) beginning on June 29. As a result, the companies lost not only their properties but also some $50 million in back payments from the Cuban government. It would be ironic if foreign exchange held back from payments due the oil companies had been used to pay for Cuban arms purchased from Eastern Europe.

The Cubans were worried about a possible cut in the sugar quota long before it actually happened, and certainly as early as December 1959 when it was made a matter of public discussion at Secretary Herter's press conference. In March, when the administration formally asked Congress for discretionary authority over the Cuban quota, Ernesto (Che) Guevara made a statement which attracted much public attention at the time:

> Why are we not a developed country? . . . The North Americans take many pains so that the country does not progress in other branches of industry [besides sugar] so that we have to buy the majority of manufactured products abroad. The North Americans control of the greater share of the Cuban import market . . . they afford us good prices for our sugar and even concede us preferential tariffs in exchange for which we reciprocate with preferential tariffs for the products the country needs for its consumption and which the North produces. . . . This influx of North American capital is translated into political dependence even after the abolition of the Platt Amendment. . . . When we struggle with all our strength to get out of this situation of economic vassalage and sign an agreement with the USSR, the representatives of the colony . . . try to sow confusion. . . . They try to show that by selling to another country we enslave ourselves and they don't stop to consider how much slavery for our country the three million tons which we sell at supposedly preferential prices represents.[158]

Guevara found the United States a handy scapegoat to explain Cuban underdevelopment, although even he would have surely admitted that there were many other reasons why Cuba had not made greater economic and social progress. Tariff protection for U.S. products in Cuba was part of the story, especially in earlier years, but Cuban dependence was also due to the much larger and sometimes more efficient productive capacity of the United States. Much of Cuban development had theretofore taken place under the impulse of trade with and investment by the United States. United States resources, including premiums on sugar sales, offered one source for capital accumulation.

The Cubans were caught on the horns of a dilemma. They wanted to rid themselves of U.S. leverage from the sugar quota, but the loss of the U.S. market would have deprived the nation of her lifeblood. Castro certainly could not have expected to survive long without help from some third party. Even if Castro was ready to break ties with the United States, it is doubtful at that date that he had commitments from the USSR to take up the slack. One would not be surprised if even Castro feared the immense risks involved. And, in view of those risks, it was much better to leave responsibility for cutting the quota to the United States rather than assuming it himself.

In June as the United States moved closer to a decision on the sugar quota, Castro said, "We will exchange the quota for investments" and estimated U.S. investments as being worth $800 million.[159] Most of the property seizures up until the sugar quota cut early in July were agricultural properties. Some of the nonagricultural seizures included the Moa Bay Mining Company in March and hotels in June. Up to the time of the sugar quota cut, the seizures were either explained as temporary interventions or expropriations and, theoretically at least, were subject to negotiation and eventual compensation.

The U.S. action in cutting the Cuban sugar quota on July 6 brought the USSR dramatically and prominently into the picture. Soviet Chairman Nikita Khrushchev declared on July 9, 1960: "Figuratively speaking, in case of need, Soviet artillerymen can support the Cuban people with their rocket fire if the aggressive forces in the Pentagon dare to launch an intervention against Cuba. . . . This, if you will, is a warning to those who would like to settle international issues by force and not by reason."[160] Castro was inclined to interpret Khrushchev literally rather than figuratively, and Soviet "complete support in maintaining Cuban independence against unprovoked aggression" was reaffirmed in a Soviet-Cuban communique on December 19, 1960.

According to Suárez, Castro pressed a suitor's case, in the face of Soviet reluctance, for Soviet military and economic support after the quota cut. The USSR hedged on the question of military guarantees, but was prepared to say enough to give the United States pause. In 1961, after a delay of more than five months, the USSR, prodded by the Chinese example, finally agreed to buy 2.7 million tons of sugar. This figure, plus agreements to buy 1 million tons by the Chinese and 300,000 tons by other socialist countries, meant that Cuba was guaranteed the sale of 4 million tons in "socialist markets."[161] In this fashion, the Communist countries came to buy the sugar the United States had spurned.

To counter congressional authorization to Eisenhower to cut the sugar quota, the Cuban Council of Ministers authorized the nationalization of U.S. properties on July 6, the same day Eisenhower suspended the Cuban sugar quota. Castro did not retaliate by new seizures until August 5, taking a month to strengthen his ties with the USSR first. On that day he announced the takeover of 26 companies wholly or partially owned by U.S. citizens; on September 17, he seized U.S.-owned banks; and on October 24, he seized 166 additional U.S.-owned properties, which largely fulfilled Castro's earlier pledge to seize U.S. investments to compensate for Cuba's loss of the sugar quota. Unlike his early seizures, Castro's expropriation measures of August 1960 were openly directed against U.S. properties, discriminating explicitly on the basis of nationality and with compensation linked to sugar sales in the United

States. Castro's post-sugar-quota-cut expropriations made the prospect of compensation so remote as to render eventual reconciliation on this issue virtually impossible. At this time, perhaps, the process had become irreversible.

The elimination of the sugar quota cast the dye in U.S.–Cuban relations. As Eisenhower himself said: "This action amounts to economic sanctions against Cuba. Now we must look ahead to other moves—economic, diplomatic, and strategic."[162] On October 19, the United States prohibited exports to Cuba except for nonsubsidized foodstuffs, medicines, and medical supplies. Alarmed by the mounting activities of the counterrevolutionary invasion forces, Castro proclaimed his fear of a U.S.-sponsored invasion and on January 2 demanded that U.S. embassy persons assigned to Havana be cut down to eleven, the same number as in the Cuban embassy in Washington. President Eisenhower responded by announcing the severance of diplomatic relations on January 3.

Castro's conduct from May 1960 to January 1961, when diplomatic relations were severed, emerges in a totally different light when viewed from the perspective of Havana. Castro must have considered himself in deadly peril, literally fighting for his life during this period, and so he was. He almost surely knew about the U.S.-sponsored organization of the counterrevolutionary force beginning in May 1960, a development that most Americans could not take seriously until almost a year later when the Cuban exiles actually landed. Nor was the American public upset about the mounting preparations to cut the sugar quota, already a real menace to Havana. Thus, the U.S. president's announcement of the cut may have come as a surprise to the uninformed North American, but it simply confirmed fears Castro expressed publicly six or more months earlier. In this light, many of Castro's acts are more understandable: his seizure of the oil companies for refusing to refine Soviet crude oil beginning June 29, 1960; his seizure of much American property in August and later; and his restrictions on the size of the American embassy staff to conform to the size of the Cuban staff in Washington in January 1961. The Castro government, let it be remembered, was not the first to take actions leading to a diplomatic break with a country mounting a hostile invasion force.

In retrospect, it is clear that the U.S. imposition of sanctions against Castro had the effect, in Ambassador Bonsal's words, of "driving the Soviet Union into Castro's arms."[163] Until these sanctions were imposed, the Soviet Union apparently did not regard the Cuban Revolution as Marxist-Leninist and had not prepared either to underwrite Castro economically or to assume strategic risks vis-à-vis the United States on Castro's behalf. Although Castro already feared an armed confrontation with the United States, he may not have had much hope of receiving the comprehensive support from the Russians necessary to weather a confrontation with the United States. In this case Eisenhower's stringent actions may have come as a severe shock. Figure 2 shows how U.S. sanctions led to the Soviet countermoves that facilitated Castro's retaliatory acts and completed the severance of U.S.–Cuban ties.

Castro was not prepared to seize the oil refineries until he was assured of the independence that the June 18 agreement with the USSR provided from western oil

FIGURE 2

CONSEQUENCES OF U.S. SANCTIONS

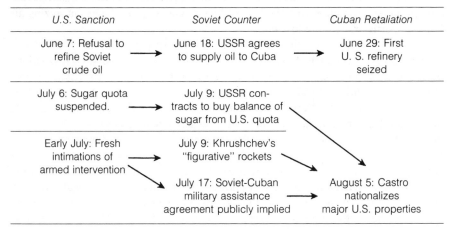

U.S. Sanction	Soviet Counter	Cuban Retaliation
June 7: Refusal to refine Soviet crude oil	June 18: USSR agrees to supply oil to Cuba	June 29: First U. S. refinery seized
July 6: Sugar quota suspended.	July 9: USSR contracts to buy balance of sugar from U.S. quota	
Early July: Fresh intimations of armed intervention	July 9: Khrushchev's "figurative" rockets	
	July 17: Soviet-Cuban military assistance agreement publicly implied	August 5: Castro nationalizes major U.S. properties

NOTE: This figure does not show who started the U.S.–Cuban conflict; one would need to go back long before June 7. It does show, however, how the United States escalated the conflict.

Soviet perceptions of the imperative necessity to come to Castro's defense against aggressive U.S. behavior are clearly shown in Akademiia Nauk SSSR, Institut Latinskoi Ameriki, *Strany Latinskoi Ameriki v Sovremennykh Mezhdunarodnykh Otnosheniiakh* (Moscow, 1967), especially pages 50–56. Page 53 substantiates the agreement on petroleum supplies and page 54 the military arrangements made with Raúl Castro on his visit to Moscow, the existence of which was implied in *Pravda* on July 17, 1960. Those arrangements must have provided for the provision of arms as well as the Soviet commitment not to permit U.S. armed intervention in Cuba. Strategic considerations became acute at this time because the suspension of the sugar quota cut made the preparations of the Cuban exile movement seem far more dangerous and imminent, not to mention other evidences in early July of a disposition in the United States to take armed action against Cuba. During those days the United States was careful not to threaten openly the unilateral use of armed force, as the USSR charged, but implicitly raised the possibility of collective military action under inter-American agreements. See *Department of State Bulletin* August 1, 1960, p. 170, and August 8, 1970, pp. 199 ff.

Another Soviet source that describes Soviet assistance to Cuba as being prompted by U.S. measures against Castro is "Sovetskii Soiuz-Kuba: Otnosheniia druzhby i sotrudnichestva," in *SSSR i Latinskaia Amerika 1917–1967* (Moscow, 1967), p. 143.

sources. Nor was he prepared to defy U.S. power directly by eliminating American influence within Cuba, symbolized primarily by U.S. business interests there, without Soviet military assistance. The threats posed by the incipient counterrevolutionary movement and the sugar quota suspension were too great. In the first part of July, Raúl Castro, the Cuban minister of defense, visited Moscow for conversations with Soviet officials. Apparently, Raúl Castro secured the commitments which he sought because Soviet spokesmen announced on July 17 that the USSR would not remain "a nonparticipant" if Cuba suffered armed intervention and that the Soviet Union would provide Cuba with "essential aid." The statement clearly implied military assistance and a military commitment to defend Cuba against the United

States.[164] Soviet commitments to take up the slack in sugar purchases caused by the U.S. suspension and to provide military and other supplies emboldened Castro to risk a full-scale confrontation with the United States. On August 5 he began seizing all U.S. properties remaining in Cuba.

Castro's relations with the Cuban Communists also support the thesis that it was Castro who was wooing the Soviet Union—not the reverse—and that U.S. sanctions made Moscow more ready to give him the support he sought. The Cuban Communists were political outsiders in Cuba before the cut in the sugar quota. By August 1960 the Communists' efforts to penetrate the Castroite leadership still had not yet borne fruit. Suárez maintains that there were no active party members in the Council of Ministers, the command posts of the rebel army, top-level administrative positions, or in the leadership of the mass organizations.[165] Nor was Suárez able to find any statement by the Cuban communists in favor of expropriation from the time expropriations were authorized in July until Castro announced the nationalizations in August.[166] In fact, the local Communists' reservations about the nationalizations were expressed both before and after the seizures were effected. Thus, it seems clear that the Soviet Union was not urging the local Communists to press nationalization on Castro. Their leader, Blas Roca, surely must have been reflecting Soviet caution in this respect because he had only just returned from an extended visit to Moscow. Despite mounting Soviet assistance, Castro continued to have differences with Moscow and with the local Communists.[167] For his own reasons, Castro pressed on with the radicalization of Cuban society almost in spite of rather than because of the local Communists. Thus, it was not Communist or Soviet pressure which caused him to characterize the Cuban Revolution as "socialist" on April 16, 1961, the day before the landing at the Bay of Pigs. More likely, the label was applied to enhance his prospects for attracting Soviet support against the impending invasion sponsored by the United States.

The Bay of Pigs

The U.S.-sponsored landing at the Bay of Pigs on April 17, 1961, did not mark any change in the objectives of American policy toward Cuba.[168] It simply marked the use of the ultimate weapon to implement a policy to overthrow Fidel Castro, decided more than a year earlier by President Eisenhower. No doubt some of Eisenhower's advisers hoped that economic measures alone would obtain Castro's political collapse. The U.S. refusal to refine Soviet oil, the cut in the Cuban sugar quota, and the trade embargo of October 1961 did not have their desired effect. The Communist countries provided Cuba with necessary petroleum, bought her unsold sugar, and provided Cuba with trade items prohibited under the embargo. The threatening U.S. posture and arms embargo strengthened Castro's appeal for arms from the East. Castro could not be brought down by economic pressures alone; therefore, only armed force gave promise of removing him.

Although the policy to overthrow Castro was initiated by the Eisenhower administration, Kennedy endorsed it in principle during the 1960 presidential campaign. Although he did not yet know about the Guatemalan training camps, he replied on September 23, 1960, to a question about the Cuban problem: "We must let the Cuban people know that we are sympathetic with their legitimate economic aspirations, that we are aware of their love for freedom, and that we will not be content until democracy is returned to Cuba. The forces fighting for freedom in exile and in the mountains of Cuba should be sustained and assisted."[169] Later Kennedy backed away from what was interpreted in some quarters as a commitment of U.S. armed support for Cuban exiles. Nonetheless, during the campaign he and Vice-President Nixon seemed to compete to see who could take the hardest anti-Castro line.

After the elections, Allen Dulles, the CIA chief, informed Kennedy about the training and arming of the Cuban exiles in Guatemala, and Kennedy was faced early in the new year with the decision of whether to permit the operation to go forward or to call it off. Kennedy felt forced to make the decision before he was fully acquainted with his major advisers and firmly established in office. Reasons for urgency were the restiveness of the Cuban exiles in Guatemala and a deadline on the evacuation of the camps imposed by the president of Guatemala. Moreover, expected deliveries of Soviet arms to Castro made action seem urgent.

Why did President Kennedy authorize a seaborne invasion of Cuban exiles against Castro? First and foremost, Kennedy would have found it extremely difficult and embarrassing to call off an operation that had been gaining momentum for a full year. The Cuban exiles were impatient to invade their homeland and could hardly have been set loose in Central America as a potential source of trouble in a traditionally unstable area. If they had been returned to the United States, as most surely would have been ordered, the exiles would have informed the press of their original plans and the Kennedy administration's unwillingness to support their efforts to restore "freedom" to Cuba.[170] Would not Kennedy be charged with having lost his nerve if he refused to challenge Communist control of Cuba?

Second, the top officials in the executive branch were either advocates of the operation or gave it tacit consent. Allen Dulles and Richard Bissell of the CIA were two of its strongest protagonists since this was an operation in which their agency had heavy vested interests. Secretary MacNamara had assumed that his senior military officers had approved the plan and that it had received careful review in the Department of State. Secretary Rusk appeared to be in accord, with suggestions only about its implementation. Security was so tight that most Latin American specialists in his department were uninformed. The joint chiefs of staff, without approving the plan as a whole, never openly opposed it and appeared to be collaborating with the CIA in its execution. Only Senator J. William Fulbright made an impassioned plea against the plan. President Kennedy's assistant, Arthur Schlesinger, Jr., opposed the plan in a critical memorandum but later regretted his "failure to do more."[171]

Third, from the early discussions to the bitter end, President Kennedy was adamant that conventional U.S. military forces would not be permitted to engage Castro's army directly. Kennedy permitted the covert use of U.S. citizens on special missions and naval support for logistic and rescue purposes, but he never wavered in his decision that the full military might of the United States would not be directed against Castro. Thus, although this decision made it impossible to turn the tide once the Cuban exiles were defeated on the beaches, it made it easier for Kennedy initially to authorize the operation with the understanding that the Cubans themselves would do the major fighting. Why should he stop them if the United States did not become openly involved? Kennedy hoped that the Cuban brigade could establish a foothold, rally other Cubans to their cause, and proclaim a new government without *overt* U.S. support. If they failed, he reasoned, the United States was not committed to intervention and the remaining brigade members could fade away into the hills and form a guerrilla movement there. Despite Kennedy's reiteration of his prohibition against massive U.S. armed intervention, the Cuban members of the brigade had been led to expect it. The political leaders in Miami and New York did not believe then that the president would let the brigade perish.[172]

The Bay of Pigs invasion failed due to faulty military planning and implementation. The 1,400 well-armed and well-trained Cuban exiles were no match for Castro's 200,000-man well-equipped and ably led army. The invaders did not gain supremacy in the air partly due to planning errors, partly due to reluctance to expose the extent of U.S. support. Castro's planes sunk the ships carrying the invaders' main stores of ammunition and other essential supplies. And the survivors never had a chance to flee into the mountains nearly eighty miles away through impenetrable jungles and swamp. Without control of the air, such a force may never have had a chance against Castro's large armies anyway. Only an insurrection in Cuba would have overcome Castro's military advantages. Moreover, when the landing occurred, Castro's police rounded up thousands of persons suspected of hostility toward the regime. The prompt crushing of the invasion eliminated the possibility of any anti-Castro bandwagon developing within the country.

The Bay of Pigs left the Cuban policies of President Eisenhower and Kennedy in ruins. Castro emerged stronger than ever within his own country, his prestige at a high point around the world. The United States had not only failed to achieve its objectives, but was revealed before the world as having resorted to means whose use by others it had long condemned. Castro drew closer to the Communist countries. Most significant, the Bay of Pigs fiasco emboldened Castro and the Soviet Union to establish nuclear missiles in Cuba, an effort which led directly to the Cuban missile crisis of 1963. Time compounded the diplomatic errors of the past. U.S. policies in Guatemala in 1954 led to the Bay of Pigs in 1961, and the latter to the Missile Crisis, one of the single most dangerous armed confrontations in human history.

Paramilitary Expeditions: How and Why

United States sponsorship of paramilitary expeditions to overthrow Presidents Arbenz and Castro were never advanced, nor defended, simply as efforts to overthrow a Guatemalan or Cuban government. Virtually no one seriously conceived of either government posing a physical threat without support from a Great Power, such as the Soviet Union or China. As a result, the rationale behind U.S. policies was to combat Soviet imperialism in the Western Hemisphere. The "menace" with which the United States sought to cope was variously described as international communism, a beachhead of communism in the Americas, an alien despotism, etc. Were the charges of Soviet penetration into the hemisphere and the American fear based upon them valid?

First, as argued above, there has never been convincing evidence that the Guatemalan Communists, while admittedly influential, dominated the Arbenz government. Party members were relatively few in number, held few if any important positions in government, and were easily swept aside by the army. In Cuba the Communists were older, more experienced, and probably a stronger party in an organizational sense than in Guatemala. They opposed Fidel Castro actively until shortly before he took power and were marginal to his success then. Thereafter, Castro kept power tightly in his own hands, staffing most major jobs with associates from the guerrilla movement. The latter have always overshadowed the pre-1959 Communists. The old Communists remained on the fringes of Cuban politics, especially in the first year and a half. Castro found their support useful against domestic opposition and, above all, as a means of attracting Soviet assistance. Castro and his closest associates used and absorbed the old Communists more than they used or manipulated him.

Similarly, there has never been much evidence of direct Soviet penetration in Guatemala in 1951–1954 nor in Cuba before early 1960. Arbenz imported arms from eastern countries only as a last resort after U.S. pressures denied him access to suppliers in the West. He only turned to the socialist countries for arms in the face of armed insurrection at home and heavily armed and hostile neighbors on his borders. Secretary Dulles railed against the Guatemalan plea for Soviet assistance in the Security Council, but even that plea was simply a public and formal request for support in the implementation of the unanimous decision of the Security Council itself. There has been made public so far little evidence of direct contact between the two governments and virtually nothing about any joint plans or high-level substantive talks.

Castro, too, had relatively little contact with the Soviet Union before 1960. Although the USSR recognized Castro on January 11, 1959, it maintained no official representative in Cuba during most of Castro's first year, and diplomatic relations were not actually established until May 8, 1960. Mikoyan's visit earlier that year attracted much attention in the press, but the February trade agreement only about doubled the level of Soviet sugar purchases under Batista in certain years. Soviet-Cuban contacts developed rapidly in 1960 but the most important agreements relating to sugar purchases, the sale of oil and arms, and other provisions for the Cuban economy occurred after Eisenhower's decision to mount a counterrevolutionary force and seek authority to cut the sugar quota. Castro—not the Russians—played the role of the suitor;[173] the latter did not demonstrate eagerness to take on new commitments in the Western Hemisphere. U.S. efforts to overthrow Castro appear to have been the most effective arguments Castro had to persuade the Soviet Union to come to his assistance.

The record does not bear out the charges of direct Soviet penetration in Guatemala in 1951–1954 nor in Cuba in 1959 and early 1960. The United States claimed to have been mobilizing exiles to fight Soviet communism in Guatemala and Cuba. Actually, the mobilizations were against the Guatemalan and the Cuban governments. The composition and support of those governments at that time were primarily, if not totally, non-Communist, and they had only minimal contact with the USSR.

Like Arbenz, Castro deserved the credit, or blame, for challenging the foundation of his relationship with the United States, and he is no doubt proud to claim it. But there were important differences between the programs and objectives of the two men. Arbenz was elected president of Guatemala, conducted the government within the established political framework, and espoused social and economic policies that were primarily capitalist, not socialist. Unlike Arbenz, Castro was never elected to public office and appears never to have wanted to risk his and Cuba's future as he saw it in an electoral contest. Moreover, Castro decided early, probably at least by late 1959, to try to lead Cuba into a socialist revolution of epic proportions. By that date Castro appears to have decided that he could not protect his own uninterrupted tenure of power and the future of the Cuban Revolution in collaborative arrangements with the United States, much less in the more likely prospect of provoking its hostility. Castro was probably right in this estimate as the discussion earlier in this chapter of his objectives, history of U.S.–Cuban relations, and U.S. interests indicates.

The implications of his position were that a more or less complete break with the United States became essential if he were to chart his chosen course. Yet Castro was reluctant to take on personally the responsibility for the inevitable wounds that cutting ties with the United States would cause. He must have realized that Cuba could survive such a break only with substantial outside support, the only likely source of which was the USSR. No doubt, too, Castro found the Communist model, subject to local variations, compatible with his own revolutionary objectives as well as facilitating the sine qua non of a break with the United States—a Cuban–Soviet alliance. (That did not mean, however, that Castro intended to turn over control to the old guard Cuban Communists.) Yet the USSR had initially shown no eagerness to assume strategic risks or economic burdens on behalf of a distant, fledgling revolutionary movement peripheral to central Soviet interests.

The U.S. decisions to arm a counterrevolutionary force and cut the sugar quota, Cuba's major export and lifeblood, had the effect of terminating the established relationship between the two countries, which termination Castro was probably unable, unwilling, or afraid to initiate himself. The United States appeared responsible for the painful consequences of this political and economic surgery. More important, the United States provided Castro with just the arguments he needed to persuade the Russians to come to his assistance. The Cuban exile force made his need for arms indisputable. The U.S. embargo on arms sales to Cuba, backed by U.S.

pressures preventing purchases from other western sources, made it easy to persuade the USSR and other socialist countries to fill his shopping list. Obviously, too, the cut in the sugar quota put the USSR in the position of either buying Cuba's surplus sugar and providing other economic assistance or being exposed before the world as having permitted the collapse of a government apparently headed toward socialism. The effect, then, of U.S. policy was not only to facilitate Castro's personal objectives but also to hasten the actual penetration of Soviet influence into Cuba by making Castro dependent on outside assistance. The failure of the Bay of Pigs emboldened Castro and tempted Khrushchev to install nuclear missiles in Cuba. Thus, the result of the Bay of Pigs, conceived and implemented by the United States, led to Soviet military intervention in the hemisphere. The effects of U.S. policies toward Cuba were diametrically opposite to their purposes, and in this sense, appear to have been totally self-defeating.

How and why did the U.S. government come to espouse such ill-conceived policies? An important part of the answer is found in the nature of the relationship with Guatemala and Cuba as it developed before Arbenz and Castro came to power. That subject was dealt with earlier and will be discussed again in chapter 7. Let us examine here only the origins of the Guatemalan and Cuban policies in the Eisenhower administration. An interesting aspect of all this is whether U.S. policymakers really believed there was a Soviet threat in Guatemala and Cuba or whether, as some maintain, these charges were simply cynical pretexts for manipulating weak neighbors for economic and political gain.

Not surprisingly, John Foster Dulles was the pivotal figure in U.S. policy toward Guatemala. Like the Republican party, Dulles had experienced long and frustrating years excluded from the central decision-making process in a position of relative impotence which may have been galling to a man of his position, wealth, and ambitions. The World Council of Churches scarcely provided sufficient scope for a man of his burgeoning talents. As a leader of the party of the outs, he was forced to develop campaign issues against the Democrats whose foreign policies had been dynamic, innovative, and widely supported. Yet the Republicans and Dulles had a point in charging that the Truman-Acheson administration had framed its politics largely in response to Communist initiatives. Dulles criticized the Democrats for not taking constructive steps of their own. It was not enough simply to contain communism—a "negative and futile policy"; democracy itself must be advanced and "liberation treated as a practical goal."[174] These views led to his advocacy of the liberation of captive peoples in Eastern Europe. Yet when Mr. Dulles became secretary of state, he was cautious about risking war with the USSR on this issue, too.

In this sense, the Arbenz government in Guatemala—a far less risky place to defeat communism and advance democracy—provided a convenient opportunity. Communists had been active and were gaining strength in Guatemala and the Arbenz government had the annoying habit of not falling into line with all U.S. Cold War requirements. In his dealings with the world, Secretary Dulles often claimed that governments which were not for him were against him. All this was a short step to the conclusion that the presence of an active and influential Communist party made the Arbenz government a Communist beachhead in the Americas. One must not forget, too, that this was the early 1950s in the thick of the Cold War.

Secretary Dulles probably believed most of what he said about Guatemala, and it suited his interests to do so. The overthrow of the Arbenz regime provided one of the great satisfactions of his tenure as secretary of state. Still elated several days after the event, Dulles referred to Arbenz's fall as "a new and glorious chapter" in the "already great traditions of the American states."[175] He and President Eisenhower did not hesitate to capitalize on their victory in the 1954 and 1956 elections.

The influence of the United Fruit Company was an important element in the early official hostility toward the Arévalo and Arbenz governments and the immensely complicated prospects for reconciliation. To explain U.S. policy as simply a maneuver of the United Fruit Company to protect its investments and future profits is facile and misleading. The U.S. antitrust action against the United Fruit Company shows that the former was not the pawn of the latter. The more likely interpretation is that private and strategic interests both played a role, with strategic, that is, Cold War, considerations dominant.

Dulles' concept of the Arbenz government as Communist and a Soviet pawn was essential to justifying his conduct in the light of his own rigid moral principles. Apparently, he did not conceive of himself simply as a political broker protecting and advancing U.S. national interests, but as a white knight leading the forces of civilization and freedom against Communist barbarism and totalitarianism. Dulles conceived of his role in moralistic and theological terms, as the leader of the faith against atheistic communism.

How else could Dulles justify the steps which his government was taking? Secretly, the CIA was doing all in its power by clandestine means, that is, by techniques which were by definition illegal or inconsistent with accepted standards of conduct, to overthrow Arbenz. In public, Secretary Dulles and his department solemnly denied any official involvement with the Liberation Movement, proclaiming his loyalty to nonintervention and other hallowed inter-American principles. No doubt Dulles told himself that the international Communist "conspiracy" used such methods and posed such a threat that the United States could only survive and fulfill its destiny as a defender of the faith by using roughly similar methods itself. Thus, Dulles tended to compartmentalize and separate the covert and the overt and may even have misled himself about the deception he wrought upon the American public and the world. Dulles was, no doubt, incapable of understanding the image he projected in Latin America, that of the big bully.

Dulles' policy was successful in the sense that Arbenz fell. Castillo Armas' military maneuvers created a political crisis in Guatemala and precipitated Arbenz's conflict with his own military. Arbenz, however, was forced to resign by the Guatemalan armed forces in a classic barracks coup—not by the Castillo Armas invasion. When communism was perceived as a threat in Cuba, U.S. officials resorted to similar techniques, hoping to repeat the success of Guatemala.[176] The situation, however, was different. Having learned from Arbenz's failures, and with still better reasons of his own, Castro had destroyed the old Cuban army and built a new one submissive to his commands. He thereby eliminated the vulnerability which led to Arbenz's fall.[177]

Eisenhower's initial policies toward Arbenz must be sharply distinguished from his early policies toward Castro. In the latter case, the Eisenhower administration appears to have sincerely sought to adjust flexibly to Castro's unprecedented challenges during most of 1959. The moderation of official policies was not shared by all private groups or officials in the United States, witness the activities of anti-Castro Cuban émigrés, U.S. press criticism of the public trials of Batista's followers, and the probably hostile reception Vice-President Nixon gave Castro during his visit to Washington. The official line of the Department of State and the embassy was, however, conciliatory as evidenced by the U.S. reaction to intervention in U.S.-owned public utilities, the official U.S. response to the land reform, and Ambassador Bonsal's posture generally. Despite this forbearance, some critics charge that the United States did not try hard enough to accommodate Castro during 1959 and thereby lost an opportunity to influence his behavior. Such comment assumes a commonality of interests between Castro and the United States that was, and is, hard to find, plus an expectation of greater adaptability of U.S. political processes than heretofore attainable. In any case, the U.S. government maintained a relatively accommodating posture through January 1960.

The sharp reversal in policy was marked initially in March 1960 by the decision to arm anti-Castro exiles and culminated in the cut in the Cuban sugar quota in July. Castro's overreaction to the United States in 1959 was followed by U.S. overreaction to Castro in 1960. The causes of Eisenhower's decision are elusive and complex. United States private interests played, in my view, only a secondary role. Castro's treatment of U.S. interests in 1959 was shameful by U.S. standards, but the damage was limited mainly to seizures in agriculture and to interference in public utilities and mining. The prospects for U.S. business in Cuba, which looked poor by late 1959, helped establish a climate of gloom in U.S. business circles. Also, the role of sugar interests in other countries seeking a slice of the Cuban quota should not be discounted.

Until the archives are open, discussion of these points will necessarily be subject to revision. Two factors, however, seem especially important. The first is U.S. resentment of Castro's, Guevara's, and other Cuban leaders' hostile statements which U.S. officials deemed insulting and provocative. There was a steady stream of such statements from the beginning of 1959, mounting in a crescendo in March 1960. This is not to say that Castro's charges were always without foundation or that his resentment of the United States was not understandable but simply that U.S. behavior, as American officials perceived it, did not warrant Castro's abuse. The conclusion Eisenhower appears to have drawn was that the United States probably could never reach a viable compromise with Castro.

A second and more important factor was Castro's early overtures to the Soviet

Union. Although his initial ties, as pointed out above, were minimal, the United States was less concerned with them as they stood in February 1960 than with Castro's potential for mischief. In any case, Castro's initial talks with the USSR touched a sore point over which the United States was traditionally jittery. These two factors come out strongly in President Eisenhower's description of the events and in the public statements of congressmen concerned. To sum up, the U.S. decision to overthrow Castro appears to have been a kind of emotional reaction arising out of Castro's defiant statements and U.S. fear of communism.

Characterization of Castro's statements as provocative causes one to wonder whether, in the light of Castro's strategies described above, Castro deliberately baited the Eisenhower administration into breaking off a relationship he was afraid, or unwilling, to break off himself. My own view is that the history of U.S.–Cuban relations and Castro's own personality are sufficient explanations for his defiance, but I do not rule out a Machiavellian calculation to lure the United States into a break.

President Eisenhower never seemed to realize that his decision to sponsor a counterrevolutionary invasionary force, a fact which could not be kept from Castro long, caused Castro to take extraordinary measures to defend himself. Similarly, the cut in the sugar quota literally put Castro at the Communists' mercy and logically led to the radicalization of the Cuban Revolution and close political and military ties with the Communist countries. In reference to these and other U.S. decisions, Ambassador Bonsal maintains, "We did not force [Castro] into the arms of the Communists, but we were, in my judgment, unwisely cooperative in removing the obstacles to his chosen path."[178] Mr. Bonsal apparently believed that Castro wanted to break off with the United States anyway and desired closer economic relations with the USSR. With domestic opposition crystallizing and the exiled community growing, Eisenhower placed Castro in grave jeopardy, and Castro interpreted it thus. Therefore, it is difficult to see what more menacing move could have been made to insure Castro's turning elsewhere for help, and where else could he go but to the Russians and Chinese?

What is puzzling and disturbing is that there is little or no evidence that leaders in the Department of State or in the Congress seemed to have been aware that their own actions would lead precisely to the circumstances they claimed they were trying to avoid. One of the few dissenting voices in the United States was that of former Ambassador Bonsal who testifies to his own strong opposition to the reversal of the January 1960 nonintervention policies. Concern about Cuba was shared equally by the Republican and Democratic parties. Except for a small circle of senior officials, leaders of both parties were ignorant of Eisenhower's decision to arm Cuban exiles and of the implications of his Cuban policies generally; and they seemed to be competing to see who could advocate the firmest anti-Castro line. Thus, when Kennedy assumed office in early 1961, he continued the main line of Eisenhower's policies.

Almost from the beginning, Castro and the United States expected the worst from each other and neither was disappointed. In retrospect, Castro emerged from the dispute remarkably well. The Cuban middle class was destroyed and that, perhaps, was a natural result of the kind of revolution Castro sought. The shock to the Cuban economy of total reorientation at the time of the break with the United States and the radicalization of the revolution was truly shattering; it was a shock from which the Cuban economy has not yet recovered. Broader social changes involving an improvement in the living standards of the rural and urban poor were achieved at immense costs to other economic and social sectors. Castro completed a literally epoch-making revolution while surviving as the dominant political power in Cuba. Castro's seeming ability to chart his own course, at least in part, did not confirm the overly facile U.S. dismissal of Castro as a leader who had exchanged American for Soviet domination.

The fruits of U.S. policy toward Guatemala and Cuba are bitter indeed. After Arbenz fell, Guatemala experienced intermittent political repression and coups. The achievement of social progress and political democracy in a reformed capitalist framework remained an unrealized goal. Guatemala was hurt by more bloody civil and guerrilla warfare than most other Latin American countries. Prospects that moderate forces would overcome extremists from the Right or Left grew more remote.

In Cuba, U.S. companies and citizens lost their investments valued at a billion dollars or more, losses larger than those suffered earlier in Russia and China. Cuba developed a Marxist-Leninist system with close ties to the Communist countries and became the principal focus of hostility to the United States in Latin America.

To sum up in the light of the analytical categories discussed in chapter 1, the impetus of revolutionary movements to seek a change in the structure of U.S. relations with their respective countries arose in large measure out of the fact of their political and economic dependence on the United States and their desire to overcome it. United States private interests controlled Guatemala's central transportation, communication, and power facilities not to mention its largest agricultural complex. United States interests also owned large shares of the Cuban economy and the latter was closely tied to the U.S. economy through the sugar quota and tariff agreements. Both countries were also dependent on the United States for arms. Economic dependence was accompanied by political dependence. Thus, the revolutionary leaders' desire to overcome dependence was one of the leading motivating forces of revolutionary change.

An understanding of the interactions discussed here requires, of course, familiarity with official relations between the two governments. And, the nature of the U.S. bureaucracy had a bearing on outcomes, too. The fact that there were few influential U.S. officials who understood or sympathized with the Guatemalan revolutionary movement, combined with the not surprising ignorance of top U.S. officials about Guatemala, made it relatively easy for the United States to adopt an antagonistic official line. It will be interesting when the archives are opened to learn whether there were ever strong efforts made within the U.S. government to moderate U.S. policy toward Arbenz. We know, for example, that the career foreign service officer, Rudolph Schoenfeld, was replaced as ambassador to Guatemala early in the Eisenhower administration by the more aggressive John Peurifoy who had been lauded for his record as a "cold warrior" in Greece. The latter's presence in Guatemala during the civil conflict, his initiatives in harmonizing Department of State efforts with those of the CIA, and the CIA's own interest in launching a successful anti-Communist operation in Central America all contributed to forming the U.S. response.

Politics within the U.S. bureaucracy, and notably conflicts between various elements, make it easier to understand why the U.S. response to Castro was initially moderate, but was then abruptly reversed when President Eisenhower took different advice. Career men in Washington and in Havana who favored moderation did not have the political influence of the party leaders and congressmen who favored a different line. Again, too, the CIA saw an opportunity in Cuba to repeat its Guatemalan "victory."

United States responses thus took place partly as outcomes of events within the U.S. government. Understanding them fully requires knowledge of far more than intragovernmental or intergovernmental developments. The hostile climate that ultimately led to U.S. support for movements to overthrow Arbenz and Castro developed initially because the two revolutionary governments took measures which U.S. private interests considered damaging. Moreover, Arbenz's and Castro's lack of responsiveness to other private groups, such as labor, contributed to official distrust. It is doubtful, however, that the perceived antagonism with U.S. private interests was what ultimately persuaded U.S. leaders to resort to paramilitary forces. Rather, it was the perception that the international Communist movement or the Soviet government might gain a foothold in the two countries and thereby pose a threat to U.S. security interests. Clearly the latter consideration could not be understood exclusively in terms of official relations between the United States and the Latin American governments concerned, nor in terms of bureaucratic politics inside the U.S. government. In Congress and in society at large, as well as within the bureaucracy, fears of Soviet and Communist activities were ultimately decisive.

After Guatemala and Cuba, new revolutionary challenges which had reverberations in the United States were posed to the status quo in several Latin American countries. United States responses to revolutionary change between the consolidation of Castro's power in Cuba in 1961 and the fall of Allende in 1973 will be discussed in chapter 8. First, however, an effort will be made to synthesize and compare U.S. responses to revolutionary change between 1910 and 1961.

7 Explaining U.S. Responses (1910–1961)

United States responses to revolutionary change in Mexico, Bolivia, Guatemala, and Cuba conformed to certain established patterns, which I will describe in the following pages. Most particularly I will discuss why U.S. leaders came to terms with the Mexican and Bolivian revolutionaries and suppressed, or attempted to suppress, the Guatemalan and Cuban revolutionaries. Some general propositions about these patterns are summarized at the end of this chapter.

Explanations of political behavior cannot be proved like mathematical equations. Moreover, U.S. policies in these cases continue to be subject to conflicting and controversial interpretations. That is why I have presented much evidence in earlier chapters to support my interpretations here.

Table 8 lists and characterizes U.S. responses in each of the three stages of the revolutionary process identified in chapter 1. Notes to that table describe the decisive episodes and refer readers to the chapters in which these episodes are discussed.

The conclusions in this chapter deal with U.S. responses up to 1961. United States reactions to the revolutionary process in Latin America since that time, for example in Peru and Chile, are discussed in chapter 8. The U.S. government has framed different responses to rebel movements and to reformist governments in other countries, such as Colombia and Venezuela, but these cases fall outside the scope of this study.

Responses Explained

Revolutionary change in these four countries posed a threat to U.S. interests in at least two major respects. First, it had an adverse impact on U.S. private interests. United States investors usually had the most at stake, but others, such as traders, the U.S. Roman Catholic hierarchy, and U.S. labor organizations, were also affected. Second, the revolutionary process threatened to diminish U.S. political influence, in that new governments tended to adopt more independent domestic and foreign policies and were less likely to conform to U.S. policies.

United States responses to revolutionary change in these four countries were not as consistently malevolent or benevolent as the bitterest critics or the most ardent

211

TABLE 8

U.S. RESPONSES TO REBEL MOVEMENTS,
REFORMIST GOVERNMENTS, AND REVOLUTIONARY GOVERNMENTS

	Date of Response	Decision Maker	Nature of Response	Decisive Consideration
Rebel movement in				
1. Mexico	1910–1911	President	Acceptance	Other
2. Bolivia	1943–1944	Secy. state	Rejection	Germany
3. Guatemala	1944	State department	Acceptance	Other
4. Cuba	1957–1959	State department	Acceptance	Other
Reformist government in				
5. Mexico	1913	Ambassador	Hostility	Private interests
6. Bolivia	1946	State department	Hostility	Private interests
7. Guatemala	1950	State department	Hostility	Private interests
8. Cuba	1959 (Jan.–May)	State department	Acceptance	Other
Revolutionary government in				
9. Mexico	1915–1917	President	Reconciliation	Germany
10.	1923	Secy. state	Reconciliation	Private interests
11.	1938–1941	President	Reconciliation	Germany
12. Bolivia	1952	State department	Acceptance	Private interests
13.	1953	State department	Reconciliation	USSR
14.	1961	State department	Support	USSR
15. Guatemala	1954	Secy. state	Suppression	USSR
16. Cuba	1960 (Jan.)	President	Acceptance	Other
17.	1960 (March)	President	Suppression	USSR
18.	1961	President	Suppression that failed	USSR

NOTE: This table lists comparatively the major U.S. responses in the three stages of the revolutionary process in selected Latin American countries according to three categories: (1) who was primarily responsible for deciding each response; (2) the nature of the response; and (3) the decisive consideration shaping each response.

The designations under "Nature of Response" are described briefly below in the notes according to the number assigned each response. In parentheses at the end of each note is the number of the chapter which describes the response further and explains the decisive consideration which shaped it and which, incidentally, represents my view of what was most decisive. Of course, many other considerations also influenced each response.

Readers will note that the decisive consideration listed in half the responses is either Germany or the USSR. That is because many of the responses were shaped by U.S. perceptions of the relationship between these Great Power rivals of the United States and the revolutionary movements.

The expression "private interests" refers to U.S. business interests in the countries concerned, usually investors. In the case of Bolivia, however, where there were few U.S. investors, private Bolivian interests (tin mine owners) appeared to have been influential as well as the official U.S. disposition to avoid creating precedents which could prove damaging to U.S. investors elsewhere.

Notes to Table 8 (continued)

"Other" is a residual category. In Mexico in 1911, President Taft was primarily concerned with maintaining order along the Mexican border. Other strategic or economic interests (except possibly the influence of arms' manufacturers who wanted to be able to sell to the revolutionaries) were not decisive one way or the other. Similarly, strategic or economic factors were not influential in dealing with the Guatemalan revolutionaries in 1944 and the Cuban revolutionaries in 1957–1959. The United States tried to maintain normal relations with Cuba during Castro's first months in power. In Cuba in January 1960, Eisenhower continued his moderate policies toward Castro not yet deterred by security concerns or the influence of private interests.

1. The Taft administration decided not to provide support for the tottering Díaz government, neutrality legislation was not strictly enforced against Madero's efforts to organize his revolt on U.S. soil, and President Taft mobilized U.S. troops to maintain order along the Mexican border and exert a stabilizing influence in Mexico. (2)

2. Secretary Hull persuaded Latin American governments, except Argentina, to refuse to recognize the Villarroel government until the MNR members had resigned from his cabinet. Hull feared Nazi influence in the MNR. (3)

3. The United States promptly recognized the governments that succeeded Ubico, after refusing to bolster incumbent governments against which the revolts had been mounted. (2)

4. The United States laid an arms embargo on the Batista government in March 1958 and promptly recognized Castro in early January 1959. (2)

5. Ambassador Henry Lane Wilson conspired with Mexican generals to force Madero's resignation from the presidency, all in defiance of Washington's instructions. (3)

6. The Department of State and the U.S. ambassador's pressures on the Villarroel government contributed to Villarroel's fall in 1946. (3)

7. Washington and Ambassador Patterson's pressures on the Arévalo government culminated in Patterson's recall at the Guatemalans' request. (3)

8. The Department of State kept communications open with the Castro government during its reformist phase in January through May of 1959 without economic sanctions or political threats. (6)

9. President Wilson recognized Carranza de facto in 1915, ordered the withdrawal of Pershing's forces unconditionally in early 1917, and recognized Carranza de jure in 1917 in order to secure his southern flank during the European war. (5)

10. Secretary Hughes agreed to recognize Obregón after provisions for the protection of U.S. investments were included in the Buccareli agreements (1923). (5)

11. President Roosevelt decided not to impose heavy economic or political sanctions following the Mexican expropriation of U.S. oil properties in 1938 and entered in negotiations which ultimately led to a compromise settlement in 1941. (5)

12. The Truman administration recognized the new MNR government after receiving assurances that property would not be expropriated without compensation. (5)

13. After the MNR government had reached an agreement with the owners of the expropriated mines, the Department of State arranged for the president to approve emergency economic assistance to Bolivia. (5)

14. The United States expanded its economic assistance in 1961 in the Plan Triangular under the Alliance for Progress. (5)

15. With Secretary Dulles acting as chief spokesman, the Eisenhower administration tried to mobilize OAS opinion against the Arbenz government at Caracas and sponsored the paramilitary invasion of Guatemala by Castillo Armas in 1954. (6)

16. As late as January 1960, President Eisenhower retained an accommodating posture toward Castro and reaffirmed nonintervention. (6)

17. In March 1960 President Eisenhower completely reversed U.S. policy, authorized the arming of Cuban émigrés for the possible future invasion of Cuba, and began steps to eliminate the Cuban sugar quota. (6)

18. President Kennedy authorized the Bay of Pigs invasion in April 1961. (6)

apologists of U.S. policies might lead one to believe. The United States tended to respond flexibly to rebel movements but then hostilely to changes instituted by reformist governments. In the last stage of the revolutionary process, when revolutionary change began, U.S. responses followed opposite patterns of either reconciliation or suppression.

Three Stages

In the first stage of the revolutionary process, the U.S. government responded flexibly to three of the four rebel movements (proposition 1). Except for the Bolivian MNR, rebel leaders were viewed as spokesmen for downtrodden peoples oppressed by brutal dictatorships. For example, the United States permitted Madero to organize the revolt against Díaz in Mexico from U.S. soil, moving belatedly to try to arrest him. United States envoys refused to aid Ubico against the Guatemalan revolutionaries in 1944 and presided over the meeting in which the latter's take-over of the government was arranged. The Eisenhower administration placed an embargo on arms deliveries to Batista in Cuba.

The United States had good reasons for opposing military dictators and adopting policies whose consequences favored the rebels. First, support of dictatorships was not considered politically expedient. The U.S. government, having decided that the dictators would soon be deposed, considered close association with a losing cause unwise. Second, the U.S. public and many officials opposed the dictatorships on ideological or political grounds, and some of the rebel leaders were popular in the United States. Finally, the rebel movements were not widely perceived initially as a threat to U.S. private or public interests.

The exception to flexible U.S. responses to rebel movements was to the Bolivian MNR. As indicated in chapter 3, British and U.S. actions led to the imprisonment of MNR leaders, stigmatized them with the Nazi label, and later forced them out of Villarroel's cabinet. The official U.S. perception of the MNR's link with a rival Great Power, Nazi Germany, was the principal reason for the hostile U.S. response. Note, too, that official U.S. hostility to the MNR was shared by oil and tin interests, which felt threatened by MNR policies.

In the second or reformist stage, the United States was consistently more hostile to revolutionary leaders than in the earlier stage, when they were fighting as rebels, or later when as government leaders they began to introduce revolutionary changes in their respective societies (proposition 2). In the reformist stage, U.S. ambassadors were involved in activities associated with the overthrow or attempted overthrow of reformist governments in Mexico (1913), Bolivia (1946), and Guatemala (1949–1951). (Cuba is not included in the following discussion about reformist governments for reasons explained at the beginning of chapter 6.)

Taken as a whole, the reformists' behavior in each of the three countries was, ironically, relatively less violent and more closely approximated U.S. ideals about peaceful change than in the other two stages. The three reformist presidents won or confirmed their offices in elections, and their record on civil liberties relative to earlier regimes was good. The social and economic reforms these men sponsored were similar to many adopted in the United States. Why, then, did the United States either oppose or ineffectively assist the kinds of government it had so long professed to favor in Latin America?

United States business interests were among the first to feel the brunt of reformist policies. Although the three reformist presidents respected property rights and the capitalist framework, they were nationalistic in the sense of reordering the nations' priorities in favor of their own rather than foreign interests. Injured or threatened U.S. interests took a hostile tone at an early stage. These were the moments when the contrast between the old and new regimes seemed especially sharp.

United States ambassadors often displayed animosity toward these governments, resented not being consulted more, and appear to have been frustrated in their aggressive efforts to shape the local situation to their liking. In several cases they acted as rivals to the reformist presidents. Ambassadors Wilson in Mexico and Patterson in Guatemala associated closely with American businessmen and were frustrated sponsors of U.S. business interests. The American embassy in La Paz sided with Bolivian and U.S. interests which opposed the Villarroel government, and high officials in Washington used their influence to support the tin interests against the government. Especially important was the fact that no influential constituency in the United States favored compromise.

There appears to have been little appreciation, either in Washington or in the American embassies, of the immensity of the obstacles to social change which the reformist presidents sought. Nor were U.S. officials sympathetic to the concrete ways the reformist governments tried to place relations with the United States on what they believed was a more equitable basis. As the examples in chapter 3 show, U.S. officials viewed these measures less as efforts to strengthen these societies and more as blows to U.S. private interests, restrictions on U.S. prerogatives, and evidence of the reformist governments' presumed hostility toward the United States. United States representatives were prepared to give lip service to the principle of equality of nations but were unwilling to collaborate in its realization when their own, their associates, or their country's interests seemed adversely affected.

United States officials did not fully appreciate that these governments could not limit reforms to internal problems. United States interests were so pervasive that reforms necessarily involved a realignment of relations with the United States as well. Reformists sometimes desired revisions of relations with the United States that were deemed essential to their country's development. As a result, the United States could not escape paying a price for social change any more than could other vested interests in these societies. What proved most difficult for U.S. officials was placing the transition to reformist regimes in the perspective of long-term U.S. national interests.

In the third stage, when revolutionary change began, there was a remarkable similarity in the problems each revolution posed for the United States. There was a clear threat to vested U.S. private interests and to U.S. political influence in the countries concerned. Tensions ultimately mounted to a climax. As chapters 5 and 6 indicate, U.S. decisions during those times of stress tended to define U.S. responses to the revolutionary regimes thereafter.

At those moments U.S. leaders selected one of two policy options. The first was to accept the revolutionary government and to undertake negotiations to achieve mutually acceptable settlements of conflicts of interests. Such a policy had some immediate disadvantages for U.S. private interests but left open the possibility of protecting and promoting those and other such interests later. In addition, this option helped establish a climate of trust in intergovernmental relations and kept open channels of communication and political influence. This was the option chosen for Mexico and Bolivia.

The second option was to discontinue serious negotiations and by covert means promote the revolutionary government's demise. This was the pattern in Guatemala and Cuba. As long as the revolutionary government survived, this option involved grave risks for U.S. public and private interests. United States authorities expected successor governments to be responsive to both interests if and when the revolutionary governments would fall.

There were two major aspects of the decision to opt for conciliation or suppression. First, U.S. leaders had to decide whether it was possible to work out mutually acceptable settlements of conflicting interests, including private interests. Could U.S. leaders establish satisfactory working relations with these governments? The second and most critical aspect of this decision was whether the establishment of such a relationship would preclude the interference of a hostile Great Power in the hemisphere. Or, put another way, could the Latin American revolutionary governments be counted on not to become pawns of a Great Power hostile to the United States? When the answers to both these questions were affirmative, U.S. leaders adopted a conciliatory posture. When either was negative, U.S. leaders initiated covert operations against the revolutionary government.

United States leaders reached their conclusions about their prospects for compromising differences with the revolutionary leaders on the basis of the latter's domestic policies, foreign policies, and public statements about the United States. An especially important early indicator was the revolutionaries' treatment of U.S. private interests. Expropriation or other threats to these interests were a source of friction from the beginning. The problem was not over the Latin American's right to expropriate; U.S. leaders explicitly recognized that right. Nor did the Latin Americans refuse to make formal provisions for compensation; even the Cuban law provided for that. The chief difficulty with respect to property issues was that the Latin Americans were unable to make effective compensation. The expropriated investments were so large and the local government resources so small that payments on terms that would ordinarily be considered satisfactory according to the standards of commercial transactions were not possible. Without outside assistance, expropriation and effective compensation were mutually exclusive. What made the confrontation so dangerous was that although the four governments did not have funds for compensation, they staked their political life on the implementation of the expropriation decrees.

The Mexicans and Bolivians persuaded U.S. leaders that they preferred a collaborative rather than an antagonistic relationship and that there were reasonable prospects of a negotiated settlement. Carranza agreed as early as 1914 to entertain foreign claims against Mexico, maintained representatives in Washington, and established a record of being able to give and take in negotiations thereafter. In the 1930s Cárdenas gave many indications of his preference for negotiations over confrontation; and in the aftermath of the oil expropriations, he announced Mexico's intention to pay compensation, and actually undertook arrangements for compensation for expropriations in agriculture. In Bolivia the new MNR government went to great lengths to reassure the United States about its willingness to pay compensation for the expropriated tin mines, about its respect for private property in general, and about its non-Communist character.

The Mexican and Bolivian revolutionaries not only preferred compromise but were also effective in making their conciliatory posture known. They were fortunate, too, because Presidents Wilson and Roosevelt were sympathetic to the Mexican revolution and Milton Eisenhower was able to pass his favorable opinion of the Bolivian revolution on to his brother, the president.

Like the Mexicans and Bolivians, the Guatemalans probably also would have preferred compromise as their best hope in the long run. Relations between the two governments under Arévalo had been so hostile, however, that the bitterness was carried over under Arbenz. Because of the domestic and international situation, Arbenz was forced to turn increasingly to the left for support, dimming U.S. hopes for compromise. Also, even before the U.S. decision to back a counterrevolutionary force, Guatemalan leaders were outspokenly critical of the United States. In spite of his meetings with Undersecretary of State Walter Bedell Smith and President Eisenhower, Guatemalan Ambassador Toriello never succeeded in making known whatever willingness Arbenz may have had to compromise.

As chapter 6 explains, Secretary Dulles needed a Communist beachhead in Guatemala to implement his policy of liberation of captive peoples, and thus he remained deaf to Guatemala's pleas. It seems doubtful that Secretary Dulles ever seriously considered offering Arbenz loans or other inducements for some mutually acceptable compromise, or if he did, that the terms would have been generous. Dulles' hopes of securing a victory against international communism rested on the perception of the Guatemalan revolutionaries as intransigent Communists.

Unlike the Guatemalans, Castro did not really want compromise with the United States because he came to believe, probably correctly, that he could not retain power in Cuba and achieve his revolutionary objectives there within the framework of a collaborative relationship with the United States. Although U.S. officials offered to discuss economic assistance with Castro's representatives during his visit to Washington in April 1959, the discussions never got started so that it is impossible to determine whether the United States might have actually extended such assistance or whether Castro would have accepted it. It seems likely that the conditions on which the United States would have insisted, while not necessarily more onerous than those for Mexico or Bolivia, would have been unacceptable to Castro. To conduct the kind of social revolution he wanted and to achieve genuine independence of the United States, Castro appears to have believed that a complete break was essential. Subsequent events would tend to bear this out.

Thus, U.S. leaders decided on conciliation with the Mexicans and Bolivians partly because U.S. officials thought they could work with them. They tried to suppress the Guatemalan and Cuban revolutions partly because they considered these governments intransigent. Closely related to and even more important than U.S. determinations of the Latin Americans' desire for a negotiated settlement in explaining the differing sets of responses were the U.S. leaders' perceptions of U.S. strategic interests in these four countries.

As chapter 5 indicates, U.S. responses to Carranza's revolutionary movement in Mexico were shaped in large measure by U.S. strategic interests in the midst of World War I. President Wilson's and Secretary Lansing's antagonistic relationships with imperial Germany and the prospects of eventual U.S. involvement in the European war made them particularly anxious to resolve conflicts with Mexico peacefully. United States recognized Carranza initially, withdrew General Pershing's troops without receiving the commitments previously demanded, and recognized Carranza de jure after the promulgation of the controversial Constitution of 1917—all in order to secure the nation's southern flank during the war with Germany. Two decades later, after tensions with Mexico peaked following the expropriations of U.S. oil companies in 1938, the strongest argument for compromise again was fear that hostile U.S. actions would force Mexico into the arms of Germany. The rapidly expanding conflict in Western Europe and in the Far East set the stage for the global settlement between Mexico and the United States in 1941.

In Bolivia the need to prevent the spread of communism was the major argument used to secure congressional approval for economic assistance to the new revolutionary government in 1953. Aid was defended as a means to shore up a friendly government and thereby prevent Bolivia from falling under Soviet control. Again in 1961, opposition to communism, especially to Khrushchev's dramatic offer of Soviet aid to Bolivia, gave the impetus for a more comprehensive program of U.S. economic assistance.

As a result of the Mexican and Bolivian desire to compromise and U.S. interpretations of its strategic interests, Wilson and Roosevelt came to terms with revolutionary governments in Mexico, and Eisenhower with the revolutionary government in Bolivia. United States leaders accepted the expropriations of oil in Mexico, tin in Bolivia, and land in both countries as an accomplished fact and provided both governments with long-term loans and other assistance that would make them both able and willing to make some effective compensations. United States government actions had the effect of encouraging the former owners to accept the compensation offered. In Bolivia U.S. private interests were so small in the 1950s that the compensation arrangements were primarily important as a precedent. In both countries the former owners may not have gotten what they thought they deserved, but they got something. The U.S. government had to commit public funds to get a settlement but friendly relations were preserved, and the United States was able to achieve many of its political objectives. Both countries continued to provide settings for profitable U.S. private investment in other economic sectors.

The pattern of U.S. responses to the Guatemalan and Cuban revolutions was the antithesis of the reconciliation sought with Mexico and Bolivia. United States leaders did not believe compromise would be viable and interpreted strategic interests as requiring an attempt to suppress the revolutionary governments in these two countries. The U.S. campaign against the Arbenz government in Guatemala culminated in the CIA-sponsored armed border-crossing of Castillo Armas, and was followed by a successful barracks coup against Arbenz in the capital. Conceived in Cold War terms from the beginning, the U.S.-sponsored armed incursion was heralded as essential to eliminate a Communist beachhead in the hemisphere. With respect to Cuba, Eisenhower's decision to arm a counterrevolutionary force of émigrés in March 1960, coming not long after the Cuban-Soviet commercial agreement, was specifically designed to meet the danger of communism in Cuba. That policy was continued by President Kennedy and failed at the Bay of Pigs in 1961.

In sum, the United States responded in the third stage according to its leaders' estimates of prospects for a negotiated settlement of outstanding issues and, most particularly, for avoiding the interference of a hostile Great Power in the hemisphere (propositions 3 and 4).

My emphasis on strategic considerations as the most important explanation of U.S. responses in the third stage of the revolutionary process does not mean that they are the *only* explanation. As previous chapters indicated, many other considerations must be taken into account for a full understanding of U.S. responses. In fact, strategic considerations did not even come up with respect to certain responses in stages one and two so that obviously other explanations are required.

Partly because of the immense influence of the international Communist and Socialist movements, the most prominent alternative explanations are economic. Marxists explain U.S. responses largely as a phenomenon of the capitalist system and particularly as an expression of the interests of trading and investing companies, the most powerful of which are huge multinational corporations. Other explanations are emphasized by the "bureaucratic politics" perspective, developed mainly by academic social scientists, who encourage the study of governmental bureaucracies for explanations of foreign-policy behaviors. Let us look at how economic and bureaucratic considerations help explain U.S. responses.

Economic Explanations

Marxist scholars and most contemporary radicals, who usually share similar views in this respect, explain U.S. responses toward revolutionary movements as public manifestations of U.S. business' efforts to exploit Latin America economically.[1] The anti-Communist posture and explicit references to strategic considerations by U.S. leaders have been interpreted mainly as pretexts for protecting and advancing business interests.

Business interests play an important role in the formulation of U.S. policies,[2] and Marxists dramatically call attention to this fact. Probably the single most important material interest affected by revolutionary change in the countries concerned initially has been U.S. direct private investment. United States investors have sometimes been well organized, financed, and politically influential. A major theme in all stages of the revolutionary process has been the impact of that process on U.S. investors, their reaction thereto, and the related U.S. official responses.

In the first stage of the revolutionary process, Marxist scholars tend to assume that the U.S. government helps suppress rebel movements around the world. They make this assertion because the U.S. helped suppress some rebel movements, notably in Latin America, in the 1960s (see chapter 8), and because they view the interests of rebels and foreign investors as contradictory. In fact, U.S. investors did not feel seriously threatened by rebel movements during the first stage of the revolutionary process in Mexico (1910), Guatemala (1944), or Cuba (1957–1958). Corporate interests were not aggressively hostile initially in these cases, nor was the U.S. government. These cases in themselves do not necessarily disprove the validity of economic explanations, but they do show that generalizations about U.S. responses to rebel movements do not always apply and that individual cases need to be examined on their own merits.

My explanations of U.S. hostility to the reformist governments of Madero in Mexico and Arévalo in Guatemala in the second stage rely primarily on economic considerations, especially private business interests. Strategic considerations are offered as the main explanation of U.S. hostility to Villarroel in Bolivia, but business interests, U.S. and Bolivian, reinforced that hostility.

Economic explanations are insufficient, however, in the third stage. In Mexico, for example, U.S. private interests were extremely incensed by provisions in the new constitution which asserted national ownership of the subsoil (including oil) as well as other revolutionary innovations in that document. Those interests failed to persuade President Wilson to make recognition of the Carranza government conditional on Mexican commitments with respect to foreign investments. Wilson feared that such pressures would force Mexico to turn toward imperial Germany, the introduction of whose influence in the Caribbean and Mexico would endanger the United States during World War I. Similarly, President Roosevelt accepted Cárdenas' expropriation of U.S. oil properties in Mexico. His administration reached a global settlement of outstanding issues with Mexico in 1941 over the oil companies' express objections in order to discourage Mexico from turning to Nazi Germany. Roosevelt also refused to support private interests who toyed with the idea of helping a Mexican general overthrow Cárdenas by force.

Economic explanations are not sufficient to explain U.S. responses to the

Bolivian revolution either. One reason is that U.S. direct investment in Bolivia was very small in the 1950s and only increased moderately in the 1960s. United States foreign assistance between 1952 and 1964 exceeded by many times the value of U.S. private investments there. The revolutionary government was careful to head off business opposition to the economic aid programs, but private interests did not play a large role in the U.S. decision to come to the revolutionary government's rescue. The government's most telling arguments in getting appropriations through Congress were that such assistance would help avoid chaos in Bolivia that could lead to communism.

Economic explanations have more plausibility in Guatemala than elsewhere because of the history of the United Fruit Company and the exaggerated charges of communism there. Much of the early antipathy between the two governments was the result of the company's campaign in the United States against the Guatemalan government. But, the charges that John Foster Dulles and his brother Allen, then director of the CIA, mounted paramilitary operations against Arbenz primarily to protect their interests as shareholders in United Fruit seem farfetched. It is unlikely that the Dulles brothers would have risked their place in history or used their high offices simply to protect one American company, even if, as seems likely, they were sympathetic toward the company's needs. The strategic reasons advanced in chapter 6 for U.S. interference seem more plausible. Moreover, the successful prosecution of an antitrust suit against the United Fruit Company later in the Eisenhower administration does not support the thesis that Eisenhower viewed U.S. national interests as identical with the company's.

United States trade and investment were so great with Cuba in the 1950s that it is tempting to rely on economic explanations to explain U.S. responses to Castro. But as chapter 6 points out, in 1960 Eisenhower sincerely believed and feared that Cuba would become a Communist state, and concern about the potential of hostile Soviet influence in Cuba was paramount in his mind. Most of what is known about the circumstances and Eisenhower's own background supports the thesis that he put the nation's military security, as he saw it, ahead of private profit. Moreover, the major U.S. interests in manufacturing, tourism, banking, and commerce were seized after President Eisenhower's decision to organize and arm a counterrevolutionary force, not before. Similarly, in authorizing the Bay of Pigs invasion, President Kennedy was more concerned about the presence of a hostile, Soviet-backed government off the coast of Florida than recovering U.S. investments there.

Marxist critics of the foregoing conclusions may point out that U.S. official hostility toward Arbenz and Castro tended to coincide with U.S. private interests in these countries. It is correct, for example, that the United Fruit Company recovered much of its property after Arbenz fell and U.S. investors who suffered from Cuba's seizures of their property have been vocal supporters of anti-Castro policies in the United States. But these facts do not prove that U.S. private interests were decisive in the decisions to attempt to overthrow Arbenz and Castro. My point is not that private interest played no role at all, only that strategic considerations were more important.

Critics who minimize the importance of strategic considerations often explain U.S. reconciliation with the Mexican and Bolivian revolutionary movements as essentially a tactical compromise or temporary concession designed to suppress revolutionary change in the long term. This argument does call attention to an important fact, namely, that U.S. influence appears to have been successful in making both revolutions more moderate. To admit such influence, however, does not explain why the United States came to terms with the Mexican revolution time and again over a period of twenty-five years and with the Bolivian revolution for over twelve years. While collaborating with U.S. leaders, these two revolutionary governments achieved significant social changes, some of which are still in effect.

Economic considerations must be taken into account in understanding most U.S. responses, and often U.S. economic and political objectives were not only compatible but mutually reinforcing. When they were not, however, strategic considerations took precedence[3] (proposition 5).

Bureaucratic Explanations

The bureaucratic perspective views U.S. policy as "the product of a series of overlapping and interlocking bargaining processes within the North American system involving both intra-governmental and extra-governmental actors."[4] Advocates of this perspective urge greater attention to a particular research arena, encouraging the study of what goes on inside government as a means of understanding foreign policy discussions. They seek explanations with special reference to such factors as the interests, values, and organizational arrangements of bureaucratic actors. Does this approach contribute fresh insights about U.S. responses to revolutionary change?

My studies show that fairly sharp distinctions may be drawn between the authority and policy outputs of top-level officials—the president and the secretary of state—on the one hand and low-level officials—those in the Department of State and ambassadors—on the other. The two groups tended to deal with decisions in different categories and framed responses which were substantively different.

The president or secretary of state actively participated in all decisions perceived as strategic, that is, involving a threat by a rival Great Power (proposition 6). Such decisions were usually made in climactic phases of the social revolutions. Woodrow Wilson and Franklin Roosevelt made such decisions on the eve of U.S. entry into World Wars I and II; John Foster Dulles was the architect of the policy against the Arbenz government in 1954 and personally approved Milton Eisenhower's recommendations of emergency assistance for Bolivia. Dwight D. Eisenhower decided in March 1960 to initiate actions designed to overthrow Castro.

Most of the nonstrategic decisions were made at lower levels and were reached during the early stages of revolutionary change in the countries concerned. Strategic challenges by a rival Great Power were not posed in either the rebel or reformist stages in Mexico (1910–1913), Guatemala (1944–1951), or Cuba (1957–May 1959). (The exception, Bolivia [1943–1946], was discussed in chapter 3). As one might expect, most of the decisions in these three cases were made by lower-ranking officials, since the president and secretary of state usually were forced to confine their personal attention to only the most pressing questions of state (proposition 7).

United States official responses decided at lower levels tended to be in accord with U.S. private interests or at least not blatantly opposed to them (proposition 8). This fact is understandable partly because it is one of the duties of officials in the Department of State and of U.S. diplomats abroad to protect and advance U.S. private interests. Moreover, such interests are often influential in Washington and in foreign capitals, as has been demonstrated time and again. Ambassadors, such as Henry Lane Wilson in Mexico and Richard Patterson in Guatemala, had close corporate ties. All such officials are not necessarily subject to direct corporate influence, but some tend to favor business as a matter of principle. In any case, U.S. officials were understandably reluctant to expose themselves to criticism from powerful private interests or the Congress without having received approval from higher authority. None of this should be surprising since bureaucracies have a status-quo bias and human institutions tend to resist change.

Concern for private interests on the part of the foreign-affairs bureaucracy has meant that ordinarily the authority of the president or the secretary of state is required for decisions strongly opposed by powerful private interests. Woodrow Wilson personally decided to recognize the Carranza government de jure in spite of provisions in the Constitution of 1917 which adversely affected U.S. oil companies' claims to subsoil rights. Franklin Roosevelt personally refused to sponsor or collaborate with U.S. interests seeking support for the Mexican opposition to Cárdenas. Eisenhower was personally associated through his brother Milton with U.S. emergency assistance for the MNR government which had expropriated the tin mines in Bolivia. In these cases, strategic considerations were used to justify U.S. responses opposed by private interests.

Clearly, the White House and the Department of State were not the only government agencies involved in the decision-making process. Other agencies which played important roles were the Department of Defense, including the armed forces, the Treasury Department, and after World War II the CIA. These agencies were especially influential when they were able to take action independent of the Department of State which had an extensive impact on U.S. foreign relations.

Intragovernmental bargaining among these agencies about responses to revolutionary change constituted the essence of the decision-making process inside the government, and familiarity with the internal workings of the government is needed to understand that process as it unfolded. Instances of intragovernmental bargaining over policy decisions include Ambassador Wilson's running dispute with his superiors in Washington about Madero; President Wilson's efforts to restrain General Pershing in Mexico; disagreements between the Departments of State, Treasury, and Interior over the Mexican oil expropriations; President Eisenhower's reversal of U.S. policy toward Castro in March 1960, contrary to Ambassador Bonsal's recommendations but in accord with those of the CIA, Vice-President Nixon, and others; and conflicting orientations of U.S. civilian and military elements in Cuba in 1958 and 1961.

Bureaucratic considerations are particularly important in understanding U.S. responses to the Bolivian Revolution. United States diplomatic and economic-assistance officials appear to have been convinced that U.S. assistance to Bolivia was in accordance with U.S. interests, if for no other reason than to promote a stable and healthy society friendly to the United States. But I believe that this position was also strongly reinforced by their humanitarian instincts, professional commitments to economic and social development, and their personal and career interests. United States officials came to identify closely with the goals of the Bolivian Revolution and were deeply involved in its domestic development and politics (proposition 9).

In the other cases of revolutionary change and even in the Bolivian case, intragovernmental bargaining was primarily a reflection of more fundamental interests and conflicts that originated outside the bureaucracy (proposition 10). The bureaucracy was one of the arenas in which these conflicts were played out. For example, considerations about protecting U.S. corporate investments from revolutionary regimes and protecting the United States from a hostile Germany or the Soviet Union were more important in determining U.S. responses than the interests, values, or operating procedure of bureaucratic organizations themselves.

The focus on the structure and functioning of political units which the bureaucratic perspective accords to national governments may also be accorded to regional and global systems. Such an approach permits more penetrating explanations of U.S. responses. The United States and Latin America are part of a geographically isolated and largely self-contained regional system. Cuba is the only populous nation south of the Rio Grande that is not a regular member of that system. Although the regional system lies wholly within the U.S. sphere of influence, Washington does not "control" all these governments in the sense of having the capacity to order their officials about. United States leaders clearly lack such power in any comprehensive or consistent sense; they do have greater influence, that is, they have a stronger bargaining position, inside the regional system than any other member, or of any other Great Power.

That position is based on the huge disparities in economic, political, and military capacities between the United States and other member governments. In fact, the U.S. armed forces are more powerful than all the other armed forces in the hemisphere put together and, in collaboration with their Canadian allies, enjoy a nuclear arms monopoly in the hemisphere. United States political preeminence is recognized not only by most Latin American governments but by the Great Powers. Soviet willingness to bow to U.S. demands that Soviet missiles be removed from Cuba was the most dramatic recent recognition of U.S. political primacy in the hemisphere.

In the light of these considerations it is not surprising that U.S. leaders framed responses to revolutionary change that sought to prevent the interference of other

Great Powers in the Americas. Such interference has been seen as undermining the U.S. position not only in the hemisphere but also in the world.

United States responses probably also served broader and longer-term strategic purposes, that is, protecting U.S. authority inside the Inter-American system. United States responses to the Guatemalan and Cuban revolutions, for example, need to be understood partly as reflex reactions to maintain informal political dominion. Dulles was angered by the Guatemalan revolutionaries' brash independence, as Eisenhower was by Castro's provocative abuse. The emotional U.S. reactions to both revolutions were partly an instinctive response to what was viewed as insubordination or impudence. In this sense, U.S. responses to revolutionary changes need to be understood as efforts to maintain U.S. political primacy within its sphere of influence.[5] Efforts to prevent external interference (proposition 4) and maintain the internal integrity of the U.S. sphere (proposition 11) were two fronts in a single power struggle. Maintenance of primacy, while important for regional purposes, was also deemed essential to U.S. global security.

It is not possible to separate out the explanations relating to strictly regional considerations in the four cases discussed in earlier chapters because external interference was perceived as an immediate and pressing issue in each case. In Chile in the early 1970s, however, the Nixon administration appears not to have considered immediate Soviet interference likely; and, as chapter 8 indicates, maintaining U.S. primacy in the area appears to have been a relatively more important explanation of U.S. responses.

Radical scholars and polemicists have been among the most vocal critics of U.S. political domination in the hemisphere. Most explain such domination, usually referred to as U.S. imperialism, as U.S. official responsiveness to corporate efforts to exploit Latin America economically. Capitalism is described as the root cause of imperialism. The more sophisticated Marxist critics do not try to explain every twist and turn in U.S. policy in terms of corporate pressures, but maintain that U.S. responses should be understood fundamentally as a means of maintaining the regional status quo for continued capitalist exploitation.

The Marxists are right about U.S. tendencies to try to maintain its position in the hemisphere, but such efforts are hardly unique to the capitalist world. The western hemisphere is not the first place where large and powerful nations have sought to dominate small and weaker ones. Such tendencies, a fact of life long before the rise of modern capitalism, are powerfully demonstrated in the political primacy of the USSR in Eastern Europe, a Soviet sphere of influence. Power politics has continued to characterize relations between socialist as well as capitalist governments.

The relative importance of strategic, economic, and bureaucratic explanations of U.S. responses in Mexico, Bolivia, Guatemala, and Cuba may be summed up by placing in rank order the categories of actors most closely associated with each explanation. My analysis suggests the following three categories of actors in descending order of influence: (1) the president acting with or through cabinet-level officers, such as the secretary of state, (2) leaders of large corporations working with members of Congress and the executive, and (3) middle-level bureaucrats (proposition 12). In these cases the president has ordinarily been able to override competing actors when he has perceived the security of the nation to be at stake. When security matters have not been an issue, business leaders have often been able to have their way, partly because of their economic and political power and partly because the U.S. political system and U.S. foreign policies are designed to protect and advance business interests. I do not mean to indicate that business interests always work together, are necessarily well coordinated, or control the U.S. bureaucracy in any consistent way, but simply that among the many groups struggling to control policy, business often seems to have had a dominant influence on policy. When the president, cabinet-level officers, or business leaders were not deeply involved, middle-level officials and "bureaucratic" considerations often proved decisive. The foregoing is offered only as a crude hypothesis, not necessarily generalizable to other cases, but worthy of further study.

Responses Evaluated

The foregoing explanations of U.S. response to revolutionary change rely heavily on strategic considerations, particularly official U.S. perceptions with respect to the activities of hostile Great Powers in the countries concerned. I will first examine whether the perceptions on which U.S. policies were based were accurate. Next the effectiveness of the policies themselves will be discussed.

The Validity of U.S. Perceptions

Wilson and Roosevelt explained their coming to terms with the Mexican Revolution in World Wars I and II as necessary in order to remain friendly to their southern neighbor and prevent German penetration on the eve of the United States' entrance into the conflicts. Similarly, U.S. leaders justified economic assistance to Bolivia in the 1950s and early 1960s as an anti-Communist measure, and, conversely, attempted to suppress the Guatemalan and Cuban revolutions to prevent the spread of communism in the hemisphere. Were U.S. fears of German influence in Mexico and of communism in Bolivia, Guatemala, and Cuba justified? My view is that U.S. official perceptions of German influence in Mexico and Soviet influence in Cuba were essentially correct, whereas perceptions of Soviet influence in Bolivia and Guatemala were exaggerated or incorrect (proposition 13).

Documents from the German archives show that Wilson's fears that Mexico might turn toward Germany were warranted. At the height of the tensions arising from Pershing's occupation of northern Mexico, the Carranza government offered to collaborate with Germany and discuss the provision of submarine bases. The Germans interpreted the Mexican overture as holding out the possibility of an alliance, and this impression encouraged Foreign Minister Zimmermann to send his notorious telegram. Wilson was also proved right in his belief that the relaxation of U.S. pressure, namely the withdrawal of Pershing's troops, would permit Mexico to cool its relations with Germany. Diplomatic records during World War II also bear out the fears of some of the leaders of Franklin Roosevelt's administration that Mexico might turn to Germany if the United States imposed heavy sanctions in retaliation for the oil expropriations. Mexico had retained ties with Germany, though not so strong as during World War I, for such an eventuality. The political and ideological affinities of the Cárdenas and Roosevelt administrations and the enlightened U.S. response meant that Mexico did not need to turn to Germany.

Similarly, U.S. perceptions of Castro's relations with the Soviet Union were essentially correct. In early 1960 the Communist old guard in Cuba was not very powerful and the USSR still had little influence and few ties with Cuba. President Eisenhower may have exaggerated the Soviet Union's importance, but the potential for close collaboration between Cuba and the USSR was present. Eisenhower perceived that Castro did not want to compromise with the United States within the framework of traditional U.S.–Cuban relations and that Castro was prepared to associate Cuba with the Soviet Union to achieve his political objectives. Eisenhower's decision in March 1960 to arm a counterrevolutionary force can be explained by his suspicions about Castro's plans to join forces with the USSR and his anger at what he viewed as Castro's inflammatory statements. By the time Eisenhower left office, Castro had become dependent on the USSR as a market for Cuban sugar and a source of fuel oil and arms.

Official U.S. perceptions of Communist influence in Bolivia and Guatemala were exaggerated or incorrect. United States leaders probably overestimated Communist and Soviet influence in Bolivia during the 1950s partly because such exaggerations were a dominant tendency in the foreign service at that stage of the Cold War and also because the alleged Communist threat helped justify the large economic-assistance program which U.S. officials favored for a variety of other reasons. Similarly, U.S. officials exaggerated Communist influence in Guatemala partly because of the rapid pace of social change there, the United Fruit's press campaign against Arbenz, and damages to other U.S. interests caused by actions of the revolutionary governments. Although Communists were politically influential, especially toward the end of the Arbenz period, no evidence has come to my attention that the Communist party ever controlled his government. The weight of evidence suggests it did not. Nor has any evidence been made public of substantial Soviet contact, much less of Soviet control. Finally, Secretary Dulles' perceptions were distorted by a number of personal and political considerations not directly relevant to the domestic situation in Guatemala.

The Efficacy of U.S. Policies

The validity of U.S. official perceptions is one subject; the efficacy of U.S. official actions is quite another. In my view, U.S. responses were functional with respect to U.S. strategic aims in Mexico and Bolivia and dysfunctional in Guatemala and Cuba (proposition 14).

Wilson's decisions to withdraw Pershing in early 1917 and maintain normal diplomatic relations with the Carranza government, in spite of the new Mexican constitution's restrictions on U.S. investments, facilitated Mexico's independent policy toward Germany. Mexico's clever concessions to German intelligence had the effect of preventing Gerban sabotage of the Mexican oil fields, from which the Western Allies continued to be supplied throughout the war. Mexico remained firmly neutral. Similarly, on the eve of World War II, Roosevelt's conciliatory policies toward Cárdenas, coupled with the latter's anti-Nazi sentiments, helped make Mexico a firm ally of the United States in World War II.

Although Bolivia was probably more susceptible to a military rather than a Communist take-over in the 1950s, massive economic assistance assured the Bolivian revolutionary government's responsiveness to U.S. interests. United States policies promoted a relatively stable government in Bolivia friendly to the United States. In this sense, U.S. policies toward Bolivia, like those toward Mexico earlier, contributed to the achievement of U.S. strategic objectives.

Although Eisenhower's appraisal in March 1960 that Castro sought to radicalize Cuban society and establish close relations with the Soviet Union was essentially correct, his decisions to arm a counterrevolutionary force and cut the sugar quota were counterproductive. His policies, confirmed by those of President Kennedy at the Bay of Pigs, facilitated Castro's rapprochement with the Cuban Communists and his efforts to strengthen his economic and military ties with the Soviet Union. This is not to say that by this time the United States could have prevented Castro, short of armed intervention, from allaying Cuba with the socialist countries, but U.S. policies seem to have removed whatever slight chances may have existed for Castro's demise and facilitated his alignment with the USSR.

Although U.S. policies toward the Guatemalan Revolution may seem to have achieved their objectives, in contrast to those toward Cuba, which did not, it is in fact doubtful that policy toward Guatemala served long-term U.S. purposes. Prospects for compromise in Guatemala in 1954 were probably better than President Eisenhower's prospects for achieving reconciliation with Castro in 1959. Unlike Castro, the Guatemalan revolutionaries would have welcomed compromise. Justifying U.S. policies on the grounds that the Communists were prevented from taking over in Guatemala requires suppositions about Communist control of Arbenz not yet supported by the record.

United States actions toward the Guatemalan revolutionaries also violated U.S. treaty commitments and political ideals. The U.S. government not only helped suppress a constitutional government, but also violated U.S. pledges not to sponsor armed intervention in the Western Hemisphere. Since 1954 Guatemala has become one of the most strife-torn countries in the Americas; nowhere else have guerrilla movements been more durable.

Origins of Error

United States policies appear to have been most counterproductive in the cases of Guatemala and Cuba. United States officials' errors sometimes resulted from hopes or fears about the impact that success or failure of a revolutionary government would have on their political positions in the United States. When hopes or fears were especially great, U.S. leaders sponsored armed action against a particular revolutionary government.

Familiarity with John Foster Dulles' personal and political objectives are essential to understanding the Guatemalan intervention of 1954. Dulles' policies toward Guatemala were in part a religious crusade against atheistic communism, in part an ideological struggle on behalf of free enterprise, and in part a political battle with Soviet expansionism. In the 1952 presidential campaign, Dulles had criticized the reactive nature of the Truman/Acheson policies, on the one hand, and favored liberating countries under communism on the other. Dulles viewed the overthrow of Arbenz as fulfilling that pledge. He regarded this "victory" as one of the major constructive achievements of the Eisenhower administration and used it as a rallying cry in the 1954 and 1956 elections. This background helps explain why he was deaf to arguments that the Arbenz government was not, in fact, a Communist beachhead in the Americas.

Eisenhower's punitive policies toward Cuba, begun in March 1960, appear to have been designed in part to strengthen the Republican party's hand in the 1960 election. Cuba became a major subject in the debates between candidates Nixon and Kennedy. Similarly, after Kennedy became president, the pressures on him to carry forward the Bay of Pigs invasion were enormous. In spite of his own reservations about the operation, his concern that calling off the invasion would have been interpreted as weakness, and thus be politically costly at home (as well as abroad), appears to have been a major factor in his decision to go ahead.

Parenthetically, President Johnson had a similar dilemma with respect to the Dominican revolt in 1965. His strong instincts told him that the political risks of armed intervention in the Dominican Republic were less than the risks of a Communist take-over there, particularly with respect to the upcoming presidential elections in 1968.

An interesting aspect of the U.S. use of armed force in response to the revolutionary process is that each instance of armed force was related to, or defended by, reference to strategic or security considerations. (See table 9, which lists the various incidents, including one case after 1961, the Dominican intervention.) Fear of a rival Great Power was an important consideration in the Guatemalan, Cuban, and Dominican interventions. (The Pershing expedition was undertaken to protect and restore order to U.S. border areas which had suffered predatory attacks by Pancho Villa's irregulars, and the Veracruz intervention was in response to alleged indignities inflicted on U.S. military forces in Mexico.) Even if one does not accept at face value U.S. official explanations for these interventions, it seems clear that the U.S. officials tended to require security justifications for the use of force (proposition 15). My view is that U.S. officials were inclined to believe in these justifications however misled or misinformed they might have been. The extent to which these armed

TABLE 9

U.S.-SPONSORED INVASIONS

Place	Dates	U.S. Military Forces	Other Forces
Mexico[1]			
Veracruz and nearby island of San Juan de Ulua	April 21, 1914 to November 23, 1914	Original invading force 787 men; by April 28, 6,000 navy and marines in occupation	
Mexico[2]			
Pershing's forces marched as far south as Parral, Chihuahua	March 17, 1916 to February 5, 1917	Three main cavalry columns, consisting of 1,109 enlisted men, 51 officers, made initial border crossing	
Guatemala[3]			
Attacks on Puerto Barrios, Zacapa and Esquipulas; air attacks on Guatemala City	June 18, 1954 to July 1, 1954		150 for infiltration 150 in paramilitary units 300 men
Cuba[4]			
Amphibious assault at Bay of Pigs on Playa Girón; air support of beach and supply drop on Girón airfield	April 17, 1961 to April 19, 1961	U.S. frogmen before invasion and one during invasion; 10 U.S. pilots involved in combat missions	1,500 men
Dominican Republic[5]			
Troop landings at Port of Haina and in Santo Domingo	April 28, 1965 to September 20, 1966	April 29 first invading forces, 1,700 were marines, 2,500 airborne troops; May 6 over 22,000 men ashore at maximum strength	IAPF (non-U.S.) forces 1,250 Bazilians 250 Hondurans 175 Nicaraguans 20 Costa Ricans 1,695

NOTE: This table covers only U.S.-sponsored invasions in cases of revolutionary change not the many other armed actions in former U.S. protectorates, such as Cuba, Panama, Nicaragua, Haiti, and the Dominican Republic.

1. Robert E. Quirk, *An Affair of Honor* (Lexington, Ky., 1962), pp. 85–86, 107, 169. Letter to author from D.C. Allard, Head, Operational Archives Branch, U.S. Naval History Division, December 26, 1970, provides these figures and adds that 4,090 army men replaced navy and marines on April 30.

2. *FR, 1916,* pp. 491–92, and *FR, 1917,* pp. 908–09; Col. Frank Tompkins, *Chasing Villa* (Harrisburg, Pa., 1934), p. 78.

3. *New York Times,* June 19, 1954, p. 1, and July 2, 1954, p. 1; *Así se gestó la Liberación,* Publicaciones de Secretaría de Divulgación, Cultura y Turismo de la Presidencia de la República, Guatemala, 1956, p. 181.

4. *New York Times,* April 18, 1961, p. 1, and April 20, 1961, p. 1; Haynes Johnson, *The Bay of Pigs* (New York, 1964), pp. 88, 118, 148–49.

5. *New York Times,* April 29, 1965, p. 1; September 21, 1966, p. 12; April 30, 1965, p. 1; May 22, 1965, p. 6; Jerome Slater, *Intervention and Negotiation* (New York, 1969), p. 54.

actions were related to the defense or promotion of U.S. private interests is discussed elsewhere, but such considerations were not very prominent in the events which led up to each particular action.

It is interesting that most of the decisions described here as dysfunctional, and thus as errors, involved the use of armed force and that all such decisions were made *within* the executive branch. They did not require specific authorization, appropriations, ratification, or other congressional approval. For example, Presidents Eisenhower and Kennedy personally authorized paramilitary operations in Guatemala and Cuba respectively—as President Nixon may have authorized covert support to Allende's opposition (see chapter 8). Both operations involved the CIA, which was then subject to only nominal congressional oversight. (Note, too, that the decision to send troops into the Dominican Republic [see chapter 8] was made by President Johnson.)

The onus of decisions to use armed force against these small Latin American countries should not fall exclusively on Dulles, Eisenhower, and Kennedy. In a sense, public opinion provided a climate fostering such decisions. This subject deserves a book in itself, but some tentative comments can be advanced here.

In attempting to mobilize U.S. resources behind the Marshall Plan and containment, the Truman administration focused public attention on the threat of communism to western democracies and to world peace. Fears of Soviet expansionism and of the international Communist movement were confirmed by the Korean War. As a result, such fears continued to be a major concern of many U.S. citizens in the 1950s and early 1960s.[6]

Aware of popular fears and sharing in them, many political leaders from both major parties attempted to identify with anti-Communist causes, and it became politically dangerous to appear soft on communism. Continuing public criticism of communism soon evoked the moral self-righteousness that had long been latent in the American character.[7] Woodrow Wilson symbolized it, as did John Foster Dulles later on. These self-righteous public attitudes about foreign policy developed partly because of the confidence gained through the rapid settlement of a wilderness continent, physical distance from Europe and Asia, relative inexperience in international affairs until World War II, and the fact that the United States had never suffered defeat in a major war. Out of this national experience emerged the evangelical policies fostering American values and American practices abroad—policies which sometimes appeared to their presumed beneficiaries indistinguishable from imperialism.

After World War II, the evangelical self-righteousness in American character was linked to overwhelming military and economic power. The American public came to believe that the United States could control the course of events beyond its shores and appeared persuaded that its leaders had the responsibility to do so. Both the Democratic and Republican administrations encouraged such beliefs in supporting the Marshall Plan, aid to Greece and Turkey, the Berlin blockade, and the Korean War. The success of the Marshall Plan bolstered American overconfidence in this respect, and the credence given Republican charges that the Democrats "lost" China perpetuated these illusions.

As a result, critics of incumbent administrations were able to argue successfully that the president had a responsibility to prevent the expansion of communism around the world. International communism was viewed as posing a threat not only to U.S. property holders ("capitalists") but also to the independence of organized labor, the press, the churches, and the universities, in fact, most of the strongest institutions in American society. For these reasons whichever party was in opposition could be expected to criticize the incumbent government and make political capital out of events abroad that were viewed adversely at home. Popular views about the responsibilities of the United States to check the advance of communism caused U.S. leaders to fear heavy political penalties against revolutionary movements associated with international communism (proposition 16). Not until the U.S. failures in Vietnam became painfully apparent did the American public at large begin to adopt a more sober and realistic view.

United States policies toward revolutionary change outside Latin America have also been affected decisively by considerations of global strategy arising in other theaters. The Wilson administration, for example, put heavy pressure on the provisional government in Russia in 1917 to stay in the war against Germany. Accepting its obligations toward the Western Allies, the provisional government refused to make a separate settlement with Germany. Ending the war was a major issue in the Bolshevik program, which together with the slogan "Land to the Peasants" contributed to the fall of the provisional government and accounted for the popular support that permitted the Bolsheviks to seize and retain power. Thereafter, both the U.S. unwillingness to release the new Soviet government from Russia's pledge not to make a separate peace and U.S. armed intervention in Russia for purposes related to the war against imperial Germany accounted in part for the diplomatic rift between the two governments that was not repaired until 1933.[8]

United States policy toward Communist China had a similar fate. After the failure of General Marshall's mission to arrange a coalition government in China, the Truman administration decided to end all military and economic assistance to the Chiang Kai-shek government. A powerful bloc in Congress, cultivated by the China lobby, insisted that the administration reverse its policy and continue aid to Chiang as the price of its votes for the Marshall Plan. In order to get the Marshall Plan passed and to "save" Western Europe, the administration, against its better judgment, agreed to continue aid to Chiang.[9] Thus, U.S. responses to the Russian and Chinese Communist revolutions were subordinated to the goals of global strategy just as they have been in the Latin American social revolutions studied here.

As table 8 shows, U.S. responses tended to be determined either by strategic considerations related to fear of a rival Great Power or, when these were not operative, by the interests of the private sector. As a result, the U.S. responses tended to be shaped by global strategy or special interests rather than by considerations of bilateral governmental relations (proposition 17).

U.S. Impact

United States influence has been so extensive and pervasive that a comprehensive evaluation of it for Mexico, Bolivia, Guatemala, and Cuba cannot be handled adequately here. However, comments will be made about two aspects of the U.S. impact: first, its effect on the pace of revolutionary change; and second, its effect on these nations' dependency on the United States, including the extent to which the revolutionary movements have been able to reduce that dependency.

With respect to pace, conciliatory U.S. policies have tended to check the momentum of revolutionary change, while suppressive policies have tended to accelerate change initially or when suppression occurred, to create potentially revolutionary situations (proposition 18).

United States conciliatory policies toward Mexico and Bolivia had a moderating and deradicalizing influence. The United States consistently opposed political extremism within those countries, either Nazi or Communist. More important, U.S. economic policies discouraged sharp departures from the status quo, particularly with respect to property rights, and exerted a dampening influence on expansion of the public sector. Policies tended to favor middle-class interests and sometimes were sharply counterpoised to organized labor, especially in Bolivia. Compromises the Mexicans and Bolivians made to insure friendly relations with the United States and to secure U.S. economic assistance served to check radical elements within the two revolutionary parties, while U.S. political, economic, and military support strengthened the hand of the moderates.

Suppressive policies toward Guatemala and Cuba tended to polarize these societies and radicalize opposition groups. United States pressures on Arbenz made him increasingly dependent on anti-American forces, including the Communists. After Arbenz fell, many of the former Guatemalan moderates, such as Juan José Arévalo, became bitterly anti-American and others, including Arbenz himself, fell increasingly under Communist influence. As chapter 6 shows, Castro veered sharply to the Left in both domestic and foreign policies when he discovered that the Eisenhower administration sought his overthrow.

A second aspect of the impact of U.S. policies is the extent to which they have helped or hindered the efforts of the revolutionary governments to reduce their dependency on the United States. To be sure, all nations are dependent to some degree and interdependence is the dominant reality. Yet the revolutionary governments discussed here all sought to gain greater control of their nations' destinies—to right an imbalance where most of the dependence had been on their side.

Resentment of foreign and especially U.S. influence in domestic affairs has been typical of all four revolutionary governments. Nationalistic aspirations are in part a product of perceived foreign dominance. The Mexicans, for example, disapproved of the special privileges foreign investors enjoyed under Díaz. The Bolivians, lacking a tin smelter within their country, charged that the lion's share of profits went for refining. Guatemalans protested against monopolistic control of their central transportation network by foreigners. Che Guevara called the U.S. sugar-quota system a form of slavery that placed the Cuban economy at the mercy of U.S. leaders who determined U.S. sugar quotas and prices.

Aware of these nationalistic feelings, the United States, as a matter of official policy, has long been on record as favoring equality and mutual respect in its relations with Latin American governments. Many U.S. leaders believed in these objectives and advanced them sincerely as matters of principle, even though U.S. "assistance" often had other self-serving purposes.

Principles, however, are one thing, and practice another.[10] Many U.S. officials and other leaders have been unwilling to accept change, especially in those areas where their individual interests have been adversely affected. The difficulty is that U.S. interests are so varied and extensive in Latin America that many important changes are likely to conflict with one or another U.S. vested interest. And these interests, particularly those of business and the U.S. economic and military bureaucracy, have been influential. United States investors were among the leading opponents of the Mexican and Guatemalan revolutions and supported punitive official policies against Cuba. Protection of creditors' rights has been an understandable restraint on lending policies. The U.S. military has strongly defended its operational facilities and opposed measures of revolutionary movements in such countries as Bolivia and Cuba. United States labor leaders have opposed the policies of revolutionary governments in Guatemala and Cuba. The Roman Catholic church in the United States was a major voice against the Mexican Revolution, especially in the 1920s and 1930s.

The effect of specific U.S. practices was to undermine U.S. principles. United States policies have generally not facilitated revolutionary governments' efforts to reduce their dependence in the United States (proposition 19). United States actions were not primarily the result of evil intentions or conspiracies, as sometimes charged, but the outcome of pressures from special interests, of political arrangements, and of prevailing values. It is, perhaps, unrealistic to expect the United States, or any other Great Power for that matter, to help significantly in reducing a client states' dependency; too many vested interests are at stake. As the United States' own experience in the eighteenth and nineteenth centuries shows, client states have had to do that largely on their own.

With respect to whether the revolutionary movements succeeded in reducing their dependence, certainly the military and technological gaps between these countries and the United States are wider now in the nuclear age than they were before the revolutions took place. Nor did economic disparities decline as evidenced in any narrowing of the gap in terms of gross national product. United States direct investment in Mexico, which was so great in 1910, fell off sharply after the revolution but is now more than double the 1910 figure.[11] Cuban dependence on sugar and a single market for exports and imports, now the Soviet Union, is as great or greater now than before Castro.[12] In these respects, both Mexico and Cuba seem to have retained their character as economic satellites.

One of the most damaging consequences of dependence in the past, both to material interests and national pride, was the capacity of powerful governments and individuals from outside to play upon the divisions within Mexico and Cuba to their own benefit and to the countries' detriment. The success of divide-and-rule policies has caused deep resentment over political dependence. One result of the revolutions in Mexico and Cuba has been to eliminate such interference, at least in part.

Mexico succeeded by strengthening and unifying the Mexican revolutionary party, subordinating the military to that party, and successfully resisting U.S. interference in internal affairs. Restrictions on foreign investment and other nationalistic foreign policies, including less participation in U.S. programs of economic and military assistance, have tended to limit avenues of U.S. influence. The result has probably been less U.S. interference in Mexican affairs than in most other Caribbean countries.

Cuba has paid a huge price in human and material terms in effecting its economic and political break with the United States. Castro eliminated U.S. influence at the cost of establishing Cuba's dependence on the Soviet Union. In late 1974 Cuba was roughly as dependent on the USSR as a market for exports, a source of oil and capital goods, and a supplier of arms and munitions as it was earlier on the United States.

An evaluation of Cuba's gains from this break goes far beyond the scope of this study. One aspect pertinent here, however, is that Cuba may be less subject today to foreign interference in its internal affairs. One reason is that Castro has concentrated almost all political and economic power in his own hands so that it is more difficult for outsiders to capitalize on divisions within Cuban society. Insofar as Cuban society is more isolated and closed than before the revolution, it may be less susceptible to external influences. Also U.S. investors and other interests may have exerted greater influence in prerevolutionary Cuba than the array of Soviet advisers exert there today. Since the USSR is a more distant sponsor than the United States, Cuba is probably in a better position to resist Soviet influence.

Unlike the Mexican and Cuban revolutions, the Bolivian Revolution appears to have resulted in more rather than less foreign interference in the nation's internal affairs. One of the reasons is that the Bolivian revolutionary party (MNR) never succeeded in dominating Bolivia as the Mexican and Cuban parties dominated their countries. Antagonisms between the MNR governmental leaders and MNR labor leaders facilitated the penetration of U.S. influence. After 1960 the Paz government increasingly relied on U.S. assistance and officials as a means of counteracting rising opposition within the country. The use of U.S. funds for the national budget, the manipulation of aid programs for political purposes, and the use of U.S. support to bolster the military and to contain unrest were symptoms of that dependence. In fact, Bolivia's earlier dependence on the tin mines, the mine owners, and British markets was superseded by Bolivian dependence on U.S. grants and loans, U.S. markets, and U.S. officials.

The foregoing suggests that the revolutionary process did not lead to a reduction of dependence but that the revolutionary governments in Mexico and Cuba, which maintained strong one-party rule and controlled the military, overcame some nega-tive consequences of dependence by making it more difficult for foreign powers to interfere in their internal affairs (proposition 20). If this proposition is valid, then social revolution will not cure dependence in and of itself. Progress toward that goal will occur under whatever system in the dependent countries results in fewer economic and political disparities with the United States.

Propositions Summarized

Three Stages

Proposition 1.   The United States responded with flexibility to rebel move-ments (first stage), which the United States did not associate with rival Great Powers (1, 3, 4),* and with hostility toward rebel movements, which it perceived as associated with such powers (2).

Proposition 2.   The United States responded hostilely toward most reformist governments (second stage) primarily because of the adverse impact these reformist governments were deemed to have on U.S. private interests (5, 6, 7).

Proposition 3.   The United States responded to revolutionary governments (third stage) according to decisions about U.S. strategic interests with respect to its strongest Great Power rival (Germany until 1945 and the Soviet Union thereafter). Strategic considerations shaped U.S. responses whether the latter were conciliatory, as in the cases of Mexico and Bolivia (9, 11, 13, 14), or suppressive, as in the cases of Guatemala and Cuba (15, 17, 18).

Proposition 4.   United States leaders opted for a conciliatory response when they determined that the revolutionary government would negotiate an acceptable settlement of issues in conflict and that such an agreement would preclude the interference of a hostile Great Power in the country concerned (9, 11, 13, 14). They opted for suppression when they determined that the revolutionary government would not negotiate such a settlement and subduing it was deemed the best means of preventing or countering the interference of a hostile Great Power (15, 17, 18).

Economic Explanations

Proposition 5.   Economic considerations, and especially private business in-terests, were important in the formulation of U.S. policies and were often compatible with policies decided primarily on strategic grounds (2, 13, 14, 15, 17, 18).

When, however, there was a conflict between economic and strategic considera-tions, the strategic factors took precedence (9, 11).

---

*The numbers in parentheses after most of the propositions refer to the episodes in table 8 which tend to support the proposition.

Bureaucratic Explanations

Proposition 6. The president or secretary of state actively participated in decisions perceived as strategic with respect to Great Power rivals (2, 9, 11, 13, 15, 17, 18, and probably 14).

Proposition 7. Departmental officials acting independently were the principal decision makers with respect to most responses that were not perceived as strategically significant (3, 4, 5, 6, 7, 8, 12). The president or secretary of state usually participated little in such decisions.

Proposition 8. Responses that were determined by departmental officials were either in accord with U.S. private interests or at least did not blatantly oppose them (3, 4, 6, 7, 8, 12).

Proposition 9. United States responses involved conflicts within the U.S. government between the Department of State and other agencies, such as the Defense Department, CIA, and Treasury (4, 5, 8, 9, 11, 16, 17). Bureaucratic considerations appear to have been more important in U.S. responses to the Bolivian Revolution than to the other revolutions (13, 14).

Proposition 10. Bureaucratic considerations per se were less decisive than strategic considerations or private interests in shaping U.S. responses. Both of the latter originated outside the U.S. bureaucracy but were reflected in its internal bargaining processes.

Proposition 11. United States responses, particularly those which were suppressive in Guatemala and Cuba, also need to be understood as efforts to maintain U.S. political primacy within its sphere of influence (15, 17, and 18).

Proposition 12. Three categories of actors appear to have shaped U.S. responses in these four cases in descending order of influence: (1) the president acting with or through cabinet-level officers, such as the secretary of state; (2) leaders of large corporations working with members of Congress and the executive, and (3) middle-level diplomats and civil servants. Their actions tended to be shaped, respectively, by security, economic, and "bureaucratic" considerations.

Responses Evaluated

Proposition 13. United States official perceptions of German influence in Mexico and Soviet influence in Cuba were essentially correct (9, 11, 17, 18); the perceptions of German influence in Bolivia and of Soviet influence in Bolivia and Guatemala were exaggerated or incorrect (2, 13, 14, 15).

Proposition 14. United States responses with respect to U.S. strategic aims were functional in Mexico and Bolivia (9, 11, 13, 14) and dysfunctional in Guatemala and Cuba (15, 17, 18).

Proposition 15. United States decisions to sponsor armed action against a particular revolutionary government were justified by security considerations, not by the need to protect a private interest (15, 17, 18).

Proposition 16. The widely held view of the U.S. public that the government had the responsibility for checking the spread of communism around the world created a situation in which U.S. leaders feared political repercussions from failure to contain international communism (15, 17, 18).

Proposition 17. Few U.S. responses were determined by broad conceptions of U.S. public interest taken within the framework of bilateral governmental relationships (1, 3, 4, 8, 16) but rather by the business and strategic considerations described in propositions 2 and 3 (2, 5, 6, 7, 9, 10, 11, 12, 13, 14, 15, 17, 18).

U.S. Impact

Proposition 18. United States conciliatory policies toward Mexico and Bolivia had a moderating and deradicalizing influence, tending to check the momentum of revolutionary change; suppressive policies toward Guatemala and Cuba tended to polarize those societies and radicalize opposition groups, creating potential revolutionary situations.

Proposition 19. United States policies have generally not facilitated the efforts of revolutionary governments to reduce their dependence on the United States in spite of the latter's sometimes sincere protestations about its desire to do so.

Proposition 20. The revolutionary process does not appear to have reduced the dependence of any of the four countries studied, but the revolutionary governments of Mexico and Cuba, by establishing firm one-party control and making the armed forces subordinate to the revolutionary leadership, overcame some of the negative consequences of dependence by making it slightly more difficult for foreign powers to interfere in their internal affairs.

Epilogue

Epilogue

U.S. Responses
Since 1961

Two countries in Latin America have experienced revolutionary change since the Bay of Pigs: Peru and Chile. Guerrilla movements tried and failed to initiate revolutionary change in several other countries in the 1960s. The Constitutionalists also probably aimed at revolutionary change in the Dominican Republic revolt in April 1965.

This chapter will describe and explain U.S. responses to these revolutionary movements and not to social change in general, so reformist governments, such as those in Colombia and Venezuela, will not be discussed. Although only Peru and Chile fit the criteria for revolutionary change established in earlier chapters, the guerrilla movements of the 1960s and the Dominican case are included here because they have so much in common with the earlier studies and were perceived by the United States as leading toward revolutionary change.

Dividing the revolutionary process into three stages—rebel movement, reformist government, and revolutionary government—is a useful ordering device for events since 1961 as well as for those prior to that date. After 1961 the three stages neatly paralleled changes of administration in the United States. The Democratic administrations of Kennedy and Johnson were concerned with the first two stages: the rebel movements of the guerrillas and the Dominican Constitutionalists; and the reformist governments of Juan Bosch in the Dominican Republic, Fernando Belaunde in Peru, and Eduardo Frei in Chile. The Republican Nixon administration faced revolutionary governments in Peru and Chile.

This chapter will also examine the extent to which U.S. responses since 1961 have been consistent with the patterns of U.S. official behavior toward revolutionary change from 1910 to 1961 summarized in chapter 7.

Kennedy/Johnson: Stick and Carrot

President Kennedy framed a two-pronged response to social change in Latin America. First, through counterinsurgency programs, his administration sponsored armed suppression of rebel movements hostile to the United States. Second, the

241

Kennedy administration provided financial support under the Alliance for Progress to popularly elected governments dedicated to social reform within existing constitutional frameworks. President Johnson continued this two-pronged policy with a change in emphasis. Whereas President Kennedy had sponsored Latin American paramilitary forces, President Johnson intervened directly with U.S. forces in the Dominican Republic in 1965. He also continued the programs of the Alliance for Progress, but with less emphasis on social reform and more on economic development.

Presidents Kennedy and Johnson both were deeply involved in decisions with respect to Latin America which were deemed strategically significant. In addition to his role in the Bay of Pigs decision, President Kennedy interpreted the national liberation movements in Latin America and elsewhere as posing a challenge to him personally as well as to the nation, and he participated in the development of the strategy and tactics of counterinsurgency. President Johnson presided at meetings in the White House that led to U.S. military intervention in the Dominican Republic in 1965.

President Kennedy was also deeply committed to the grand design of the Alliance for Progress, particularly its elements favoring rapid social change at the risk of social revolution. Kennedy authorized the display of naval might which appears to have been decisive in ousting the remnants of the Trujillo family's control of the Dominican Republic.[1] He was prepared under exceptional circumstances to restrain U.S. companies in Latin America in the interests of broader social objectives.[2] Yet, it also seems clear that Kennedy was unable to devote the attention that would have been required to maintain the momentum of the social idealism expressed in the Alliance charter in the face of the inertia of a status-quo-oriented bureaucracy and the opposition of entrenched private interests. The inability of his administration to provide effective support to Juan Bosch's reformist government in the Dominican Republic, on which Kennedy had counted so much, demonstrated the gulf between U.S. official behavior and the U.S.-sponsored ideals.[3] President Johnson probably never fully shared this idealism with respect to Latin America, and U.S. officials ceased to press for it during his administration.

My conclusions in chapter 7 which need to be tested with respect to the Kennedy and Johnson administrations relate to U.S. responses in the first and second stages of the revolutionary process. Were the Kennedy and Johnson responses to rebel movements determined by their perceptions of the rebels' associations with rival Great Powers? Was U.S. hostility or opposition to reformist governments based on the foregoing strategic considerations, and, if not, did U.S. private interests tend to determine U.S. policy? Were official U.S. perceptions of strategic threats posed by rival Great Powers valid and were U.S. responses in such cases functional to U.S. interests?

Armed Suppression

Guerrillas. Guerrilla movements sprang up in the early 1960s in Latin America numbering dozens of men in Peru and Bolivia, hundreds in Guatemala,

Colombia, and Venezuela, and thousands in Uruguay (see table 10). The guerrillas of the 1960s, like earlier rebels described in chapter 2, sought to overthrow incumbent governments, but they were dissimilar in other ways.

In the first place, the guerrillas of the 1960s sought to overthrow governments of a reformist democratic persuasion, such as those of Méndez Montenegro in Guatemala, Leoni in Venezuela, and Lleras Restrepo in Colombia. These presidents were not brutal dictators like Huerta, Batista, and Trujillo. Second, the guerrillas of the 1960s were openly anti-American and espoused radical Marxist programs. Many of the earlier rebels had not been anti-American initially and stood for moderate policies. The reasons that recent rebels were more radical are that they believed that reformism had failed, that the United States had opposed and would continue to oppose needed social change, and that the Cuban Revolution demonstrated that radical strategies can succeed.

The policies that President Kennedy framed to cope with guerrilla movements arose less from experience with these movements in Latin America (many sprung up *after* counterinsurgency operations began) and were more a result of his assumptions about Soviet ties with national liberation movements generally and his personal confrontations with First Secretary Khrushchev. In championing peaceful coexistence between the USSR and the United States, Khrushchev had to find a formula for reconciling Soviet revolutionary ideology, with peaceful coexistence with "U.S. capitalism and imperialism." In his efforts to maintain the Soviet claim to leadership of revolution in the Third World, he reiterated time and again Soviet support for national liberation movements.[4] Early in his term, President Kennedy suffered humiliating defeat at the Bay of Pigs. Thus, when personally confronted shortly thereafter at Vienna by Khrushchev's explicit challenge with respect to national liberation movements, Kennedy felt impelled to respond forcefully with counterinsurgency programs. Latin America became a major arena for the implementation of such programs.

The rationale for U.S. military assistance in Latin America shifted from the prevention of external attack to the prevention and suppression of subversion in the hemisphere which was perceived as externally sponsored. United States security agencies launched a comprehensive program of counterinsurgency operations supported by military and police assistance. Military advisers on counterinsurgency operations were assigned to Latin American armed forces; training to deal with guerrilla warfare was provided in Panama and the United States; and special supplies, such as helicopters, small arms, and communications equipment, were given to the armed forces. Between 1950 and 1970, 54,270 Latin Americans were trained under the U.S. military assistance program.[5] Simultaneously, funds were provided Latin American armed forces for civic action (construction of roads, schools, etc.) to serve restive populations.

The Agency for International Development (AID) under its public safety program provided equipment and training to police and other internal security forces in many Latin American countries. Also made available were special techniques of the Federal Bureau of Investigation, as well as some of the more sophisticated

TABLE 10
SELECTED GUERRILLA MOVEMENTS

	Movement	Leaders	Dates	Place	Maximum Strength	External Ties	Status in 1972
Bolivia	Army of National Liberation (ELN)	"Che" Guevara "Ricardo" Inti Peredo	1965–1967	Foothills southeast of La Paz	41[1]	Training in Cuba	Nearly destroyed after death of "Che"
Colombia	Revolutionary Armed Forces of Colombia (FARC)	Manuel Marulanda	1965–	Mountains south of Bogotá	400	Pro-Moscow	Crippled by counterinsurgency operations and internal feuding
	National Liberation Army (ELN)	Fabio Vázquez Castaño Camilo Torres	1965–	Middle Magdalena Valley	80	Cuban subsidies	
	Peoples Liberation Army (EPL)	Gonzalo Gonzalez	1968–	Córdoba Province	150[2]	Pro-Maoist	
Guatemala[3]	Revolutionary Movement of Nov. 13 (MR-13)	Yon Sosa	1963–	Guatemala City and environs	300[4]	—	Urban terrorism and political kidnappings
	Revolutionary Armed Forces (FAR)	Turcios Lima César Montes	1963–	Mountains of Sierra de los Minas		—	
Peru	Movement of the Revolutionary Left (MIR)	Hugo Blanco Luis de la Puente	1962-1965	Cordillera de Urubamba	100[5]	—	Nearly destroyed after deaths of leaders

Country	Organization		Leaders	Dates	Location	Numbers	Support	Status
Uruguay	Tupamaros (MLN)	Pluralistic		1965–	Montevideo and eastern urban section	1,000–3,000[6]	Largely independent (populist)	Organization destroyed, thousands of members/collaborators in military prisons
Venezuela	Revolutionary Armed Forces and Armed Forces of National Liberation (FAR/FALN)		Douglas Bravo Fabricio Ojeda	1963–	Mountains and small towns of the northwest Central university in Caracas	800[7]	Cuban subsidies and training	Quiescent except for sporadic city uprisings

Table prepared by Judith Ludvik.

SOURCES: Richard Gott, *Guerrilla Movements in Latin America* (New York, 1971), and Luis Mercier Vega, *Guerrillas in Latin America: The Techniques of the Counter-State* (New York, 1969). Other sources are listed in the table notes below.

1. As recorded by Che Guevara in March, 1967, Daniel James, ed., *The Complete Bolivian Diaires of Che Guevara and Other Captured Documents* (New York, 1968), p. 323.

2. As reported by Colombian military officers, *New York Times*, January 24, 1971, p. 13. This source provides figures on all three major Colombian guerrilla movements and information on other guerrilla movements beyond those appearing on the table.

3. Table includes leftist movements. For listing of rightest movements in Guatemala see H. Jon Rosenbaum, *Arms and Security in Latin America: Recent Developments* (Washington, D.C., 1971), p. 20. This source also includes a more complete table of guerrilla movements in various Latin American countries than is offered here.

4. Apparently as reported by Guatemalan military officers, *New York Times*, June 13, 1971, p. 50.

5. As estimated by Peruvian military intelligence, *New York Times*, September 28, 1965, p. 4.

6. Rosenbaum, *Arms and Security*, p. 21. Greatest strength after Che's death.

7. U.S. Congress, Senate, "Insurgency in Latin America," January 15, 1968, p. 15. Report by David Burks for the Subcommittee on American Republic Affairs, Committee on Foreign Relations.

methods of crowd control. Between 1966 and 1970, 3,543 Latin American police officers were trained in the United States and abroad under this program.[6]

Most of the guerrilla detachments were wiped out or rendered relatively harmless by 1967. In that year Bolivian units trained by the U.S. Green Berets wiped out Ernesto Che Guevara's small detachment in Bolivia, marking a dramatic climax to counterinsurgency operations. United States training and equipment played an important part in suppressing Guevara's detachment. Since Guevara's death, guerrilla activities have persisted sporadically in Guatemala and a few other places. A large group of guerrillas, the Tupamaros in Uruguay, which remained intact longer than any other, was largely destroyed by 1972.[7]

The Dominican Intervention.   United States officers and men have rarely participated in direct confrontations with Latin American rebels. Nevertheless, President Lyndon Johnson's decision to order U.S. troops into the Dominican Republic in 1965 was a logical extension of the counterinsurgency operations begun under President Kennedy.

The Dominican crisis began on Saturday, April 24, when pro-Bosch military officers revolted to depose Donald Reid and restore Juan Bosch to the presidency, an office to which Bosch had been elected in 1962 and deposed in September 1963. In the five days after April 24, 1965, the tide of battle swung back and forth between the pro- and anti-Bosch forces. On Wednesday, April 28, the pro-Bosch forces appeared on the verge of seizing control and a junta of anti-Bosch colonels requested U.S. assistance. Late that afternoon in Washington, President Johnson authorized the landing of U.S. forces that very evening. More than twenty-two thousand troops were landed in the next few weeks.[8]

President Johnson's initial justification for U.S. intervention was "to give protection to hundreds of Americans who are still in the Dominican Republic and escort them safely back to this country."[9] However, four days later after thousands of men had come ashore, the president justified the intervention as a way to prevent "the establishment of another Communist government in the Western Hemisphere."[10] In fact, the evidence seems conclusive that the prevention of another Cuba was the real explanation from the beginning of the intervention.[11]

Once U.S. troops were firmly in control and had the pro-Bosch forces bottled up in downtown Santo Domingo, the United States moved toward more neutral policies with respect to the opposing Dominican forces. Impressed by popular support for the pro-Bosch forces and opposition to the anti-Bosch military, the Johnson administration wished to minimize armed encounters and undercut adverse criticism of the Dominican intervention. Ultimately the United States sought and achieved a negotiated settlement among the parties. This agreement led to presidential elections on June 1, 1966, when Joaquín Balaguer defeated Juan Bosch for the presidency by a wide margin.[12]

Why Armed Suppression?   United States official perceptions of the guerrilla movements and the Dominican revolt had much in common. The rebels in both cases were perceived primarily as tools of the international Communist movement—most particularly the Soviet Union—for fomenting wars of national liberation and spreading international communism.

Some critics of U.S. policies charge that the description of the rebels that the Kennedy and Johnson administrations made explicit in explaining their policies to the American people was part of a cynical maneuver to veil their efforts to dominate these societies economically and politically.[13] It is true that the U.S. government was influenced by its desire to protect and advance private American business interests in the countries concerned. Like other Great Powers in its relations with small powers, the United States also sought to have its way, that is, to impose its will on its smaller neighbors. These two practices, however, are not incompatible with the earlier perception of the Communist threat. My own view is that Presidents Kennedy and Johnson actually perceived the guerrillas and Dominican rebels as instruments of Soviet policy. But were their perceptions valid?

Most of the guerrilla leaders and many of their followers were Marxist-Leninists, but their relations with the orthodox Communist parties were strained or overtly hostile. Cuba served as a model for some of the movements; others tended to identify with Peking. Castro provided some material assistance, but there is little evidence of much material support from Moscow or Peking. The guerrilla movements were organized, composed, and led almost exclusively by local nationals. Che Guevara's small *foco*, manned by many Cubans, was the main exception and was easily eliminated partly because it was repudiated by the local Moscow-oriented Communist party. Thus, the guerrilla movements could properly be described as Marxist-Leninist in orientation but hardly as instruments of Soviet policy in any conscious or disciplined sense.

Unlike the guerrillas, the leaders and most of the participants in the Dominican revolt were anti-Communist or non-Communist. The Johnson administration never proved that Communists actually took control, and the extent to which they posed a threat of doing so is a matter of judgment. Several dozen Communists, some trained in Cuba, did participate after the revolt broke out. On the basis of embassy estimates, Johnson claimed that about one-third of the armed civilians were Communist *led*.[14] Other figures that take into account the Constitutionalist military—and have more convincing support—suggest that about one out of twelve rebels was Communist led.[15] In any case, the core of the revolt was not civilian but made up of units of the regular armed forces. United States officials have asserted, but never proved, that there were Communists among the top civilian and military leadership of the revolt.[16] However, the men holding appointments in the cabinet of the Constitutionalist government and the top leaders of the armed forces were non-Communists,[17] and the Constitutionalists' revolt appears to have been dominated by non-Communists. The official U.S. version emphasizing Communist control is not only misleading, but incorrect.

United States counterinsurgency programs and the Dominican revolt were also justified as being responsive to official requests by incumbent governments whose independence the United States felt duty-bound to protect. Military assistance against many of the guerrillas was extended on the expressed request of popularly elected constitutional regimes. Such assistance was widely regarded as consistent with international law, but in the Dominican revolt that justification was a sham, and the U.S. intervention violated the OAS charter. The intervention came in response to a request from a hastily formed junta headed by Colonel Pedro Benoit at the San Isidro Air Force Base.[18] The latter had formed the "government" only a few hours earlier on the recommendation of the American embassy.

In the light of the foregoing, why did the United States sponsor counterinsurgency and intervene in the Dominican Republic? The counterinsurgency programs have been criticized as U.S. vehicles for defending the status quo. Yet this explanation does not square with President Kennedy's commitment to social change under the Alliance for Progress, which will be described below. The Alliance was, in fact, designed to promote gradual change of the sort which would result in minimal damage in the long term to U.S. economic and political interests.[19] Kennedy's Latin American policy contained contradictory elements: counterinsurgency operations and U.S.-sponsored change. Although counterinsurgency had the effect of strengthening the status quo, it originated in John Kennedy's conception of his role as leader of the free world against the international Communist movement. It was a reflection of the ideological and political conflict of the Cold War.

When Khrushchev directly challenged him with his national-liberation theses, Kennedy felt obliged to respond in the established spirit of Soviet-American rivalry.[20] Kennedy and his advisers probably gave more credence to Khrushchev's implied pretensions with respect to the leadership or control of these movements than they deserved. The counterinsurgency programs in Latin America also received high priority because of Castro's seizure of control in Cuba, his revolutionary proselytizing, and, more importantly, Kennedy's desire to counter the stinging defeat administered at the Bay of Pigs. They were introduced in many countries where guerrillas were not active, and the political costs of such programs as against their anticipated advantages apparently were not viewed as significant.

The causes of the U.S. response to the Dominican revolt involve the foregoing considerations plus others. The paternalistic and proprietary attitudes of the United States toward the Caribbean countries played a role. More important was the U.S. psychological climate in the Cold War. Anti-Communist emotionalism did not facilitate dispassionate analysis nor measured responses in threatening situations. United States diplomatic officers in Santo Domingo knew well how foreign service officers, whose views and actions regarding revolutions in China and Cuba did not conform to contemporary orthodoxies, were pursued and persecuted. With their careers at stake, U.S. diplomats in Santo Domingo in April 1965 opted for what they had learned was a lesser evil: it is better to overestimate than underestimate the "Communist threat." Always sensitive to public criticism and still a potential contender for reelection in 1968, President Johnson knew the political penalties implicit in "another Cuba." So sensitive to these pressures were he and his advisers—as well as the embassy in Santo Domingo—that the president authorized intervention only four days after the outbreak of what he described as a "popular democratic revolution."[21]

The anti-Communist obsession dimmed the vision and disturbed the equilibrium of American officials. A vast bureaucracy in Washington and a large section of the American embassy in Santo Domingo devoted their major energies to ferreting out and describing the activity of Communists in the republic. Poised in Santo Domingo as elsewhere to defend the free world against communism, the military attachés and military-assistance missions kept close touch with old-guard Dominican military officers. The embassy knew relatively little about the Constitutionalist forces, had little contact with them in the first week of the revolt, and thus was unable to place in broad perspective the vast accumulation of reports on the observed or rumored activities of the local Communists.[22] Sharing a similar mentality and far removed from the conflict, Washington lacked means of rectifying the distorted reports emanating from Santo Domingo.

Fear of communism, established U.S. pretensions to leadership of the free world, and misperceptions of the Latin American political scene caused the United States to become deeply embroiled in internal conflict by providing military assistance to one side against another. The experiences of the Kennedy and Johnson administrations with rebel movements amply bear out the conclusions of chapter 7 (proposition 1) that the United States responded hostilely to rebel movements perceived as associated with rival Great Powers.

Social Reform

One major objective of the Kennedy administration's Latin American policies was to promote social change under the Alliance for Progress. In an address to members of the Congress and to Latin American diplomats at the White House on March 13, 1961, President Kennedy summed up the purposes of the Alliance:

> We propose to complete the revolution of the Americas, to build a hemisphere where all men can hope for a suitable standard of living, and all can live out their lives in dignity and freedom. To achieve this goal political freedom must accompany material progress. . . . This political freedom must be accompanied by social change. For unless necessary social reform, including tax and land reform, are freely made . . . our alliance, our revolution, our dream, our freedom will fail. Let us once again transform the American continent into a vast crucible of revolutionary ideas and efforts.[23]

Kennedy's strategy was to encourage the basic reforms in social structure that traditional societies in Latin America had resisted for so long, by providing incentives, especially economic loans and grants, to those countries which cooperated in the Alliance for Progress (see table 11). A few members of the Kennedy administration, including probably the president himself, knew that efforts to promote change might cause social disorder, even violence, and were prepared to take such risks. The

TABLE 11

U.S. ASSISTANCE TO LATIN AMERICA IN THE 1960s
(U. S. Dollars, Millions)

Fiscal Year	Economic[1]	Public[2] Safety	Military[3]	Civic Action[4]	Transfer of Military Surplus[5]
1961	847.7	—	111.3	—	See note
1962	1,012.2	—	174.0	5.7	See note
1963	978.5	7.1	122.5	14.1	See note
1964	1,202.8	4.5	112.3	10.3	7.7
1965	1,199.5	5.5	89.1	9.2	9.5
1966	1,254.0	7.1	122.8	8.4	10.5
1967	1,343.0	5.3	87.0	4.2	4.1
1968	1,335.2	4.0	76.2	1.4	2.5
1969	986.3	3.9	44.8	1.0	2.1
1970	1,085.7	4.2	22.1	1.1	5.5

Table prepared by Judith Ludvik.

1. *U.S. Overseas Loans and Grants and Assistance from International Organizations: Obligations and Loan Authorizations, July 1, 1945–June 30, 1971,* Office of Statistics and Reports, Bureau for Program and Policy Coordination, Agency for International Development, May 24, 1972. See especially pp. 6, 33. 1961 figures from *U.S. Overseas Loans and Grants, July 1, 1945–June 30, 1967.*

2. Included in economic assistance totals (column 1); program initiated in fiscal year 1963. Office of Public Safety, Agency for International Development, Report U203, May 21, 1971.

3. *U.S. Overseas Loans and Grants, July 1, 1945–June 30, 1967,* and *July 1, 1945–June 30, 1971.*

4. Included in military assistance totals (column 3); program initiated in fiscal year 1962. U.S., Congress, House, Hearings before the Subcommittee of the Committee on Appropriations, *Foreign Assistance and Related Agencies Appropriations for 1968,* 90th Cong., 1st sess., pt. 1:571, pp. 68–70; U.S., Congress, House, Hearings before the Subcommittee of the Committee on Appropriations, *Foreign Assistance and Related Agencies Appropriations for 1972,* 92d Cong., 1st sess., pt. 1:101.

5. Included in military assistance totals (column 3). Military surpluses granted during 1950–1963 totaled $150 million. Breakdown by year not available. This and the figures 1964–1970 are from data processing files of the Defense Security Assistance Agency, Department of Defense, provided me by letter dated July 3, 1973. The agency was unable to provide figures on military sales of military surplus equipment for the years 1961–1970.

central purpose of this strategy, however, was to achieve a sufficient amount of social change through reform so that Latin American societies would evolve in a relatively peaceful fashion in the long term, thereby avoiding the costly and bloody revolutions which often follow intransigent regimes.

Kennedy's natural allies to achieve these purposes were the moderate, democratic governments in Latin America, which were more numerous in the early 1960s than a decade later. (A few middle-of-the-road regimes survived into the early 1970s, notably in Colombia and Venezuela.) Most of the reformist governments, however, were succeeded either by authoritarian governments of the Right or revolutionary governments of the Left. The reformist governments of João Goulart in Brazil and Juan Bosch in the Dominican Republic, for example, were overthrown by military coups. Both successor governments sought a return to the status quo ante. Reformist governments in Peru and Chile were succeeded by revolutionary governments of the Left—the Peruvian by left-wing military leaders, the Chilean by a coalition dominated by Marxist parties.

The central purpose here is to examine briefly U.S. responses to the reformist governments of Juan Bosch, Fernando Belaunde, and Eduardo Frei.

Bosch. President Kennedy considered the Dominican Republic the "show window" of the Alliance for Progress. He sought to promote social reform and establish a democratic regime there to prove the ability of the Alliance to meet its expressed goals. In the Dominican Republic progress toward these goals would be in dramatic contrast to the defunct Trujillo regime. The Eisenhower administration had already played an important role in Trujillo's demise by supporting political and economic sanctions against the dictator in August 1960 following the latter's attempts to assassinate the president of Venezuela.

After Trujillo himself had been assassinated in May 1961, President Kennedy ordered elements of the U.S. fleet to the horizon near Santo Domingo as a demonstration of support for local efforts to rid the republic of Trujillo's heirs. His action appears to have tipped the balance. Subsequently, the Kennedy administration threatened economic and military sanctions and provided economic assistance to insure free elections in 1962. Juan Bosch was elected president and assumed the presidency in February 1963. The Kennedy administration had a heavy investment in the new governments' fate.

Tensions between the two governments, however, began to develop from the start. Although they had many political views in common, U.S. Ambassador John Bartlow Martin, a liberal Democrat, and President Bosch did not have the best personal relations. Bosch was proud and was sensitive about Dominican weaknesses and dependence on the United States. Martin, who loved to deal directly with Dominican political figures, was annoyed that Bosch did not consult him more. When Bosch became president, military officers hostile to him controlled the armed forces and Martin refused to support Bosch in his desire to remove them.[24]

Numerous issues arose to cloud the two countries' relations. Martin was critical of Bosch's trip to Europe on the eve of his assumption of the presidency and his success in securing a Swiss line of credit. Martin thought Bosch's abrogation of a contract with Esso for building an oil refinery would discourage much-needed foreign investment. He was not enthusiastic about Bosch's plans for agrarian reform, and officials in Washington frowned on it. Martin also insisted, over Bosch's strong objections, on the fulfillment of a sugar sales contract whose terms Bosch considered unfair. Although Martin and other senior officials did not consider Bosch a Communist, many doubted his capacity to cope with the Communists, and there were continuing rumors, picked up by journalists, about Communist activities in the republic.[25]

As a result of the absence of support for and faith in Bosch, plus U.S. balance-of-payments difficulties, the United States made only minor commitments of economic assistance to Bosch's government in contrast to the much larger loans to his predecessor.[26] Bosch was too proud to press for aid, Martin hesitated to take the initiative in offering it, and later, when he did so, U.S. congressmen were not responsive.

Part of Bosch's political problem was mobilizing mass support and developing organizations to counter the hostile military. Agrarian reform was one way he hoped to do this, but U.S. officials discouraged him.[27] Another was to build a strong, united labor organization, but U.S. labor leaders who disposed of large funds, many from official U.S. sources, opposed politicizing and unifying Dominican labor.[28] Finally, U.S. military officers assigned in the Dominican Republic developed rapport with their military counterparts and were critical of what seemed to some an indecisive and unreliable civilian president.

When the military defied Bosch's authority in September 1963, the United States refused to bring in the fleet unless the embassy certified that a Communist take-over might occur. When the military confronted Bosch directly, Ambassador Martin decided to "let him go," much to the relief of his military adviser.[29]

The scope and intensity of U.S. influence in the Dominican Republic immediately before and during the presidency of Juan Bosch was truly remarkable. The United States was deeply involved in the military, police, labor, governmental, business, and educational institutions of the republic. Martin and the U.S. government claimed to seek—no doubt believed they sought—a victory for Dominican democracy under Juan Bosch. Yet the United States failed in its objective of maintaining Bosch, a popularly elected president, in office in an orderly transition to a democratic system.

In seeking to promote democratization and economic development, Juan Bosch faced formidable opposition among the Dominican military and vested economic interests. The United States was unable to bring to bear its significant military and economic power to save him. Distracted by the Communist "threat," U.S. officials were reluctant to back him firmly against the military.

Nor was the United States able to provide Bosch effective economic assistance when he needed it most. Charges of communism in the Dominican Republic sapped the necessary congressional support. Moreover, Bosch's actions affecting U.S. private interests cooled Washington's efforts in his behalf.

Not only did the United States prove an ineffective ally against Bosch's domestic opponents, but U.S. pressures hampered his efforts to mobilize mass political support behind his regime from his most likely sources—rural and industrial labor. With respect to Bosch's political strategy generally, Ambassador Martin deliberately sought to lessen Bosch's ties with the Left and move him toward business groups.[30]

In sum, the announced U.S. goal of promoting democracy in the Dominican Republic, at least insofar as Juan Bosch and his political party the PRD were its bearers, was subordinated to U.S. private and public vested interests. Concern for

U.S. investors and traders caused the United States to take actions hampering Bosch's strategies for building a broad base of popular support through social reform and nationalist appeals. Opposition to the perceived threats of communism was given priority over the defense of Bosch's Constitutional government.

The United States did not respond as hostilely to Bosch's reformist government as it did to those of Madero in Mexico, Villarroel in Bolivia, and Arévalo in Guatemala. But its indifference or hostility to social reform under Bosch's leadership was due to some of the same factors as in the other three cases. Bosch's differences with U.S. private interests were partly responsible. Such interests, however, appear to have been less influential than in Mexico in 1911–1913 and Guatemala in the late 1940s. United States investment in the Dominican Republic was much smaller in 1962, only $108 million,[31] much of which was in sugar. Fears of communism also accounted for U.S. hesitancy but were less important than fears of naziism in Bolivia in early 1944.

The United States tended to support social change as embodied in Kennedy's goals for the Alliance for Progress when such change did not interfere with U.S. private interests and public policies. When such change, however, conflicted, as it was bound to do in a country so close and dependent, the United States did not sustain active support for social reform.

Belaunde. The government of Fernando Belaunde in Peru (1963–1968) linked development and reform in accordance with the goals of the Alliance for Progress. Popularly elected, Belaunde sought to modernize Peru through agrarian reform, increased expenditures for education, and rural development. Educated at the University of Texas and speaking good English, Belaunde was friendly to the United States. At the same time, however, he took a moderately nationalistic line, pressing Peru's claims against the International Petroleum Company (IPC) and against U.S. fishing boats operating off the Peruvian coast.

Lacking a majority in Congress, Belaunde had difficulty implementing his programs, particularly agrarian reform. His bitterest opposition was the landowners who faced possible expropriation. The APRA, (Alianza Popular Revolucionaria Americana), the party which had so long claimed to represent the interests of peasants and organized labor and itself had been the leading proponent of such reform, also was not well disposed to see its rival, Belaunde, reap its political benefits. Belaunde succeeded in getting through the Congress a compromise bill which permitted compensation in bonds, but also provided many exceptions for certain types of property, including the sugar lands owned by U.S. interests. Belaunde's reforms faced massive technical problems, bureaucratic complications, and political resistance. Small parcels of land were distributed to some eleven thousand families,[32] but his achievements during five years in office fell far short not only of the massive reform for which the parties of the Left dreamed but also of his own goals.

The tensions between the United States and the Belaunde administration arose not so much out of the moderate reforms he introduced but rather out of a long smoldering dispute between Peru and the IPC. In his address to the Congress on taking office, Belaunde promised to take steps to resolve the conflict with the IPC in Peru's national interest. In the years that followed, the United States suspended or slowed payments of economic assistance in order to achieve a favorable settlement of the IPC case; the AID loans to Peru were suspended or slowed down from early 1964 to early 1966.[33] In February of 1966 the development loan commitments to Peru were resumed. By that time, however, Belaunde no longer had the political power necessary to implement some of the austerity measures required as a condition of the loans. A further difficulty arose in 1967 when the Peruvian government ordered Mirage jets from France. As a result of congressional restrictions on U.S. economic assistance to developing countries with high military expenditures, the United States froze the two loans to Peru then under negotiation.[34]

As a result of these restrictions, Belaunde received relatively few development loans during his administration. Chile and Colombia, with far smaller populations, received much more.[35]

In August 1968 Belaunde negotiated a settlement with the IPC in which the company ceded its subsoil rights to the government and the latter gave up its tax claims against the company. The parties also negotiated a mutually acceptable operating contract. All appeared well until September when a dispute exploded in public over how the company would pay for oil purchased from the wells. The controversy provided a pretext for the military charge that Belaunde had sold out Peru to the IPC. The Peruvian military under General Juan Velasco Alvarado took over the government in a palace coup and sent Belaunde into exile in October 1968.

The freeze in new commitments and slowdown in the flow of development assistance to Peru in 1964 and 1965 are clear from foreign-aid statistics (see table 12). According to Richard Goodwin, U.S. leaders attributed the stoppages to bureaucratic red tape when in fact Assistant Secretary of State Thomas Mann had made the decision to suspend aid until Belaunde reached an agreement with the IPC.[36] Belaunde was expected to get the idea without being told directly. Many other observers with access to U.S. officials also attributed the aid slowdown to U.S. efforts to secure a settlement favorable to IPC.[37] The result was that U.S. pressures on Belaunde through slowdowns or suspensions of economic assistance not only did not greatly assist him in achieving the social goals of the Alliance but also hampered his efforts to cope with the domestic opposition which ultimately overcame him.

Frei.   Eduardo Frei's program for rapid social reform in Chile, the "revolution in liberty," was predicated on friendly and collaborative relations with the United States. He was prepared to accept U.S. ground rules because the ideals and program of the Alliance for Progress, as enunciated by President Kennedy, were "precisely the same" as those he envisaged for the Latin American revolution.[38] Moreover, Frei was well aware of the political preeminence of the United States in the hemisphere, the importance of the U.S. market for Chilean exports, and the fact that the United States was the most promising foreign source of financial and capital resources for Chilean development.

TABLE 12

U.S. AND INTERNATIONAL ASSISTANCE TO PERU

(U.S. Dollars, Millions; Fiscal Years)

	1964	1965	1966	1967	1968	1969	1970	1971	1972	1973
U.S. assistance										
Total economic	82.9	36.1	42.5	33.0	18.5	22.9	16.9	19.5	75.3	9.0
Loans	67.2	21.0	24.9	23.2	4.8	9.8	—	7.3	58.7	—
Grants	15.7	15.1	17.6	9.8	13.7	13.1	16.9	12.2	16.6	9.0
Total military	8.7	11.5	9.9	4.8	1.4	0.6	0.6	0.5	1.0	0.8
International organizations										
World Bank (IBRD)	18.0	21.5	42.1	10.0	17.5	—	—	30.0	—	—
International Finance Corporation	1.6	—	—	*	0.1	—	—	—	—	—
Inter-American Development Bank	6.7	7.7	38.5	27.2	21.6	—	9.0	70.6	13.1	10.5
United Nations	2.6	2.8	2.8	3.3	1.9	2.4	2.2	6.0	3.0	3.5
Total international organizations	29.0	32.0	83.4	40.5	41.1	2.4	11.2	106.6	16.1	14.0

SOURCES: 1964–1965, Agency for International Development, *U.S. Overseas Loans and Grants from International Organizations, July 1, 1945–June 30, 1971* (Washington, D.C., 1972), p. 56; 1966–1972, *ibid., July 1, 1945–June 30, 1972* (Washington, D.C., 1973), pp. 58, 183; and 1973, *ibid., July 1, 1945–June 30, 1973* (Washington, D.C., 1974), pp. 57, 185.

*Less than $50,000

Frei's core reform programs involved the Chilean copper industry, land reform, and social welfare programs. Reforms of the copper industry posed the main potential threat to U.S. private interests. Yet there appears to have been "an unchallenged consensus among [Chilean] policy makers that the establishment of close, cooperative relations with the United States required that mutually satisfactory working relationships with the copper companies be arranged."[39] Frei put greater emphasis on expanding copper production as a means of accelerating economic growth and fiscal revenues than on introducing structural reforms in the industry. He believed that nationalization would injure necessary technological ties, recognized that Chile lacked the means to compensate U.S. owners, and rightly feared that nationalization would severely disrupt relations with the United States.

Frei's views thus led to the "Chileanization" of most of the copper industry. The Chilean government arranged to acquire a 51 percent interest in the Kennecott company and a minority interest in two other major U.S. copper companies. Compensation was arranged with the companies, which accepted the new arrangements in a negotiated settlement. (Late in Frei's term one company arranged to sell out to the government.) The agreements resulted initially in a spurt in copper output and in new investment in the industry.

During his campaign for the Chilean presidency in 1964, Frei set the goal of distributing land to 100,000 families with provisions to compensate the former owners mainly in bonds. In fact, U.S. private interests owned relatively little agricultural land in Chile and Frei's reform did not therefore pose a threat to them. In the face of political opposition and insufficient funds to implement the program, Frei was able to distribute land to probably less than a third of his goal of 100,000.[40] What is relevant here, however, is that the land reforms caused few repercussions in the United States partly because Americans owned little of Chilean agriculture. Similarly, his other reforms with respect to housing, education, health, taxes, etc., had repercussions which were mainly domestic in character.

Since Frei appears to have set out deliberately not to pose a major threat to U.S. interests, public or private, it is not surprising that the U.S. response was, in the main, sympathetic and cooperative. President Kennedy was assassinated nearly a year before Frei's election to the presidency and at the time of his death, late 1963, the emphasis of Kennedy's policy had begun to shift from social reform to economic development. United States policy toward the Frei government in the Johnson administration became a kind of legacy of Kennedy's reformist aspirations. Ralph Dungan, one of Kennedy's White House aides, was made ambassador to Chile and enjoyed close and friendly relations with the Frei government thereafter. The Chilean ambassador to the United States was a leading figure in Frei's party.

Economic assistance to Chile was given a high priority during the Johnson administration and became among the highest in the world on a per capita basis (see table 13 on p. 264). Nonetheless, that assistance was composed primarily of long-term loans which, despite relatively low rates of interest, sharply increased Chile's foreign debt. During the Vietnam War the Frei government reciprocated in a number of ways, including sales of copper to the United States at relatively favorable prices.[41] During these years there appears to have been relatively little friction between the U.S. and Chilean governments with respect to Frei's domestic programs. If such did exist, it was resolved with relatively little public acrimony. What needs to be determined when confidential aspects of bilateral relations become more widely known is what price the Frei government may have been forced to pay with respect to domestic programs in order to receive U.S. assistance. The price actually may not have been large since Frei's original program was conceived within the framework of collaborative relations with the United States.

The Frei government's foreign policy appears to have caused more friction with the United States than its domestic policies. Chile was sharply critical of the U.S. intervention in the Dominican Republic and opposed the establishment of the Inter-American Peace Force there. Nor did Frei support U.S. sanctions against Cuba and opposition to the admission of Communist China to the United Nations. All of this was part of Chile's "independent foreign policy" which was designed to safeguard its own international interests without unduly provoking the United States. Later in the Frei administration, when the goals of collaboration with the United States and social reform had not met expectations, the Chilean government stepped out more boldly for a revision of the structure of inter-American relations in Latin America's favor. The Andean Pact was one expression of that policy and the Consensus of Viña del Mar another. With respect to the latter, Chile seized the leadership in presenting to the United States for the first time collective and comprehensive Latin American demands devised in an independent forum.[42]

The U.S. responses to the Chilean reformist government of Eduardo Frei came closer to meeting the ideals of the Alliance for Progress than did its responses to most other Latin American governments. The United States provided relatively large long-term loans and Frei began social reforms, even if they fell far short of his own and the Alliance's original goals. Frei's close relations with the Johnson administration ruled out close collaboration with Great Power rivals of the United States, and clearly no strategic threat was ever posed. Moreover, Frei's interest in working with rather than against U.S. private interests ruled out serious friction in the private sector.

Conclusions.   United States responses to the reformist governments of Bosch and Belaunde had much in common with U.S. responses to the reformist governments discussed in chapter 3 and summarized in chapter 7 (proposition 2). In both sets of cases, U.S. responses tended to be shaped in large measure by U.S. private interests. The impact of U.S. business interests was probably greater in Peru where new commitments for economic assistance were suspended for two years in an effort to prevent nationalization of the IPC properties. The United States had less direct investment in the Dominican Republic than in Peru, but Bosch's refusal to grant a concession to Standard Oil and his interests in agrarian reform were unwelcome in the U.S. embassy and in Washington.

Vested public as well as private interests also helped shape the responses in both countries. In the Dominican Republic, U.S. balance of payments problems contributed to the relatively little assistance extended to Bosch, and U.S. labor and other policies hampered Bosch's efforts to build a mass political following. In Peru the flow of U.S. economic assistance to Belaunde was slowed by U.S. congressional restrictions on Peruvian expenditures for expensive military aircraft.

United States responses to Bosch and Belaunde, although not so hostile as the U.S. ambassadors' policies toward Madero and Arévalo earlier, had a destructive impact. United States official fears and criticisms, cultivated by special interests and intensified by policy conflicts, were evidence of resistance within the Inter-American system to the innovations the reformist governments sought to effect. As a result, while the rhetoric of the Alliance for Progress called for strong support for popularly elected, reform-oriented governments, the United States provided relatively little material or moral support to Bosch and Belaunde and appears to have contributed to their vulnerability to military coups.

United States responses to the Frei government in Chile did not follow the patterns of the other reformist governments discussed elsewhere on these pages; the United States appeared to be doing its utmost to provide Chile with morale and material support. Implementation of Alliance for Progress policies in this respect was easier in Chile than in the Dominican Republic or Peru because Frei decided to collaborate closely with U.S. private interests, especially in copper, and because providing him support was perceived as the best means of checking the influence of his Socialist and Communist opposition.

Nixon: Contrasting Patterns

By the time Richard Nixon became president, many of the popularly elected governments seeking social reform, which had been the great hope of the Alliance for Progress, had been succeeded by authoritarian regimes. The Alliance's original preoccupation with social reform in the early part of the Kennedy administration had subsided rapidly under President Johnson and was nonexistent under President Nixon. Most of the guerrilla movements in Latin America had also been defeated by 1969.

As a result, coping with rebel movements and reformist governments was not a major item on the Nixon administration's Latin American agenda. However, the new president did have to face governments in Peru and Chile bent on introducing revolutionary changes. The military leaders, who overthrew President Belaunde of Peru in a palace coup in October 1968, began a revolution characterized by nationalistic defense of Peru's interests with respect to foreign powers and by the introduction of sweeping domestic changes especially regarding government control of national resources, agrarian reform, and centrally planned economic development. The nationalization of IPC properties in northern Peru on October 9, 1968, meant, for example, that on assuming office Nixon faced a major challenge to established U.S. policy on expropriations.

The election of Salvador Allende backed by a Marxist coalition as president of Chile in late 1970 was perceived initially in the United States as marking the biggest crisis in U.S.–Latin American relations since the Dominican revolt of 1965. Allende promptly began to nationalize major U.S. investments, redistribute agricultural lands, revolutionize Chilean social institutions, and reorient Chilean foreign policy.

The Nixon administration initially reacted in similar fashion toward both Peru and Chile, introducing a policy of economic denial, that is, sponsoring cutbacks in U.S. bilateral economic assistance and loans by international agencies. In the case of Peru, the most serious issues were eventually resolved in a negotiated settlement announced in February 1974. The Nixon administration's policies toward Chile went in the opposite direction, particularly after an impasse over the expropriation of U.S. properties. As President Ford subsequently admitted, the United States provided covert support to opposition political parties, whose conflicts with Allende ultimately came to a climax in September 1973. At that point the armed forces overthrew the government and Allende was killed in the Presidential Palace.

Although many questions remain unanswered, preliminary explanations may be offered as to why the United States responded to revolutionary change in Peru in a conciliatory way and in Chile by supporting opposition groups against the beleaguered president. As previous chapters have indicated, U.S. responses to revolutionary governments in Mexico, Bolivia, Guatemala, and Cuba were explained partly in terms of U.S. fears about their ties with hostile Great Powers, either Germany or the Soviet Union. Similarly, the Nixon administration was concerned about the possible ties with the USSR of the new revolutionary governments in Peru and Chile.

Soviet Ties

The initial grounds for U.S. uneasiness were that both governments moved to strengthen their political and economic ties with socialist countries almost immediately. Peru established diplomatic relations with the USSR in 1969, with Communist China in 1971, and with Cuba in 1972. The Peruvian government also entered into trade and credit agreements with several socialist countries.[43] Chile under Frei had already established diplomatic relations with the Soviet Union, but Allende did so with Cuba in 1970 and with China in 1971. The USSR and other socialist countries began to provide Allende with long-term loans. Following socialist models (at least in part), the new Peruvian and Chilean governments favored more centralized economic planning and controls over the economy, greater restriction on foreign investment, the nationalization of mining and other important properties, and foreign policies generally less responsive to U.S. influence.

Peru was a cause of far less concern than Chile. While explicitly opposing Peruvian dependence on "capitalism," the Velasco government also spoke out openly against Communist ideologies and policies.[44] It was clear almost from the beginning that the Velasco government, some of whose members had crushed the Peruvian guerrillas several years earlier, opposed rather than supported the international Communist movement. The Nixon administration had no grounds to perceive the Velasco government as falling under Soviet control.

Well aware of U.S. sensitivity on strategic questions and Chile's vulnerability to U.S. sanctions whether economic or military, Allende sought to reassure the United States about his independence of Great Power control from whatever source. In an interview with the *New York Times* in early 1971, Allende declared that he would never provide a military base that might be used against the United States, nor permit Chile to be used for such purposes by any foreign power.[45] He also denied that the Chilean Revolution should be copied by other countries in South America. When visiting Chile in late 1971, Castro denied that violence was the only road to revolution and reportedly advised Allende not to provoke U.S. reprisals.[46]

Socialist countries reportedly extended about $450 million in credits to the Allende government through 1972.[47] Much of this was tied to purchases in the socialist countries and was associated with projects requiring several years. The result was that much of this sum was never drawn down. The USSR is not known to have provided Allende with any military assistance.

In early 1973 a high State Department official, although reaffirming Soviet interest and ties with the Allende government, expressed the view that the Soviet Union was being "quite circumspect" in relations with Chile, that it had not embraced the Allende government and was not pursuing an "aggressive role" there.[48] One reason for U.S. confidence on that point was that the ultimate arbiters of Chile's fate during the Allende years were the Chilean armed forces, whose officers had apparently convinced the U.S. government that they would not permit Chile to fall under Soviet control. Evidence of U.S. confidence in that respect was the substantial military assistance extended to the armed forces during Allende's administration, an amount which eventually exceeded on an annual basis that provided to the Frei government.[49] Most important, the United States was developing increasingly close relations with the USSR in the era of détente.

Thus, fears of Soviet imperialism were less important in U.S. relations with the Velasco and Allende governments than they had been in relations with the revolutionary governments in Guatemala and Cuba. Other major considerations must have shaped the Nixon administration's responses.

Peru

Conflict over the expropriation of U.S.-owned properties was the central issue in U.S. relations with the Peruvian revolutionary government. Objections to Belaunde's agreement with the IPC were the pretext for Belaunde's overthrow. His successor, General Juan Velasco, seized the IPC's properties shortly after coming to power. The Peruvian government refused to compensate the company on the grounds that it owed the government $690 million for crude oil extracted under an invalid title and with invalid tax arrangements.[50] That amount exceeded the value of the property. The Velasco government later took land under the agrarian reform decree[51] and certain other properties from W. R. Grace and other U.S. companies. It also seized telephone properties belonging to the International Telephone and Telegraph Corporation, later buying out ITT's interests in a negotiated settlement.[52]

The Peruvian expropriation of IPC was among the first problems that the new Nixon administration was forced to deal with on assuming office in 1969. The question promptly arose whether the Nixon administration would invoke the Hickenlooper Amendment requiring the president to cut off economic assistance and sugar quotas to governments failing to take appropriate steps to provide compensation for expropriated properties where at least 50 percent of the property was owned by U.S. citizens. Although the Nixon administration avoided formally invoking the amendment on a technicality, "the foreign aid program to Peru simply died quietly."[53] Loans from the United States and from international agencies in which the United States had an important voice fell far below the levels they had reached under Belaunde when loan slowdowns or suspensions were not in effect.

The United States continued to follow the spirit if not the letter of the Hickenlooper Amendment for several years. Then, in 1972, U.S. bilateral assistance to Peru rose, much of it for relief following the Peruvian earthquake.[54] Thus, in spite of disagreements between Washington and Lima on a number of other issues (such as fishing and arms purchases), the Peruvian government appeared to have convinced the United States that it would not serve as an anti-American pawn in the East-West conflict and that it genuinely sought to attract foreign capital, albeit on its own terms. Meanwhile, too, sharper conflict had begun between neighboring Chile and the United States. There were grounds for speculation that the Nixon administration wished to reinforce the greater responsiveness of Velasco, in contrast to that of Allende, through more flexible policies on economic assistance toward Peru than Chile.

On February 19, 1974, the two governments reached agreements on the dispute over Peruvian expropriations of U.S.-owned property, arranged in part by a New York banker, James Greene. Peru authorized remittances of $74 million to five companies, including the Cerro Corporation, W. R. Grace, and H. J. Heinz. Cerro received $67 million of this amount on condition that Peru receive $38.5 million blocked abroad. Another $76 million was paid to the U.S. government for distribution to these and other U.S. claimants. Funds for payment were obtained from loans from the First National Bank of Boston.[55] Reports at the time of signature suggested that large loans by the Export-Import Bank, the World Bank, the Inter-American Development Bank, and private U.S. banks would follow the agreement.

The most interesting aspect of the bilateral agreement relates to the IPC claim. In a joint statement issued six months earlier, in August 1973, the two governments explicitly ruled out the IPC case as a subject of the negotiations. In addition, the Peruvian government listed in Annex A to the February 1974 agreement the companies covered, and the IPC was not included. Nonetheless, Article III of the agreement provided that the distribution of the $76 million should fall within the "exclusive competence of the Government of the United States," and Annex B to the agreement stipulated that the Peruvian government's statement in Annex A should not otherwise modify the agreement. On December 19, 1974, the Department of State paid Esso Standard $22 million for the expropriation of the IPC and distributed the balance of the $76 million to other claimants, such as W. R. Grace, Cerro de Pasco, and Star Kist Foods. Since the agreement was signed, loans mounting into the hundreds of millions of dollars have been extended to Peru by various national and international agencies and private banks.[56]

Chile

Just as the expropriation of the IPC was the major but not the sole difficulty in U.S. relations with Velasco in Peru, the seizure of the copper mines was a grave issue in U.S. relations with Allende in Chile. The largest copper properties nationalized belonged to Kennecott and Anaconda, whose claims against Chile mounted into the hundreds of millions of dollars. The Allende government refused to pay these corporations on the grounds that excess profits removed from the country earlier exceeded valid claims. The Allende government also took over under a variety of arrangements most of the remaining U.S. investments, including the telephone company controlled by ITT, banks, and manufacturing concerns. Cash payments and deferred compensation were arranged for some of these expropriations as part of negotiated settlements; but many of the owners who accepted the government's terms did so unhappily, claiming privately that the negotiations occurred under conditions of duress.

In early 1973 a high State Department official reported that the Chilean government had taken over about $680 million book value of U.S. private investment in Chile.[57] This included about $400 million of nationalized copper properties, $70 million of "bought out" mineral, manufacturing, and other properties, and $210 million "intervened or requisitioned" properties, including movie distributorships and manufacturing concerns. He estimated that about twelve to thirteen other U.S. companies valued at about $70 million remained in Chile.

As a result of these seizures, the Nixon administration reasserted U.S. policy with respect to expropriations in general and to Chile in particular. In a formal statement on January 24, 1972, President Nixon said that the United States would not extend new bilateral economic benefits to countries that expropriate U.S. properties "until it is determined that a country is taking reasonable steps to provide adequate compensation or that there are major factors affecting U.S. interests which require continuance of all or part of these benefits." He added that "the United States government will withhold its support from loans under consideration in multilateral development banks."[58] With respect to Chile, President Nixon explicitly linked bilateral and multilateral assistance to Allende's expropriation without compensation of certain U.S.-owned copper companies. In describing the expropriations as "not encouraging," he maintained, "We and other public and private sources of development investment will take account of whether or not the Chilean Government meets its international obligations." An interesting aspect of this statement was his assertion that U.S. relations with Chile's leaders would "not hinge on their ideology [which is] frankly in conflict with ours [but on] their conduct towards the outside world."[59]

Meanwhile, the United States claimed to be pursuing a policy of open communications with Chile, or as President Nixon put it, "We are prepared to have the kind of relationship with the Chilean government that it is prepared to have with us."[60] The administration rather consistently attempted to assert its flexibility toward Chile and particularly Chile's right to conduct its own internal affairs, while in fact there were intermittent signs that some officials, at least, were hostile toward Allende. Dr. Kissinger was reported to have been the official in an off-the-record press briefing in September 1970 who said Allende's election would pose a threat to Chile's neighbors.[61] President Nixon did not congratulate Allende on his election to office. The visit of the U.S. chief of naval operations to Chile was canceled under awkward circumstances. White House aides Herbert G. Klein and Robert H. Finch were reported to have the feeling that Allende "won't last long."[62] Other dramatic signs of U.S. hostility were various discussions conducted between representatives of ITT and high Nixon administration officials. Company and Government officials exchanged views and made proposals for covert activities to prevent Allende from taking office or, later, to precipitate his fall from office.[63] United States hostility to Allende was reflected in its economic policies toward Chile and in covert operations there.

United States measures contributed in an important way to decline in the Chilean economy. Massive U.S. economic assistance to the Frei government (1964–1969), mainly in the form of long-term loans, resulted in a huge foreign indebtedness, some $3 billion by late 1971. About $864 million was owed to U.S. government agencies and $493 million to U.S. private creditors.[64] The Allende government had to generate several hundred million dollars a year in foreign exchange to meet payments on that debt, a large portion of which fell due in the early 1970s.

The United States took several steps which were damaging to the Chilean economy. First, when Allende became president, the United States discontinued most new economic assistance to Chile, sharply cutting back a major source of foreign exchange. Note in table 13 that U.S. economic assistance fell from about $80 million in the fiscal year ending in June 1969, Frei's last in office, to less than $9 million in fiscal year 1971. The freeze also applied to credits from the Export-Import Bank to finance Chilean purchases in the United States, deferred on the explicit grounds that satisfactory arrangements to compensate the U.S. copper companies had not been made.[65] Allende did not insist that the United States had an obligation to provide him with economic assistance, but its sharp reduction faced his government with cruel alternatives. Even under Frei, U.S. economic assistance had largely provided the margin to make debt service possible.

Second, the United States also used its influence to reduce economic assistance to Chile from international agencies. Such assistance dropped from $49 million in fiscal year 1969 to $9.4 million in fiscal year 1973,[66] attributed in part to plausible questions about Chile's credit worthiness. Chilean representatives at the Inter-American Development Bank, supported by Peru, were especially incensed that U.S. influence, including its veto power, deprived the government of loans from a bank in which it had invested capital.[67]

TABLE 13

U.S. AND INTERNATIONAL ASSISTANCE TO CHILE
(U.S. Dollars, Millions; Fiscal Years)

	1964	1965	1966	1967	1968	1969	1970	1971	1972	1973
U.S. assistance										
Total economic	127.1	130.4	111.4	238.1	96.3	80.3	26.3	8.6	9.0	3.8
Loans	112.9	110.6	100.6	224.8	83.5	71.0	15.0	—	1.6	—
Grants	14.2	19.8	10.8	13.3	12.8	9.3	11.3	8.6	7.4	3.8
Total military	9.0	9.9	10.2	4.2	7.8	11.7	0.8	5.7	12.3	15.0
International organizations										
World Bank (IBRD)	22.6	4.4	2.7	60.0	—	11.6	19.3	—	—	—
International Finance Corporation	—	0.3	1.2	—	—	—	10.9	—	—	—
Inter-American Development Bank	16.6	4.9	62.2	31.0	16.5	31.9	45.6	12.0	2.4	5.2
United Nations	2.2	2.8	5.9	2.9	2.9	5.5	0.6	3.4	6.1	4.2
Total international organizations	41.4	12.4	72.0	93.8	19.4	49.0	76.4	15.4	8.5	9.4

SOURCES: 1964-1965, Agency for International Development, U.S. Overseas Loans and Grants from International Organizations, July 1, 1945–June 30, 1971 (Washington, D.C., 1972), p. 40; 1966–1972, ibid., July 1, 1945–June 30, 1972 (Washington, D.C., 1973), pp. 42, 181; 1973, ibid., July 1, 1945–June 30, 1973 (Washington, D.C., 1974), pp. 41, 183.

Third, the United States was slow to respond when the Allende government, unable to make payments, declared a moratorium on the foreign debt in November 1971. Although Chile negotiated the new repayment arrangements with its creditors, including the United States, in the Paris Club, and the agreement was implemented with several European creditors, it was not implemented with the United States.[68]

The Chilean economy suffered also as a result of measures taken by private foreign corporations. Short-term credit provided by U.S. banks dried up. Chile did succeed in securing substitute short-term credits from several European countries, but total availability of such credits as well as the amounts actually drawn down declined sharply.[69] In addition, the Kennecott Corporation took its case with respect to compensation into French and other European courts and managed to tie up Chilean copper receipts and discourage Western European purchasers. Chilean sales were thus a problem, but maintaining copper production for export was even more difficult. These various factors affected Chile's capacity to import needed items such as spare parts, raw materials, and medicine.

Political and social conflict in Chile grew increasingly intense during the opening months of 1973 as class antagonisms intensified throughout Chilean society. The breakdown of the economy was painfully apparent. Nationalization of industry and agrarian seizures seriously shook the economy. Some of the symptoms included the fall of output with concomitant shortages and price distortions, runaway inflation which eventually exceeded 300 percent for the year, and the collapse of Chile's economic relations with other countries. The domestic struggle over the control of property and the distribution of income surged toward a climax. And the financial measures taken by U.S. officials and U.S. companies described above helped intensify the economic crisis, thereby feeding the massive social unrest which preceded Allende's fall.

Covert activities of the United States in Chile, as well as the policy of economic denial, hurt Allende. William E. Colby, the director of the Central Intelligence Agency (CIA), was reported to have told the House Armed Services Subcommittee on Intelligence in April 1974 that the CIA provided $8 million to opposition groups in Chile.[70]

On September 16, 1974, President Gerald Ford admitted at a press conference: "The effort that was made in this case [Chile] was to help and assist the preservation of opposition newspapers and electronic media and to preserve opposition political parties. I think this is in the best interest of the people in Chile, and certainly in our best interest."[71] Accordingly, the president's own testimony confirms that the United States conducted a covert policy of political interference in Chile.

Persuasive evidence has also come to the light that CIA funds paid to opposition political groups, or possibly private corporations, made their way to the truck drivers and other strikers and demonstrators whose activities were so important in precipitating the national political crisis that preceded the military coup.[72] Confirmation is needed about the amounts, channels, and significance of these alleged transfers.

This evidence raises the question whether CIA activities were designed to protect the multiparty system and a free press in Chile, as President Ford has indicated, or to help overthrow Allende. It seems certain that many U.S. officials, particularly in the State Department, though not wishing to see Allende expand his political support, preferred that he survive until the next presidential elections, when he would be succeeded by an opposition candidate. It is not clear, however, that this was the dominant view of the U.S. government, particularly of the administration's officials who authorized CIA interference in Chile.

In the light of the various U.S. official measures unfriendly to Allende, the *intent* of U.S. actions seems far less important than their *effect*. If U.S. funds did reach the strikers and demonstrators, as now seems likely, they clearly had a subversive effect.

President Ford, Secretary Kissinger, and other U.S. officials have consistently denied that the United States had "involvement in anyway whatsoever in the coup itself."[73] By this they probably mean that U.S. officials did not help plan, initiate, or conduct the military operations that overthrew Allende. In the absence of information to the contrary, these denials are plausible. In the first place, the Chilean armed forces did not need external assistance to overthrow Allende, as events proved; nor did they lack reasons of their own for overthrowing him. Second, there are many obvious reasons why U.S. officials would not want to be closely associated with any such effort, particularly since their help was not needed. What was most important was the Chilean military leaders' certainty, which was confirmed later, that the United States would welcome Allende's fall and cooperate with the successor government.

So much public attention has been devoted to CIA activities in Chile that it is necessary to keep in perspective the role of U.S.-Chilean relations in Allende's fall. Chilean society became sharply polarized toward the end of the Allende administration, and there was widespread opposition to his continuing in office in many sectors of the population. And of course, it was the Chilean armed forces which actually overthrew him. The extent to which U.S. policies contributed to his fall is difficult, probably impossible, to measure. My view is that domestic factors were primarily responsible for the coup, but that U.S. policies, even if playing only a minor role, might have made the difference between Allende's demise or survival until the next election. We will never know for sure.

Responses Explained

Much remains to be made public about the Nixon administration's relations with the revolutionary governments in Peru and Chile so explanations of what happened must remain tentative. Since it may take a long time to learn the full story, it seems worthwhile to attempt preliminary explanations about why the Nixon administration opposed Allende and compromised with Velasco.[74]

Expropriations of U.S. direct private investment was the most prominent public issue in U.S. relations with the two governments (proposition 5). Both expropriated and refused to pay compensation for the largest U.S. investments in their respective countries, the IPC oil properties in Peru and most of the U.S. copper properties in

United States presidential emissary, John N. Irwin (left), with Peruvian President Juan Velasco Alvarado in Lima, Peru, April 1969. (Wide World Photos)

James Greene, chief U.S. negotiator, speaks at the signing of the general settlement between the United States and Peru, February 1974.

Salvador Allende, president of Chile, 1970–1973, at a press conference at the United Nations, New York, with his minister of foreign affairs, Clodomiro Almeyda (left), and a UN official. (United Nations)

Chile. Velasco and Allende also expropriated other U.S. properties and negotiated compensation settlements. Allende expropriated a larger number of U.S. firms than Velasco but also negotiated more compensation agreements. Even so, in 1973 there were a number of unsettled claims in both countries, in addition to the more dramatic disputes over oil and copper.

Would it be fair to say that the United States came to terms with Peru and not with Chile because Velasco demonstrated more willingness to negotiate than Allende? Without access to the records of the negotiations, it is hard to say. It appears that Allende would have welcomed a negotiated settlement because his domestic political position was weaker and he was extremely vulnerable to U.S. economic and political sanctions. This hypothesis is born out by the relatively large number of compensation agreements he negotiated before his fall.

Nevertheless, Allende's policies posed a greater threat to U.S. companies than Velasco's. First, Allende was moving toward full socialism and was expropriating more firms than Velasco. Velasco favored maintaining a dynamic private sector, and his government energetically sought foreign capital to develop certain branches of the economy under government regulations. Companies still had the opportunity to make large profits in Peru. Second, Allende's revolutionary reorganization of society and the downward trends in that economy, whatever their causes, made Chile far less attractive to U.S. investors. Thus, however much Allende might have wished to blunt U.S. hostility and to work out compensation arrangements in order to do so, he did not have anything like Velasco's capacity to make such compensation effective. Peru's policies on foreign investment tended to isolate the IPC. Whereas there were some U.S. investors who wished to work with Velasco, U.S. business sentiment was almost uniformly critical of Allende. As a result, Allende was viewed as posing a greater threat to U.S. private interests than Velasco. The influence those interests exercised on U.S. policies was indicated in an exchange between Congressman Dante Fascell and Deputy Assistant Secretary of State for American Republic Affairs, John Crimmins:

> FASCELL: The issue is who is making foreign policy. If private enterprise is to continue to be the flag carrier of U.S. foreign policy, then it is inevitable that whenever there is a dispute the U.S. government will be subrogated to whatever the problem is. That has been the difficulty, has it not?
> CRIMMINS: Yes.[75]

To what extent did strategic considerations account for tensions between Washington and Santiago? Did the Nixon administration fear a Communist beachhead in Chile as much as the Eisenhower administration feared one in Guatemala? Probably not, partly because of Allende's efforts to lay those fears to rest and because of close ties with the Chilean armed forces. Perhaps more importantly, détente and the closer Soviet-American relations which made it possible gave U.S. leaders a greater sense of security with respect to Soviet designs on the hemisphere.

There was, however, another major difference; Castro had not yet come to power in Cuba at the time of the Guatemalan episode. But the Nixon administration had to put up with Chile as one more Marxist government independent of and hostile to the United States. Henry Kissinger appears to have been concerned about any increase in the numbers of such governments in the hemisphere. Cuba was enough. In the revolutionary restructuring of Chilean society and its explicit ties with Cuba, Allende appeared to be following in Castro's footsteps. Kissinger was also reported to have feared that Allende's policies might be contagious among Chile's neighbors in South America.[76]

President Nixon's disclaimer that ideological differences in themselves were not a serious obstacle to friendly relations may have accurately reflected his intentions, but in fact such differences appear to have prejudiced the administration against Allende. Nixon and Kissinger were willing to come to terms with Communists in the Soviet Union and China. The ideology of those two countries was really beyond their reach; nor was there any realistic prospect of unseating either leadership. Chile was different. Nixon might have been willing in a theoretical sense to live with Allende's socialism, but not with Chile's resistance to U.S. policies.

But what could Nixon do about it? United States military intervention in Chile may or may not have been given serious consideration. However, U.S. failures in Vietnam, the widespread popular disillusion with U.S. intervention abroad, and looming economic problems would have made military action in Chile extremely unwise politically. Nonetheless, Allende posed a challenge to U.S. political influence in the hemisphere and a threat to the integrity of the U.S. sphere of influence (proposition 11).

The Nixon administration was far from helpless when it came to opposing this threat to what it apparently viewed as a vital U.S. interest. Allende became president with a slim electoral plurality. He was literally at the mercy of the Chilean military from the day of his inauguration, and the United States moved to strengthen its ties with the armed forces by increasing military assistance. The CIA apparently had maintained close ties with the Christian Democrats and other groups opposed to Allende, and had been committed, at least since the 1964 presidential elections, to preventing his assumption of the presidency. Thus, covert support for the opposition established earlier did not involve creating new networks but simply continuing or modifying old ones. By presumably long established sponsorship of political operations against totalitarian Marxist movements elsewhere in the world, the CIA had developed momentum difficult to check when Marxists won in Chile. The agency appears not to have been able to make the crucial distinction between the earlier totalitarian Marxists and the unique Chilean case in which Allende was freely elected under the constitution and initially, at least, respected representative institutions. In this sense "bureaucratic" considerations with respect to the CIA played a role in Chile, as such considerations with respect to diplomatic and economic officials had in Bolivia (proposition 9).

The situation in Peru was much different. While the revolutionary changes sought by the Peruvian military government were extensive, they were less than in Chile and allowed far greater opportunity for foreign investment. While cordial to Castro and the USSR, the Velasco government maintained greater distance than Allende. Most important, the impetus to Peru's revolution came from the military itself. Unlike Allende, Peru's rulers could count on the loyal support of the armed forces and allowed little or no organized political opposition. With far less political involvement in Peru under Belaunde than in Chile under Frei, the United States had far less capacity to interfere in Peru's domestic affairs than in Chile's.

The Nixon administration appears to have decided to adopt relatively flexible policies toward Peru and more hostile policies toward Chile. Peru was less resistant to U.S. investment, less radical politically, less sympathetic toward Cuba and the Soviet Union, and less critical of U.S. policies. United States leaders may have reasoned that since U.S. interests would not be served by a sharp conflict with both countries, coming to terms with the government that represented the lesser evil would prevent a tight alignment of Peru and Chile against the United States. More important, the revolutionary government in Peru posed a challenge of less magnitude to U.S. political supremacy in the hemisphere than the revolutionary government in Chile (propositions 4 and 11).

These explanations of U.S. responses to the Peruvian and Chilean revolutions conform rather closely to the conclusions reached in chapter 7 about U.S. responses to the other four revolutionary governments. The conditioning factor which is different in the two sets of cases is the international setting. The climaxes of U.S. responses to the four earlier revolutionary governments all occurred at moments of military tensions with a rival Great Power, Germany or the Soviet Union (propositions 3, 4, and 5). In the 1970s détente softened U.S. fears of Soviet penetration in Peru and Chile. Castro's coming to power in Cuba, however, led to the presence in the hemisphere of a Marxist government independent of U.S. influence, and this had never existed before.

Fear of Soviet interference was much more important in shaping U.S. responses to the Guatemalan and Cuban revolutions than it was to the revolution in Chile. With respect to Chile, strategic considerations were relevant not so much in terms of a prospective threat of Soviet aggression or subversion but in terms of sphere-of-influence politics. Allende's links with Castro widened the challenge to U.S. influence from within the hemisphere. In this sense, proposition 11, dealing with the maintenance of U.S. political primacy in the hemisphere, is more applicable to the Chilean case than proposition 4, dealing with fears of Soviet interference. The other relevant propositions in chapter 7 are, in the main, valid in the Peruvian and Chilean cases.

The U.S. settlement with Peru had a good deal in common with the U.S. settlement with Mexico thirty years previously. The Peruvians and Mexicans succeeded in nationalizing the nation's largest oil properties, both with substantial U.S. participation. They agreed to pay compensation (the Peruvians in fact if not always in form) in exchange for long-term credits and other economic inducements.

United States responses to Allende were most similar to its earlier responses to Arbenz in Guatemala. Allende, like Arbenz, had a fairly weak political grip on the country, and the Chilean armed forces were even less reliable than in Guatemala. United States penetration of Chilean society appears to have been greater than in Guatemala. The course of events led to similar results, a barracks coup against the constitutional president. In Guatemala, this was precipitated by a paramilitary action sponsored from abroad, whereas in Chile organized domestic political opposition sparked the coup. The role of U.S. investors in the conflict was similar in both countries. Both societies experienced political polarization during and after the conflict. The successor governments promptly suppressed the remnants of Arbenz's or Allende's forces, moved promptly to reach agreements with U.S. investors whose property had been expropriated, and resumed relations with the U.S. and other foreign governments.

Lessons of History

Analysis of U.S. responses to revolutionary change since 1910 yields useful lessons for both sides, Latin American revolutionaries and U.S. leaders alike. Neither side is likely to escape the repercussions of acts of the other; men representing the often conflicting interests of these constituencies are likely to be facing each other in various countries for generations to come. The mix of programs and tactics on both sides is constantly shifting, but underlying problems and behavior patterns recur.

For revolutionaries the historical record suggests that control over the armed forces is essential to make and sustain a social revolution. The political leaders of all the revolutions that have endured have dominated the military, as in Mexico and Cuba, or were the military, as in Peru. All the other revolutionary regimes were defeated by military coups: Arbenz in Guatemala, Paz Estenssoro in Bolivia, and Allende in Chile. Note, too, that the enduring revolutions in fact, if not always in form, were one-party systems, as in Mexico, Cuba, and Peru. Social revolution in Latin America has not lasted in pluralist societies. Allende's fall to a military coup was a dramatic reaffirmation of what many democratically oriented Latin American leaders had long feared, that rapid social change cannot be achieved in pluralist settings.

Failure to maintain control of the armed forces and the presence of powerful opposition parties have made revolutionary regimes vulnerable to foreign interference. United States political interference was most effective against Arbenz in 1954 and Allende in 1973. United States leaders, however, did not provide effective support to opposition leaders within Cuba in 1960 or in Peru after 1968. They were explicit about their refusal to support opposition to the revolutionary governments in Mexico after 1914. Similarly, U.S. diplomats strongly favored Paz Estenssoro in 1964; the role of the U.S. military in Bolivia at that time, as in the Dominican Republic in 1963, was equivocal. Thus, organized political and military opposition to incumbent revolutionary regimes has presented opportunities for foreign interference, but U.S. officials have not always seized them.

Revolutionary governments in Latin America have seldom been able to count on effective support from extrahemispheric Great Powers. In both world wars Mexico regarded Germany as a most unpromising ally. What we have since learned about German policy confirms the Mexicans' judgment in this respect. Since World War II the Soviet Union appears to have had virtually no significant contact with, much less offered any effective support to, Arbenz in Guatemala or pro-Bosch forces in the Dominican Republic in 1965. Khrushchev's offer to help finance a tin smelter in Bolivia was regarded on all sides as primarily a political gesture rather than a project likely to materialize.

Soviet inability to provide adequate economic assistance to Allende in 1973 when he needed it so desperately spoke loudly to revolutionaries around the world. Like other Great Powers, the Soviet Union puts its own national interests ahead of those of other states, socialist as well as capitalist. Allende's fate had a low priority, strategically and politically, for the USSR, which appears not to have wanted to invest many of its scarce resources in Chile. Perhaps the Soviet government reasoned that if the U.S. government was expected not to interfere in Eastern Europe, then it should not interfere in Chile, particularly when détente represented such an important part of its global policy.

Soviet economic and military assistance to Castro has stood in sharp contrast to the absence of effective Soviet support for other revolutionary governments. But Soviet leaders came to Castro's assistance largely on his initiative, not theirs. Castro used political blackmail effectively to make support of his government essential if the USSR still had aspirations of continuing leadership in the international Communist movement. For the present, however, the Soviet government apparently prefers to regard Castro as an exceptional case. The USSR may come to the rescue of revolutionary movements in the hemisphere in the future, but they cannot afford to count on it.

In the light of these realities, revolutionary regimes may be better off to try to avoid hostile U.S. reactions. The fact that the Mexican, Bolivian, and Peruvian revolutionary movements all succeeded in coming to terms with the U.S. government and received extensive economic assistance shows that reconciliation is by no means impossible. The experience of these revolutionary movements suggests that there are at least two important ways of facilitating reconciliation. The first is to attempt negotiated settlements of disputes over expropriated U.S. investments. United States leaders have not opposed most expropriations in principle. Nor have revolutionary regimes been forced to make huge sacrifices in terms of compensation; such settlements have been accompanied by large loans from U.S. and international agencies as well as private credits. External financing has not only eased the burdens of compensation payments but contributed importantly to national development.

The second way involves convincing U.S. leaders that a collaborative relationship with a revolutionary government is the best way of avoiding the interference of other Great Powers in this hemisphere. Judicious contact with such powers is not ruled out, as the Mexican and Peruvian experiences have indicated, but means need to be found to prevent U.S. leaders from making strategic justifications for interference. Revolutionary governments, such as the one in Bolivia, that have taken full advantage of their opportunities to influence U.S. policy through the press, Congress, and other means have made the most of their opportunities in this and other respects.

It must be admitted that Allende appears to have been aware of these considerations and attempted to take them into account in his relations with the United States. It is still too soon to know for sure why he was unable to prevent U.S. interference. No doubt powerful groups which he counted on for support may have prevented some of the necessary conciliatory gestures or tactics, and, of course, he was a "minority" president who was never really in full control of the Chilean armed forces. Although he negotiated many property settlements, Allende, unlike the Mexicans and Peruvians, alienated virtually the entire international financial community and provided them almost no incentives to urge conciliatory policies on U.S. officials. Allende also happened to be elected president of Chile at a time when the U.S. administration was not in the hands of those likely to understand his point of view, nor for that matter, to check hostile action by such agencies as the CIA.

The extent to which the foregoing considerations about revolutionary movements' strategies vis-à-vis the U.S. government are relevant to the future remains to be seen. In the first place, revolutionary movements were in retreat throughout the Americas in the mid-1970s. Authoritarian military regimes rode the rising waves. Second, the world situation has been changing so rapidly that such Great Powers as the United States and the Soviet Union may no longer be able to act in neighboring countries as they have in the past. A reorientation of U.S. policies in which U.S. officials no longer consider Latin America as part of the U.S. sphere of influence has to be seen to be believed. Such a fundamental change in policy would require comparable changes in U.S. public opinion as well.

History's lessons suggest that U.S. policy makers, like Latin American revolutionaries, also need to face up to realities. United States leaders on the right side of the political spectrum can hardly afford to ignore the claims of revolutionary movements in the idle hope that they will somehow go away. Nor has suppression worked, except in the short run, only postponing the day of reckoning. Recognition must be given to the fact that U.S. private investments and other vested interests in Latin America which stand in the way of social change are potential hostages to revolutionary movements and for this and other reasons are an important U.S. vulnerability.

As for critics of U.S. policy on the left, the claims of U.S. investors abroad can hardly be ignored either—given the history of U.S. relations and the political influence and durability of multinational corporations in the U.S. system. Dismissing property rights does not represent viable public policy as long as prospects for radical changes in that system are as poor as they were in the mid-1970s.

At the same time, U.S. officials violate their public trust when they equate the public interest with specific private interests, but the U.S. government has been deeply involved in U.S. private investment abroad for so long that it cannot detach itself overnight. One possible way out is for them to maintain a certain distance from both U.S. investors and revolutionary governments which threaten the investors' interest, using the great weight of governmental power to encourage negotiated settlements between the parties. Settlements with the revolutionary governments of Mexico in 1941, Bolivia in 1953, and Peru in 1974 show that such a conciliatory role can be successful. Now, too, is the time to review policies on direct private foreign investment which, as a potential source of conflict, may jeopardize U.S. relations in the future.

The fate of the Alliance for Progress shows how difficult it is for the United States to implement and sustain *positive* programs for coping with social change. Developments in the United States and the world since the effective end of the Alliance reduce, if anything, U.S. capacities in this regard. Although the United States has difficulty in taking positive steps, perhaps it can at least avoid errors of commission.

For example, U.S. leaders should take greater care in identifying those governments in Latin America whose survival best suits U.S. national interests. If the United States is unable to support those governments effectively, U.S. officials should at least not undermine them. United States actions contributed to the fall of Madero, threatened Arévalo, and weakened Bosch and Belaunde. All such actions were counterproductive in the sense that these governments better suited U.S. political and economic objectives than the governments which immediately preceded and succeeded them.

Similarly, U.S. leaders should try to minimize the negative impact that U.S. global policies sometimes have on U.S.–Latin American relations. It is, perhaps, unrealistic to expect the United States or any other Great Power to set aside what are perceived as vital security interests and deal with small nations solely on the merits of bilateral relationships. If the cordial bilateral relations must be sacrificed to broader U.S. concerns, then U.S. leaders should try to avoid making the mistakes of the past. The pursuit of global strategies, for example, should not blind them to Latin American realities. Ignorance and fear of a rival Great Power, the Soviet Union, resulted in mistaken U.S. perceptions of external penetration and strategic threats in Guatemala and the Dominican Republic and clouded an objective evaluation of events. Moreover, if global strategies are given priority, as seems certain, then at least Latin American policies should be consistent with these larger strategies. I have argued, for example, that U.S. policies toward Guatemala in 1954 and Cuba in 1960 tended to defeat these goals.

The United States has often brought on itself what it most seeks to avoid, the interference of rival Great Powers in the hemisphere. In this sense, the United States has long been its own worst enemy in Latin America. Latin American governments tend not to appeal to extrahemispheric powers for assistance, especially military assistance, without good reason. Too often that reason has been an effort to maintain their independence in the face of U.S. pressures. The Carranza government in Mexico did not offer submarine bases to imperial Germany in World War I until

Pershing's forces reached deep into Mexico. When Pershing withdrew and U.S. pressures were relaxed, Mexico cooled toward Germany. Similarly, Cárdenas kept open communications with the Nazis in the late 1930s until the Roosevelt administration assured him that the United States would not undertake punitive policies because of the oil expropriations. Mexico subsequently became a loyal U.S. ally in World War II.

Secretary Dulles made a great fuss about the shipment of arms from Eastern Europe to Arbenz in 1954, but the Guatemalan government placed that order as a last resort because the United States had refused to sell arms to Guatemala for years and prevented it from securing them from Western Europe as well. Arbenz needed the arms to protect his government from U.S.-supplied paramilitary forces. The Soviet Union came to Castro's assistance only after U.S. countermeasures guaranteed that only Soviet assistance could save him. Juan Bosch was a firm believer in representative political institutions and a friend of the United States until the Dominican intervention in 1965. It was later that he turned to more authoritarian solutions on the Left.

United States errors in its Guatemalan and Cuban policies contributed to the rise of guerrilla movements in the 1960s. Roving bands overtly hostile to the United States sprinkled the Americas from north to south for the first time in history. Ironically, they too recognized that the United States can be its own worst enemy. Their one hope for victory was that the United States would so expand its suppressive military activities in Latin America (other "Vietnams in the Americas") that the mass popular reaction might ignite liberation movements which would sweep them to power. Luckily for U.S. policies, the guerrillas had little success in attracting mass support or securing assistance from foreign powers. United States-sponsored counterinsurgency programs achieved certain temporary and limited objectives at immense long-term political and other costs.

The history of U.S. responses suggests what is both good policy and good morals, namely, that the U.S. government should not use military or paramilitary forces against its Latin American neighbors, most of whom are largely weak and defenseless. If the United States, given its immense economic and political power, cannot achieve its goals through negotiation, then it probably would be unwise to try to achieve them by the use of force. Force is almost by definition the worst way to resolve conflicting interests because an imposed settlement is inherently unstable in the long term.

Note that the U.S. decisions to use force in Guatemala in 1954, Cuba in 1960 and 1961, and the Dominican Republic in 1965, and what now appears almost certain, its decision to support political subversion in Chile in the early 1970s were all made and implemented exclusively within the executive branch. The president or his immediate subordinates had the power to turn the armed forces or the CIA against Latin American countries without other specific legislative authority. These governmental arrangements facilitated serious abuses of power, however well meaning a particular administration may have been, and argue for the establishment of real rather than nominal congressional oversight.

When international tensions have been low in the past, as in the mid-1970s, private interests, particularly investors, have tended to increase their influence over U.S. policies toward Latin America. Larger national interests toward the area have been neglected or ignored. As a result, the mid-1970s have been a good time to reaffirm the stake in Latin America of U.S. citizens in general, that is, taxpayers, traders, creditors, organized labor, religious organizations, educational institutions, etc., as well as private investors.

If the relaxation of international tensions persists, the presidency and the Congress will have one of their best opportunities in recent history to reexamine and reformulate U.S. policies so that the United States is better able than in the past to come to terms with revolutionary change in Latin America in accordance with broader conceptions of the national interest.

Notes

Index

Notes

The following abbreviations are used throughout the notes:

DS Unpublished documents from the archives of the U.S. Department of State.

FR *Foreign Relations of the United States* (U.S. Government Printing Office: Washington, D.C.) Published annually in one or more volumes. Contains selected documents from the archives of the Department of State. The latest year used here is 1948.

Chapter 1. Introduction: Revolutionary Change

1. Wilbert E. Moore defines social change as "significant alteration of social structures (that is, of patterns of social action and interaction), including consequences and manifestations of such structures embodied in norms (rules of conduct), values, and cultural products and symbols" (*International Encyclopedia of the Social Sciences* [New York, 1968], 14:366. See entry "Social Change").

In its political dimensions, social change involves a redistribution of the capacity of social groups to influence a society's authoritative mechanisms, such as government, the armed forces, and the police. The social groups concerned include, among others, agricultural laborers of various types, urban wage earners, salaried employees, professional persons, and the owners of property. Their respective relations to land and capital, as well as to authoritative decision-making bodies, are of special interest.

2. See James M. Malloy, *Bolivia: The Uncompleted Revolution* (Pittsburgh, 1971), p. 4. Malloy defines revolution as a "form of internal war that results in (a) a redistribution of the capacity of groups to influence a society's authoritative mechanisms; (b) the exclusion of groups with a previously high authoritative capacity from any future access to power; (c) the redefinition of a society's concepts and principles of authority; and (d) a redefinition of the goals which governmental authority usually pursues." Harry Eckstein has defined internal war as denoting "any resort to violence within a political order to change its constitution, rulers or policies." See "On the Etiology of Internal War," *History and Theory*, 4, no. 2 (1965): 133.

A good introduction to theories of revolutions is Lawrence Stone, "Theories of Revolutions," *World Politics*, 18 (January 1966): 159–76. Other basic studies include Crane Brinton, *The Anatomy of a Revolution*, rev. ed. (New York, 1965); James C. Davies, "Toward a Theory of Revolution," *American Sociological Review*, 27, no. 1 (February 1962), 5–19; and Chalmers Johnson, *Revolution and the Social System* (Stanford, 1964) and *Revolutionary Change* (Boston, 1966). See also Eckstein cited above.

3. See table 7, chapter 4.

4. United States direct private investment in Mexico in 1913 totaled $800 million and in Cuba in 1959, $956 million. United States investments in Russia on the eve of World War I were about $59 million and in China in 1940, $47 million.

Accurate figures on U.S. investments in prerevolutionary Mexico are difficult to find. The sum above is from Max Winkler, *Investments of United States Capital in Latin America* (Port Washington, N.Y., 1971), p. 275. See also Luis Nicolau D'Oliver in Daniel Cosío Villegas, *Historia moderna de México, el*

Porfiriato, la vida económica (Mexico, 1965), 7:1154-55. For source of Cuban figures see herein, table 6, note 34, chapter 4.

The Russian figure is from Leonard J. Lewery, *Foreign Capital Investments in Russian Industries and Commerce*, Report of U.S., Department of Commerce, Bureau of Foreign and Domestic Commerce, Miscellaneous Series 124 (Washington, D.C., 1923), pp. 5–6 (117,750,000 rubles converted at $0.5146). The Chinese total is from Robert L. Sammons and Milton Abelson, *American Direct Investments in Foreign Countries, 1940*, Report of U.S., Department of Commerce, Bureau of Foreign and Domestic Commerce, Economic Series 20 (Washington, D.C., 1940), p. 5.

5. See figures on U.S. exports and imports in U.S., Department of Commerce, Bureau of the Census, *Statistical Abstract of the United States 1971*, 92d annual edition (Washington, D.C., 1972), pp. 768–71.

6. Some of the sources in the rapidly growing literature of "dependencia" include: R. H. Chilcote and J. C. Edelstein, *Latin America: The Struggle with Dependency and Beyond* (Cambridge, Mass., 1974); James D. Cockcroft, André Gunder Frank, and Dale L. Johnson, *Dependence and Underdevelopment: Latin America's Political Economy* (New York, 1972); Celso Furtado, *Economic Development of Latin America* (Cambridge, 1970), especially chapters 17 and 18; and Oswaldo Sunkel, "National Development Policy and External Dependence in Latin America," in *Contemporary Inter-American Relations*, ed. Yale H. Ferguson (Englewood Cliffs, N.J., 1972).

7. Morton H. Halperin and Arnold Kanter, *Readings in American Foreign Policy: A Bureaucratic Perspective* (Boston, 1973), pp. 2–3. See also Graham T. Allison, *Essence of Decision: Explaining the Cuban Missile Crisis* (Boston, 1971) and Abraham F. Lowenthal, "United States Policy Toward Latin America: 'Liberal,' 'Radical,' and 'Bureaucratic' Perspectives," *Latin American Research Review*, 8, no. 3 (Fall 1973): 3–25.

8. Robert O. Keohane and Joseph S. Nye, Jr., eds., *Transnational Relations and World Politics* (Cambridge, Mass., 1971), pp. xii ff.

9. Friedrich Katz called my attention to the importance of the fact that the "fear of contagion" distinguishes the post–1945 revolutions from the Mexican Revolution.

Chapter 2. Rebel Movements: Flexibility

1. Fidel Castro, *La historia me absolverá* (Havana, 1961), pp. 59–60.

2. Lee Lockwood, *Castro's Cuba, Cuba's Fidel* (New York, 1969), p. 142. Castro's letter to Celia Sánchez of June 5, 1958, was a rare outburst against North Americans prompted by his seeing U.S.–supplied rockets fired at a friend's house. He said "waging war" against North Americans was his true destiny. This letter was made public in 1967. See Rolando E. Bonachea and Nelson P. Valdés, eds., *Revolutionary Struggle 1947–1958*, vol. 1, *Selected Works of Fidel Castro* (Cambridge, Mass., 1972), p. 379.

3. Lockwood, *Castro's Cuba*, p. 141.

4. Juan José Arévalo, *The Shark and the Sardines* (New York, 1961).

5. Henry Lane Wilson to secretary of state, dispatch, October 31, 1910: DS 812.00/355.

6. See also Henry Lane Wilson to secretary of state, dispatch, April 26, 1911: DS 812.00/1543 and May 23, 1911: DS 812.00/1981.

7. H. F. Pringle, *The Life and Times of William Howard Taft* (New York, 1939), 1: Taft to Helen Taft, October 15, 1909, p. 462.

8. Green H. Hackworth, *Digest of International Law* (Washington, D.C., 1943), 3:394.

9. "The mere fact that a man is engaged in revolutionary undertakings in another country does not render his presence in the United States illegal. . . . the sale of arms and ammunition to individuals, so long as it is not forbidden by our neutrality statutes, does not constitute unneutral conduct. . . . It is not an offense against the United States to transport arms, ammunition, and munitions of war from this country to any foreign country, whether they are to be used in war or not; nor is it an offense against the United States to transport persons out of this country and land them in foreign countries, although such persons have an

intent to enlist in foreign armies; nor is it an offense against the United States to transport from this country persons intending to enlist in foreign armies and munitions of war in the same ship. . . . what it prohibits is a military expedition or a military enterprise from this country against any foreign power at peace with the United States" (*FR, 1911*, p. 397).

10. *FR, 1911*, p. 371.

11. Isidro Fabela, ed., *Documentos históricos de la revolución y régimen maderista* (Mexico, 1965), 5:162.

12. See the carefully documented opinion of Edward J. Berbusse, "United States and Mexico, 1910–1911," *The Americas,* 12, no. 2 (1965): 265–83.

13. Francisco Léon de la Barra, *El internato presidencial de 1911* (Mexico, 1912), p. 10, as quoted by Berbusse, "United States and Mexico."

14. Peter Calvert, *The Mexican Revolution 1910–1914* (Cambridge, 1968), pp. 80 ff.

15. The foregoing interpretation about the financial sources for the Madero revolution follows the argument of Calvert, *The Mexican Revolution,* pp. 73 ff. Calvert's version conflicts with but appears to take fully into account the contrary arguments found in M. S. Alperovich and B. T. Rudenko, *La revolución mexicana de 1910–1917,* 2d ed. (Mexico, 1966), pp. 88 ff.

16. *FR, 1911*, p. 401.

17. Stanley R. Ross, *Francisco I. Madero: Apostle of Mexican Democracy* (New York, 1955), p. 135.

18. *FR, 1911*, p. 437.

19. Jules Dubois, *Fidel Castro: Rebel-Liberator or Dictator?* (Indianapolis, 1959), p. 105.

20. Ibid., pp. 133, 136, and Herbert L. Matthews, *Fidel Castro* (New York, 1969), p. 90.

21. Interview with Ernesto Betancourt, Washington, D.C., June 9, 1970. Mr. Betancourt was a Castro spokesman in Washington before 1959.

22. U.S., Congress, Senate, Subcommittee of the Committee on the Judiciary, *Hearing on State Department Security, Testimony of William Wieland,* 87th Cong., January 9, 1961, pt. 5:554.

23. U.S., Congress, House, *Congressional Record,* 85th Cong., 2d sess., 1958, 104, pt. 4:5497.

24. U.S., Congress, Senate, Committee on the Judiciary, *Hearing on State Department Security,* pt. 5:554.

25. U.S., Congress, Senate, Committee on Foreign Relations, *Hearing on Review of Foreign Policy 1958,* 85th Cong., 2d sess., 1958, pt. 1:359.

26. U.S., Department of State, *American Foreign Policy: Current Documents, 1958,* No. 7322, (Washington, D.C., 1962), p. 343.

27. Dubois, *Fidel Castro,* p. 313.

28. Earl E. T. Smith, *The Fourth Floor* (New York, 1962), p. 144.

29. Ibid., p. 35.

30. Ernesto Che Guevara, *Obra revolucionaria,* 2d ed. (Mexico, 1968), pp. 161, 207.

31. *FR, 1911*, p. xii.

32. *FR, 1911*, p. 432.

33. *FR, 1911*, p. 431.

34. Dispatch 508, April 29, 1911: DS 812.00/1618, to which was attached a clipping from *El Imparcial* of April 27, 1911, containing the quote attributed to Vice-President Corral.

35. Henry Lane Wilson to secretary of state, May 13, 1911: DS 812.00/1874. For a further description of the tensions between the two governments in the spring of 1911 see Daniel Cosío Villegas, *Historia moderna de México: El Porfiriato, la vida política exterior* (Mexico, 1963), pt. 2, pp. 445–75.

36. *FR, 1911*, p. 483.

37. *FR, 1911*, p. 481.

38. Fabela, *Documentos históricos,* 1:367.

39. *FR, 1911*, pp. 495–96. For further information on this period see Berta Ulloa, "Las relaciones mexicano-norteamericanas 1910–1911," *Historia Mexicana,* 15, no. 1 (July–September 1965): 25–46.

40. Smith, *The Fourth Floor,* p. 155.

41. Ibid., p. 60.

42. U.S., Congress, Senate, Committee on the Judiciary, Subcommittee to Investigate the Administration of the Internal Security Act and Other Internal Security Laws, 86th Cong., 2d sess., September 2
and 8, 1960, p.739.

43. Smith, *The Fourth Floor,* p. 182.

44. Bonachea and Valdés, eds., *Revolutionary Struggle,* pp. 354–55.

45. *New York Times,* November 2, 1958, p. 11.

46. Letter from Philip Bonsal, July 31, 1972, and telephone conversation, May 31, 1973, with
William Wieland, who was on the Cuban desk in 1959, correct my earlier version in "The Elimination of
United States Influence," in *Revolutionary Change in Cuba,* ed. Carmelo Mesa-Lago (Pittsburgh, 1971),
p. 48.

47. Dubois, *Fidel Castro,* p. 345.

48. Ibid., pp. 345, 347.

49. Interview with Ernesto Rivas, Guatemala City, July 15, 1969.

50. *FR, 1944,* 7:1132.

51. Ibid., p. 1133.

52. Memorandum, June 26, 1944: DS 814.00/6-2644.

53. Dispatch 1282, July 4, 1944: DS 814.00/7-444.

54. *FR, 1944,* 7:1139.

55. Ibid., p. 1140.

56. Dispatch 1658, October 23, 1944: DS 814.00/10-2344.

57. Ibid.

58. *FR, 1944,* 7:1142–43. The concluding sentence was taken from a telegram sent later the same
evening, p. 1144.

59. For further details, see Cole Blasier, "The United States and the Revolution," in *Beyond the
Revolution: Bolivia Since 1952,* eds. James Malloy and Richard Thorn (Pittsburgh, 1971), pp. 53–109.

60. Cole Blasier, "The United States, Germany, and the Bolivian Revolutionaries (1941–1946),"
Hispanic American Historical Review, 52, no. 1 (February 1972): 26–54.

61. United States relations with the Bolivian revolutionaries were an exception with respect to prompt
recognition. The U.S. nonrecognition policy against the Villarroel government is described in chapter 3.

62. This chapter is based in part on my "Studies of Social Revolution: Origins in Mexico, Bolivia,
and Cuba," *Latin American Research Review,* 2, no. 3 (1967): 28–64. Howard F. Cline encouraged me to
write this, my first article on this theme; and his works, particularly those on Mexico, have been helpful to
me on many occasions.

Chapter 3. Reformist Governments: Hostility

1. Dispatch, July 11, 1911: DS 812.00/2219.

2. See, for example, his candid admission of the use of "work not compatible with my diplomatic
character," (Dispatch, August 28, 1912: DS 812.00/4899).

3. Dispatch, March 26, 1912: DS 812.00/3443.

4. Peter Calvert, *The Mexican Revolution, 1910–1914* (Cambridge, 1968), pp. 121–22. With
respect to the arms embargo of March 12, 1912, Taft frequently made exceptions on shipments to the
Mexican government during Madero's presidential term thereby showing his partiality vis-à-vis the
revolutionary opposition. See Donna Marie Wolf, "American Regulations of Arms Exports to Mexico,
1910–1915" (unpublished manuscript, April 1971), pp. 18 ff.

5. Calvert, *The Mexican Revolution,* pp. 123–24.

6. Friedrich Katz, *Deutschland, Díaz und die mexikanische Revolution: die deutsche Politik in
Mexiko 1870–1920* (Berlin, 1964), p. 214.

7. Telegram, April 3, 1912: DS 812.00/3484A.

8. U.S., Department of State, *Foreign Relations of the United States, 1912* (Washington, D.C.,
1919), pp. 842 ff.

9. *FR, 1912,* pp. 871 ff.

10. Secretary of state to American ambassador, dispatch, February 21, 1913: DS 812.00/6325a.

11. For sources on that visit see Cole Blasier, "The United States and Madero," *Journal of Latin American Studies,* 2 (November 1972): 230.

12. See Katz, *Deutschland, Díaz,* p. 216, and Knox to American ambassador, dispatch, January 7, 1913: DS 312.11/1031c.

13. The text of Madero's wire was reprinted in Henry Lane Wilson, *Diplomatic Episodes in Mexico, Belgium, and Chile* (New York, 1927), p. 234.

14. Dispatch, February 4, 1913: DS 812.00/6068.

15. Telegram, October 23, 1912: DS 812.00/5333.

16. DS 312.11/1048.

17. Knox to Taft, January 27, 1913: DS 812.00/7229A.

18. M. Márquez Sterling, *Los últimos días del presidente Madero,* 2d ed. (Mexico, 1958), p. 183. The section on Madero's overthrow is based on Blasier, "United States and Madero."

19. Telegram to secretary of state, February 15, 1913: DS 812.00/6174.

20. Secretary of navy to secretary of state, February 12, 1913: DS 812.00/6095.

21. Telegram to secretary of state, February 12, 1913: DS 812.00/6192.

22. Katz, *Deutschland, Díaz,* p. 220, using the Hintze diary. See also, "Por la verdad," a confidential statement made by Bernardo J. Cologán y Cologán, the Spanish ambassador, on August 2, 1914. The statement is reprinted in Isidro Fabela, ed., *Documentos históricos de la revolución mexicana* (Mexico, 1965), 5:227.

23. Hintze's diary entry of February 14, as quoted in Katz, *Deutschland, Díaz,* p. 221.

24. Cologán y Cologán, "Por la verdad," in Fabela, *Documentos históricos,* 5:233.

25. For the British version, see Calvert, *Mexican Revolution,* pp. 142–43. For the German minister's statement see telegram to Foreign Office, February 17, 1913, Imperial German Archives.

26. Fabela, *Documentos históricos,* 5:78.

27. February 15, 1913: DS 812.00/612c.

28. Calvert, *The Mexican Revolution,* p. 138; Katz, *Deutschland, Díaz,* p. 223; and Fabela, *Documentos históricos,* 5:85.

29. Manuel Bonilla, Jr., *El regimen maderista* (Mexico, 1962), p. 178; *Memorias del general Victoriano Huerta* (Mexico, probably 1915), pp. 21 ff; Kenneth J. Grieb, *The United States and Huerta* (Lincoln, Nebr., 1969), p. 14; Sterling, *Los últimos días,* p. 195.

30. Wilson to secretary of state, February 9, 1913: DS 812.00/6058.

31. Report of President Woodrow Wilson's confidential agent, William Bayard Hale, June 13, 1913, pp. 10-12: DS 812.00/7864 1/2.

32. Wilson to secretary of state, February 17, 1913: DS 812.00/6225.

33. See note 31, passim.

34. Wilson to secretary of state, February 18, 1913: DS 812.00/6246.

35. Katz, *Deutschland, Díaz,* p. 218.

36. Wilson to secretary of state, February 23, 1913: DS 812.00/6325.

37. Wilson to secretary of state, February 19, 1913: DS 812.00/6271.

38. Two messages from the Department of State to Mexico City, February 12, 1913, and a message on February 14, 1913: DS 812.00 Documents 6092, 61770A, and 1073.

39. Secretary of state to Wilson, February 12, 1913: DS 812.00/6092.

40. Secretary of state to Wilson, February 14, 1913: DS 812.00/6149.

41. Secretary of state to Wilson, February 20 and 21, 1913: DS 812.00/6271 and DS 812.00/6294A.

42. A good case can be made for considering the military socialist governments of David Toro (1936–1937) and Germán Busch (1937–1939) as reformist governments, that is, as representing the same phase in the Bolivian revolutionary process. I have not so classified them here partly because military dominance was even more marked than under Villarroel. Also, the young men who later came to lead the classic Bolivian revolutionary movement, the MNR, were less influential earlier than under Villarroel.

43. Cole Blasier, "The United States, Germany, and the Bolivian Revolutionaries (1941–1946)," *Hispanic American Historical Review,* 52, no. 1 (February 1972): 26–54.

44. For further information on the Standard Oil dispute and settlement see Bryce Wood, *The Making of the Good Neighbor Policy* (New York, 1961), chapter 7.

45. The text of Galarza's letter to Sumner Welles was carried in *The Nation,* January 9, 1943, p. 59. See in the same issue, "Did Hull and Welles Tell the Truth?," pp. 42–44. See also Carlton Beals, "Inside the Good Neighbor Policy," *Harper's* (August 1943), pp. 213–21.

46. *FR, 1943,* 5:536.

47. *FR, 1944,* 7:431 ff. For original see DS 824.00/1491.

48. *FR, 1944,* 7:445–46.

49. The Villarroel government was bicephalic in the sense that there was a strong military wing and a civilian wing dominated by the MNR. The contradictions between these two factions were sufficiently great as to raise questions about the MNR's continued participation even in the absence of U.S. pressure. Thus, recognition of the Villarroel government should be considered as only one of the factors contributing to the MNR's leaving the cabinet.

50. Víctor Paz Estenssoro, *Discursos parlementarios* (La Paz, 1955), pp. 222–23.

51. Embassy Dispatch 1586, April 29, 1943. This quote was requoted and reaffirmed in Dispatch 3162, February 15, 1944, from La Paz: DS 824.00/1825. The conclusions described above are elaborated in my article on this period (see note 43).

52. U.S., Department of State, *Consultation Among the American Republics with Respect to the Argentine Situation,* Inter-American Series 29, Publication 2473 (Washington, D.C., 1946).

53. Augusto Céspedes, *El presidente colgado* (La Paz, 1966), p. 207. Céspedes, an early leader of the MNR, was a novelist and publicist.

54. *FR, 1946,* 11:376.

55. Ibid.

56. *FR, 1946,* 11:379.

57. Ibid., p. 380.

58. Ernesto Galarza, *The Case of Bolivia,* Inter-American Reports No. 6 (Washington, D.C., 1949).

59. *FR, 1946,* 11:392.

60. Ibid., p. 393.

61. Ibid., p. 352.

62. Ibid., p. 357.

63. Ibid., p. 359.

64. Joseph Flack, "Diary of a Revolution," *Foreign Service Journal,* September 1946, pp. 22 ff.

65. Alfonso Bauer Paiz, *Como opera el capital yanqui en Centroamérica: el consul de Guatemala* (Mexico, 1956), p. 408, table 5.

66. International Bank for Reconstruction and Development, *The Economic Development of Guatemala* (Washington, D.C., 1951), p. 219.

67. Bauer Paiz, *Como opera el capital yanqui,* pp. 55–56. Estrada Cabrera, railroad contract of 1904; José María Orellana, railroad and electric power contracts of 1923; Lázaro Chacón, United Fruit contract of 1930; Jorge Ubico, United Fruit contract of 1936; Carlos Castillo Armas, United Fruit and other contracts with U.S. companies of 1955.

68. Ibid., p. 355.

69. Stacy May and Galo Plaza, *The United Fruit Company in Latin America* (Washington, D.C., 1958), p. 242.

70. Ibid., pp. 229–30. Italics in the original.

71. Ibid., p. 240.

72. Archer C. Bush, *Organized Labor in Guatemala: 1944–1949* (Hamilton, N.Y., 1950), part 4, p. 28.

73. Ronald M. Schneider, *Communism in Guatemala, 1944–1954* (New York, 1958), chapter 4.

74. Bush, *Organized Labor in Guatemala,* pt. 4, pp. 29–30. The CIO, however, got in touch with Pinto Usaga in the summer of 1949 and helped him in a dispute with the United Fruit Company.

75. Bauer Paiz, *Como opera el capital yanqui,* p. 20.

76. Richard N. Adams, *Crucifixion by Power: Essays on Guatemalan National Social Structure, 1944–46* (Austin, Tex., 1970), p. 188.

77. Ibid., p. 189.

78. U.S., Congress, Senate, *Congressional Record,* 81st Cong., 1st sess., XCV, pt. 2:1353. See also *FR, 1947,* VIII:705–19.

79. Interview with Alfonso Bauer Paiz, Guatemala City, July 14, 1969.

80. Ibid.; see also *Business Week,* February 26, 1949, pp. 128–29. Juan José Arévalo alleged that rights to exploit oil were also linked to economic assistance in his *Guatemala: la democracia y el imperio,* 7th ed. (Buenos Aires, 1964), p. 81.

81. Luis Cardoza y Aragón, *La revolución guatemalteca* (Montevideo, 1956), pp. 73, 91.

82. Raúl Osegueda, *Operación guatemala* (Mexico, 1954), pp. 47, 49; see also Guillermo Toriello, *La batalla de Guatemala* (Santiago, Chile, 1955), p. 45.

83. *New York Times,* February 27, 1950, p. 11.

84. *El Imparcial,* April 11, 1950, quoting a statement of the ministry of foreign affairs.

85. Medardo Mejía, *Juan José Arévalo: humanismo en la presidencia* (Guatemala City, 1951), p. 163. Quotes from Arévalo's presidential report for the period beginning March 15, 1950, and ending March 15, 1951.

86. Arévalo, *Guatemala: la democracia,* p. 120. Elaborated and confirmed in a personal interview with Raúl Osegueda, Guatemala City, July 16, 1969.

87. U.S., Department of State, *The Ninth International Conference of American States, Bogotá, Colombia, March 30 to May 2, 1948,* Publication 3263 (Washington, D.C., 1948), p. 86.

88. *Inter-American Conference for the Maintenance of Continental Peace and Security, Quitandinha, Brazil, August 15–December 2, 1947* (Washington, D.C., 1948), p. 79.

89. U.S., Dept. of State, *Ninth International Conference,* p. 216.

90. Arévalo, *Guatemala: la democracia,* p. 120.

91. Ibid., p. 27.

92. *New York Times,* July 18, 1950, p. 6.

93. U.S., Congress, House, *Congressional Record,* 81st Cong., 1st sess., 1949, 95, pt. 2:1464.

94. U.S., Congress, Senate, *Congressional Record,* 81st Cong., 1st sess., 1949, 95, pt. 1:1353.

95. U.S., Congress, Senate, *Congressional Record,* 81st Cong., 1st sess., 1949, 95, pt. 1:1172.

96. U.S., Congress, Senate, *Congressional Record,* 81st Cong., 2d sess., 1950, 96, pt. 5:5880–5881.

97. *New York Times,* April 8, 1950, p. 12; *New York Herald Tribune,* April 16, 1950.

98. G. E. Britnell, "Problems of Economic and Social Change in Guatemala," *Canadian Journal of Economics and Political Science* (November 1951), p. 480.

99. International Bank, *Economic Development,* p. 283.

100. Arévalo, *Guatemala: la democracia,* pp. 230–34.

101. My "United States and Madero," cited above, contends that Ambassador Wilson's involvement in Madero's overthrow was in poorly concealed defiance of U.S. official policy in spite of some conflicting and inconclusive evidence cited in note 82 of that article. Friedrich Katz has since sent me further information suggesting the possibility of the Taft administration's involvement. He considers this evidence inconclusive but said it showed that "the innocence of the Taft administration is somewhat more doubtful than you would imply." Since there is conclusive evidence that Wilson disobeyed Washington's orders about interfering, the original interpretation seems justified to me until there is firm evidence of Washington's actual rather than possible complicity.

I gratefully acknowledge Professor Katz's assistance on this and many other points.

Chapter 4. Seizures of U.S. Properties: Compensation Required

1. Other seizures include that of American and Foreign Power interests in Argentina in 1958 (settled later that year) and of American and Foreign Power and International Telephone and Telegraph interests in Brazil in 1959 and 1962 respectively (both settled in 1963). See Legislative Reference Service, Library of

Congress, for the Committee on Foreign Affairs, *Expropriation of American-Owned Property by Foreign Governments in the Twentieth Century* (Washington, D.C., 1963), pp. 18 ff. See also George Jackson Eder, "Expropriation: Hickenlooper and Hereafter," *The International Lawyer*, 4, no. 4 (July 1970): 612–13.

2. Green H. Hackworth, *Digest of International Law* (Washington, D.C., 1943), 3:656.

3. See, for example, Ibid., 3:652, and Marjorie M. Whiteman, *Digest of International Law* (Washington, D.C., 1967), 8:1085. See also John Basset Moore, *Digest of International Law* (Washington, D.C., 1906), passim. B. A. Wortley gives a list of some precedents before 1914 in *Expropriation of Public International Law* (Cambridge, 1959), pp. 58 ff.

4. Wortley, *Expropriation*, p. 121.

5. The Cuban authority is Miguel A. D'Estéfano Pisani, "Las nacionalizaciones del gobierno revolucionario y el derecho internacional," *Política Internacional*, 1, no. 3 (Havana, 1963): 53, 63, 88. See also Andreas F. Lowenfeld, *Expropriation in the Americas* (New York, 1971). Jorge D. Dominguez describes the Swiss and French settlements in "Taming the Cuban Shrew," *Foreign Policy* (Spring 1973), pp. 101–02.

6. *FR, 1917,* p. 947.

7. Ibid., p. 1072.

8. Frank Tannenbaum, *Mexico: The Struggle for Peace and Bread* (New York, 1950), pp. 140–41. Professor Tannenbaum presents the figures in detail and in authoritative fashion, but no census reference is given.

9. Proceedings of the United States–Mexican Commission convened in Mexico City, May 14, 1923 (Washington, D.C., 1925), passim.

10. A convenient table of land distribution to ejidos based on presidential reports is presented in Frank Brandenburg, *The Making of Modern Mexico* (Englewood Cliffs, N.J. 1965), p. 254.

11. *FR, 1935,* 4:770–76.

12. Josephus Daniels, *Shirt-Sleeve Diplomat* (Chapel Hill, N.C., 1947), p. 234.

13. Ibid., p. 235. Bryce Wood, *The Making of the Good Neighbor Policy* (New York, 1961), pp. 213 ff.

14. E. David Cronon, *Josephus Daniels in Mexico* (Madison, 1960), p. 198. Ramón Beteta, undersecretary of state for foreign affairs, told Cronon that Mexico would have broken diplomatic relations if Ambassador Daniels had presented the note officially. Note also that the Mexicans did break relations with Britain a few weeks later in retaliation for a strong British protest.

15. Ibid., p. 199.

16. *FR, 1938,* 5:713 ff.

17. U.S., *Department of State Bulletin*, November 22, 1941, pp. 400 ff., and *New York Times,* November 20, 1941, p. 1.

18. Wood, *Good Neighbor Policy*, p. 258, and *FR, 1943*, 6:592; see also *New York Times,* October 2, 1943, p. 21.

19. Cronon, *Josephus Daniels,* p. 268, and *FR, 1941,* 7:300–02; see also note 17.

20. José Felman Velarde, *Víctor Paz Estenssoro: El hombre y la revolución* (La Paz, 1954), pp. 88 ff.

21. Wood, *Good Neighbor Policy,* p. 171.

22. Ibid., p. 189.

23. Cole Blasier, "The United States, Germany, and the Bolivian Revolutionaries (1941–1946)," *Hispanic American Historical Review*, 52, no. 1 (February 1972), 32 ff.

24. *New York Times,* April 13, 1952, p. 1.

25. *New York Times,* April 19, 1952, p. 3.

26. Víctor Andrade, *Bolivia: Problems and Promise* (Washington, D.C., 1956), p. 12.

27. *U.S. News and World Report,* June 5, 1953, pp. 69–70.

28. John Moors Cabot, *Toward Our Common Destiny* (Medford, Mass., 1954), p. 186. See also U.S., *Department of State Bulletin,* October 26, 1953, pp. 554–55.

29. Former Bolivian ambassador to the United States, Víctor Andrade, confirmed both conditions in an interview with the author in La Paz, July 27, 1969.

30. U.S., *Department of State Bulletin*, November 2, 1953, pp. 584–87. Bolivian expropriation of the properties of Gulf Oil in 1969 and the subsequent settlement are outside the scope of this study. See George M. Ingram, *Expropriation of U.S. Property in South America, Nationalization of Oil and Copper Companies in Peru, Bolivia, and Chile* (New York, 1974).

31. The text of the Guatemalan note of June 26 was contained in Guillermo Toriello, *La batalla de Guatemala* (Santiago, Chile, 1955), pp. 171 ff. The text of the U.S. note of August 28 is contained in U.S., *Department of State Bulletin*, September 14, 1953, pp. 357 ff.

32. U.S., *Department of State Bulletin*, May 3, 1954, p. 678.

33. Note of the Guatemalan government of May 24, 1954, to the U.S. government, in Toriello, *La batalla*, p. 176.

34. Ibid., pp. 175–77.

35. Luis Cardoza y Aragón, *La revolución guatemalteca* (Montevideo, 1956), p. 30. According to a U.S. source, *Area Handbook for Guatemala* (Washington, D.C., 1970), p. 274, United Fruit lands represented less than 40% of the lands expropriated.

36. Stacy May and Galo Plaza, *The United Fruit Company in Latin America* (Washington, D.C., 1958), p. 164.

37. Philip W. Bonsal, *Cuba, Castro, and the United States* (Pittsburgh, 1971), p. 47.

38. Ibid., pp. 72–73.

39. U.S., *Department of State Bulletin*, June 29, 1959, p. 958.

40. Bonsal, *Cuba, Castro*, p. 74.

41. Ibid., pp. 117–18.

42. The October 12 note was not published, but for the ambassador's official statement see U.S., *Department of State Bulletin*, November 16, 1959, pp. 715 ff.

43. Ibid., February 1, 1960, p. 158.

44. Ibid., February 15, 1960, pp. 237 ff.

45. Bonsal, *Cuba, Castro*, p. 97.

46. *Revolución*, June 25, 1960, and U.S. Department of Commerce, *Balance of Payments, Statistical Supplement, 1961* (Washington, D.C., 1961), p. 215.

47. U.S., *Department of State Bulletin*, August 1960, p. 171.

48. Ibid., August 29, 1960, p. 316, and October 17, 1960, p. 604.

49. Foreign Claims Settlement Commission of the United States, *Annual Report to the Congress for the Period January 1–December 31, 1971* (Washington, D.C., 1972), p. 35.

50. What constitutes fair and adequate compensation will continue to be subject to dispute. Some settlements cover interest, others do not. Some are based on book value rather than market value which might be much higher. The fact that a negotiated settlement is reached does not necessarily indicate that compensation is "fair." For views often expressed by claimants see Eder, "Expropriation: Hickenlooper and Hereafter."

51. Wood, *Good Neighbor Policy*, p. 194.

52. Marina Von Neumann Whitman, *Government Risk-Sharing in Foreign Investment* (Princeton, N.J., 1965), pp. 84 ff.

53. Agency for International Development, *Operations Report* (Washington, D.C., 1971), pp. 124–25 (data as of June 30, 1971).

54. U.S., Congress, House, Hearings before the Subcommittee on Inter-American Affairs of the Committee on Foreign Affairs, *Recent Developments in Chile, October 1971*, 92nd Cong., 1st sess., October 15, 1971, pp. 6–7.

55. Albert O. Hirschman, *How to Divest in Latin America and Why*, Princeton University, Essays in International Finance, no. 76 (Princeton, N.J., 1969), pp. 8, 9, and passim.

56. Ibid., p. 9.

57. Statement of January 19, 1972, *Weekly Compilation of Presidential Documents*.

58. *Survey of Current Business* (November 1972), p. 24.

59. For additional information on seizures of U.S. property see Ingram, *Expropriation of U.S. Property in South America* and Eric N. Baklanoff, *Expropriations of U.S. Investments in Cuba, Mexico, and Chile* (New York, 1975). Both are from Praeger Publishers.

Chapter 5. Mexico and Bolivia: Reconciliation

1. Ray Stannard Baker and William E. Dodd, eds., *The Public Papers of Woodrow Wilson*, vol. 1, *The New Democracy* (New York, 1925), pp. 111–12. Also quoted by P. Edward Haley, *Revolution and Intervention: The Diplomacy of Taft and Wilson with Mexico, 1910–1917* (Cambridge, Mass., 1970), p. 137.

2. José Vasconcelos, "A Mexican's Point of View," in J. Fred Rippy, et al., *American Policies Abroad: Mexico* (Chicago, 1928), pp. 104–05.

3. Secretary of state to U.S. embassies accredited to certain foreign powers, November 24, 1913, as quoted by Arthur S. Link, *Wilson: The New Freedom* (Princeton, N.J., 1956), p. 387.

4. Robert E. Quirk, *An Affair of Honor* (Lexington, Ky., 1962), p. 75.

5. Carranza's letter to González Gante of May 14, 1913, informing of the issuance of the decree, as quoted in Isidro Fabela, ed., *Documentos históricos de la revolución mexicana: revolución y régimen constitutionalista* (Mexico, 1960), 1:44.

6. *FR, 1914*, pp. 438–84. Carranza to Wilson, text transmitted April 22, 1914: DS 812.00/11618.

7. W. B. Hale to secretary of state, November 14, 1913, State Department Papers, as quoted by Link, *Wilson: The New Freedom*, p. 383.

8. General Carranza to the mediators, May 3, 1914, *FR, 1914*, p. 518.

9. Arthur S. Link, *Wilson Campaigns for Progressivism and Peace, 1916–1917* (Princeton, N.J., 1965), p. 121.

10. See, for example, Lind to Secretary of State Bryan, April 3, 1914: DS 812.00/11396; Silliman to secretary of state, August 26, 1914: DS 812.00/13015; and Silliman to secretary of state, September 5, 1914: DS 812.00/13116. The subject is briefly mentioned in John Womack, Jr., *Zapata and the Mexican Revolution* (New York, 1969), passim.

11. Duval West report of May 11, 1915: DS 812.00/19181.

12. Diary, October 10, 1915, Lansing Papers, as quoted by Haley, *Revolution and Intervention,* pp. 183–84.

13. Louis G. Kahle, "Robert Lansing and the Recognition of Venustiano Carranza," *Hispanic American Historical Review,* 38, no. 3 (August 1958): 353–72.

14. Joseph P. Tumulty, *Woodrow Wilson as I Know Him* (Garden City, N.Y., 1921), pp. 159, 160.

15. Link, *Wilson Campaigns for Progressivism,* p. 335. Professor Link quotes from Lansing's letter to E. N. Smith of March 3, 1917, in the Lansing Papers. See also Philip Holt Lowry, "The Mexican Policy of Woodrow Wilson" (Ph.D. diss., Yale University, 1949), p. 173.

16. Link, *Wilson Campaigns for Progressivism,* pp. 337–38.

17. Link, *Wilson Campaigns for Progressivism,* pp. 336–37, describes the oil and mining interests' pressures on Lansing and Wilson. Link cites an entry of March 10, 1917, in the diary of Chandler P. Anderson in the collection of the Library of Congress to substantiate Wilson's fears of German influences on Carranza. As chapter 4 of this study indicates (see note 7), Carranza gave *oral* assurances that his government would not take over properties in exploitation or confiscate them. Lansing also temporarily relaxed prohibitions on arms shipments to Carranza in response to the latter's request. See Lowry, "The Mexican Policy," p. 188.

18. Friedrich Katz, *Deutschland, Díaz und die mexikanische Revolution: die deutsche Politik in Mexiko 1870–1920* (Berlin, 1964), p. 271. Hintze's preference for Huerta over Díaz is described on p. 223.

19. Gerard to secretary of state, October 17, 1913, *FR, 1913,* p. 842.

20. Franz von Papen, *Memoirs* (London, 1952), p. 44.

21. Franz Rintelen von Kleist, *The Dark Invader* (New York, 1933), p. 175.

22. Ibid., p. 177; see also p. 223.

23. One of the most cautious accounts about charges of German involvement in Huerta's attempted coup is that of Kenneth J. Grieb, *The United States and Huerta* (Lincoln, Nebr., 1969), pp. 182 ff., in which he speculates that the large quantity of arms Huerta's group possessed may well have been provided by the German agent, Rintelen.

Emanuel Victor Voska, who led a Czech counterespionage and propaganda organization in the United States, provides some of the most authoritative evidence of assistance the Germans offered Huerta, in Voska, *Spy and Counterspy* (New York, 1940). Voska's men were stationed in the room next to that in which Huerta and the Germans negotiated and overheard the negotiations with a listening device. Voska reports on p. 192 that the Germans had set aside $500,000 for Boy-Ed's work in Mexico, which money was later transferred to Franz Rintelen von Kleist. The Germans offered Huerta arms from the German-owned arms factory. Voska describes later on pp. 196–97 German shipments of arms to Mexico including some to Pancho Villa.

Barbara Tuchman reports in *The Zimmerman Telegram* (London, 1959), p. 79, that eight million rounds of ammunition were purchased in St. Louis, orders placed for a further three million in New York, some $800,000 deposited to Huerta's account at the Deutsche Bank in Havana, and $95,000 in a Mexican account. Miss Tuchman does not indicate the source of these figures. Some of them may have originated in the unsubstantiated account on pages 288–95 of John Price Jones, *The German Secret Service in America 1914–1918* (Boston, 1918). Other authors who have looked closely into this subject and use these same figures include: Katz, *Deutschland, Díaz,* pp. 339–40; Michael C. Meyer, "The Mexican-German Conspiracy of 1915," *The Americas,* 23, no. 1 (July 1966): 84 ff.; and George J. Rausch, Jr., "The Exile and Death of Victoriano Huerta," *Hispanic American Historical Review,* 41, no. 2 (May 1962): 137.

24. Allen Gerlach discusses German involvement in the "diversion" in "Conditions along the Border—1915, The Plan de San Diego," *New Mexico Historical Review* (July 1968), p. 201. Michael C. Meyer has called attention to a still earlier document of November 26, 1914, signed by Francisco Alvarez Tostado, calling for a reannexation of Mexico's lost territories. See Meyer, *Huerta, A Political Portrait* (Lincoln, Nebr., 1972), pp. 215, 217.

25. Katz, *Deutschland, Díaz,* pp. 342–44, quotes from Dernberg's message to Berlin and the Foreign Office's reply.

26. Ibid., pp. 344–48, gives a lengthy discussion of Villa's probable ties with German agents. See also Katz's earlier "Alemania y Francisco Villa," *Historia Mexicana,* 12, no. 1 (July–September 1962): 88–102. See also note 23 above. For information on Dr. Rauschbaum and speculation about German involvement in the Columbus raid see James A. Sandos, "German Involvement in Northern Mexico, 1915–1916: A New Look at the Columbus Raid," *Hispanic American Historical Review,* 50, no. 1 (February 1970): 70–88.

27. Katz, *Deutschland, Díaz,* p. 346, quoting a letter from Ambassador Bernstorff to foreign minister, May 4, 1916.

28. See notes 14, 15, 16, and 17 above.

29. Katz, *Deutschland, Díaz,* pp. 354–55.

30. Ibid., p. 354, summarizes the note. The text of the Mexican note, according to Katz, is in the Potsdam Archives, AAII, No. 4462.

31. *Official German Documents Relating to the World War* (New York, 1923), 2:1337. Translated under the supervision of the Carnegie Endowment for International Peace.

32. Ibid., p. 1338.

33. Katz, *Deutschland, Díaz,* p. 357.

34. Eckhardt's telegram to the foreign minister, March 2, 1917, is quoted in full in Burton J. Hendrick, *The Life and Letters of Walter H. Page* (Garden City, N.Y., 1926), 3:351.

35. Katz, *Deutschland, Díaz,* p. 366. Professor Katz's source is a personal interview.

36. Ibid., pp. 366, 367.

37. Hendrick, *The Life and Letters,* 3:350–55, provides the texts of messages between Eckhardt and the Foreign Office regarding arms, munitions, and financial assistance.

38. Fletcher to secretary of state, February 26, 1917, *FR, 1917,* supplement 1, p. 235.

39. Fletcher to secretary of state, March 10, 1917, *FR, 1917,* supplement 1, pp. 238–39.

40. Katz, *Deutschland, Díaz,* pp. 368–69.

41. Ibid., p. 369.

42. Hendrick, *The Life and Letters,* 3:354.

43. Katz, *Deutschland, Díaz,* p. 470.

44. Ibid., pp. 466–67.

45. Ibid., p. 431.

46. Ibid., p. 468.

47. Carl W. Ackerman, *Mexico's Dilemma* (New York, 1917), p. 45.

48. Katz, *Deutschland, Díaz,* p. 418.

49. In *Deutschland, Díaz und die mexikanische Revolution,* Professor Katz discusses German secret service activities in Mexico on pp. 418–45 and propaganda activities from pp. 446–64.

50. Katz, *Deutschland, Díaz,* pp. 403–04.

51. Katz, *Deutschland, Díaz,* p. 432, cites Potsdam Archives, Reichskanzlei, No. 2477, Aufzeichnung über die Besprechung in Spa Am 2/3.7.1918 and 27.7.1918.

52. Secretary of state to Summerlin, telegram, June 8, 1921, quoting public statement of June 7, 1921. See *FR, 1912,* 2, p. 406 f.; see also Charles Ignasias, "Reluctant Recognition: The United States and the Recognition of Alvaro Obregón of Mexico, 1920–1924" (Ann Arbor, Mich., 1967), pp. 92, 248.

53. *FR, 1917,* p. 1072.

54. Ignasias, "Reluctant Recognition," p. 93.

55. Ackerman, *Mexico's Dilemma,* p. 45.

56. Ignasias, "Reluctant Recognition," p. 156.

57. Ibid., p. 185. Text is found in Edgar Turlington, *Mexico and Her Foreign Creditors* (New York, 1930), pp. 379–86.

58. Ignasias, "Reluctant Recognition," p. 177.

59. Ibid., p. 194.

60. Elton Atwater, *American Regulation of Arms and Exports* (Washington, D.C., 1941), chapter 2, passim.

61. Division of Mexican affairs memorandum, January 30, 1922, to Ambassador Fletcher: DS 812.113/9324.

62. Harding to Fletcher, March 2, 1922: DS 812.113/9306; see also DS 812.113/9305 and DS/712.113/9310.

63. Ignasias, "Reluctant Recognition," p. 297.

64. Charles Evans Hughes, "Recent Questions in Negotiations," *American Journal of International Law,* 18, no. 2 (April 1924): 235–36.

65. Ignasias, "Reluctant Recognition," pp. 297–98.

66. Ibid., p. 303.

67. Stanley Robert Ross, "Dwight Morrow and the Mexican Revolution," *Hispanic American Historical Review,* 38, no. 4 (November 1958): 506–28.

68. Comprehensive and authoritative treatment of U.S.–Mexican relations from 1916 to 1932 is found in Robert Freeman Smith, *The United States and Revolutionary Nationalism in Mexico, 1916–1932* (Chicago, 1972), received after my research on Mexico was largely completed.

69. U.S., Department of State, Report to the secretary of state, American-Mexican Claims Commission (Washington, D.C., 1948), p. 72.

70. Josephus Daniels, *Shirt-Sleeve Diplomat* (Chapel Hill, N.C., 1947), pp. 67–68.

71. *FR, 1938,* 5:728; Daniels to secretary of state, telegram, March 21, 1938: DS 812.6363/3109.

72. For further information see E. David Cronon, *Josephus Daniels in Mexico* (Madison, 1960), chapter 8, and Bryce Wood, *The Making of the Good Neighbor Policy* (New York, 1961), chapter 8.

73. *FR, 1938,* 5:727; secretary of state to Daniels, telegram, March 19, 1938: DS 812.6363/3096A.

74. *FR, 1938,* 5:728; Daniels to secretary of state, telegram, March 21, 1938: DS 812.6363/3109.

75. Memorandum of conversation of March 21, 1938: DS 812.6363/3153; *FR, 1938,* 5:732.

76. Morganthau diary entry of December 16, 1937, as quoted in Allan Seymour Everest, *Morgenthau, the New Deal and Silver* (New York, 1950), p. 86.

77. Morgenthau diary entry of December 31, 1937, as quoted in Everest, *Morgenthau,* pp. 87–88.

78. John Morton Blum, *From the Morgenthau Diaries: Years of Crisis, 1928–1938* (Boston, 1959), p. 496.

79. Everest, *Morgenthau*, pp. 96–97.

80. Harold L. Ickes, *The Secret Diary of Harold L. Ickes*, vol. 2, *The Inside Struggle* (New York, 1954), p. 353.

81. For evidence of links between the Nazis and the Sinarquistas see Mario Gill, *Sinarquismo, su origen, su essencia, y su misión*, 3d ed. (Mexico, 1972), p. 316.

82. Friedrich Katz, "Einige Grundzüge der Politik des deutschen Imperialismus in Lateinamerika von 1898 bis 1941," in *Der Deutsche Faschismus in Lateinamerika, 1933–1943*, ed. Friedrich Katz, et al., (Berlin, 1966), p. 29.

83. U.S., Department of State, *Documents on German Foreign Policy, 1918–1945* (Washington, D.C., 1953), Series D., vol. 5, p. 829. Rüdt to Foreign Office, April 8, 1938. Although dated after the oil seizures, the message appears to be an assessment made before the implications of the seizure were fully realized. This minister's views had changed by May (see note 88).

84. Wood, *Good Neighbor Policy*, p. 232.

85. Ruth Sheldon, "Marketing Harasses Mexican Oil Industry Officials," *Gas and Oil Journal*, June 1, 1939, pp. 18 ff.

86. Rüdt to Foreign Office, April 8, 1938: Roll 2726, Frame E417090.

87. Rüdt to Foreign Office, May 4, 1938: Roll 2727, Frame E417160.

88. Rüdt to Foreign Office, May 6, 1938: Roll 2727, Frame E417249.

89. Jesús Silva Herzog, *Historia de la expropiación de las impresas petroleras*, 3d ed. (Mexico, 1964), p. 193.

90. Some believed that von Merck had ties with the German minister. See Gill, *Sinarquismo*, pp. 25 f. In fact, the German Foreign Office and military appeared to know little about him. The former queried Rüdt about him, and Rüdt replied tersely that he was a Mexican citizen (May 30, 1938, to Berlin: Roll 1304, Frame 487668). The high command also had no information (see memorandum to Foreign Office, July 8, 1938: Roll 1304, Frame 487669). Clandestine support, while possible, was also inconsistent with the official German opposition to Cedillo (see note 91).

91. Rüdt to Foreign Office, April 14, 1938: Roll 2727, Frame E417277.

92. Silva Herzog, *Historia de la expropriación*, p. 146; see also Nathaniel and Sylvia Weyl, *The Reconquest of Mexico* (New York, 1939), pp. 300–01.

93. Both the foregoing points are treated by Cronon, *Josephus Daniels*, p. 212. He cites the Daniels papers.

94. U.S., Department of State, *Documents on German Foreign Policy*, pp. 876 ff. Rüdt to Foreign Office, October 22, 1938.

95. Cronon, *Josephus Daniels*, p. 234, also quoting the Daniels Papers.

96. Silva Herzog, *Historia de la expropriación*, p. 193.

97. National Industrial Conference Board, *The Petroleum Almanac*, 3d ed. (New York, 1946), p. 115.

98. Foreign Office to Madrid, October 8, 1940: Roll 143, Frame 84763.

99. Laurence Duggan, *The Americas: The Search for Hemisphere Security* (New York, 1949), p. 70.

100. Rüdt to Foreign Office, June 10, 1940: Roll 143, Frame 84737. For an account of Axis influence in Mexico in the late 1930s and early 1940s, see Betty Kirk, *Covering the Mexican Front* (Norman, Oklahoma, 1972), especially chapter 12.

101. Cronon, *Josephus Daniels*, p. 257, quoting from the Roosevelt Papers.

102. *FR, 1940*, 5:135 ff.

103. *FR, 1941*, 7:403 ff.

104. *New York Times*, April 20, 1952, p. 22.

105. *New York Times*, April 13, 1952, p. 1.

106. Marjorie M. Whiteman, *Digest of International Law* (Washington, D.C., 1963), 2:262.

107. *New York Times*, April 19, 1952, p. 3.

108. *New York Times*, May 4, 1952, p. 29.

109. Whiteman, *International Law*, p. 262.

110. Carter Goodrich, "Bolivia in Time of Revolution," in *Beyond the Revolution: Bolivia Since 1952*, ed. James M. Malloy and Richard Thorn (Pittsburgh, 1971), p. 12.

111. Henry W. Berger, "Union Diplomacy: American Labor's Foreign Policy in Latin America 1932–1955" (Ph.D. diss., University of Wisconsin, 1966), p. 326.

112. *New York Times*, June 3, 1952, p. 10.

113. U.S., Department of State, *World Strength of the Communist Party Organizations* (Washington, D.C., 1953).

114. Partido Comunista de Bolivia, *Primer congreso, documentos* (La Paz, 1959).

115. Víctor Andrade, *Bolivia—Problems and Promise* (Washington, D.C., 1956), p. 15.

116. Wálter Guevara Arze, *Planteamientos de la revolución en la décima conferencia inter-americana* (La Paz, 1954), p. 21.

117. Ibid., p. 19.

118. Víctor Paz Estenssoro, *Discursos parlementarios* (La Paz, 1955), pp. 220–22.

119. Luis Peñaloza C., *Historia del Movimiento Nacionalista Revolucionario, 1941–1952* (La Paz, 1963), p. 21.

120. Milton Eisenhower, *The Wine Is Bitter* (New York, 1963), pp. 67–8, for the quotes in this and the preceding paragraph.

121. Ibid., p. 68.

122. U.S., Congress, Senate, Committee on Foreign Relations, *Hearings on the Mutual Security Act of 1953* (Washington, D.C., 1953), p. 368.

123. *New York Times*, June 17, 1953, p. 26.

124. U.S., Department of State, *Bulletin*, July 20, 1953, p. 82.

125. Eisenhower, *The Wine Is Bitter*, p. 194.

126. Interview, 1969 (name of source withheld).

127. U.S., Department of State, *Bulletin*, November 2, 1953, pp. 584–87.

128. U.S., Department of State, *Bulletin*, October 26, 1953, p. 555.

129. Interview with Andrade, La Paz, June 27, 1969. During a tense moment for Andrade on the links, the president had reassured him about a U.S. subsidy for the Bolivian budget. Bob Hope, who started out with the presidential foursome, later asked the president about the golf stakes. The president reportedly replied he would bet only one dollar since he "just lost three million to the Bolivian ambassador."

130. U.S., Congress, Senate, Committee on Banking and Currency, *Study of Latin American Countries*, Report No. 2 (Washington, D.C., 1954), p. 63.

131. U.S., Congress, House of Representatives, *Hearings Before the Committee on Foreign Affairs on the Mutual Security Act of 1955* (Washington, D.C., 1955), p. 306. Mr. Holland's testimony was on June 14, 1955.

132. Cornelius H. Zondag, *The Bolivian Economy, 1952–65* (New York, 1966), p. 114.

133. An authoritative explanation of the inflation is contained in George Jackson Eder, *Inflation and Development in Latin America: A Case History of Inflation and Stabilization in Bolivia* (Ann Arbor, Mich., 1968), pp. viii–ix, and chapters 5, 6, and 7.

134. Zondag, *Bolivian Economy*, p. 56.

135. Eder, *Inflation and Development in Latin America*, p. ix.

136. Ibid., chapter 7, pp. 128–35.

137. Ibid., pp. 234, 720.

138. The opposition's criticism of the plan is contained in Ñuflo Chavez, *El signo del estaño* (La Paz, 1961), pp. 109–55.

139. Eder, *Inflation and Development in Latin America*, p. 177.

140. *Hispanic American Report*, No. 7 (1957), p. 375.

141. *New York Times*, August 7, 1957, p. 9.

142. The foreign debt had been in default since 1931. Agreements were worked out with the Foreign Bondholders Protective Association to resume payments on the debt, thus fulfilling one of the requirements qualifying Bolivia for loans from the World Bank (IBRD) as well as for the stabilization loan. Many of Bolivia's defaulted bonds were not in the hands of the original owners but had been bought up by

speculators. Payments on the debt have been suspended and resumed several times since the agreement was announced in 1957.

143. Eder, *Inflation and Development in Latin America,* p. 148.

144. Ibid., p. 220.

145. Since 1958 the Bolivian peso was stabilized for years at slightly less than twelve pesos to the U.S. dollar.

146. A hint of the far-reaching nature of the fund's role is contained in International Monetary Fund, *Annual Report of the Executive Directors for the Fiscal Year Ended April 30, 1957* (Washington, D.C., 1957), p. 139.

147. Zondag, *Bolivian Economy,* p. 90.

148. Interview, Lima, July 7, 1969.

149. Eder, *Inflation and Development in Latin America,* p. 163.

150. Ibid., p. 460.

151. *Hispanic American Report,* No. 7 (1957), p. 375.

152. Víctor Paz Estenssoro, *Contra la restauración por la revolución nacional* (Lima, March 1965), pp. 35–36.

153. Interview with Víctor Paz, Lima, July 7, 1969.

154. U.S., Agency for International Development, *Overseas Loans and Grants and Assistance from International Organizations: Obligations and Loan Authorizations, July 1, 1945–June 30, 1967* (March 29, 1968), table 1. Comparisons were made for the years 1953–1964 inclusive. In Latin America, Chile came closest to Bolivia in per capita economic assistance. A selective review of this publication suggests that the only country to receive more per capita economic assistance than Bolivia during this period may have been Israel.

155. An AP correspondent quoted Paz in *El Mercurio* (Santiago, Chile), April 8, 1955.

156. *New York Times,* August 7, 1957, p. 9.

157. Sergio Almaraz Paz, *Requiem para una república* (La Paz, 1969), p. 20. Víctor Paz confirmed this version in an interview in Lima, July 9, 1969.

158. For further information on Paz's fall see Cole Blasier, "The United States and the Revolution," in *Beyond the Revolution,* ed. Malloy and Thorn, pp. 95 ff.

159. Friedrich Katz's emphasis would be different. In a letter to me dated May 31, 1973, he writes: "Up to 1916 Woodrow Wilson's policy towards Mexico was not opposed by the great majority of American businessmen. Quite the contrary, very large business interests, especially the oil companies, were actively cooperating with the different Mexican Revolutionary factions. In the Senate hearings in 1919, Doheny testified that he actively supported Carranza until 1915. Interventionism began to develop among business interests in 1917 on a large scale and at that time World War I made any kind of intervention in Mexico extremely difficult. It was only in 1919 that a serious split developed between American business interests on the one hand, and Woodrow Wilson on the other." For further discussion of the general subject, especially with respect to the 1930s, see Wood, *Good Neighbor Policy,* pp. 344–47.

160. For further treatment of U.S.–Bolivian relations (1952–1964) see Blasier, "The United States and the Revolution"; James W. Wilkie, *The Bolivian Revolution and U.S. Aid Since 1952* (Los Angeles, 1970); and Laurence Whitehead, *The United States and Bolivia: A Case of Neo-Colonialism* (London, 1969).

Chapter 6: Guatemala and Cuba: Paramilitary Expeditions

1. The most useful secondary sources on the Arbenz regime, by nonparticipants, include: S. A. Gonionskii, "Agressiia protiv Gvatemaly (1954g)," chapter 4 of *Latinskaia Amerika i SSHA 1939–1951* (Moscow, 1960); Daniel James, *Red Design for the Americas* (New York, 1954); Friedrich Katz, "Der Sturz der demokratischen Regierung in Guatemala im Jahre 1954," *Wissenschaftliche Zeitschrift der Humboldt-Universität zu Berlin,* no. 9 (1959–1960): 45–52; John D. Martz, *Communist Infiltration in Guatemala* (New York, 1956); Ronald M. Schneider, *Communism in Guatemala, 1944–1954* (New York, 1959); Philip B. Taylor, Jr., "The Guatemalan Affair: A Critique of United States Foreign Policy,"

The American Political Science Review, vol. 50 (1956): 787–806; and David Wise and Thomas B. Ross, "Guatemala: CIA's Banana Revolt," in *The Invisible Government* (New York, 1964), chapter 11.

2. Carlos Samayoa Chinchilla, *El quetzal no es rojo* (Guatemala, 1956), pp. 125–33; Manuel Galich, *¿Por qué lucha Guatemala?* (Buenos Aires, 1956), pp. 201–07; and Schneider, *Communism in Guatemala,* pp. 28–31.

3. *New York Times,* November 14, 1950, p. 16.

4. Quoted from Arbenz's "Programa de gobierno" of 1951 by Jaime Díaz Rozzotto, *El caracter de la revolución guatemalteca* (Mexico, 1958), p. 267.

5. Thomas and Marjorie Melville, *Guatemala: The Politics of Land Ownership* (New York, 1971), p. 58; and Comité Interamericano de Desarrollo Agrícola (CIDA), *Tenencia de la tierra y desarrollo socio-económico del sector agrícola: Guatemala* (Washington, D.C., 1965), p. 41.

6. CIDA, *Tenencia de la tierra,* p. 53.

7. United Fruit sales in the six countries of Central America in 1955 were about $150 million. See Stacy May and Galo Plaza, *The United Fruit Company in Latin America* (Washington, D.C., 1958), p. 122. Revenues of the Guatemalan government for July–December 1953 were equivalent to $29 million which if doubled is still well below half of the United Fruit sales two years later. See *Informe del ciudadano presidente de la república, Colonel Jacobo Arbenz Guzmán, al congreso nacional,* March 1, 1954, p. xxxvi.

8. Galich, *¿Por qué lucha Guatemala?,* p. 237; see also, Guatemala, Secretaría de Relaciones Exteriores, *Guatemala ante América, la verdad sobre la cuarta reunión de consulta de cancilleres americanos* (Guatemala, 1951), passim.

9. Juan José Arévalo, *Escritos políticos y discursos* (Havana, 1953), pp. 411 ff.; see also Schneider, *Communism in Guatemala,* pp. 22 ff.

10. Schneider, *Communism in Guatemala,* pp. 186 ff., and Chinchilla, *El quetzal no es rojo,* pp. 162 ff.

11. In Chile and Cuba, for example, Presidents González Videla and Grau San Martín turned against the Communist party and were instrumental in helping anti-Communist labor leaders split the national labor federations, over which the Communists had gained dominance and established strong anti-Communist labor centrals. With the support of labor leaders in the United States, the new labor organizations in other countries threw off the influence of the Confederación de Trabajadores de América Latina (CTAL) of Vicente Lombardo Toledano and ultimately joined together in the Organización Regional Interamericana de Trabajo (ORIT). The CTAL remained affiliated with the Soviet-sponsored World Federation of Trade Unions (WFTU) and the ORIT joined into the anti-Communist U.S.-sponsored International Confederation of Free Trade Unions (ICFTU). The U.S. Central Intelligence Agency backed the anti-Communist labor movement. See chapter 3, notes 141, 142, and 143.

12. Schneider, *Communism in Guatemala,* pp. 158 ff.

13. Ibid., p. 57. See also my *Cuban and Chilean Communist Parties, Instruments of Soviet Policy (1935–1948)* (University Microfilms, 1956).

14. Schneider, *Communism in Guatemala,* p. 101.

15. *Informe del ciudadano presidente,* pp. xlix ff.

16. Schneider, *Communism in Guatemala,* p. 279.

17. See note 4 above.

18. Akademiia Nauk SSSR, Institut Latinskoi Ameriki, *Politicheskie Partii Stran Latinskoi Ameriki* (Moscow, 1965), p. 143.

19. Schneider, *Communism in Guatemala,* p. 294.

20. One of the first authoritative Soviet treatments of the Guatemalan affair of 1954 appeared in *Kommunist,* no. 10, 1954, by V. Chichkov, "Respublika Gvatemala i imperializm SSHA," pp. 102–10. Chichkov described the Arbenz government as "formed from representatives of the Guatemalan middle class and army officers" and explained that the major political forces behind Arbenz were "three large bourgeois parties" (p. 105). He clearly did not consider the Arbenz government as Communist though he described how the Communists were permitted to join and support this "democratic electoral front."

One of the most authoritative Soviet treatments is Gonionskii, "Agressiia protiv Gvatemaly

(1954g)." Gonionskii's study draws widely on the available material and represents a serious Marxist-Leninist treatment of the episode. The two Soviet treatments use essentially the same sources as do U.S. and Latin American scholars and provide virtually no new information. One would not be surprised if the USSR had clandestine sources providing special insight on developments, but if so, there is no sign that such sources are made available to Soviet scholars any more than such U.S. sources are to U.S. scholars. Moreover, there is nothing in either of these articles showing any conspiratorial relationship or joint planning between the Arbenz and Soviet governments.

Another authoritative treatment from a Marxist-Leninist perspective is Katz, "Der Sturz der demokratischen Regierung." Like the Soviet writers, Katz marshals many of the same primary sources as others without providing any new light on the Soviet-Arbenz relationship.

21. For contrary views see James, *Red Design for the Americas;* U.S., Department of State, *Intervention of International Communism in Guatemala,* Publication 5556 (Washington, D.C., 1954); and U.S., Department of State, *A Case History of Communist Penetration,* Publication 6465 (Washington, D.C., 1957).

Bryce Wood convincingly shows how the study of the Guatemalan Communist party contained in Part Two of the first Department of State publication (1954) was twisted in the second (1957)—the two publications cited in the paragraph above. The 1957 publication was based largely on the 1954 publication but omitted many parts of the original which were in conflict with Secretary Dulles' own explanation of the growth of communism in Guatemala as "an intrusion of Soviet despotism." The 1954 publication, for example, described Guatemalan intellectuals' views on p. 44 as "a glaze of nationalism and Marxism, a scrambled compound which was short of the full strength of militant Communism." See Bryce Wood, "Self-Plagiarism and Foreign Policy," *Latin American Research Review,* 3, no. 3 (Summer 1968): 184–91.

22. Galich, *¿Por qué lucha Guatemala?*, p. 247.

23. Ibid., p. 252.

24. Raúl Osegueda, *Operación Guatemala $$ OK $$* (Mexico, 1955), pp. 156–57, and Galich, *¿Por qué lucha Guatemala?*, p. 254.

25. Salvador, Secretaría de Información, *De la neutralidad vigilante a la mediación con Guatemala* (El Salvador, 1954?), pp. 25 ff., and Osegueda, *Operación Guatemala,* p. 159.

26. Guillermo Toriello, *La batalla de Guatemala* (Santiago, Chile, 1955), p. 46.

27. *New York Times,* February 25, 1953, p. 7.

28. Ibid., March 13, 1953, p. 14.

29. Spruille Braden, *Diplomats and Demagogues* (New Rochelle, N.Y., 1971), p. 409.

30. Osegueda, *Operación Guatemala,* pp. 163 ff.

31. John Moors Cabot, *Toward Our Common Destiny* (New York, n.d.), p. 88.

32. *New York Times,* October 17, 1953, p. 13, and October 18, 1953, p. 22.

33. Guatemala, Secretaría de Propaganda y Divulgación, *La democracia amenazada, el caso de guatemala* (Guatemala, 1954), pp. 28 ff.

34. Ibid., pp. 15–16; see also Miguel Ydígoras Fuentes, *My War with Communism* (Englewood Cliffs, N.J., 1963), p. 50, who wrote: "Colonel Castillo Armas then paid me a visit in San Salvador. He told me that he had the promise of assistance from official U.S. agencies, an offer from the Government of Honduras to give him asylum and allow the common border with Guatemala to be used for the attack, that the Government of Nicaragua had also offered him arms and bases for training troops, and that Generalissimo Rafael Leonidas Trujillo of Santo Domingo was generously supplying him with substantial economic assistance and large quantities of arms. We agreed on conditions and the 'gentlemen's pact,' as it was later called, was drawn up and signed."

See also Robert Crassweller, *Trujillo: The Life and Times of a Caribbean Dictator* (New York, 1966), p. 335.

35. Guatemala, *La democracia amenazada,* pp. 33 ff., provides photocopies of the alleged letters.

36. Marta Cehelsky, "Guatemala's Frustrated Revolution: The 'Liberation' of 1954," (Master's thesis, Columbia University, 196?). See especially pages 44 and 53–56. Ms. Cehelsky has done some of the most extensive interviewing on the Liberation Movement.

37. The letters were published on January 29, 1954, in the Guatemalan press and were reprinted in Guatemala, *La democracia amenazada,* cited above. See also, Guatemala, Secretaría de Divulgación, Cultura y Turismo de la Presidencia de la República, *Así se gestó la liberación* (Guatemala, 1956), p. 177.

38. Guatemala, *La democracia amenazada,* p. 92.

39. Ibid., p. 46.

40. U.S., Congress, Senate, Committee on the Judiciary, Hearings Before the Subcommittee to Investigate the Administration of the Internal Security Act, *Communist Threat to the United States Through the Caribbean,* 87th Cong., July 27, 1961, pt. 13:866.

41. Dwight D. Eisenhower, *The White House Years: Mandate for Change, 1953–1956* (New York, 1963), pp. 425–26.

42. Allen Dulles, *The Craft of Intelligence* (New York, 1963), p. 224. Allen Dulles discussed "our Guatemalan operation" with President Kennedy in 1961; see Theodore C. Sorenson, *Kennedy* (New York, 1965), p. 296.

43. Robert Murphy, *Diplomat Among Warriors* (New York, 1964), p. 372.

44. Ydígoras, *My War with Communism,* pp. 49–50. Ydígoras wrote: "A former executive of the United Fruit Company, Mr. Walter Trumbull, came to see me with two gentlemen whom he introduced as agents of the CIA. They said that I was a popular figure in Guatemala and that they wanted to lend their assistance to overthrow Arbenz. When I asked their conditions for the assistance I found them unacceptable. Among other things I was to promise to favor the United Fruit Company and the International Railways of Central America; to destroy the railroad workers' labor union; to suspend claims against Great Britain for the Belize territory; to establish a strong-arm government, on the style of Ubico."

45. Toriello, *La batalla,* p. 121.

46. Juan José Arévalo in *Guatemala: la democracia y el imperio,* 7th ed. (Buenos Aires, 1964), p. 143, contends that Castillo Armas said the liberation of Guatemala did not cost $5 million.

47. Braden, *Diplomats and Demagogues,* p. 411.

48. *Time,* January 11, 1954, p. 27.

49. Osegueda, *Operación Guatemala,* pp. 203–05.

50. Cehelsky, "Guatemala's Frustrated Revolution," p. 56.

51. *Department of State Bulletin,* February 15, 1954, p. 251.

52. Toriello, *La batalla,* p. 46. The extent of Dulles' and his firm's legal relationships with United Fruit needs to be verified. I do not have additional evidence.

53. Ibid., p. 56.

54. Ibid., pp. 56–57.

55. Osegueda, *Operación Guatemala,* p. 166.

56. *Department of State Bulletin,* September 14, 1953, pp. 357–60.

57. *New York Times,* July 3, 1954, p. 1.

58. Ibid., February 5, 1958, p. 1.

59. U.S., Department of State, *Tenth Inter-American Conference, Caracas, Venezuela, March 1–28, 1954,* Publication 5692, (Washington, D.C., 1955), p. 8.

60. Toriello, *La batalla,* pp. 192–94.

61. Ibid., p. 185.

62. U.S., Dept. of State, *Tenth Conference,* p. 62.

63. See M. Margaret Ball, *The OAS Transition* (Durham, 1969), p. 446, on the Bogotá conference and p. 447 on the foreign ministers' meeting of 1951.

64. Arévalo, *Guatemala: la democracia,* pp. 27 ff.

65. *The Memoirs of Anthony Eden: Full Circle* (Boston, 1960), p. 151.

66. *New York Times,* May 20, 1954, p. 12.

67. U.S., Congress, House, Subcommittee on Latin America of the Select Committee on Communist Aggression, *Ninth Interim Report of Hearings. Communist Aggression in Latin America,* 83rd Cong., 2d sess., September 27–October 15, 1954, pp. 119–20. See also Emma Moya Posas, *La jornada épica de Castillo Armas vista desde Honduras* (Tegucigalpa, 1954?), pp. 19 ff.

68. Guatemala, Secretaría de Propaganda y Divulgación de la Presidencia de la República de Guatemala, *Genocidio sobre Guatemala* (Guatemala, 1954), passim.

69. United Nations, Security Council, *Official Records, Supplement,* Document S/3232, April, May, and June 1954.

70. United Nations, Security Council, *Official Records,* 675th meeting, June 20, 1954, pp. 2–3.

71. Ibid., p. 31.

72. Ibid., p. 38.

73. Eisenhower, *Mandate for Change,* pp. 425–26.

74. Excerpts from the text of these two messages are found in Katz, "Der Sturz der demokratischen Regierung," pp. 49–50. Katz's source was the *Neue Züricher Zeitung,* June 27, 1954.

75. *New York Times,* July 1, 1954, p. 2.

76. United Nations, Security Council, *Official Records,* 676th meeting, June 25, 1954.

77. *The Memoirs of Anthony Eden,* p. 154.

78. *New York Times,* July 1, 1954, p. 2.

79. Guatemala, Secretaría de Divulgación, *Así se gestó la liberación,* pp. 181–208, summarizes the military operations.

80. Ibid., p. 195; Toriello, *La battala,* p. 122, denies that it was ever possible for Armas to move general headquarters to Guatemalan territory before Arbenz's resignation.

81. Toriello, *La batalla,* p. 121.

82. Ibid., p. 122.

83. Eisenhower, *Mandate for Change,* p. 425.

84. Guatemala, Secretaría de Divulgación, *Así se gestó la liberación,* p. 235.

85. Jorge del Valle Matheu, *La verdad sobre el "caso de Guatemala"* (Guatemala, 1956?), pp. 141 ff.

86. *La Prensa Libre* (San José, Costa Rica), October 25, 1955, pp. 9, 14. This appears to be a reprint of an article published in the Chilean magazine, *Vistazo,* the account of an interview with Arbenz in Prague, Czechoslovakia, by a Guatemalan architectural student, Ronaldo Ramirez. Arbenz's statement about the excellent offer of the U.S. ambassador appears to be a thinly veiled and unsubstantiated reference to bribery.

87. Ibid. Peurifoy may not have been active in the planning and development of Castillo Armas' Liberation Movement, at least he denied having been so in congressional hearings. See Congress, House, *Communist Aggression in Latin America,* p. 114, and Ydígoras, *My War with Communism,* p. 54. In this connection, it is interesting that Ambassador Peurifoy did take full credit for lending his "good offices to assist in negotiating the truce between the forces of Colonel Castillo and the military junta." Galich, *¿Por qué lucha Guatemala?,* p. 361, accuses Ambassador Peurifoy of paying a $60,000 bribe to an army officer who surrendered his troops and arms to the army of liberation.

88. *La Pensa Libre,* October 25, 1955, p. 14.

89. Guatemala, Secretaría de Divulgación, *Así se gestó la liberación,* p. 247. The complete text of his radio address is reprinted here.

90. *La Prensa Libre,* October 25, 1955, p. 14.

91. Toriello, *La batalla,* p. 129.

92. *New York Times,* July 1, 1954, p. 3.

93. Salvador, Secretaría de Información, *De la neutralidad vigilante,* pp. 83–85, contains the text of their agreement.

94. Cehelsky, "Guatemala's Frustrated Revolution," p. 63. According to Ms. Cehelsky, most reports place the figure at $100,000 which, however, she called "unverified."

95. See the *Hispanic American Report* for the balance of 1954.

96. *New York Times,* December 12, 1954, p. 48.

97. U.S., Congress, Senate, Committee on Foreign Relations, *Mutual Security Act of 1955,* 84th Cong., 1st sess., May 5–23, 1955, p. 313.

98. Dwight D. Eisenhower, *Public Papers of the President of the United States, 1954* (Washington, D.C., 1960), radio and television address, August 23, 1954, p. 746; at the Iowa State Fair, August 30, 1954, p. 789; at the Hollywood Bowl, September 23, 1954, p. 870; at the American Jewish Tercentenary Dinner, New York City, October 20, 1954, p. 925; at the Eisenhower Day Dinner, Washington, D.C., October 28, 1954, p. 981.

99. Dwight D. Eisenhower, *Public Papers of the President of the United States, 1956* (Washington, D.C., 1958), pp. 738, 782, 833.

100. Standard sources on this period include chapter 2 on the Cuban Revolution and international relations in Akademiia Nauk SSSR, *Strany Latinskoi Ameriki v Sovremennykh Mezhdunarodnykh Otnosheniiakh* (Moscow, 1967); Philip W. Bonsal, *Cuba, Castro, and the United States* (Pittsburgh, 1971); Knud Krakau, *Die kubanische Revolution und die Monroe-Doktrin* (Frankfurt, 1968); Karl E. Meyer and Tad Szulc, *The Cuban Invasion: Chronicle of a Disaster* (New York, 1962); John Plank, ed., *Cuba and the United States: Long Range Perspectives* (Washington, D.C., 1967); Manuela Semidei, *Les Etats-Unis et la Revolution Cubaine* (Paris, 1968); and Maurice Zeitlin and Robert Scheer, *Cuba: Tragedy in Our Hemisphere* (New York, 1963).

This section is largely based on my "The Elimination of United States Influence," in *Revolutionary Change in Cuba*, ed. Carmelo Mesa-Lago (Pittsburgh, 1971).

101. See Hugo Gambini, *El Che Guevara* (Buenos Aires, 1968), pp. 89–98, and Ricardo Rojo, *My Friend Che* (New York, 1968), pp. 53–59.

102. Gambini, *El Che Guevara*, p. 216.

103. After the Bay of Pigs, Fidel Castro distinguished between the Guatemalan response to the U.S. intervention and his own, noting that he had dispersed the old army. See *Revolución*, April 24, 1961, p. 4.

104. Luis E. Aguilar, "Cuba, 1933: The Frustrated Revolution" (Ph.D. diss., University Microfilms, 1968), passim.

105. See, for example, José R. Alvarez Díaz et al., *Un estudio sobre Cuba* (Miami, 1963), pp. 783–88, and Julio Le Riverend, *La república dependencia y revolución* (Havana, 1969), pp. 328–38.

106. Cole Blasier, "Studies of Social Revolution: Origins in Mexico, Bolivia, and Cuba," *Latin American Research Review*, 2 (Summer 1967), p. 43. discusses conflicting estimates of the numbers of armed guerrillas.

107. Rufo López-Fresquet, *My Fourteen Months with Castro* (Cleveland, 1966), p. 106.

108. Ibid., p. 108.

109. Richard M. Nixon, *Six Crises* (New York, 1962), p. 352.

110. The U.S. government and international agencies could not be expected to make grants or loans to Cuba in the face of Castro's radical domestic program—especially the expropriation of foreign investment without effective compensation—and Castro knew it. In *The United States, Cuba and Castro* (New York, 1962), pp. 101 ff., William Appleman Williams suggests that the probable conditions for any International Monetary Fund (IMF) loan to Cuba—a stabilization program with credit restraint and a balanced budget—were economically and politically unacceptable to Castro. He argues that the IMF was Castro's best option, and the latter concluded after his Washington trip that the price of such a loan would have meant giving up his social revolution.

111. López-Fresquet, *My Fourteen Months*, p. 106. In *Cuba, Castro*, Bonsal puts the date at the "spring of 1959," p. 67.

112. *New York Times*, December 17, 1959, p. 1.

113. *Revolución*, April 25, 1959.

114. *Revolución*, January 1, 1960, quote reprinted from original article entitled "Ante la prensa" in the August 14, 1959 issue.

115. U.S., Department of Commerce, Bureau for Foreign Commerce, *Investment in Cuba: Basic Information for United States Businessmen* (Washington, D.C., 1956), p. 10.

116. International Sugar Council, *The World Sugar Economy*, vol. 2, *The World Picture* (London, 1963), pp. 176, 181–82.

117. David F. Healy, *United States in Cuba: 1898–1902* (Madison, Wisc., 1963), pp. 150, 178.

118. Bryce Wood, *The Making of the Good Neighbor Policy* (New York, 1967), pp. 81 ff., 101 ff. There is, of course, no assurance that Batista would not have eliminated Grau later anyway.

119. Earl E. T. Smith, *The Fourth Floor* (New York, 1962), p. 172.

120. *Revolución*, April 18, 1959, p. 10.

121. Meyer and Szulc, *The Cuban Invasion,*, p. 22. The interviewer was "one of the authors."

122. *Revolución*, January 21, 1960, p. 2.

123. Ibid.

124. U.S., Department of State, *American Foreign Policy: Current Documents, 1959,* no. 7492 (Washington, D.C., 1963), pp. 383–84.

125. Letter to author, October 1, 1970.

126. Castro's estimate is quoted in *Revolución,* June 25, 1960. An official U.S. figure for 1960 can be found in U.S., Department of Commerce, *Balance of Payments: Statistical Supplement, 1961* (Washington, D.C., 1961), p. 215.

127. See chapter 7 and Ernesto F. Betancourt, "Exporting the Revolution to Latin America," in *Revolutionary Change in Cuba,* ed. Carmelo Mesa-Lago (Pittsburgh, 1971), pp. 105–25.

128. López-Fresquet, *My Fourteen Months,* p. 82; Andrés Suárez, *Cuba: Castroism and Communism, 1959–1966* (Cambridge, Mass., 1967), p. 72. Arms might also have come up in a meeting Guevara reportedly had with a Soviet representative during the former's visit to Cairo in the summer of 1959. See Edward Gonzalez, "Castro's Revolution, Cuban Communist Appeals, and the Soviet Response," *World Politics,* 21, no. 1 (October 1968): 50.

129. U.S., Department of State, *Current Documents 1959,* p. 380.

130. *Revolución,* March 7, 1960, pp. 5–6.

131. *New York Times,* March 11, 1960, p. 1.

132. U.S., Congress, Senate, Committee on Foreign Relations, *Events in United States–Cuban Relations: A chronology from 1957 to 1963,* 88th Cong., 1st sess., 1963, p. 12. Prepared by the Department of State for the Committee on Foreign Relations and quoted in Suárez, *Cuba.*

133. Dwight D. Eisenhower, *The White House Years: Waging Peace, 1956–1961* (New York, 1965), p. 524.

134. *Revolución,* January 21, 1960, p. 6.

135. See U.S. statements of June 11, and October 27, 1959, in Department of State, *American Foreign Policy: Current Documents, 1959,* pp. 342–43, 377–82.

136. Bonsal, *Cuba, Castro,* p. 59.

137. Philip W. Bonsal, "Cuba, Castro and the United States," *Foreign Affairs,* 45 (January 1967): 271.

138. See Bonsal's memoirs, *Cuba, Castro,* pp. 134–35.

139. Haynes Johnson, *The Bay of Pigs* (New York, 1964), p. 26.

140. Eisenhower, *Waging Peace,* p. 533.

141. Nixon, *Six Crises,* p. 352.

142. Bonsal reported that the oil companies "would probably have reluctantly gone along with the government's request, seeking remedies through the courts and eventually, if necessary, through channels provided under international law." He reported, however, that the secretary of the treasury had strongly urged the companies to refuse to refine the Soviet crude oil. See Bonsal, "Cuba, Castro," p. 272.

143. U.S., Congress, House, Committee on Agriculture, *Extension of Sugar Acts in 1948 as Amended,* 86th Cong., 2d sess., June 22, 1960, HR12311, HR12534, HR12624, p. 4.

144. Ibid., p. 8.

145. Eisenhower, *Waging Peace,* p. 535.

146. U.S., Congress, House, *Congressional Record,* 86th Cong., 2d sess., 1960, 106, pt. 11, p. 15228.

147. Ibid., p. 15230.

148. Ibid., p. 15232.

149. Ibid., p. 15245.

150. Adolph A. Berle's diary entry of February 17, 1960, in Beatrice B. Berle and Travis B. Jacobs, eds., *Navigating the Rapids, 1918–1971* (New York, 1973), p. 703. Meyer and Szulc, *The Cuban Invasion,* p. 64, reported that the political pressures were so great that Eisenhower opted to eliminate the entire balance of the quota.

151. U.S., Congress, Senate, *Events in United States–Cuban Relations,* p. 16. Readers should not confuse the nationalizations referred to in this paragraph with Castro's seizures of the oil refineries beginning on June 29, 1960.

152. U.S., Congress, House, *Congressional Record,* 86th Cong., 2d sess., 1960, 106, pt. 11, p. 15232.

153. Ibid., p. 15245.

154. *Revolución,* May 2, 1960.

155. Gregorio Selser, *De Dulles a Raborn* (Buenos Aires, 1967), p. 97.

156. Suárez, *Cuba,* pp. 92 ff.

157. U.S., Department of State, *Current Documents, 1960,* p. 246.

158. *Revolución,* March 3, 1960, p. 12.

159. Ibid., June 25, 1960.

160. U.S., Department of State, *Current Documents, 1960,* p. 207.

161. Suárez's interpretation can be found in Suárez, *Cuba,* pp. 113, 119.

162. Eisenhower, *Waging Peace,* p. 535.

163. Bonsal, *Cuba, Castro,* p. 154.

164. See Akademiia Nuak, *Strany Latinskoi Ameriki,* p. 54. *Pravda,* July 17, 1960, p. 5.

165. Suárez, *Cuba,* p. 100.

166. Ibid., p. 97.

167. Ibid., chapter 5, passim.

168. Standard sources include Johnson, *The Bay of Pigs;* Meyer and Szulc, *The Cuban Invasion;* Arthur Schlesinger, Jr., *A Thousand Days: John F. Kennedy in the White House* (Boston, 1965), especially chapters 10 and 11; and *Playa Girón, derrota del imperialismo* (Havana, 1961), vols. 1–4.

169. U.S. Congress, Senate, Freedom of Communications, Final Report of the Committee on Commerce, Part III, *The Joint Appearances of Senator John F. Kennedy and Vice-President Richard M. Nixon and Other 1960 Campaign Presentations,* 87th Cong., 1st sess., 1961, p. 432.

170. Schlesinger, *A Thousand Days,* p. 242. See also Sorenson, *Kennedy,* p. 304.

171. Schlesinger, *A Thousand Days,* pp. 241–55, describes the positions of the various members of the administration. See also p. 258.

172. Ibid., pp. 265, 268.

173. Castro, for example, misrepresented and exaggerated Khrushchev's July 1960 pledge of support after the U.S. sugar quota cut. See Suárez, *Cuba,* pp. 93, 113; see also Gonzalez, "Castro's Revolution," pp. 67–68.

174. John Foster Dulles, "The Republican Perspective," *Foreign Policy Bulletin,* 32, no. 1 (September 15, 1952): 4; see also the *New York Times,* August 28, 1952, p. 12; September 4, 1952, pp. 1, 20; and October 11, 1952, p. 14.

175. *New York Times,* July 1, 1954, p. 2.

176. Richard M. Bissell, Jr., deputy director of the CIA (1959–1962), wrote the author on May 14, 1973, that it is "correct to say that the success of the operation in Guatemala did contribute to the decision to support the Bay of Pigs invasion."

177. At the time of the Bay of Pigs invasion, Castro referred to the Guatemalan episode and his own "destruction" of the professional army in *Revolución,* April 24, 1961, p. 4. The lessons he drew from Guatemala should not, however, be exaggerated. He had many other reasons to destroy the old army which initially constituted the chief threat to his long-term hold over Cuba.

178. Bonsal, "Cuba, Castro," p. 272. On July 31, 1972, Mr. Bonsal wrote to me: "Until the U-2 incident in May of 1960 Washington and Moscow were more or less basking in 'the spirit of Camp David.' My thesis is that we could have caused Castro and Guevara considerable embarrassment if we had avoided the oil crisis and the sugar quota cut in June and July of 1960 and that the Russians would have been glad to continue in the relatively innocuous framework of the Mikoyan agreement of February of 1960. Local resistance in the absence of challenges to the Revolution 'made in the United States' would I believe have developed in a form far more challenging than that which flowered at the Bay of Pigs."

Chapter 7. Explaining U.S. Responses (1910–1961)

1. See, for example, Harry Magdoff, *The Age of Imperialism* (New York, 1969), pp. 27 ff. Ronald H. Chilcothe and Joel C. Edelstein, *Latin America: The Struggle with Dependency and Beyond* (Cambridge, Mass., 1974), pp. 74–81, contains a bibliography listing the works of many well-known Marxist writers as well as of the new dependency theorists. Authoritative replies to both are contained in Robert W. Tucker, *The Radical Left and American Foreign Policy* (Baltimore, 1971) and Benjamin J. Cohen, *The Question of Imperialism* (New York, 1973).

2. Several U.S. scholars have attempted to test empirically assertions that foreign policies are primarily determined by economic interests in Steven J. Rosen and James R. Kurth, eds., *Testing Theories of Economic Imperialism* (Lexington, Mass., 1974). One of the contributors, John S. Odell, found that "the level of American military assistance given to a nation during the Cold War years varied with the importance of the nation to the United States as a supplier of critical raw materials, as a field for private investment, and as a trade partner" ("Correlates of U.S. Military Assistance and Military Intervention," p. 155). In the same book Steven J. Rosen found in a study of five cases that U.S. foreign military and economic assistance tended to correlate with the openness of a country to U.S. trade and investment in "The Open Door Imperative and U.S. Foreign Policy," pp. 117–42.

3. In the Rosen and Kurth book, Odell found "very little support for the hypotheses that variations in [military] intervention could be accounted for by raw materials value or private investment amounts, either among nations or regions" (p. 155). In his introductory chapter, Kurth found in a study of major cases of U.S. intervention since 1945 that "the economic explanation for U.S. interventions is afflicted with serious flaws. And at best it is only equal to several, alternative non-economic explanations for U.S. interventions" (p. 6).

Cohen, in *The Question of Imperialism* also rejects radical arguments and maintains that government authorities seek "to bend the corporation to serve the will and interests of the state, rather than the reverse" (p. 130).

4. Abraham F. Lowenthal, " 'Liberal,' 'Radical' and 'Bureaucratic' Perspectives on U.S. Latin American Policy: The Alliance for Progress in Retrospect," in *Latin America and the United States: The Changing Political Realities,* ed. Julio Cotler and Richard R. Fagen (Stanford, Calif., 1974), p. 227. See rejoinders by Jorge Graciena (pp. 205–11) and Heraclio Bonilla (pp. 236–37). See also Abraham Lowenthal's modifications and reassertion of the validity of the "bureaucratic" perspective in "Bureaucratic Politics and United States Policy Toward Latin America: An Interim Research Report" (Paper delivered at the Annual Meeting of the American Political Science Association, Chicago, 1974).

5. Tucker in *The Radical Left,* pp. 111 and 151, maintains that U.S. opposition to radical revolution is based partly on fear that the revolution will be resistant to U.S. control and that men with power sometimes want to use it simply to rule over others. Cohen in *The Question of Imperialism* maintains that "nations yield to the temptations of domination because they are driven to maximize their individual power position" as a result of the anarchic organization of the international system of states (p. 245). See also earlier formulations of Kenneth N. Waltz, *Man, the State and War* (New York, 1959).

6. Samuel A. Stouffer, *Communism, Conformity and Civil Liberties* (Garden City, New York, 1955), p. 156; Lloyd A. Free and Hadley Cantril, *The Political Beliefs of Americans: A Study of Public Opinion* (New York, 1968), p. 52; and Albert H. Cantril and Charles W. Roll, Jr., *Hopes and Fears of the American People* (New York, 1971), p. 23.

7. George F. Kennan touches on the U.S. "legalistic-moralistic" approach to international problems in *American Diplomacy, 1900–1950* (Chicago, 1951), pp. 95 ff.

8. George F. Kennan, *Soviet-American Relations, 1917–1920,* vol. 1, *Russia Leaves the War* (New York, 1967), pp. 23 ff., discusses the incompatibility of the U.S. desires for Russia to remain in the war and for the provisional government to survive. Page 158 describes U.S. "disappointment and amazement" at the Bolshevik desire to withdraw from the war in explaining U.S. nonrecognition policy. Volume 2, *The Decision to Intervene,* discusses the military considerations related to World War I in the decisions to land U.S. troops in Archangel, p. 379, and for the landings in Siberia, pp. 398 ff.

9. Tang Tsou, *America's Failure in China 1941–50* (Chicago, 1963), II: 462 ff.

10. A classic example of the gap between principles and practice is U.S. policy toward the Bosch government in the Dominican Republic in 1963 (see chapter 8).

11. Harry K. Wright, *Foreign Enterprise in Mexico: Law and Policies* (Chapel Hill, N.C., 1971), pp. 54, 77. For a discussion of the revolution and Mexican dependence see Lorenzo Meyer, "Cambio político y dependencia, Mexico en el siglo XX," in Centro de Estudios Internacionales, *La política exterior de México: realidad y perspectivas* (Mexico, 1972).

12. Carmelo Mesa-Lago, ed., *Revolutionary Change in Cuba* (Pittsburgh, 1971), pp. 260–61.

Chapter 8. Epilogue: U.S. Responses Since 1961

1. Arthur M. Schlesinger, Jr., *A Thousand Days: John F. Kennedy in the White House* (Boston, 1965), p. 771.

2. Juan Bosch, *The Unfinished Experiment: Democracy in the Dominican Republic* (New York, 1965), p. 165.

3. This and other conclusions set forth in this chapter regarding the Dominican Republic are based on my studies of U.S.–Dominican Relations which are too long to be included here, but which I hope to publish elsewhere at a later time. See also note 5, chapter 7.

4. Nikita S. Khrushchov [Khrushchev], *The National Liberation Movement: Selected Passages, 1956–1963* (Moscow, 1963), pp. 43–44.

5. U.S., Department of Defense, Office of the Assistant Secretary of Defense for International Security Affairs, *Military Assistance and Foreign Military Sales Facts* (Washington, D.C., March 1971), p. 15.

6. H. Jon Rosenbaum, *Arms and Security in Latin America: Recent Developments* (Washington, D.C., 1971), p. 27.

7. Arturo Porzecanski, *Uruguay's Tupamaros, The Urban Guerrillas* (New York, 1973), p. 70.

8. Lyndon Johnson, *The Vantage Point* (New York, 1971), p. 202.

9. U.S., *Department of State Bulletin,* May 17, 1965, p. 738.

10. Ibid., pp. 744–48.

11. Abraham F. Lowenthal, *The Dominican Intervention* (Cambridge, Mass., 1972), pp. 137–38.

12. Jerome Slater, *Intervention and Negotiation: The United States and the Dominican Revolution* (New York, 1970), p. 171.

13. Fred Goff and Michael Locker, "The Violence of Domination: U.S. Power in the Dominican Republic," in *Latin American Radicalism* ed. Irving L. Horowitz (New York, 1969), p. 280, and Lowenthal, *The Dominican Intervention,* pp. 139–42. E. V. Ananova maintains that Johnson and Rusk did not believe charges about Communist influence over Caamaño in "Vooruzhenaia interventsiia SSHA v Dominikanskoi respublike," *Novaia i Noveishaia Istoriia,* no. 1. (1969): 34.

14. Johnson, *The Vantage Point,* p. 200.

15. José Moreno, *Barrios in Arms* (Pittsburgh, 1970), pp. 210–11, lists the strength of the commando units, based on photostatic copies of the constitutionalist personnel records. I calculated the one-to-twelve ratio on the basis of Moreno's identification of units led by Communists and hope to publish the names of the units, the calculations, and analysis at a later date.

16. Lowenthal, *The Dominican Intervention,* p. 215.

17. Caamaño's cabinet was listed in *La Nación,* May 6, 1965, pp. 3–4. The Department of State's list of Communists is contained in U.S., Congress, Senate, *Testimony of Brigadier General Elias Wessin y Wessin,* 89th Cong., 1st sess., October 1, 1965, pp. 207–20.

18. Lowenthal, *The Dominican Intervention,* p. 99.

19. Jerome Levinson and Juan de Onis, *The Alliance That Lost Its Way* (Chicago, 1970), pp. 30–3.

20. Schlesinger, *A Thousand Days,* p. 340.

21. U.S., *Department of State Bulletin,* May 17, 1965, p. 744.

22. Lowenthal, *The Dominican Intervention,* pp. 153–54.

23. John F. Kennedy, "Address at a White House Reception for Members of Congress and for the

Diplomatic Corps of the Latin American Republics," March 13, 1961, *Public Papers of the Presidents of the United States, 1961* (Washington, D.C., 1962), pp. 170–75.

24. John Bartlow Martin, *Overtaken by Events: The Dominican Crisis from the Fall of Trujillo to the Civil War* (New York, 1966), pp. 322–23.

25. Ibid., pp. 451, 454, 495, and passim.

26. All or almost all AID loans and grants for fiscal year 1963 were committed before Bosch became president and the account had a negative balance for fiscal year 1964. AID records made available to me show only a $3.5 million loan for housing under the Social Progress Fund signed on February 28, 1963, and the authorization of a $4.8 million loan in fiscal year 1964 to complete a prior Food for Peace Agreement. AID Statistics and Reports Division provided data which answered my inquiries in part.

27. Martin, *Overtaken by Events*, pp. 473, 477.

28. Ibid., pp. 126, 309; see also Howard J. Wiarda, "The Development of the Labor Movement in the Dominican Republic," *Inter-American Economic Affairs*, 20 (Summer 1966): 57–59.

29. Martin, *Overtaken by Events*, p. 573.

30. Ibid., p. 453.

31. U.S., Department of Commerce, Bureau of International Commerce, "Basic Data on the Economy of the Dominican Republic," *Overseas Business Reports* (Washington, D.C., 1964), p. 17.

32. James L. Petras and Robert La Porte, Jr., *Cultivating Revolution: The United States and Agrarian Reform in Latin America* (New York, 1971), p. 257.

33. Levinson and de Onis, *The Alliance That Lost Its Way*, pp. 152–53, and Charles T. Goodsell, "Diplomatic Protection of U.S. Business in Peru," in *United States Foreign Policy and Peru*, ed. Daniel A. Sharp (Austin, Texas, 1972), p. 248. See also Charles T. Goodsell, *American Corporations and Peruvian Politics* (Cambridge, Mass., 1974), received after this section was completed.

34. Levinson and de Onis, *The Alliance That Lost Its Way*, pp. 153–55. See also Luigi Einaudi, "U.S. Relations with the Peruvian Military," in *United States Foreign Policy and Peru*, ed. Sharp, p. 43.

35. In fiscal years 1965 and 1966, Chile received a total of $241.8 million and Colombia received $125.6 million in U.S. economic assistance. In these same years, Peru received $78.6 million. (See tables 12 and 13 and references for same.) Slight variations occur in aid extended for a given period in publications from different years.

36. Richard N. Goodwin, "Letter from Peru," *The New Yorker*, May 17, 1969, p. 60.

37. Goodsell, "Diplomatic Protection," p. 248, and William J. McIntire, "U.S. Labor Policy," p. 304, in *United States Foreign Policy and Peru*, ed. Sharp; and Jane S. Jaquette, "The Politics of Development in Peru," (Ph.D. diss., Cornell University, June 1971), p. 172.

38. Eduardo Frei Montalva, "The Alliance That Lost Its Way," *Foreign Affairs*, 45, no. 3 (April 1967): 438.

39. M. Wilhelmy Von Wolff, "Chilean Foreign Policy: The Frei Government, 1964–1970," (Ph.D. diss., Princeton University, 1973), p. 186.

40. Petras and La Porte, *Cultivating Revolutions*, p. 201.

41. Wilhelmy, "Chilean Foreign Policy," pp. 281–82.

42. Gabriel Valdés Sotomayor, *Conciencia latinoamericana y realidad internacional* (Santiago, Chile, 1970), pp. 225–33.

43. James F. Petras and Robert La Porte, *Perú: ¿Transformación revolucionaria o modernización?* (Buenos Aires, 1971), pp. 132–33.

44. Juan Velasco Alvarado, "Discursos pronunciados por el Señor General de División Don Juan Velasco Alvarado, Presidente de la República en la Clausura de la IX Conferencia de Ejecutivos (Cade 70)," *Discursos pronunciados por el Señor General de División Don Juan Velasco Alvarado* (Lima, 1970), pp. 6–11.

45. *New York Times*, March 28, 1971, p. 1.

46. *New York Times*, November 21, 1971, p. 3.

47. U.S., Congress, House, Committee on Foreign Affairs, Subcommittee on Inter-American Affairs, Hearing, *United States–Chilean Relations*, 93d Cong., 1st sess., March 6, 1973 (Washington,

D.C., 1973), pp. 5, 26. Statement by John H. Crimmins, acting assistant secretary of state for inter-American affairs.

48. Ibid., p. 16.

49. U.S., Agency for International Development, *U.S. Overseas Loans and Grants and Assistance from International Organizations: Obligations and Loan Authorizations, July 1, 1945–June 30, 1973* (Washington, D.C., 1974), p. 41.

50. Peru's claim against IPC was more than five times the valuation of $120 million that the company had put on its holdings. *New York Times,* March 26, 1970, p. 8, and U.S., Congress, Senate, Committee on Foreign Relations, Subcommittee on Western Hemispheric Affairs, Hearings, *United States Relations with Peru,* 91st Cong., 1st sess., April 14, 15, and 17, 1969. (Washington, D.C., 1969), pp. 103–04.

51. Expropriation occurred June 27, 1969. Peru took over Grace's sugar plantations (25,000 acres valued at $10 million) and sugar mills (valued at $15 million). *New York Times,* June 28, 1969, p. 6, and *Fortune,* 80 (October 1969): 108.

The Peruvian government occupied the $80 million chemical and paper complex on August 22, 1969, but the occupation of the latter was only temporary. *New York Times,* August 23, 1969, p. 1, and August 28, 1969, p. 38.

52. The Peruvian government ultimately agreed to nationalize the Lima telephone company by purchasing the controlling bloc shares from ITT at an agreed price of $17.9 million. *New York Times,* October 30, 1969, p. 4.

53. Goodsell, "Diplomatic Protection," p. 251.

54. U.S., AID, *U.S. Overseas Loans and Grants,* p. 57.

55. *The Wall Street Journal,* February 20, 1974, p. 4, and *New York Times,* February 20, 1974, p. 4.

56. *Andean Times,* February 22, 1974, p. 35. See also *The Wall Street Journal,* December 20, 1974, p. 4.

57. U.S., Congress, House, *United States–Chilean Affairs,* pp. 6–7.

58. Richard Nixon, "Economic Assistance and Investment Security in Developing Nations" (The President's Policy Statement, January 19, 1972), *Weekly Compilation of Presidential Documents* (Washington, D.C., week ending January 22, 1972), vol. 8, pt. 1, p. 65.

59. Richard Nixon, "United States Foreign Policy for the 1970's: The Emerging Structure of Peace" (The President's Report to the Congress, February 9, 1972), *Weekly Compilation of Presidential Documents* (Washington, D.C., week ending February 12, 1972), vol. 8, pt. 1, pp. 315–16.

60. Ibid.

61. *New York Times,* September 20, 1970, p. 24.

62. *New York Times,* December 1, 1971, p. 20.

63. U.S., Congress, Senate, Committee on Foreign Relations, Subcommittee on Multinational Corporations, *The International Telephone and Telegraph Company and Chile, 1970–71,* 93d Cong., 1st sess., June 21, 1973 (Washington, D.C., 1973), pp. 16–17.

64. U.S., Congress, House, *United States–Chilean Affairs,* p. 2.

65. Paul E. Sigmund, "The Invisible Blockade and the Overthrow of Allende," *Foreign Affairs,* 52, no. 4 (January 1974): 330.

66. U.S., AID, *U.S. Overseas Loans and Grants,* p. 183.

67. Américo Zorrilla and Brig. Gen. Francisco Morales Bermúdez, *Inter-American Development Bank: Proceedings,* 13th Meeting of the Board of Governors (Quito, Ecuador, 1972), pp. 57, 98.

68. Sigmund, "The Invisible Blockade," p. 335.

69. Zorrilla and Morales Bermúdez, *Proceedings,* p. 97; Sigmund, "The Invisible Blockade," pp. 332–33.

70. *New York Times,* September 8, 1974, pp. 1, 26, and September 14, 1974, p. 2.

71. *New York Times,* September 17, 1974, p. 22.

72. *New York Times,* September 20, pp. 1, and 10. Ray Cline, former director of the Bureau of Intelligence and Research for the Department of State, was reported to have said that the striking truckers benefited from U.S. assistance to opposition political parties. See *New York Times,* October 17, 1974, p.

9, and October 20, 1974, p. 43. Corporate support for the truckers was discussed in *New York Times,* October 16, 1974, p. 8. See also *New York Times,* February 10, 1975, pp. 1, 18.

73. *New York Times,* September 17, 1974, p. 22. See also Assistant Secretary Jack Kubisch's statement in *IDOC, International North America Edition,* no. 58 (December 1973): 60. This issue contains other documents including an article by Laurence Birns from *New York Review of Books,* November 1, 1973; a statement by Senator Kennedy; an article by Tad Szulc which appeared in the *Washington Post,* October 21, 1973; and Chilean documents.

74. See "Chile: What Was the U.S. Role?" *Foreign Policy,* no. 16 (Fall 1974): 127–56 (includes Elizabeth Farnworth, "More Than Admitted," pp. 127–41, and Paul Sigmund, "Less Than Charged," pp. 142–56); Richard R. Fagen, "The United States and Chile: Roots and Branches," *Foreign Affairs,* 53, no. 2 (January 1975): 297–313, and exchange of correspondence between Paul Sigmund and Richard Fagen on pp. 376 and 377 of same issue.

75. U.S., Congress, House, *United States–Chilean Affairs,* p. 20.

76. *New York Times,* September 20, 1970, p. 24.

Index